The Meaning of the Scrolls (a) for the Bible
(b) for the Church
(c) " Christology

THE MEANING OF THE QUMRÂN SCROLLS
FOR THE BIBLE

The Meaning of
The Qumrân Scrolls for The Bible

WITH SPECIAL ATTENTION TO THE BOOK OF ISAIAH

WILLIAM HUGH BROWNLEE

THE JAMES W. RICHARD LECTURES
IN CHRISTIAN RELIGION
GIVEN AT THE UNIVERSITY OF VIRGINIA

NEW YORK · OXFORD UNIVERSITY PRESS
1964

TO MY FORMER PROFESSORS

JAMES L. KELSO, *Pittsburgh [-Xenia] Theological Seminary,*
JUDAH GOLDIN, *formerly at Duke University, now at Yale,*
WILLIAM F. STINESPRING, *Duke University Divinity School.*

Table of Contents

Foreword

Archaeologists of the Near East have made innumerable discoveries helpful to the understanding of the Bible. Such discoveries have occurred with ever increasing rapidity since the time of Napoleon, when the famous Rosetta Stone which led to the decipherment of the ancient Egyptian hieroglyphs was found. Yet the continuing recovery of documents from caves near the Dead Sea, ever since 1947, has a unique importance for students of the Bible. Here are ancient manuscripts from the Holy Land, witnessing to the text and interpretation of the Old Testament and setting the stage of religious thought whereon were enacted the critical events of the great drama of redemption set forth in the New Testament. No other single series of related discoveries has such broad and profound import for the Bible as a whole.

The present book does not deal with all the literature from the wilderness west of the Dead Sea. It is limited to the documents known as the Qumrân Scrolls from the northwest shore of that great salt lake; these belong to a common segment of Jewish sectarian life to be classified as Essene. As I have argued from the first, the term Essene, as employed by the ancient Jewish historians Philo and Josephus, probably covers a multiplicity of small related sects, including the society at Khirbet Qumrân.[1] This society had its inception in pre-Christian times and continued down into the time of Christ and the Apostles. Other documents from the region west of the Dead Sea are unrelated and are mostly of later date. These include historical documents from the period of the Second Jewish Revolt against Rome (A.D. 132–135) and also Christian manuscripts from the ruins of an ancient monastery at a site known as Khirbet Mird, a few miles inland from the area of Qumrân. These works are largely irrelevant for the present study. The documents with which we are concerned, then, are the Qumrân Scrolls; and, as a popular synonym, I also employ the name Dead Sea Scrolls, which I use with reference to the Qumrân literature alone, inasmuch

1. "A Comparison of the Covenanters of the Dead Sea Scrolls with Pre-Christian Jewish Sects," *Biblical Archaeologist,* Sept. 1950.

as the title was first coined as a designation of this particular group of manuscripts.

Not all aspects of the Qumrân literature can be discussed here, nor even all the scrolls (many of which remain unpublished), for the vastness of the subject forbids it. One roll will receive more attention than any other, the great Isaiah Scroll. Part II, consisting of seven chapters, will be devoted to this roll alone, by way of analyzing its text and delineating its significance; but even here the treatment will be far from exhaustive. It will merely illustrate the varied aspects of the document and its importance for the understanding of Isaiah. This treatment of the prophet will be set against the background of the general significance of the scrolls for the interpretation of the Old Testament, and also of the Bible as a whole, which we will discuss in Part I. However, the New Testament will receive less attention than the Old, because once more limitation seems necessary. The Old Testament is therefore our major concern; and yet it is hoped that this work will convey a qualitative, if not a quantitative, impression as to the signal importance of the scrolls for Christianity. Discussion of the implications of these documents for New Testament scholarship will be found in Chapters Five and Six, but occasional references to the New Testament will also be found throughout the book.

The book is intended to be interesting, not by reason of any special talent in telling, or retelling, the already familiar story of the Dead Sea Scrolls (which will be omitted here), but by portraying before the eyes of the reader the methods of Biblical criticism. For this reason, the texts will be presented in translation, even when variant readings of different sources are compared. When the original languages are quoted, the words will be transliterated into the familiar Latin alphabet of our everyday use, in order that the lay reader may see for himself the degrees of similarity and dissimilarity between readings, without the nuisance of puzzling over unfamiliar characters. The method of transliteration will be explained below.

The book is intended to be popular, not in the sense, however, of being light reading; for some sections will require careful study, which will slow the reader to a snail's pace. Yet the aim is to write with such lucidity that no subject, no matter how technical, need be incomprehensible to anyone with an eager mind. Many subheads are employed in the chapters in order that the reader may know where he can lay the book aside and take it up again, without any serious break in continuity.

It is hoped that this book will be inspiring, not by giving eloquent expression to familiar truth or by championing some holy cause, but by guiding the student of the Bible (learned or unlearned) to summits from which he can see new horizons of religious thought — or by leading him to some unexplored Garden of God, tucked away in a hidden valley, beneath whose trees he may gather an occasional wildflower of Biblical interpretation different from anything he has seen before.

The views of other scholars are often referred to, but this book is not intended to be a survey of current opinion regarding the Qumrân literature. The author wishes, rather, to invite into his study whosoever will come, and to explain through an examination of the texts themselves what he believes to be the real meaning of the Qumrân Scrolls.

It is this emphasis upon meaning which explains in large measure both the arrangement and the contents of the book. Thus we shall explore the different ways in which the Old Testament had meaning for the Qumrân Community and the different ways in which their literature may assist us to a better understanding of the Bible. These avenues of approach should disclose to the reader not merely the results of scroll studies, but the methods of their investigation. Consequently, we shall have a reasoned presentation, whose authority is appeal to evidence, rather than to scholarly opinion. The reader should not look for quick and easy answers as to what the Qumrân Community believed; for he will not find a systematic discussion of a given theme confined to a single section of the book. New, or complementary, aspects of the same doctrine may appear from time to time as they are encountered in the texts; or, again, some areas of scroll interest may not be discussed at all, since it is not at all my intention to give a systematic presentation of all Qumrân ideas. Many good books have already been written on the Dead Sea Scrolls and many more will need to be written in order that the varied aspects of this growing body of ancient literature may be adequately understood.

The inspiration for the present book was the invitation to deliver the James W. Richard Lectures in Christian Religion at the University of Virginia, in February, 1958. The lectures actually delivered (which were diminished by one by reason of a snow storm) were: an illustrated lecture on the discoveries of the Qumrân Scrolls, a second entitled

"The Teacher of Righteousness and the Uniqueness of Christ" (which had already been delivered substantially at the first Southern Regional Ecumenical Institute held at Lake Junaluska, North Carolina, June, 1957), and a third dealing with the Isaiah Scroll. At that time, I had written Chapters Six through Eleven of this book, except for the footnotes. Chapter Five was first delivered in October, 1958, at a convocation held in the Claremont Church by the Southern California School of Theology at Claremont. Later, that same fall, I presented the substance of Chapter Thirteen before a meeting of the North Carolina Teachers of Religion held at Wake Forest College, Winston-Salem, North Carolina. It was first written as a formal paper early in 1960 and was read before the Twenty-fifth International Congress of Orientalists, which was held at Moscow University in August 1960. Since then I have revised it in order to make it more popular and in order to include a few more New Testament illustrations. Two of the lectures were read to the Pacific Coast Section of the National Association of Biblical Instructors: Chapter Thirteen at a meeting held at the University of Redlands, California, in October 1960; and Chapter Four (selections only) in a meeting held at the University of Southern California, Los Angeles, October 1961.

To a certain extent, then, the present work is an anthology, but the occasion for the production of the book is the obligation of presenting for publication the James W. Richard Lectures. I had hoped to include here an account of the discoveries, but several months of labor in trying to write such a narrative, with full attention given to the varied phases of the subject, have convinced me that this cannot be done adequately without writing another whole book. For a presentation of the discoveries, I recommend the reading of Millar Burrows, *The Dead Sea Scrolls,* and *More Light on the Dead Sea Scrolls,* published by the Viking Press, in 1955 and 1958, respectively. It was in February, 1948, while Burrows was director of the American School of Oriental Research in Jerusalem, that he, John C. Trever, and I began the first researches on the Dead Sea Scrolls of the St. Mark's Monastery. Since then, other documents have come to light (including those even then possessed by Dr. E. L. Sukenik of Hebrew University); and the continuing discoveries have been my absorbing interest, second only to the study and teaching of the Bible itself.

The present book presents many Qumrân Biblical texts in original translation, a feature generally absent from books on the Qumrân

Scrolls. An effort has been made to represent the assonance and rhythm of the Biblical poetry in translation. Usually this can be done without any sacrifice of the literal sense; but, in order to achieve the necessary terseness of expression to represent the Hebrew rhythm, it has sometimes been necessary to introduce contractions in the English verbal forms. These are to be excused as the poetic license of the translator. Some Qumrân non-Biblical texts also appear in original translation here, but they are only excerpts designed to illustrate specific points of interpretation. For the most complete collection of Qumrân texts in reliable English translation, I recommend the reading of Géza Vermès, *The Dead Sea Scrolls in English,* published in Baltimore, Maryland, by Penguin Books, in 1962.

I wish to acknowledge the careful reading of most of this manuscript by the Rev. Mr. Jack Sanders, a student of the Claremont Graduate School, and the Rev. Mr. William Richard Denton, the Order Librarian of the Southern California School of Theology. For their suggestions affecting the style of the presentation, I am very grateful. Particular gratitude is due to the Oxford University Press for its careful handling of my manuscript. I also wish to acknowledge the help of Mrs. Catherine H. Tramz, who as a departmental secretary at the Claremont Graduate School so ably and willingly typed and retyped the pages of this book as it was being prepared for publication. I am also grateful to the Reverend Richard Denton for his assistance in the preparation of the indexes.

Transcriptions

Since the Latin alphabet is not wholly adequate for indicating the pronunciation of Semitic consonants, certain diacritical marks will appear above or under certain of them in order to indicate to linguists the precise letter of Hebrew, Aramaic, or Arabic which is involved in a given spelling. Students who are untrained in these languages should ignore such markings, except as they form part of the visual imagery by which variant readings may be compared. Two letters *'Âlef* and *'Ain* are so alien to English that they are transcribed as ' and ', respectively. They may be omitted in pronunciation by the layman who may wish to quote orally any of the arguments of this book. Indeed, as we shall see, these letters were probably silent in the speech of some of the scribes of the Qumrân Scrolls.[1]

Two methods of transcription are presented in the present book, one with an attempt to vocalize (or pronounce) the words, and another without any such attempt. The advantage of not vocalizing is that it enables even the layman to see visually the slight difference between two Hebrew or Aramaic words in an unpointed consonantal text, whereas an English vocalization which supplies vowels makes the words appear more pronouncedly different than they actually do in the ancient manuscripts. Vocalization involves not only a utilization of vowels, but also a modification of the consonants. Thus *B*, *K*, and *P* are softened (or aspirated) as *v*, *kh*, and *f*, respectively, whenever they stand after a vowel and the consonant is not reduplicated. The choice of *v* and *f* in the place of *bh* and *ph* is motivated by the desire for simplicity. Moreover, *bh* is an unintelligible combination of letters in English. The same may be said of *kh*, which is pronounced similar to a German *ch;* but this cannot be avoided in English transcription. In classical Hebrew, aspiration also applies to *G*, *D*, and *T;* but I have omitted this distinction out of deference to modern Hebrew usage which has affected also the teaching of classical Hebrew in universities and theological seminaries. On the other hand, I transcribe the letter *Wâw* with a *W* (or *w*), and never with a *v* — even though in modern

1. Cf. below, p. 165.

xv

(Germanized) pronunciation *Wâw* is always pronounced like an English *v*. One other distinction between vocalized and non-vocalized transcription is that *Shîn* (*Š*) is identified as *sh* when vocalized. When transliterating words with no attempt to vocalize, I print all the letters as capitals; but when vocalizing a word by introducing the vowel sounds, I print all the letters small. Thus a simple consonantal transliteration yields *SPR;* but a vocalization of the same letters may produce various words: *sippêr, suppâr, sôfêr, sêfer,* etc., according to the sense agreeable to a given context. For the convenience of Hebrew and Aramaic students who are accustomed to reading only the printed, or "square Hebrew," characters, I present here a table of consonantal transcriptions, listing the lower case forms of the same letters only where different pronunciations are involved:

'Âlef	'	*Lâmed*	L
Bêt	B (*b* or *v*)	*Mêm*	M
Gimel	G	*Nûn*	N
Dâlet	D	*Sâmekh*	S
Hê	H	*'Ayin*	'
Hê when sounded at close of syllable, after vowel	(*ḣ*)	*Pê*	P (*p* or *f*)
Wâw	W	*Ṣâde*	Ṣ
Zayin	Z	*Qôf*	Q
Ḥêt	Ḥ	*Rêsh*	R
Ṭet	Ṭ	*Śîn*	Ś
Yôd	Y	*Shîn*	Š
Kaf	K (*k* or *kh*)	*Tâw*	T

The transcription of the vowels calls for special comment. Although it has become customary among scholars to distinguish between long vowels by using two different diacritical marks in transcription, shifting according to need between the circumflex (^) and the macron (‾), I have chosen the exclusive use of the circumflex. The reason that scholars make this distinction is that in certain words the vowel is always long, whereas in other words the vowel may become short when inflected. By marking the former with a circumflex, they bring this matter to the attention of the reader. However, if one approaches the matter phonetically, there is no reason for making this distinction, for the long vowel in question is in either case pronounced the same. It happens also that in English the macron indicates phonetic values for the vowels which are different from those of the Hebrew and Aramaic. Consequently, I have avoided the macron and have employed the circumflex alone. For the sake of simplicity, I have placed no diacritical marks over the short vowels, leaving it to the intelligence of the reader to note that unmarked vowels are short vowels. My method of transcribing the full Hebrew and Aramaic vowels is displayed in the following table:

VOWEL	TRANSCRIPTION	ENGLISH SOUND
Qâmeṣ	â	ä as in *arm*
Pataḥ	a	ȧ as in *ask*
Hôlem	ô	ō as in *vote*
Qâmeṣ Ḥâṭûf	o	ŏ as in *dog*
Shûreq	û	ōō as in *boot*
Qibbûṣ	u	ŏŏ as in *nook*
Long *Hireq*	î	ē as in *cedar*
Short *Hireq*	i	ĭ as in *it*
Ṣêrê	ê	ā as in *cave*
Səgôl in closed syllable	e	ĕ as in *fed*
Səgôl in stressed, open syllable	è	a prolonged "short e" without analogy in English
Shəwâ' (schwa)	ə	ə as in *the* before consonants in non-emphatic speech

In addition to these vowels, Hebrew and Aramaic also use the Ḥaṭef, or half, vowels, in which a given short vowel becomes even shorter, almost like the schwa. In my transliterations they are represented by the appropriate raised letters, so that all ambiguities are avoided. The silent and so-called medial *Shəwâ's* of the Massoretic text are entirely omitted in transcription, since both were probably really silent and served largely as visual syllable dividers.[2] Mention may also be made of the diphthongs *oi* and *ai*, as in English "oil" and "aisle." Usually the first vowel of the diphthong *ai* is vocalized with a *Pataḥ*, but in other

---

2. It is obviously impossible to conceive of something halfway between vocal and silent, when dealing with so slight a vowel. The phenomenon to which the so-called medial *Shəwâ'* points is that of exceptions to the rule that the *bəghadh-kəfath* consonants are not to be aspirated after a closed syllable. These exceptions are probably to be explained as occasioned by the dropping out of a vowel which originally stood in such positions — the aspiration having been retained after the dropping out of the vowel.

cases (as Adonai, vocalized *'ªdônâi*) with a *Qâmeṣ*. In the latter case
the vowel is prónounced much the same (*ī*), except that it receives
greater stress. No attempt has been made to mark the accents of the
Hebrew and Aramaic words; but these have more to do with actual
length (defined as stress and duration) than the particular vowel involved. Thus the sound represented by *Səgôl* is classified in English
as a short *e;* but, whenever it stands in an accented open syllable in
Hebrew or Aramaic, it is prolonged in good Semitic pronunciation.

When Greek words are transliterated, *Ômega* is distinguished from
Omicron, by placing a circumflex over it. Similarly, *Êta* is distinguished
from *Epsilon* by the use of the circumflex. The phonetic values thus
differentiated are the same as in the case of Hebrew and Aramaic.

ABBREVIATIONS USED IN FOOTNOTES

AASOR	*Annual of the American Schools of Oriental Research*
ADAJ	*Annual of the Department of Antiquities of Jordan*
ASV	American Standard Version
BA	*Biblical Archaeologist*
BASOR	*Bulletin of the American Schools of Oriental Research*
BJRL	*Bulletin of John Rylands Library*
CC	*Christian Century*
CDC	*Cairo Fragments of a Damascus Covenant*
DJD	J. Milik, *Discoveries in the Judean Desert*
E	Ephraimite tradition
HTR	*Harvard Theological Review*
IB	*Interpreter's Bible*
J	Judean tradition
JA	Josephus, *Jewish Antiquities*
JBL	*Journal of Biblical Literature*
JQR	*Jewish Quarterly Review*
JThS	*Journal of Theological Studies*
JW	Josephus, *Jewish Wars*
KJV	King James Version
NTS	*New Testament Studies*
RB	*Revue Biblique*
Rech. Bib.	*Recherches Bibliques*
RQ	*Revue de Qumran*
RSV	Revised Standard Version
ThLZ	*Theologische Literaturzeitung*
ZAW	*Zeitschrift für die Alttestamentliche Wissenschaft*
ZNW	*Zeitschrift für die Neutestamentliche Wissenschaft*

Scroll Nomenclature and Abbreviations

In 1950, Millar Burrows published a very simple system of designating the Dead Sea Scrolls for the documents that had been discovered,[1] all of which came from a single cave near the Dead Sea. This nomenclature was in English, as were the abbreviations based upon it, so that it was not suitable for universal usage. Within two years it became outmoded by the discovery of many more manuscript caves, some of them in areas near the Dead Sea, but with an unrelated literature. It became necessary, therefore, to distinguish localities from one another, by employing the Arabic proper noun for each locality. Thus the caves near Khirbet Qumrân were labeled Q caves and their documents as Q documents. Those of the Wady Murabba'ât were designated by the letter M. It was also necessary to number the caves, in order to indicate from which particular cave in a given area a manuscript came. Thus 4Q and 2M refer, respectively, to the fourth cave of the Qumrân area and the second cave of the Wady Murabba'ât. Individual copies of the same work within a given cave continue to be distinguished from one another by raised letters of the alphabet, as first proposed by Burrows.

Another feature of the new nomenclature (as proposed by Roland de Vaux in 1953) [2] is that each of the newly discovered documents be given a Hebrew or Aramaic name appropriate to its contents. One tacit modification in the use of Hebrew, or Aramaic, concerns the names of Biblical books (based ultimately upon the Hebrew), where a person is free to abbreviate the names of these books according to their familiar forms in the language in which he is writing. Thus the Prophet *Yəhezqê'l* (Hebrew) is known as *Hesekiel* in German and as *Ezekiel* in English, so that the prophet's name will be abbreviated differently in each language. Often this must mean the use of more than one letter, so that (for example) Ezekiel in English needs to be abbreviated as Ezek (not as E or Ez), if it is to be readily distinguished

---

1. Millar Burrows, with the assistance of John C. Trever and William H. Brownlee. *The Dead Sea Scrolls of St. Mark's Monastery,* I, New Haven: The American Schools of Oriental Research, 1950, p. xi.
2. In the *Revue Biblique* (hereafter cited as *RB*), lx, 1953, pp. 87f.

from Ezra. It would be helpful if all scholars made a clear distinction between the mode of referring to column and line numbers, as distinct from chapter and verse. Thus 42:1 designates chapter 42, verse 1; whereas xxv, 10f. refers to the manuscript location as column 25, lines 10 and 11. The practice of distinguishing chapters by Arabic numerals and columns by Roman numerals is followed in the present book.

Another feature of the new nomenclature is the use of the word *pêsher* as designating a new type of Biblical commentary (or *midrâsh*). This is a typically Qumrân word (borrowed from the Aramaic of Daniel), which is used frequently in the Qumrân literature for the introduction of comments explaining the hidden prophetic meaning of passages. The symbol for a *pêsher* of a book, as distinct from a straight manuscript of the work, is a small *p* prefixed to the name of the book which is thus interpreted.

In reading the literature on the Qumrân Scrolls, we find many different names for the same works and correspondingly different abbreviations, although more and more the new system of reference proposed by de Vaux is being used. In order to promote the use of this new nomenclature, I have proposed a renaming of certain of the documents in English so that the new system of abbreviations may be more easily remembered by laymen who do not read Hebrew or Aramaic.[3] Even if these new names never really become current, perhaps the very proposing of them may serve as a memory aid to non-linguists. In the following table of the principal documents of the first Qumrân cave, the first column gives the name formally (or officially) assigned a document, and beneath it, within parentheses, the proposed new name, if any. The second column gives the old abbreviation; and the third, the new and now standard abbreviation. Beneath the new abbreviation the Hebrew word which is abbreviated in the new mode of reference appears within parentheses.

NAME OF DOCUMENT	OLD ABBREVIATION	NEW ABBREVIATION
Isaiah A	DSI[a]	1Q Isa[a]
Isaiah B	DSI[b]	1Q Isa[b]
Habukkuk Commentary	DSH	1Q pHab
(Predictions of Habakkuk)		(*pêsher*)

3. I first suggested this in *New Testament Studies* (hereafter cited as *NTS*), Vol. III, No. 1 (Nov. 1956), p. 13, n. 1.

NAME OF DOCUMENT	OLD ABBREVIATION	NEW ABBREVIATION
Manual of Discipline, or Rule of the Community (Socicty Manual)	DSD	1Q S (*serekh*)
Rule of the Congregation [4] (Society Manual Annex)	(none)	1Q Sa
Collection of Benedictions (Society Benedictions, or Blessings)	(none)	1Q Sb
Thanksgiving Psalms (Thanksgiving Hymns, or simply Hymns)	DST	1Q H (*hôdâyôt*, or *hôdôt*)
War of the Sons of Light against the Sons of Darkness (Military Manual)	DSW	1Q M (*milḥâmâh*)
Lamech Apocalypse (a misnomer) (Genesis Apocryphon [now in use])	DSL	1Q Gen[apoc] (both *Genesis* and *apocryphon* are Greek words)

The manuscripts from the other caves have not been involved in the same changes of abbreviation (or mode of reference), and do not figure in the above table; but their standard abbreviations will be appropriately explained as they are introduced in the footnotes.[5] The same method will be employed in introducing abbreviations to periodicals and standard reference works.

4. This and the following portion of the Manual of Discipline were purchased from Mr. Khalil Iskander (alias, Kando), a merchant of Bethlehem, in 1949, through the patient negotiations of Mr. Joseph Saad. See G. Lankester Harding in D. Barthélemy and J. T. Milik, *Discoveries in the Judaean Desert* (hereafter cited as DJD), I. *Qumrân Cave I*, Oxford, Clarendon Press, 1955, p. 4; John M. Allegro, *The Dead Sea Scrolls*, Harmondsworth, Middlesex, Penguin Books, 1956, pp. 27–33. It was not known that these additional materials should be classified as separate literary compositions until after the publication of the Manual of Discipline by the American Schools of Oriental Research in 1951.

5. The problem of giving documents appropriate Hebrew names is beginning to be avoided by assigning numbers to the manuscripts. In the case of small fragmentary texts of previously unknown works, this is doubtless the easiest and best way of handling them. However, it seems quite unnecessary and undesirable for the Copper Scroll from Cave Three with its record of buried treasure to be called 3Q 15.

PART I

THE MEANING OF THE SCROLLS FOR THE BIBLE

CHAPTER ONE

The Text and Composition of the Old Testament

The most obvious value of the Qumrân Scrolls is for determining the authentic text of the Old Testament, since indeed every book of the Hebrew Bible (unless it be Esther) is represented among the manuscript fragments of the fourth Qumrân cave alone.

THE TRADITIONAL HEBREW TEXT

Prior to the discovery of the Qumrân Scrolls our direct knowledge of the Hebrew Old Testament text was limited largely to the text of Rabbinic Judaism, which is known as the Massoretic text. The term "Massoretic," meaning "traditional," stands related to two different Hebrew words, *Massôret* and *Massôrâh*,[1] both of which mean "tradition." The former was used in Rabbinic literature to designate the text written only in consonants (which alone belonged to the traditional text) as distinct from that indicating the pronunciation (which would include the vowels). Although the term *Massôret* may sometimes have been used more inclusively, it is the term *Massôrâh* which is generally used to refer to the entire text: consonants, vowel indications, and accompanying textual notations.[2] It is this text which has been the basis of most English translations of the Bible, although in recent years increasing efforts have been made to correct that text on the basis of ancient versions.

The Massoretic text as we now possess it contains both vowels and

1. Alternative spellings are with one *s*; and thus *Webster's New Collegiate Dictionary* (Springfield, Mass., G. & C. Merriam Co., 1961) lists the words: "Masora, Masorah" and "Masoretic." However, preferred usage among contemporary scholars employs two *s*'s. Cf. Bleddyn J. Roberts, *The Old Testament Text and Versions*, Cardiff, University of Wales Press, 1951, pp. 40–42.
2. The more extensive Massoretic notes are not included in the standard editions of the Hebrew Bible, but they are published separately under the title *Massôrâh*.

consonants; but its oldest ancestors were without vowels.[3] The consonantal base of the Massoretic text is very ancient, much more ancient than it was thought to be. The once standard view, now known to be erroneous, traced it back in substantially its present form only to the second century A.D. Without clear indication of vowels, anyone reading such a text had to supply the vowels himself from context or depend upon the guidance of oral tradition. Finally, however, the Rabbinic scholars saw the wisdom of indicating the vowels directly in the manuscripts themselves. Scholars in Palestine and Babylonia experimented with different methods of doing this from the sixth to the eighth centuries A.D. The system developed at Tiberias, in Palestine, came into general use during the ninth and tenth centuries A.D. Our oldest extensive manuscripts of the Massoretic text come from this period.[4] Prior to the discovery of the Qumrân (or Dead Sea) Scrolls, these were our primary source of knowledge concerning the original Hebrew text.

THE ANCIENT VERSIONS

Fortunately, in the case of the five Books of Moses, we could consult the Samaritan Pentateuch, which was an independent transmission of the Hebrew text from pre-Christian times. For the whole Old Testament we could also consult ancient translations from the Hebrew into other languages. Such translations are called "versions," and chief among them are the following: the Septuagint (the primary Greek translation), the Targums (free translations into Aramaic),[5] the

---

3. Shortly before the Babylonian Exile, there was an occasional adaptation of consonants to vowel usage. In post-Exilic times this practice became more common and was developed to its fullest during the second century B.C.; but thereafter the popularity of such spellings (especially for Biblical manuscripts) declined.

4. For a discussion of these, see B. J. Roberts, *op. cit.,* pp. 8of.

5. The word *targûm* (hereafter cited as Targum) means "translation" and is sometimes used in Rabbinic literature for translations into any language. However, the word usually refers to the oral Aramaic translations which accompanied the reading of the Scriptures in the Synagogue. According to Rabbinic tradition, the practice of "Targuming" the Scriptures in Aramaic originated in the time of Ezra and the last Old Testament prophets. The Targum of the Pentateuch was subject to restoration (or revision?) by a man named Onkelos and the Targum of the Prophets was restored (or revised) by a man named Jonathan. These men lived after the destruction of Jerusalem by the Romans in A.D. 70, and they have given their names to the later written editions of the Targums of the Pentateuch and of the Prophets. In referring to these translations in subsequent pages of this book, I shall speak simply of the Targum, since the Biblical reference is sufficient indication as to which Targum is referred to. Traditions are vague with regard to the origin and development of other Targums to the Old Testament.

Peshitta (the principal Syriac translation), the Old Latin, the Coptic, and the Vulgate (Jerome's Latin translation).[6] The advantage of a version is that it may help in the interpretation of the Hebrew text, yet one must constantly seek to determine whether the translator of the version read the same Hebrew known to us, or whether his Hebrew readings were different. Although this study is often helpful, it does not always lead to sure results.

THE IMPORTANCE OF THE QUMRÂN SCROLLS

The manuscripts from the caves near the Dead Sea are mostly in the original languages of the Old Testament. (Although we have been speaking of the Old Testament as though it were all originally written in Hebrew, about 1½ per cent has come down to us in Aramaic.) The Biblical manuscripts of these important finds may therefore be used directly for correcting the Old Testament text. By their sometimes free use of vowel letters, whereby consonants were adapted to vowel usage,[7] they occasionally lead us to see new ways of reading the old words. Yet these documents must be scrutinized with care; for ancient copyists made mistakes. Moreover, there were different editions of the Biblical books which circulated at the same time. A prolonged and meticulous examination of a variant is often required before one can judge fairly as to its superiority or inferiority. Most of the texts are not even published as yet, so that one may safely say that many years of study lie ahead before any full and definitive use of the Dead Sea Scrolls can be made in the area of textual criticism of the Old Testament.

In certain cases, the scrolls contribute to the discussion of dating the composition of a Biblical work. Theories of composition stand related to readings and contents; and, in certain cases, to the dates of the manuscripts themselves. Although the present chapter will be focused chiefly upon matters of text, some attention will be devoted also to the significance of the scrolls in determining when certain books were written or compiled.

6. For a history of these and other ancient versions, see B. J. Roberts, *op. cit.;* F. F. Bruce, *The Books and the Parchments, Some Chapters on the Transmission of the Bible,* London, Pickering Inglis, 1950, rev. ed., 1953; Stanley Rypins, *The Book of Thirty Centuries, an Introduction to Modern Study of the Bible,* New York, Macmillan, 1951.
7. See above, pp. xvif., below, p. 165.

The Pentateuch

The text of the Pentateuch (or Torah) appears in three different forms. Most of the manuscripts differ little from the consonantal base of the Massoretic text. This type of manuscript alone is found among the Bar Kokhba manuscripts of the second century A.D.; and the Qumrân Scrolls prove that it is as ancient as the first two centuries B.C. It was once supposed that Rabbinic scholars of the second century A.D. created this text by selecting readings which pleased them from a wide variety of manuscript types. It now appears more probable that they chose one type of manuscript which already existed and undertook to standardize its readings in detail. Efforts to standardize this text may have begun earlier than is generally supposed.

A second form of Pentateuchal text found at Qumrân resembles that employed by those who translated the Pentateuch into Greek in the third century B.C. This Greek version is commonly called the Septuagint, or LXX, because according to Egyptian tradition it was prepared by seventy (or seventy-two) translators during the reign of Ptolemy Philadelphus (285–246 B.C.). This tradition seems to be reliable for the dating of the translation of the Pentateuch. The prophets were translated later that century; and the rest of the Old Testament, gradually, during the next two centuries. A variant view of the origin of the Septuagint is that of Paul Kahle, according to whom there were many different Greek translations prepared in the third and second centuries B.C., the Septuagint being the revised standard version which was produced in Alexandria about 100 B.C.[8] Whatever the origin of the Septuagint, this is the primary Greek version; and because of its antiquity and frequent divergence from the Massoretic text, it is the most important version for Old Testament criticism. Moreover, copies of this version dating from the third to the fifth centuries A.D. were our most ancient Old Testament manuscripts prior to the Qumrân Scroll

---

8. *Masoreten des Westens,* Vol. II, Beiträge zur Wissenschaft vom Alten und Neuen Testament, 3 Folge, Heft 14, 1930; *The Cairo Geniza,* London, London Academy, Oxford University Press, 1947, pp. 132–79. Kahle's views have been challenged by D. Barthélemy, "Redécouverte d'un chaînon manquant de l'histoire de la Septante," *Revue Biblique* (hereafter cited as *RB*), LX, 1953, pp. 18–29. To Barthélemy's views, Kahle has replied in "Die im August 1952 entdeckte Lederrolle mit dem griechischen Text der kleinen Propheten und das Problem der Septuaginta," *Theologische Literaturzeitung* (hereafter cited as *ThLZ*), Vol. 79, 1954, cols. 81–94. See, however, F. M. Cross, Jr., *The Ancient Library of Qumran and Biblical Studies,* Garden City, N.Y., Doubleday Company, Anchor Books, rev. ed., 1961, p. 171.

discoveries. Some scholars regarded the text of the Septuagint as definitely superior to the Massoretic text; while others largely repudiated the Septuagint, claiming that the translators employed great freedom in preparing this version. Between these two extremes, there were wide varieties of opinion; however, among the recent scroll finds are texts in Hebrew which support many of the Greek readings. These scrolls show that there existed a type (or family) of manuscript in Hebrew containing many of the same readings as found in the Septuagint.

The discovery of Hebrew manuscripts in such close agreement with the Septuagint indicates that we should not exaggerate the amount of freedom employed by the Septuagint translators. Some liberties were doubtless taken, especially where the Hebrew text was obscure and it required valiant effort for one to make sense out of a passage. Some Hebrew words were misunderstood. In the main, however, the "Seventy" translated faithfully the text which was before them — their degree of error being probably no greater than that of those who prepared the King James Version of the Holy Bible, who also sometimes misunderstood the Hebrew text from which they worked.

There are some very interesting examples of these newly found Hebrew readings which support the Septuagint. In Ex. 1:5, one scroll text reads seventy-five (rather than seventy) as the number of Jacob's offspring in Egypt.[9] The larger number is also found in the speech of Stephen recorded in Acts 7 (v. 14). For the first time we have proof that this reading once existed in Hebrew.

At Deut. 32:8, the Massoretic text reads:

When the Most High gave to the nations their inheritance,
    when He separated the children of men,
He set the number of the peoples
    according to the number of the children of Israel.
                                    (American Standard Version)

In the Septuagint the last clause reads: "according to the number of *the angels* of God." Now it happens that one expression for angels in the Old Testament is "sons of God" (as in Job 1:6), so scholars not unreasonably argued that the Hebrew which the "Seventy" rendered

9. See F. M. Cross, Jr., "The Scrolls and the Old Testament," *The Christian Century* (hereafter abbreviated as *CC*), August 10, 1955, p. 921.

as "angels" read literally "sons of God" rather than "children [literally, sons] of Israel." Many modern versions, including the Revised Standard Version, adopted this reading on the authority of the Septuagint version. It is precisely this reading "sons of God" which now finds attestation in a scroll fragment.[10]

The meaning of Deut. 32:8 differs according to which of the above readings we adopt. Rabbinic authorities, basing their contention upon the Massoretic text, argued that there are exactly seventy nations of mankind — the number of peoples exactly equaling the number of Israel's (i.e. Jacob's) children mentioned at Ex. 1:5 (cited above). The Septuagint reading indicates rather that the number of nations corresponds with the number of angels, so that each nation has a patron angel. This idea is found in Daniel, where one reads of the princes (or archangels) of Greece, Persia, and Israel (Dan. 10:10–21; 12:1). The role of angelic mediation in Daniel is not quite the same as in the scroll- and Septuagint-supported text of Deuteronomy, however, for Deut. 32:9 declares that the Lord Himself is the sole ruler of Israel, so that God's relationship to Israel is immediate, unmediated by any angel. This view of the direct relationship of God to the Hebrews is repeated in the Wisdom of Sirach (at 17:17) and is spelled out with precision in the Book of Jubilees, a work which seems to have attained canonical status with the Essenes. Jub. 15:30–32 defines God's election of Israel as a relationship of immediacy, in contrast with the abandoned, remote connection of God with heathen nations who are governed by angels that have led them astray. The errant behavior of these angels is like that of the gods of Psalm 82, whom the Lord threatens with destruction in order to make all nations His personal possession. In the thought of Jubilees there are also good angels, and they minister to Israel. Their special missions manifest God's constant and direct concern for His people. Along this line of reasoning, the Qumrân Community was probably able to reconcile its text of Deuteronomy with belief in Michael as Israel's guardian — Michael not acting on his own, but intervening only when sent by the Lord.[11]

10. See Patrick W. Skehan, "A Fragment of the 'Song of Moses' (Deut. 32) from Qumran," *The Bulletin of the American Schools of Oriental Research* (hereafter abbreviated as *BASOR*), No. 136 (Dec. 1954), p. 12.
11. On the eschatological intervention of Michael, see 1Q M xvii, 6ff. For an important study of this scroll, see Yigael Yadin, *The Scroll of the War of the Sons of Light against the Sons of Darkness* (translated from the Hebrew by Batya and Chaim Rabin), London, Oxford University Press, 1962.

A fragment of the Song of Moses in Deut. 32, which was found in Cave Four, has each stich (or half-line of Hebrew poetry) one above the other, as in modern translations of the Bible. Its text of verse 43 makes interesting comparison with our previously known Hebrew and Greek texts:

MASSORETIC TEXT

Sing joyfully, O nations, of His people;
    for the blood of His servants He avenges,
And takes vengeance on His adversaries,
    and purges His land, His people.

SEPTUAGINT

Rejoice, O heavens, with Him;
    and do obeisance to Him, all sons of God.
Rejoice, O nations, with His people
    and ascribe Him strength, all angels [or sons] of God;
For the blood of His sons He avenges,
    and takes vengeance and repays (His) adversaries,
And requites those who hate him (Him);
    and the Lord purges the land of His people.

SCROLL

Rejoice, O heavens, with Him;
    and do obeisance to Him, all ye gods;
For the blood of His sons He avenges,
    and takes vengeance on His adversaries,
And requites those who hate Him,
    and purges the land of His people.

In the first stich, the only difference in the consonantal text is the vocative "heavens" in the Septuagint and scroll texts where the Massoretic text reads "nations." The other differences are due to the Massoretic pointing, which makes "His people" the object of the Hebrew verb "sing joyfully of." The second stich of the scroll text reads "gods" for the Greek "sons of God." When the passage is quoted in the New Testament (Heb. 1:6), the phrase is appropriately rendered "angels of God." The third stich of the Greek is a doublet, or variant reading, of its first stich (as comparison with the Massoretic text shows). The reading of "His sons" for "His servants" in the fifth stich of the Greek text (in contrast with the second stich of the Massoretic text) requires that God's sons be understood differently here from what they are in the preceding lines, for the sons whose blood the Lord avenges are Israelites rather than angels. Though this shift in meaning is not impossible, it is noteworthy that it is avoided in the scoll reading of "gods" in stich 2, rather than "sons of God." At present we can only conjecture how the original text read. Patrick W. Skehan suggests the restoration:

> Rejoice, O heavens, with Him,
> and ascribe Him strength, all sons of God:
> For the blood of His sons He avenges,
> and purges the land of His people.[12]

In favor of Skehan's second stich is its greater dissimilarity to Psalm 97:7 ("Do obeisance to him, all ye gods"), a verse which may have influenced the wording of the present passage. Similarly, Skehan omits the description of God as taking vengeance on His adversaries and on those who hate Him, as perhaps taken over from verse 41 (the person being altered from the first to the third). In these views, Skehan may well be correct; yet other reconstructions are possible, such as the following:

> Rejoice, O heavens, with Him;
> and do obeisance to Him all ye gods,
> and ascribe Him strength, all angels of God.
> For the blood of His sons He avenges,
> and takes vengeance on His adversaries,
> and purges the land of His people.

This deletes only two clauses of the Greek text as doublets or later embellishments. At the same time, it retains the clause "takes vengeance on His adversaries" which appears in all three ancient recensions of the text. Both lines of the verse have three rather than two stichs. Uncertainty, however, must attach to any such suggestions. The simplest alternative would be the adoption of the scroll text as it stands; but this easy solution is not necessarily correct. The Septuagint is more ancient than the scroll fragment and may well preserve something of the

---

12. *Op. cit.*, p. 15, but without English translation; but see now Frank Cross, *The Ancient Library of Qumran*, pp. 182f. For still another reconstruction of the text, which appeared too late for consideration here, see G. Ernest Wright, "The Lawsuit of God: a Form-Critical Study of Deuteronomy 32," in *Israel's Prophetic Heritage* (Essays in honor of James Muilenburg, edited by Bernhard W. Anderson and Walter Harrelson), New York, Harper, 1962, pp. 26–67, with attention here to p. 33.

original wording lost in the other textual recensions. The Massoretic text is also old and must not be ignored.

Alongside these two types of Hebrew texts, the Massoretic and manuscripts with affinities to those used by the translators of the Septuagint, there is a third type of text resembling the Samaritan Pentateuch. The Samaritans were of Hebrew background and lived mostly in the region of the former northern kingdom of Israel. They adhered to the ancient tradition of worship at Mount Gerizim adjacent to Shechem, rather than at Mount Zion. When the schism occurred between them and the Judeans, probably in the fourth century B.C., they recognized as Scripture the Pentateuch alone. They did, however, possess also the Book of Joshua as a necessary historical work indicating fulfillment of the Lord's promises to the Patriarchs and to Moses. Characteristic of their Torah are not only many peculiar spellings, but a fullness of text, in which the laws given in one place are supplemented by additional information found elsewhere. Likewise, when Moses is given a divine injunction to perform a task, the text is never satisfied (as it usually is in the Jewish Bible) to declare in summary fashion that the assignment was performed. Rather in the account of the performance all the details of the divine command are spelled out one by one. There are also numerous readings at variance with the Jewish Torah, but sometimes supported by the Septuagint and other ancient versions. The Samaritan Pentateuch was also written in a form of pre-Exilic, paleo-Hebrew script in contrast with ordinary Jewish copies in which the Aramaic script was adopted for the writing of Hebrew.

Manuscripts with many features of the Samaritan recension have shown up in the Qumrân caves. They are fragmentary, and, insofar as their texts have been published or described, special readings supporting Samaritan beliefs and practices have not been discovered.[13] In view of the fragmentary character of the documents, this may be wholly accidental. Still, pro-Samaritan readings would hardly be expected in the documents of Qumrân, since the sectaries of the scrolls revered the Hebrew prophets, some of whom had associated Messianic hopes with the Jerusalem temple. The discovery, nevertheless, of Hebrew manuscripts having other affinities with the Samaritan Pentateuch is solid proof that the Samaritans adopted as authoritative a Pentateuchal text largely similar to that possessed by many loyal

13. See Patrick W. Skehan, "Exodus in the Samaritan Recension from Qumran," *The Journal of Biblical Literature* (hereafter abbreviated as *JBL*), LXXIV, 1955, pp. 182–7.

Judeans who believed that the true temple was at Jerusalem. The Samaritans did not develop their Torah in complete independence of the Jews; but it is possible that some of the repetitiousness of the Samaritan Pentateuch (excepting enrichment from parallel passages) is original, for this repetitive quality is characteristic of much ancient Near Eastern literature, including the mythological tablets of ancient Ugarit.

The above survey indicates the richness of the resources for Pentateuchal textual criticism brought to us by the Qumrân manuscripts. They not only attest the existence of a pre-Christian Old Testament text which was almost identical with that of the traditional Jewish Scriptures; but they also attest the antiquity of texts similar to the Samaritan Pentateuch and to the Septuagint. The scrolls will aid the textual critic in tracing the origin and development of these recensions, and at the same time stimulate him to sift them all with greater diligence for possibly original readings which may have survived in one recension only.

THE TEXT OF THE FORMER PROPHETS

Joshua, Judges, Samuel, and Kings are classified in the Hebrew Bible as the Former Prophets.[14] The designation indicates Jewish belief that these works consist not only of history but of a prophetic interpretation of Israel's life in relation to her God.

From this section of the Old Testament little has yet been published of the Qumrân finds, except important samplings from I Samuel. Three different manuscripts ranging from the late third century B.C. to the first century B.C. are more closely related to the Hebrew text which the "Seventy" translated into Greek than to the traditional text employed as the basis of most modern versions. The same situation is said to exist in connection with some fragments of Kings. There are also other manuscript materials similar to the Massoretic text; but in the Former Prophets' case the superiority of Septuagint readings is more often demonstrable than elsewhere in the Old Testament. This judgment had often been made before the discovery of the scrolls, and we are therefore most happy to have documentary evidence that the Septuagint version of these books was a careful translation from Hebrew prototypes.

An extensive section of text already published is I Sam. 1:22b—2:6.

14. The books of Ruth and Chronicles are omitted from this list, for they are found among the Writings, rather than the Prophets, in the Hebrew canon.

The Hebrew was pieced together from numerous fragments by Frank M. Cross, Jr.[15] To facilitate our study, I have followed the Revised Standard Version, except where variant readings of the scroll represent translatable differences. I have placed within brackets the restorations of missing text, mostly those of Cross, but partly my own. In italics are readings which agree with the presumed Hebrew text employed by the translators of the Greek Septuagint. In CAPITAL LETTERS is material peculiar to the scroll text. I have interpolated the verse numbers, which, of course, are absent from the original text.

[But Hannah did not go up *with him,* for she sa]id to her husband, "As soon as [the child is weaned, I will bring him, that he may appear] in the presence of the Lord, and abide [there] BEFORE [THE LORD for ever. AND I WILL] MAKE HIM A NAZIRITE FOR EVER, FOR THE FULL EXTENT OF [HIS LIFE." (23) Elkanah, her husband, said to her,] "Do what seems best to you, wait until [you have weaned him; only may the Lor]d establish *that which proceeds from your mouth.*" So the woman remained [and nursed her son until she weaned h]im. (24) *Then she took him up to Shiloh* WHEN [HER HUSBAND WAS GOING UP TO SACRIFICE TO THE LORD, *with*] a *three-year-old* [*bull*], and [LEAVENED] *bread,* [and an ephah of flour, and a skin of wine; and she brought them to the house of] the Lord at Shiloh; and the child was [*with them. They came into the presence of the Lord; and his father slew*] *the sacrifi*[*ce, just*] *as* [*he was accustomed to do from year to year to the Lord. So they brought the* child, (25) and h]e slew [the bull, while Hannah, the child's mother, brought him* to Eli. (26) And she said, "Oh,] My lord! [As you live, I am the woman who was standing here in your presence, praying to] the Lord. (27) [For this child I prayed; and the Lord has granted me my petition which I made to Him. (28). Therefore I have lent him to the Lo]rd; as long [*as he lives,* he is lent to the Lord." THUS SHE LEFT] HIM THERE and worshiped [the Lord, (2:1) and said:

"My heart exults in the Lord;]
   my strength is exalted in the L[or]d.
[My mouth derides my enemies.
   I rejoice in Thy salvation.

(2) Be]*cause there is none holy like the Lo*[*rd,*
   and none so righteous as our God.

15. "A New Qumran Biblical Fragment Related to the Original Hebrew Underlying the Septuagint," *BASOR*, No. 132 (Dec. 1953), pp. 15–26.

> There is none besides] Thee;
>   there is no rock like our God.
> (3) Talk no more so very proudly,
>   let *not* arrogance come from your mouth;
>   For [the Lord] is a God of *knowledge*
>   [*and a God who weighs actions.*
> (4) The bow of the migh]ty *is broken,*
>   but the f[ee]ble gir[d on strength.
> (5) Those who are full have hired themselves out for bread,
>   and are hungry.]
>   AS FOR [the barre]n, she has borne [seven,
>   but she who has many children is forlorn.
> (6) The Lord kills and brings to life;]
>   He brings down [to Sheol and raises up]."

Interest in the above passage of the Samuel Scroll attaches not only to the large amount of material agreeing with the Septuagint (here italicized), but also to the additional matter (here in CAPITALS). The information that Samuel was made a Nazirite (v. 22) is probably authentic. The omission of this from both the Hebrew and Greek texts previously known is readily explained. The eye of an early scribe skipped from the first "for ever" to the second "for ever," omitting all intervening material. This explanation implies that the following words "for the full extent of his life" are not original to the text but are an interpolated explanation as to what "for ever" means here. This is a true gloss and an important proof that "for ever" (literally, "for the age") in Old Testament usage often means something quite different from "eternally."

A precisely similar omission occurred in the traditional Hebrew text of verse 24, the Massoretic text skipping from the word "child" in the middle of the verse to the same word at the end of the verse. The resultant text would run literally, "The child (was) a child," which in the Revised Standard Version is rendered: "The child was young." In this case the intervening material is fully preserved in the Septuagint, enabling us to restore the large lacunae in the scroll.

Some of the above translation is italicized as in agreement with the Septuagint, even though the English wording agrees with the Revised Standard Version. In these cases, the English version has emended the text, either tacitly (that is, without footnote) or explicitly (with footnote), so as to agree with the Greek version. Thus the scroll reading, "a three-year-old bull" (v. 24), agrees with the Greek and justifies the Standard Bible Committee's alteration of the text from the Hebrew reading, "three bulls" (as indicated in the RSV footnote). In the first clause of 2:4, the Massoretic Hebrew reads, literally, "The bow of the mighty broken ones." Contextually, "broken" should refer to the "bow," not to the "mighty." Here the RSV presents a tacit emendation, rendering, "The bows of the mighty *are broken.*" The scroll text once more vindicates the rendering of the Standard Bible Committee.

One must constantly stress that *no* manuscript is free from scribal error. Thus, in the above quotation of I Sam. 2:5 the text involves a serious omission and partial corruption of the verse. The original text of 2:5 should be read, according to the unanimous textual evidence of other sources, precisely as translated in the Revised Standard Version:

> Those who were full have hired themselves out for bread,
>> but those who were hungry have ceased to hunger.
> The barren has borne seven,
>> but she who has many children is forlorn.

The errors in the scroll are chargeable either to the copyist of this document or to an earlier scribe whose work he copied. In either case, it is clear that this tremendously valuable scroll, like all other manuscripts, must be used critically.

Dr. Cross believes that the readings of this Samuel Scroll are frequently superior to both the Massoretic and Septuagint texts. One of the many examples he gives is that of I Sam. 23:10–12, where we may make the following comparisons (following and modifying the RSV). A few focal points of the text which figure in our subsequent discussion are italicized. Again, brackets indicate extensive lacunae in the scroll text, but the restorations within the brackets are governed by careful measurements of the amount of text to be restored.[16]

MASSORETIC TEXT

Then said David, "O LORD, the God of Israel, thy servant has surely heard that Saul seeks to come to Keilah, to destroy the city on my account. *Will the men of Keilah surrender me into his hand?* Will Saul come down, as thy servant has heard? O LORD, the God of Israel, I beseech thee, tell thy servant." And the LORD said, "He will come

16. Cf. Cross in *CC*, Aug. 10, 1955, p. 921.

down." Then said David, *"Will the men of Keilah surrender me and my men into the hand of Saul?"* And the LORD said, "They will surrender you."

SEPTUAGINT

Then said David, "O Lord, the God of Israel, Thy servant has surely heard that Saul seeks to come to Keilah, to destroy the city on my account. *Will they shut (me) out?* And now, will Saul come down, as Thy servant heard? O Lord, the God of Israel, tell thy servant." And the Lord said, "They will shut you out."

SCROLL

[Then said David, "O LORD, the God of Israel,] Thy servant [has surely] heard that Saul seeks [to come to Keilah, to destroy the city on my account. And now, will Saul come down, as Thy servant heard? O LORD,] the God of Israel, tell [Thy] servant." [*And the* LORD *said,* "He will come down." Then said David, "Will the men of Keilah surrender me and my men into the hand of Sa]ul?" *And the* LORD *said,* "They will sur[render you."]

In the italicized portions of the Massoretic text, one will notice that the question "Will the men of Keilah surrender me?" is asked twice, but only the second time is it followed by the answer. Doubtless the scroll text as restored by Dr. Cross is correct in omitting the first posing of this query. It seems probable also that the Septuagint version's very short form of the question was not a part of its Hebrew original. With the scroll text taken into account, one can readily see that the eye of the translator (or copyist) of the Septuagint skipped from the first to the second "And the LORD said," with the result that to the question, "And now, will Saul come down?" came the inappropriate reply, "They will shut you out." Puzzled by this lack of congruity, a later scribe of the Septuagint reintroduced the lost question in a truncated form. However, he made no attempt to supply the lost answer to the question, "Will Saul come down?" The scroll is more accurate here than either of the previously known texts.

Dr. Cross has been able to piece together some fragments of most of the chapters of I and II Samuel in the third century B.C. manuscript alone. Fragments of two other scrolls of later date are less extensive but bear witness to a Hebrew text of Samuel often similar to that used by the translators of the Septuagint. The evidence is sufficient to establish the fact that the Massoretic text is very faulty and often guilty of omissions. It should not be of serious concern, therefore, that parts of the Samuel text have not survived; for with discretion we may use the Septuagint itself in all such cases. Thus, the original text of II Sam. 13:17 probably read as in the Septuagint:

> But Absalom pressed him until he allowed to go
> with him Amnon and all the sons of the king.
> *And Absalom prepared a feast like the feast of a king.*

It is easy to understand how a scribe could accidentally omit the second half of the verse (italicized above), since it begins and ends similarly as the first half. Support for the Septuagint reading may appear when all the scroll fragments are published; but whether or not it does, we may well adopt this fuller reading.

Another verse for which we shall eagerly await the textual evidence is II Sam. 13:39; the Hebrew text according to most scholars is untranslatable, but it should mean, "And King David longed to go forth to Absalom." The Septuagint reads here, *"The spirit of* the king longed to go forth to Absalom." In favor of this reading is the feminine gender of the Hebrew verb, "longed," which could hardly take King David as its subject! The gender agrees, however, with the Hebrew word *rûah* ("spirit"). Hence, all the English versions, including the King James, supply the word "spirit" from the Greek text. A careful scrutiny of the Massoretic pointing of the Hebrew, however, convinces me that the verse is not ungrammatical. David is not the subject of the verb, but the object, so that the Massoretic text should be translated: "To go forth to Absalom consumed King David." The infinitive phrase is the subject of the verb which is pointed transitively by the Massoretes. This more difficult (yet grammatically correct) construction may or may not be original; but the commonly recognized principle of giving preference to the more difficult (yet defensible) reading would favor this hitherto misunderstood Hebrew text of II Sam. 13:39.[17]

Not only do all the reported fragmentary texts of Samuel tend to support Septuagint readings rather than peculiarly Massoretic readings, but they also attest a Hebrew text which in parallel passages agrees more closely with Chronicles than the Massoretic text. As scholars have long theorized, the author of Chronicles made use of Samuel and

17. The reason for favoring the more difficult reading is that the tendency of ancient scribes was to substitute easier readings for hard ones, not vice versa. However, this principle can be applied too rigidly by failure to recognize that accidental errors may alter the text to something more difficult (if not impossible) to understand.

Kings, together with additional sources, in preparing his account of the same history. Some of the differences between Chronicles and Samuel-Kings are due to these additional sources. Others are attributable to the different interests and viewpoints of the authors. According to Cross, some are also to be accounted for by the Chronicler's possession of a text of Samuel unlike the Hebrew recension previously known to us. This Samuel text was shared both by Palestine (as the Qumrân texts show) and by Egypt (where the Septuagint was prepared). Therefore, the ancestry of the Massoretic edition of Samuel must derive from some other quarter, most probably from Babylonia.[18] This is a reasonable suggestion, for in Babylonia there was a large Jewish population which was sufficiently remote as to have its own special editions of Biblical books. Unless fragments of this Massoretic type of Samuel text are found in the area of Qumrân, we may well conclude that it was introduced into Palestine after the First Jewish Revolt against Rome, which resulted in the concealing and destruction of so many Palestinian manuscripts that copies of many Biblical books had to be imported from Babylonia.

THE TEXT OF THE LATTER PROPHETS

Isaiah, Jeremiah, Ezekiel, and the Twelve are the four books called "the Latter Prophets" in the Hebrew Bible. Our English Bibles group Lamentations and Daniel with the first three, which then are classified as "Major Prophets" as distinguished from the twelve "Minor Prophets" — the designations "major" and "minor" referring to the size of the books, not to the importance of their contents.

Fragments of many scrolls of Isaiah appear in the Qumrân caves. One scroll has survived with almost perfect preservation in Cave One. It is the scroll that deviates most frequently from the traditional Hebrew text. Still, it more often agrees with the Massoretic text against the ancient versions than with them against the Massoretic text. The text of this scroll is so very important that I have reserved a major part of the present book for an examination of it.

In the case of Jeremiah we are confronted with fragments of two different editions of the book. We are familiar with the fact that modern books often undergo revision in subsequent editions, and that a revised edition may be altered, enlarged, and even have some

---

18. Cross, *op. cit.*, pp. 188–92. See also his article in *The Interpreter's Bible* (hereafter cited as *IB*), Nashville and New York, Abingdon, 1957, Vol. 12, p. 656.

of the material rearranged. Revised editions may be prepared by the author, or posthumously by another author. Not only is this true of modern times, however; the same thing occurred in the composition of Biblical books. The awareness of such a phenomenon has called forth a new science devoted to the task of determining the authorship, date, nature, and form of the original composition. This science is known as higher criticism. Such "criticism" is an attempt to understand and appreciate a book more fully through discovery of the literary processes through which it passed. In most cases only one major edition of the text of a book has survived; but study of the text often suggests that certain materials may have originally, and more logically, stood in a different order. Certain other materials are suspected to be later additions. The religious value of these interpolations may be as great as (or even greater than) the contributions of the original author; but they are more readily understood and adequately appreciated in a different historical setting from that of the principal author. Higher criticism is ideally, therefore, a higher appreciation of a composition.

Now it happens that in the Septuagint and Hebrew texts of Jeremiah there are important differences. This Greek version is about one-eighth shorter and some of the materials are in a different order. Though a few critics have claimed that the translators of the Septuagint are responsible for a disarranged and truncated text, other scholars have attributed the differences to variant editions of the Hebrew Book of Jeremiah, claiming that the "Seventy" translated quite faithfully the Hebrew text which they possessed. The latter position is supported by some important scroll fragments found in Cave Four, for some of the materials appear in the Septuagint order and with its briefer form of text.[19] Obviously, at least two different editions of Jeremiah existed in Hebrew. Back of them must have existed still earlier editions of the prophetic book. The earliest of these was the scroll which was hacked to pieces and burned by King Jehoiakim (Jer. 36:20ff.). At the conclusion of this account, we are explicitly told:

"Then Jeremiah took another scroll and gave it to Baruch the scribe, the son of Neriah, who wrote on it at the dictation of Jeremiah all the words of the scroll which Jehoiakim king of Judah had burned in the fire; *and many similar words were added to them.*" (36:32)

19. Cross, *The Ancient Library,* rev. ed., p. 187.

There is no evidence to identify either the shorter or longer editions of Jeremiah's scroll mentioned in this verse with the Septuagint or Massoretic text types which have come down to us. On the contrary, both of these known text types probably contain passages of later date than the two scrolls referred to in Jer. 36.

One may raise here an interesting question relating to the Biblical canon. Which form of Jeremiah, that of the Septuagint or that of the Massoretic text, should be included in our Bible? Protestants and Jews have hitherto resolved this problem by turning to the supposed "original" Hebrew text. At one time, however, more than one edition existed in Hebrew. Suppose a Hebrew text similar to the one on which the Septuagint was based had been fully preserved (as the Complete Isaiah Scroll in Cave One), which Hebrew form should we adopt for Biblical translation? In the textual criticism of the New Testament, the effort has been to discover the more primitive text and to translate it, even though this means leaving out whole passages. Thus the discovery of ancient Greek manuscripts of the New Testament has altered considerably the textual base of modern versions from that followed by the translators of the earliest English versions. This has involved the omission of verses here and there, and most notably the dropping of Mark 16:9–20 and John 7:53—8:11.

All this is mild, however, compared with the differences between the two surviving recensions of Jeremiah. An adoption of the Septuagint form of text for translation would confuse many a Bible lover, who would need to look for familiar passages of Jeremiah under differing chapter numbers, or who would look in vain for certain verses which had disappeared. An answer to the canonical question might well be that, despite the possibility that the shorter recension of the Septuagint may be earlier, the longer recension is canonical, for it was the one finally adopted and perpetuated by the Jews. In that case, the shorter recension would be used by Biblical translators only for the correction of scribal errors that occurred in the transmission of the longer edition. With similar logic, one may argue against current translation practices regarding Mark 16:9–20 and John 7:53—8:11, that these passages are worthy of recognition as Scripture. In that case, they should be included within the text of Mark and John (or handled as appendices) and printed in the same size of type as the rest of these gospels. In view of our textual knowledge, they should be bracketed, and footnotes should indicate that they are not in the most ancient manuscripts; but probably no aspersion should be cast upon them on this ground alone.[20] Present practice usually denies the Scriptural value of the passages, and the type size employed in the footnotes where they are cited is too small to encourage general reading. The New English Bible is a commendable exception to this practice.

Almost nothing has been published yet of the fragmentary Ezekiel manuscripts. As so far reported they are in harmony with the Massoretic text. A fragment removed by Dr. John Strugnell from the outside of the 11Q Ezekiel (whose preserved text begins with Chap. 4) possibly supports an RSV emendation of Ezek. 5:15. An attempt to open this scroll was largely a failure, since the document had almost completely disintegrated into an unstratified mass of desiccated gelatin. A few small fragments (or scales) of text were recoverable from the outside and seem to indicate a general agreement with the familiar Massoretic text.[21]

THE TEXT OF HABAKKUK

In the case of the Minor Prophets (also included in the Latter Prophets) the numerous small manuscript fragments are as yet unpublished, as also the reputedly more extensive material from Qumrân. Large parts of a Minor Prophets Scroll from Murabba'ât have been published, but this scroll is in almost full agreement with the Massoretic text. It is quite otherwise in the case of the text of the Habakkuk Midrash found in Cave One. It quotes only the first two chapters of the prophet, and a few lines of text are missing from each column at the bottom of the scroll, and yet of these chapters about 85 per cent of the text survives in a form extremely rich with variants. In all they total 135. The greatest number of variants affects spelling only, or at most the pronunciation of the Hebrew, without altering the grammatical form or sense. Of fifty-six major variants in which questions of grammar and sense are

20. The late Dr. John McNaugher, who for fifty-four years taught New Testament at Pittsburgh-Xenia Theological Seminary, used to distinguish between non-authentic and spurious. He classified the Pericope of John as non-authentic (as not written by John); but he regarded the long addition at the end of Mark as not only non-authentic but spurious (by reason of objectionable elements in it). Printing the passages in the same size of type as the rest would not only make for easier reading, it would also tend to prevent an automatic repudiation of these passages as unworthy of a place in Scripture. The average reader regards the removal of a passage to a mere footnote as tantamount to its removal from the Bible.

21. See Wm. H. Brownlee, "The Scroll of Ezekiel from the Eleventh Qumran Cave," *Revue de Qumran* (hereafter abbreviated as *RQ*), No. 13, 1963, pp. 11–28.

involved, thirty have been judged to be superior readings — that is, deemed more likely to be original than those in our traditional text.[22] This is a very rich gleaning, and yet only about a third of these appreciably affect translation.

The text of Hab. 1:5 is not wholly preserved in the scroll, but the interpretation of the verse repeatedly refers to "traitors" (or "faithless ones"), so that there is no room for doubt that the reading of the scroll was: "Look, O traitors, and see," rather than "Look among the nations, and see." The former is the reading followed by the Greek, Acts 13:41 ("scoffers"), and the Syriac. Contextually, this reading joins well with the preceding verse where the lawless in Judah, who have repudiated the Deuteronomic reform in its social and ethical implications, are condemned. The readings "O traitors (*BGDYM*) and "among the nations" (*BGWYM*) resemble each other so closely that a scribal error could easily have been made from one to the other.

The scroll text of Hab. 1:8 involves several slight changes which present us with poetic structure a bit different from the Massoretic text but similar to the Greek version.

MASSORETIC TEXT

Swifter than panthers are their horses
and fiercer than evening wolves,
   and their horsemen press forth.

Their horsemen come from afar;
   they fly as a vulture
   hastening to devour.

SEPTUAGINT

More bounding than panthers are their horses
and fiercer than Arabian wolves.

Their horsemen press forth,
   and course on from afar.
They fly as a vulture
hastening to devour.

SCROLL

Swifter than panthers are their horses
and fiercer than evening (or, Arabian) wolves.

22. See Wm. H. Brownlee, *The Text of Habakkuk in the Ancient Commentary from Qumran*, *JBL* Monograph Series, XI, 1959.

> They press forth and course on,
> their horsemen from afar.
> They fly as a vulture
> hastening to devour.

In the Massoretic text, the two occurrences of horsemen seem unduly repetitious, but this may be partially relieved by dividing the verse so as to put one in the first half and the other in the second half. In both the Septuagint and scroll texts one occurrence of "horsemen" yields its place to a verb.[23] In the Septuagint it is the second occurrence; in the scroll it is the first. The verb "come" is also omitted from both texts. The result of these variants is that four short stichs come together to yield the galloping rhythm suited to the portrayal of rushing cavalry. The Hebrew assonance (represented in translation above) also adds to the poetic beauty of the verse. It is probable that either the Septuagint or the scroll text is original. Possibly the moving forward of the subject in the Greek version is simply a matter of translation. It would therefore be safer to follow the scroll in ascertaining the original Hebrew order.

Several variants occur likewise in the text of Hab. 1:17, which may be compared as follows:

MASSORETIC TEXT

Shall he therefore empty his *net, and that* continually,
to slay nations without showing pity?

SCROLL

He shall therefore draw his *sword* continually,
to slay nations, *and that* without showing pity.

Most of the ancient versions (including the Septuagint) support the declarative rather than the interrogative character of the verse. The Coptic version, one Greek manuscript of the Lucian recension, and a newly found Greek text believed to have come from the Murraba'ât Caves support the reading "sword." The Targum and the Syriac versions support the scroll's placement of the conjunctional stress "and that." Many interpreters have preferred to read "empty his net" for "draw his sword," in view of the references to "net" and "seine" in the preceding verse. One slays "nations," however, with swords rather than nets. It is therefore probable that "sword" (*herev*) rather than "net" (*herem*) is the original reading. Here we have a literal application of the figurative language of the preceding verse.

23. See Brownlee, *op. cit.,* § 11–14, pp. 11–17.

At 2:1a, the Habakkuk Commentary reads:

> I will stand upon my watch,
> and set me upon *my* tower.

The second "my" is supported only by the Targum, but it is favored by the internal evidence of parallelism and the absence of any article with "tower" in the traditional text, where the definiteness of the possessive in *"my* watch" might well have been matched by *"the* tower." Stylistically the scroll reading is better, but the traditional Hebrew reading is more strongly attested.

At 2:15 and 16, the Revised Standard Version has twice emended the text, altering "your wrath" to "his wrath" and "be uncircumcised" to "stagger." In the case of the latter, the Greek and Syriac versions are cited. In both cases the Habakkuk Commentary supports the emendations.

In the above examples, I have chosen simple passages where the presentation is easily followed by the general reader. Often in textual criticism, however, it is not a matter of merely following one text or another, but of drawing upon the readings of many texts and versions. Conjectural emendation may also be required in order to achieve a text most likely original. An example of this kind is Hab. 2:4–5. Any reader who finds the discussion too intricate may skip the remainder of this section; but for those who are willing to try to follow, I shall present as clearly as possible to the non-technical reader the process involved in the restoration of this highly important passage to its approximately original form. I begin by presenting a three-way comparison of Hab. 2:5a:

MASSORETIC TEXT

> Moreover, wine is a traitor,
> a presumptuous and restless man.

SCROLL

> Moreover, wealth betrays the presumptuous
> man, and he shall not abide (or succeed?).

SEPTUAGINT

> But the audacious and scornful man is
> a braggart, yet he shall not succeed.

The Septuagint version was translated from a Hebrew text fairly close to that quoted by the Habakkuk Commentary from Qumrân. The same word translated "audacious" by the "Seventy" was taken to mean "wealth" in the interpretation of the Habakkuk Commentary.[24] Indeed different vocalization of the same consonants is alone involved, since Hebrew originally was written without vowels. The scroll's verb "betrays" (*YBGD*) appears closer to the Greek "and scornful" (*WBGD*) than to the Massoretic "traitor" (*BGD*), when one considers that, in the script of this scroll, rarely, if ever, is there a clear distinction between *W* and *Y*. In the next clause, though the translations differ, the underlying Hebrew is probably identical. Dr. W. F. Albright suggests that the Septuagint understanding of the verb (which occurs only here in the Old Testament) is correct. He also believes that the word "audacious" (*hayyân* or *hawwân*) referred originally to the Canaanite Hayyân, whose role as the god of craftsmanship is similar to that of the Mediterranean Hermes, the crafty inventor of legend. With some slight emendations and with partial reliance upon the Habakkuk Commentary, he would read and translate:

> Even though he be tricky as Hayyân,
> the presumptuous man shall not succeed.[25]

"Even though" is a possible rendering of the introductory particles *af kî*, instead of "moreover." With this understanding of the construction, and with close adherence to the Hebrew prototype of the Septuagint, one could read and translate:

> Even though audacious and treacherous,
> the presumptuous man shall not succeed (or, abide?).

Another possible meaning of the particles is "much more," or, as when following a statement of negation, "much less." Contextually, however, such meanings are unsuitable.[26] My preferred reconstruction of the text which Habakkuk was to inscribe upon plaques is as follows:

---

24. The word *HWN* when vocalized as *huwwân* means "audacious," but when vocalized as *hôn*, it means "wealth." A possible variant spelling for *HWN* would be *HYN* (*hayyân* = *hawwân*). A very ancient spelling for "wine" was *YN* (attested in the Samaritan Ostraca of the ninth century B.C.). Thus it is easy to see how an original *HYN* came to be interpreted as meaning *hay-yân* ("the wine") and was later given the longer, revised spelling *HYYN* (*hay-yayin*) which is found in the Massoretic text.

25. Cited by Brownlee, *op. cit.,* p. 48.

26. In the extant order of the text, only the meaning "much less" would be appropriate, but it does not follow the negative immediately. In the order of the text as reconstructed below, either comparison would introduce a distinction between more or less heinous sinners, which is alien to the context.

4a Behold, [the naughty] is haughty;
    his soul is not humble within him.
5a Even though audacious and treacherous,
    the presumptuous man shall not abide;
4b   but the righteous by his faithfulness shall live.

In the above reconstruction, it is suggested that a word has fallen out of the first stich of 2:4, most probably a word resembling "haughty" (literally, "puffed up"), just as "naughty" and "haughty" resemble one another in English. It is next suggested that 2:5a fits best after 2:4a and that 2:4b stood originally as an antithetical conclusion. In this position the uncertainty of the meaning of the verb translated "abide" or "succeed" is resolved on the side of the former, since it is the antithesis of *live*. This accords with the Targum's rendering: "shall not survive." One will notice also the climactic force of 4b as rearranged.[27] There are uncertainties with regard to details of the text, but I believe this is an approximate picture of Habakkuk's placarded revelation.

The rest of Hab. 2 is best interpreted as an oracle against Assyria, whose introduction is in 2:5b:

Assyria enlarged his appetite as Sheol,
    and he as death could never be satisfied.
He gathered to himself all the nations
    and amassed to himself all the peoples.

The first word ('ŠR) has universally been interpreted as "who," but it can also be read as "Assyria."[28] The meaning "who" required that 2:5b stand in immediate connection with 2:5a for it to have an appropriate antecedent. In fact, it is this misinterpretation which probably led to the displacement of 2:4b. The reading of "Assyria" here need not involve any denial of the correctness of the reading "Chaldeans" at 1:6 — a read-

27. One need not suspect the genuineness of 4b on the grounds that the preceding line is a distich, rather than a tristich. The function of the third stich in a tristich is often to achieve the sort of emphasis that this passage illusrates. Alternation between distichs and tristichs is common in Hebrew poetry. For the whole passage, see my revision of the article on Habakkuk in *Dictionary of the Bible* (edited by James Hastings, Revised Edition by Frederick C. Grant and H. H. Rowley), New York, Scribner, 1963, p. 356. For a technical treatment, see my article, "The Placarded Revelation of Habakkuk," *JBL*, LXXXII, Part III (Sept. 1963).
28. In the Massoretic text the word is vocalized as *'ᵃsher* (who); but the same consonants may be vocalized as *'ashshûr* (Assyria). For the defective spelling of the latter, see I Chron. 5:6. For another example of the wrong Massoretic vocalization of the word, see Isa. 5:28: "As for Assyria, his arrows are sharp" — rather than, "Who, his arrows . . ." (i.e., "Whose arrows . . .").

ing fully attested in all our sources, including the Habakkuk Commentary from Cave One. Since the collapse of Assyria was concurrent with the rise of Chaldea mentioned at 1:6, it is not surprising to find oracles dealing with both Chaldea and Assyria by the same prophet. The taunting dirge of 2:5b–20 would be admirably appropriate after either 612 B.C. or 605 B.C. — the former date being that of the fall of Nineveh, the latter, that of the destruction of the last vestige of the Assyrian kingdom. We may recall here Nahum's dirge upon the fall of Nineveh.

The result of this venture in textual restoration is, I believe, the clarification of Habakkuk's fundamental message of 2:4–5a and the recovery of the proper historical reference in 2:5b–20. Both are basic to an understanding of Habakkuk's teaching and place in history. Textual criticism is no mere academic exercise; it often achieves results which are exciting for the Biblical interpreter.

THE TEXT OF THE SACRED WRITINGS

The third division of the Hebrew Bible, after the Law and the Prophets, is called the Kətûvîm (Writings). A Greek equivalent to this term is Hagiographa (Sacred Writings). In Kittel's Biblia Hebraica, the orders of the Writings is as follows:

Psalms	Lamentations
Job	Esther
Proverbs	Daniel
Ruth	Ezra-Nehemiah
Song of Songs	Chronicles
Ecclesiastes	

Variations of this list appear in other Hebrew Bibles, as also in the canonical lists found in Rabbinic sources. One listing which appeals to the present author is that which puts Chronicles before the Psalms,[29]

29. Cf. the table given by C. D. Ginsburg, Introduction to the Masoretico-Critical Edition of the Hebrew Bible, London, 1897, p. 7. Ginsburg's presentation is discussed by Ludwig Blau, "Bible Canon," in The Jewish Encyclopedia, New York and London, Funk and Wagnalls Co., 1902, Vol. III, p. 144. According to his analysis, the Massoretic tradition begins the Kətûvîm with Chonicles; whereas the Talmudic (that of Baba Batra 14b) places Ruth before Psalms and concludes the canon with Chronicles. Ginsburg's fifth order gives the beginning sequence as Chronicles, Ruth, Psalms. One is puzzled to explain why Chronicles was placed after Ezra-Nehemiah, unless the earliest order placed Chronicles at the head of the list and was later replaced by Ruth in the listing given by Baba Batra. The genealogy at the end of Ruth with its reference to David doubtless contributed to the choice of Ruth as an introduction to the Psalter.

for it would give a possible explanation for the unexpected sequence of Ezra-Nehemiah before, rather than after, Chronicles. If Chronicles were placed at the head of the list, the Chronicler's treatment of the origin of the temple cult and of the development of psalmody would serve as an apt introduction to the Psalms. The Writings would also be suitably rounded out at the end with Ezra-Nehemiah, the companion and concluding volume of the Chronicler's work. It would be as though the Chronicler's historical treatises were separated and used as the frame into which the other Writings were inserted. Perhaps this was the original sequence, and at a later date Chronicles was moved to the end in order to give precedence to some other book. Sometimes the Psalms are given first place, and other times the Book of Ruth.

Job

Jewish tradition often attributed the composition of the Book of Job to Moses, and located the story of Job either in the Patriarchal Age or shortly before the time of Moses. Though no modern critical scholar trusts this tradition, some reasons for its origin are obvious: (1) Job, even in his most pious moments, never recalls the Law of Moses, and so, presumably, he lived before Moses. (2) The Chaldeans are described as nomadic raiders, who are not yet a civilized world power (Job 1:17). (3) The earliest author of Biblical literature must be Moses; hence to him must be ascribed the composition of the Book of Job. Reason No. 1 may be readily explained by noting that Job is an Edomite and is represented as debating with other Edomites.[30] True to this background, the author of the book avoids citations of the Torah of Moses. Reason No. 2 is highly significant in indicating the antiquity of the legend concerning Job which was utilized as the framework into which the later, more sophisticated, author inserted the debates concerning human suffering and theodicy. The viewpoint expressed in No. 3 need not seem sur-

---

30. Robert H. Pfeiffer (*Introduction to the Old Testament,* New York and London, Harper, 3rd ed., 1941, pp. 678–83) went so far as to argue that the author of Job was himself an Edomite, which seems unlikely when one considers that the monotheism of the book far exceeds even the monotheistic tendencies of the famed sun-worshipper Pharaoh Akhnaton. Cf. Job 31:24–28. The ethical standards of Job (Chaps. 29–31) are the highest in the Old Testament and must surely have as their antecedent the preaching of the Hebrew prophets — whatever the nationality of the author. Pfeiffer asserted that the author of Job "could easily have read Israelite writings such as Jer. 20:14–18, which may have inspired Job 3." On ancient conjectures concerning the antiquity of Job, see Peter Katz in the *Zeitschrift für die neutestamentliche Wissenschaft* (hereafter abbreviated as *ZNW*), Vol. 47, 1956, p. 208.

prising, if we consider the pre-eminent place of Moses as the assumed author of the Pentateuch. Although the Essenes may have entertained the possibility of other early figures writing their own books, the fact that only certain copies of the Pentateuch and Job are written in their entirety in the paleo-Hebrew script strongly suggests that presumed Mosaic authorship was the basis for this practice.

The paleo-Hebrew script, which was probably a Hebrew borrowing from the Canaanites, was largely given up in post-Exilic times in favor of the more universal script of Aramaic for the writing of Hebrew. The paleo-Hebrew is used in a few of the Qumrân manuscripts for the writing of the divine name (especially Yahweh, the ineffable Tetragrammaton). It was also employed on Hasmonean coins. The Aramaic calligraphy is referred to popularly today as "square Hebrew," even though it is of Aramaic origin and is used in Hebrew Bibles for both Hebrew and Aramaic. The vast majority of the Qumrân manuscripts are written in this "square Hebrew," but Job and the Pentateuch have the distinction of being sometimes represented in paleo-Hebrew. This probably indicates belief in a common Mosaic authorship for these books. Perhaps the unpublished Aramaic Targum of Job from Cave Eleven will shed some light upon this question. In any case, the existence of such a written Targum stresses the importance attached to the book.

Psalms

Although many different manuscripts of the Psalms have been found in the Qumrân Caves, little of this material has been published. A large part of this work appears among the documents of Cave Eleven, and ten or more copies are to be found among the Cave Four documents. From published notices, it appears that the psalms are not always in the same order in which they appear in the Massoretic text. In some cases, perhaps, a more original order may be attested which will be of help in studying the growth of the Psalter (or Book of Psalms) as a bringing together of collections of grouped psalms,[31] but one wonders whether special cultic practices in the Qumrân Community may have influenced the arrangement in special cases.

Frank Cross has indicated that one of the Psalms manuscripts from

---

31. On "The Psalter as a Compilation," see W. Stewart McCullough in the *IB*, Vol. 4, pp. 7f.; John Paterson, *The Praises of Israel*, New York, Scribner's, 1950, Chap. 2, pp. 12–22.

Cave Four attests so-called Maccabean psalms at a period which is roughly contemporary with their supposed composition.[32] If this is true, it would seem that we should abandon the idea of any of the canonical psalms being of Maccabean date, for each song had to win its way in the esteem of the people before it could be included in the sacred compilation of the Psalter. Immediate entrée for any of them is highly improbable.

The radically different character of the manuscript 11Q Ps[a] is a challenge to this view, for this Psalm Scroll contains not only thirty-six canonical psalms (nos. 101–103, 109, 105, 146, 148, 121–130, 132, 119, 135, 136, 118, 145, 139, 137, 138, 93, 141, 133, 144, 142, 143, 149, 150, 140, 134) but also eight non-canonical compositions![33] The beginning of this scroll is missing, so we cannot be sure at what point it began; nor can we be certain of the exact order of the first four listed here, since they are represented by detached fragments. Since approximately the bottom third of each column is also missing, we may wonder whether a brief psalm like 131 could be missing from this list merely because it appeared at the bottom of a column.

This intermingling of the non-canonical compositions with the canonical indicates a certain liberality toward the Book of Psalms which made possible later insertions. These occur in a manuscript dated paleographically to the middle of the first century A.D.; and there are some indications that most, if not all of these, may have been composed prior to the establishment of the Qumrân Community. In other words, even though these psalms represent a late insertion into this special Psalter, they had first of all circulated in various Jewish quarters for as much as one to two hundred years. They had thus come to be regarded as ancient, even as Davidic. One of the added compositions is, indeed, a prose passage ascribing to David the composition of 4,050 psalms; and its insertion may well have served as a defense for the generous inclusion in this Psalter of psalms not found in other manuscripts, even those at Qumrân.

The eight non-canonical compositions in this edition of the Psalms

---

32. *Op. cit.*, pp. 165ff.

33. James A. Sanders, "The Scroll of Psalms (11Q Pss) from Cave 11: a Preliminary Report," *BASOR*, No. 165 (Feb. 1962), pp. 11–15; "Ps. 151 in 11Q Pss," *Zeitschrift für die alttestamentliche Wissenschaft* (hereafter abbreviated as *ZAW*), Band 75, Heft 1 (Jan. 1963), with a continuation in Oct. 1963. See also Jean Carmignac, "La Forme poétique du Psaume 151 de la Grotte 11," and W. H. Brownlee, "The 11Q Counterpart to Psalm 151:1–5"—both articles appear in *RQ*, No. 15 (Oct. 1963).

include the prose passage just referred to and seven psalms, one of which is represented only by a fragmentary superscription. The prose section seems to be patterned after I Kings 4:29–34 and contains what may be legendary lore as to the number of psalms that David composed for various holy days and cultic occasions. One of the newly found psalms has been known previously as Psalm 151 of the Septuagint, Old Latin, and Syriac versions. It is somewhat longer in the Qumrân scroll, however; and yet it lacks the reference to David's slaying of Goliath which appears in the last two verses of this lyric as previously known. Below this psalm is the tattered edge of the lower margin showing traces of a title, or superscription, which mentions a "Philistine." Dr. James A. Sanders, who first opened and studied this manuscript in Jerusalem in the winter of 1961–62, believes that this superscription was followed by a psalm dealing with an account of David's slaying of Goliath; but unfortunately it is lost from the bottom of the manuscript. The old Psalm 151 of the Septuagint is, in his view, a condensation of two psalms: one contained in verses 1–5 of that version, and the other in verses 6–7. The fact that both were included in the Septuagint, even in this summary fashion, indicates that they were of wider currency than the Qumrân Community and probably also more ancient. If the Septuagint version of the Psalms was prepared in about 50 B.C., as is commonly believed, the composition of the two psalms which it condenses as Psalm 151 must be no later than the second century B.C. Fortunately, the former of the two is fully preserved in 11Q Ps[a]. James Sanders believes that he has found certain Hellenistic overtones in this psalm which explain why a more conservative-minded Jew would have omitted portions of this psalm when translating it into the Greek.[34]

Two other non-canonical psalms of 11Q Ps[a] were previously known in a Syriac translation found in a medieval Syriac book of church discipline. They are grouped there with three other Syriac hymns (one of which is a translation of the Septuagintal Ps. 151).[35] In 1930 Martin Noth reconstructed the Hebrew text from which he believed three of these to have been translated, and, of these, two are now found in the Hebrew of 11Q Ps[a].[36] Before this scroll was opened, two scholars of the

34. Sanders actually prefers the view that the two psalms were combined in their compressed form in Hebrew before being translated into Greek. This would call for an additional step between the composition of the psalms and their translation into Greek.
35. W. Wright in *Proceedings of the Society of Biblical Archaeology*, IX, 1887, pp. 257ff.
36. "Die funf syrisch uberlieferten apokryphen Psalmen," *ZAW*, Vol. 48 (1930), pp. 1ff.

Qumrân literature had theorized that these hymns were Qumrân compositions; they tried to restore the original Hebrew on the basis of the distinctive phraseology of the Dead Sea Scrolls.[37] A comparison of these varied attempts at restoration with the text of 11Q Ps[a] shows, according to Sanders, that Martin Noth, who based his reconstruction on Old Testament Hebrew, came very much closer to the original Hebrew text. This probably points to a non-Qumrânian authorship and to a pre-Qumrânian date. We must await the publication of the texts before we can draw definite conclusions, but a reasonable hypothesis would be that these psalms were inherited by the people of Qumrân from their forebears, the Hasidim (pronounced *H^{a}sîdîm*). These Hasidim (sometimes called Hasideans) were the pietists who opposed the Hellenizing and paganizing of Judaism under the pressures of the Syrian government during the second quarter of the second century B.C. They should not be confused with a medieval Jewish sect of the same name.

One of the remaining three non-canonical psalms of 11Q Ps[a] has been published by James Sanders in English translation. He has labeled it "an apostrophe to Zion." This beautiful psalm reads as follows:[38]

1   I remember thee for blessing, O Zion;
        with all my might have I loved thee.
2   May thy memory be blessed for ever.
        Great is thy hope, O Zion!

3   Peace and hope are thy salvation
        that generation after generation come to thee.
4   And generations of saints are thy splendor,
        those who yearn for the day of thy salvation;
5   They will rejoice in the greatness of thy glory:
        On the abundance of thy glory they are nourished,
        and in the expanses of thy splendor they totter.
6   The merits of the saints wilt thou remember,
        and in the deeds of thy saints wilt thou glory.

7   He who pronounces violence clean and announces lies,
        yea, the unjust, will be cut off from thee.

37. Matthias Delcor, "Cinq nouveaux psaumes esseniens?' *RQ*, Vol. I, No. 1 (1958), pp. 85ff.; Philonenko, "L'origine essenienne des cinq psaumes syriaques de David," *Semitica*, IX (1959), pp. 35ff.
38. The psalm has been adapted by me from the publication in the *New York Times*, March 8, 1962, pp. 1 & 10. I have arranged the material poetically, corrected misprints (pointed out by Sanders), and revised the translation slightly.

8 Thy sons will rejoice in thy midst;
   and thy precious ones will be united with thee.
9 How have they hoped for thy salvation;
   thy pure ones, how have they mourned for thee!

10 Hope for thee does not perish, O Zion,
   nor is hope for thee forgotten.
11 Who has ever perished in righteousness,
   or who has ever survived in his iniquity?
12 Man is tested according to his way;
   every man is requited according to his deeds.
13 All about are thine enemies cut off, O Zion,
   and all who hate thee are scattered.

14 Praise of thee is sweet to the nose, O Zion,
   ascending through all the world.
15 Many times do I remember thee for blessing;
   with all my heart do I bless thee.

16 Mayest thou attain to everlasting righteousness;
   and ponderous blessings mayest thou receive.
17 Accept a vision bespoken of thee,
   and dreams of prophets mayest thou receive.
18 Arise and stir thyself, O Zion!
   Praise the Most High, thy Savior.
   Let my soul be glad in thy glory.

The author of this lovely lyric was the member of a religious community which felt itself separated from the central sanctuary in Zion (= Jerusalem), which in his view was dominated by a wicked man described in verse 7 as "he who pronounces violence clean and announces lies." Some historical event seems to have led the psalmist to conclude in verse 13: "All about are thine enemies cut off, O Zion" One could easily identify the wicked man of verse 7 with Alexander Jannaeus (103–76 B.C.), the Hasmonean priest-king who figures in many theories of the historical allusions of the Qumrân Scrolls; and he might think of one of Jannaeus' military defeats as the background of verse 13. However, one might equally guess that the occasion of the psalm's composition was some earlier situation when Jerusalem was dominated by one of the Hellenizing chief priests (Jason, Alcimus, or Menelaus), who during the early Maccabean struggle co-operated with the Syrian government in persecuting the Hasidim. Although some scholars place the rise of the Qumrân sect back in this period, more probably the sectaries of the scrolls were a later defection of Hasidim which occurred after the Maccabees (or Hasmoneans) came to power. In this case, the psalm, which had previously arisen in Hasidic circles, continued to be used and cherished by the Qumrân sect because it suited so well their own situation of separation from Jerusalem. In favor of this prior dating of the psalm is the fact that, according to Sanders, the Hebrew which underlies the phrase "who announces lies" is not the same as that found habitually in the Qumrân literature in the expression "dripper [or preacher] of lies." In favor of dating the psalm no earlier than the Maccabean period not only is the historical situation implied, but also a probable echo in vv. 16f. (above) of Dan. 9:24: "to bring in *everlasting righteousness,* to seal *vision* and *prophet.*" [39] Since Daniel, according to scholars, was written by a Hasid (one of the Hasidim) in about 165 B.C., the 11Q Ps[a] apostrophe to Zion was most probably written after that date. An alternative to direct literary influence of Daniel on verses 16–17 would be the possibility that both authors were giving independent expression to vocabulary current within Hasidic circles. In either case, we should date this psalm to the early Maccabean period.

We are eagerly awaiting the publication of this psalm and all others in this manuscript in order to determine, if possible, from style and implied historical background the probable dating of their composition. If they confirm for the second century B.C. a different type of psalmody from that of the latest canonical psalms, they will reinforce the view that none of the canonicals is to be dated later than the third or fourth century B.C.[40] More than this, these newly found Hebrew

---

39. There are doubtless many literary echoes in the psalm. Thus verse 11 is reminiscent of Job 4:7, and verse 18a seems to echo Isa. 52:2 (cf. also 60:1). The combination "vision" (singular) and "dreams" (plural) in verse 17 may be further compared with Daniel 1:17, where the word "vision" is doubtless a collective noun meaning "visions." The expectation of renewed prophetic gifts is Messianic and reminds one not only of the promised gift of the Spirit in Joel 3:1–2 (English, 2:28–29), but of the expected Messianic prophet of Deut. 18:15–18. Concerning this figure, see below, pp. 98, 149. The expectant attitude of the devout in this psalm (at verse 4) is strikingly similar to that of the saints in Luke 1—2. See especially Luke 2:38.

40. The so-called Maccabean Psalms of the Psalter include a number of royal psalms (e.g., Ps. 2; 45; 110), supposedly composed to honor the Hasmonean priest-kings. If these must be dated earlier, it is no simple matter of shoving them back into the third century B.C., for the kings which inspired such psalms would need in most cases to be pre-Exilic. Other literary evidence, such as the correlation of the royal psalms with the ancient ideas of sacral kingship and the linguistic similarities of many psalms with

lyrics will find their place in the study of the development of late Hebrew psalmody by helping bridge the period between the last canonical psalms and the sectarian Hymn Scroll (1Q H) which was probably composed in the last decades of the second century B.C.

Daniel

The Book of Daniel is usually dated at about 165 B.C. for the following reasons: (1) Its knowledge of history is more thorough and accurate for the Greek period which is predicted than it is for the Babylonian and Persian periods during which the supposed author Daniel lived. (2) The message of the book was especially designed for the last days, the time of Jewish persecution (168–165 B.C.) when Antiochus Epiphanes, King of Syria, sought to make pagans out of the Jews. Although one might try to explain away this theory of composition by supposing that Daniel represented a sort of person who was confused about current history, but who under divine inspiration could unfold the future, it is much more reasonable to suppose that collections of legends from the Babylonian Exile were the springboard from which the author of Daniel leaped into the presumed prophecies of the prophet Daniel. The book is neatly divided into these two types of material. Six chapters are devoted to stories of heroic faith during the Exile and six to prophecies of the Antiochian persecution at the end of time, which will again demand this same kind of faith. The "Little Horn" of chapters 7 and 8 is clearly Antiochus Epiphanes, and his history is written large in 11:21–39. The predicted end of Antiochus in 11:40–45 differs from the stories of his death in I and II Maccabees and hence it pre-

---

ancient Ugaritic literature, had led most critics (even prior to the Dead Sea Scroll discoveries) to conclude that large numbers of the Old Testament psalms were of pre-Exilic origin. See Aubrey R. Johnson in H. H. Rowley, *The Old Testament and Modern Study,* Oxford, Clarendon Press, 1951, Chap. VI, pp. 162–207. When the late Robert H. Pfeiffer declared in his famous *Introduction to the Old Testament,* p. 631, that one, or at most two, psalms were definitely of pre-Exilic origin, he was speaking from an already outdated point of view. Pfeiffer was able to find room for the development of Hebrew psalmody almost wholly in the post-Exilic period by employing the commonly held critical dating of the Chronicler which placed him (author-editor of I–II Chron. and Ezra-Nehemiah) in the third century B.C. However, if the Chronicler (who quotes psalms from all parts of the Psalter and refers to all the Levitical singing guilds) wrote no later than about 350 B.C., one is left with one century less for the development and full flowering of psalmody in post-Exilic times, so that at least the beginnings of psalmody must be pushed back to the time of the first temple. On the dating of the Chronicler, see W. F. Albright, "The Date and Personality of the Chronicler," *JBL,* Vol. 40 (1921), pp. 104–24; W. A. L. Elmslie, in *IB,* Vol. 3, pp. 345f.; N. H. Snaith, in Rowley, *op. cit.,* pp. 107–14.

sumably represents real prediction on the part of the author of Daniel which was never fulfilled.[41] The great worth of Daniel has never been in its predictions, however, but in the type of faith and action it has been able to inspire. A partial corroboration of the late date of Daniel is the fact that in the Hebrew Bible his book appears among the Sacred Writings rather than among the Prophets.

None of the Dead Sea Scroll copies of Daniel are so early as to dispute the usual critical view concerning the book's authorship, although one Daniel manuscript from Cave Four is to be dated not more than fifty years later than its composition. The texts are largely unpublished, but we are informed that one scroll fragment overlaps the change from Hebrew to the Aramaic language which occurs in the middle of 2:4 and still another overlaps the change back into Hebrew after chapter 7 (at 8:1). Other fragments of Daniel are consistent with these changes, and thus the same portions of Daniel which appear as Aramaic or as Hebrew in our Hebrew Bible appear in the same languages in the scroll. This is of interest since some critics have argued that certain Hebrew materials of Daniel were translated out of the Aramaic, or even that some Aramaic sections were translated out of the Hebrew. One should not assert dogmatically that translation theories are disproved, for such could have taken place almost at once, before any wide dissemination of the text; yet it must be a source of disappointment to persons holding translation theories that no support is afforded from the Qumrân literature. An analogy to the translation theory, however, is to be found in the discovery of fragments of the Book of Tobit, some according to a Hebrew version of the apocryphal book, but others according to an Aramaic edition. It will require special study to determine which edition preserves the original tongue.[42]

Of even greater interest for the Book of Daniel is the fragmentary manuscript concerning the Babylonian King Nabonidus. This king is never mentioned in the Biblical book. In fact, Belshazzar is represented there as the son of Nebuchadnezzar, although we know from the ancient inscriptions of Babylonia that in reality he was the son and co-

---

41. On the historical allusions in Dan. 11, see Frederick W. Farrar, "The Book of Daniel," in *The Expositor's Bible, ad loc.,* or Arthur Jeffery, in *IB, ad loc.* See also H. H. Rowley, *Darius the Mede and the Four World Empires in the Book of Daniel,* Cardiff, University of Wales Press Board, 1935.
42. See J. T. Milik in "Editing the Manuscript Fragments from Qumran," *The Biblical Archaeologist* (hereafter cited as *BA*), Vol. XIX, No. 4 (Dec. 1956), p. 88. Tobit and Tobias in these new documents are called, respectively, Tobi and Tobiah.

regent of Nabonidus. During the early part of his reign, Nabonidus retired to the Arabian oasis of Tema, where he resided many years before returning to Babylonia. Ruling at Babylon on his behalf, although never assuming the title of king, was his son Belshazzar, with whom he maintained regular communications by caravan. Different guesses have been made as to the reason of Nabonidus' secluded life. According to one view, there was in his family ancestry a tradition of worshipping the gods of the Arabian desert; and it was therefore a religious quest which sent the king there. Others have speculated that he suffered from malaria while residing in the lower Euphrates, and so retired into the arid wilderness for the sake of his health. An early Persian inscription said he was mad.[43] The following sensational story appears among the Aramaic texts of Cave Four.[44]

> The words of the prayer which Nabonidus, the king of Assyria and Babylonia, the [great] king, prayed, while he was afflicted with a severe inflammation, by the decree of the [Most High] G[od], in the City of Teman:
>
> "I was afflicted with a severe inflammation seven years, so away from [men I] used to dwell; [but when I confessed my errors] and my sins, I was granted an exorcist. He was a Jew of [the exiles at Babylon. He] explained in a letter that glory and g[reat majes]ty should be ascribed to the name of G[od Most High. He wrote thus:
>
> " 'While] you have been afflicted with a se[vere] inflammation [in the City of Teman by the decree of God Most High] seven years, [you have] kept praying to the gods of silver and of gold, of brass, iron, wood, and stone, who [can not] . . . for they are [not real] gods . . . . . [your] health . . . . . .' "

The story is remarkable for its memory of Nabonidus, whose name appears in no other Jewish source. It is even more remarkable for its memory of the fact that "the great king" (or emperor) had lived for seven years at Tema in Arabia. It correlates interestingly with two of the guesses of why he retired there; for reasons of health and religion are tied together, as indeed they may have been in real life. Even the letter sent by the Jewish exile is convincing, in that regular communica-

43. R. P. Dougherty, *Nabonidus and Belshazzar,* Yale Oriental Series, 15, New Haven, Yale University Press, 1929, pp. 130–60, 181, 196, n. 649.
44. For the text, see J. T. Milik, " 'Prière de Nabonide' et autres écrits d'un cycle de Daniel," *RB,* LXIII, 1956, pp. 407–15. Some rather serious lacunae are involved in this text, and quite different restorations are given by A. Dupont-Sommer in *Les Écrits esséniens découverts près de la Mer Morte,* Paris, Payot, 1959, pp. 337f.

tions were maintained between Tema and Babylon. This story contains too much historical data to be sheer fiction. It appears probable therefore that here we have a Jewish tradition of the type found in the first six chapters of Daniel. The fact that it shares the same repetitious style as Daniel makes possible the restoration of many lacunae. Similarities of vocabulary are also helpful. If we compare the form of this story with the Danielic legends, we may even reconstruct the principal purport of the missing text. The letter must have concluded with the advice that Nabonidus should pray to God Most High in order to be healed. We may be sure that the king followed this advice and was restored to health. Next he probably returned to Babylonia where he met the Jewish exorcist (or astrologer?) and promoted him to great honor.

Another portion of the Nabonidus story is too fragmentary to translate, but according to it the king had a dream which required interpretation. At one point he exclaimed, "How much like . . . you look." J. T. Milik thinks that this is addressed to an angelic figure, the guardian angel of the Jewish exile, and that at this point the name of this exorcist (perhaps Daniel) appeared. In any case, the same Aramaic phraseology is employed in a copy of Tobit from Qumrân, in which the parents of Tobias (Tobiah in the scroll) exclaim over the close resemblance between their son's guide (an angel incognito) and the son himself. If this be the setting of Nabonidus' remark, we would seem to have moved on to a new story of what happened after the king met the exile. However, the reverse may be the case. In a dream the emperor, perchance, saw an angelic figure who gave him important advice. Then, afterward, he met the Jewish exile and exclaimed over his close resemblance to the angelic figure he had seen before.[44a] In either reconstruction of what happened, we would have a trace in Judaism of the Zoroastrian belief that every man has his angelic double. Another trace of this is found in the Acts of the Apostles, where Rhoda's report that imprisoned Peter was standing outside the gate was rejected by the insistence that the girl must have seen his guardian angel (Acts 12:15).

The main significance of this Nabonidus story is the evidence of the preservation of genuine Exilic legends among the Jews who had been

---

44a. The story would then be similar to that of the Rabbinic commentary, Midrash Rabbah, according to which Jacob wrestled with Esau's guardian angel and later said to Esau, "Your face resembles that of your guardian angel." See Midrash Rabbah, Song of Songs III, § 6, ¶ 3.

in Babylonia. Like the stories in Daniel, this may be only folklore; but if so, it had its origin in Babylonia at a time sufficiently early that it is colored with genuine historical reminiscences. Some scholars have interpreted the stories in Dan. 1—6 as purely fiction, but this is unsatisfactory by reason of some authentic historical information conveyed by these stories. It is also evident from inconsistencies in the stories of Daniel that some were independent of one another. Thus when Shadrach, Meshach, and Abednego were thrown into the burning fiery furnace, Daniel nowhere figures because this is an independent tale unrelated to the Daniel legends. For the same reason, these three youths do not make their appearance in the lion's den with Daniel. The author of Daniel was therefore a collector, who brought together the stories concerning the three youths and Daniel. In the first two stories (Chaps. 1—2), he grouped their names together, although Daniel emerges as the real hero of the second. After that, there is one story concerning the three youths and everything that follows concerns Daniel alone. The collector of these stories seems not to have known of Nabonidus, since he makes Belshazzar the son of Nebuchadnezzar. However, many scholars have seen a distorted reminiscence of Nabonidus in the story of Nebuchadnezzar's madness. The king went out into the wild and ate straw like an ox. After "seven times" (probably seven years) he recognized that the Most High rules in human affairs and was restored to sanity and resumed the rule of his kingdom. This story very likely had as its starting point Nabonidus' lengthy absence in Arabia, together with the rumor that the king was mad. It is therefore a doublet, and an historically inferior one at that, to the Nabonidus story at Qumrân.

Why did the author of the Book of Daniel not include the Nabonidus legend? Perhaps he did not know it. Frank Cross, following W. F. Albright, has suggested that memory of Nabonidus was preserved only among the Jews who remained in the Babylonian Exile until after the Book of Daniel was written by its Palestinian author. Then in the middle of the second century B.C. a fresh migration of Jews to the Holy Land from Babylonia brought with it the story of Nabonidus, which was later written down at the Qumrân Community. According to Albright, the strongly Zoroastrian character of Essene faith was derived from these latecomers from the Exile.[45] Although this is an attractive explanation, it is also possible that the author of Daniel knew both

45. "New Light on Early Recensions of the Hebrew Bible," *BASOR*, No. 140 (Dec. 1955), pp. 27–33.

stories; but he chose to include the tale concerning Nebuchadnezzar's madness because it served his purpose best, since just then his compatriots were castigating Antiochus Epiphanes as Epimanes (the mad man). Similarly he may have known the tales of Susannah and of Bel and the Dragon, but did not include them. In any case, these stories in the Apocrypha may also have had a long oral transmission before they came to be a part of the Greek Old Testament.

D. N. Freedman believes that the Qumrân Prayer of Nabonidus may lead us to a better understanding of the handwriting on the wall (Dan. 5:24ff.).[46] His view springs from a theory first advanced by Ch. Clermont-Ganneau, in 1886, that the words which comprise the writing are the names of weights, or money values: *mənê* being the Persian mina, *təkêl* standing for the shekel (according to a familiar orthographic difference between Aramaic and Hebrew), and *parsîn* meaning two half-shekels (or half-minas).[47] These monetary values in turn represent the worth of individual men according to a familiar idiom attested in Rabbinic literature. The origin of the handwriting on the wall was the answer to a riddle, "What were the successors to Nebuchadnezzar like?" The answer given was: "A mina, a mina, a shekel, and two half-minas." The kings involved were:

> Amel-Marduk (Biblical Evil-merodach), 562–556 B.C.
> Nergal-shar-usur, 560–556 B.C.
> Labashi-Marduk, 556 B.C.
> Nabonidus, 556–539 B.C.
> Belshazzar, as co-regent with Nabonidus.

According to this theory, the two half-shekels (or half-minas) preserved the memory of Nabonidus and Belshazzar as co-regents. The scroll fragments attest a memory of Nabonidus, so that Freedman feels this basic theory is supported. However, Freedman wishes to follow the shorter Septuagint reading: "*mənê, təkêl,* and *pərês*" (i.e. a mina, a shekel, and one half-shekel). H. L. Ginsberg had years before adopted this reading, but had changed the question of the riddle to: "What were the kings of Babylon like?" The answer according to the briefer text referred to Nebuchadnezzar, Evil-merodach, and Belshazzar

---

46. "The Prayer of Nabonidus," *BASOR*, No. 145 (Feb. 1957), pp. 31–2.
47. "*Mané, Thécel, Pharès* et le Festin de Balthasar," *Journal Asiatique*, Series 8, Vol. I 1886, pp. 36–67. This view has been taken up and developed by Hans Bauer, "Menetekel," *Vierter Deutscher Münzforschertag zu Halle/Saale, Festgabe,* 1925, pp. 27–30; and Emil G. Kraeling, "The Handwriting on the Wall," *JBL*, LXIII, 1944, pp. 11–18.

—the only neo-Babylonian kings mentioned in the Bible.[48] Now that we know that Nabonidus figured in Jewish lore, Freedman would substitute Nabonidus for Evil-merodach. He points out that if we recognize that the story of Nebuchadnezzar's madness referred originally to Nabonidus, the three kings are precisely those which figured originally in the Daniel legends: Nebuchadnezzar, Nabonidus, and Belshazzar.

Although this is probably a correct conjecture as to the earliest form of the traditions, there is one fatal weakness to this method of interpreting the handwriting on the wall: It is not so interpreted in the Book of Daniel itself! According to the story the words were without any obvious meaning except as God disclosed it through Daniel: "*Manê*, God has numbered (*manâh*) the days of your kingdom and brought it to an end; *takêl*, you have been weighed (*takiltâh*) in the balances and found wanting; *parês*, your kingdom is divided (*parîsat*) and given to the Medes and Persians (*pârâs*)." Here is a punning interpretation which is much more inspiring and inspired than the modern substitutes. If indeed these words were the names of money, their prophetic meaning was not clear until Daniel disclosed it. An interesting aspect of the two half-shekels (*parsîn*) is that they receive a double interpretation: one *parês* means "divided," the other "Persian." [49] This argues for the originality of the Aramaic reading *parsîn* at 5:25, rather than *parês* as at 5:28. Lack of agreement between the text of the inscription and the simpler citation given in the interpretation led to the abbreviated reading of 5:25 in the Septuagint.

At two points only may the tradition of Nabonidus illumine the story of Belshazzar. First of all, the words of the queen at 5:11 become intelligible, if we substitute Nabonidus for Nebuchadnezzar both here and in the preceding chapter. Her role also is seen to be more than that of queen mother, for she is the wife of the reigning king Nabonidus. To be sure, the Biblical editor of the legends did not understand this, but thought she was referring to the earlier reign of Nebuchadnezzar.

48. *Studies in Daniel,* New York, Jewish Theological Seminary of America, 1948.
49. Double meanings are not only characteristic of midrashic (or Rabbinic) exegesis, but they also occur in apocalyptic literature. Cf. the explicit double interpretation of the seven heads of the beast in Rev. 17:9. Otto Eissfeldt, "Die Mene-Tekel Inschrift," *ZAW*, Vol. 63 (1951), p. 105, has argued on the basis of the Habakkuk Commentary that inconsistency between the text and the exposition is also characteristic of such literature, especially of the Book of Daniel. However, inconsistency is not a necessary presupposition here, as Emil G. Kraeling, *op. cit.,* has shown.

A second point which stands related to the first is that Belshazzar exalted Daniel only to the third place in his kingdom (5:29), as compared with Joseph's exaltation in a similar situation to the second place (Gen. 41:39-43). Various interpretations of this aspect of the story are possible,[50] but it is not at all improbable that at the earliest stage of the tradition one understood that Belshazzar as co-regent with his father already himself occupied the second place and that the highest place left to offer Daniel was third. These points are based upon the assumption that the traditions really originated in the Exile and are not wholly fictional — a position to which the Prayer of Nabonidus has led us. We are still plagued with the historical enigma of where Nabonidus was on the night of Belshazzar's feast. Apparently he had returned from Tema, according to the ancient monuments; but was he now in Babylon, or was he conveniently out of town?

50. In the present context of Daniel, one would easily surmise that the second place was occupied by the queen-mother and that Daniel would be third after her. On still other interpretations of the "third ruler," cf. Jeffery, *op. cit.*, regarding Dan. 5:7. For possible historical elements in the legends of Daniel, see R. P. Dougherty, *op. cit.*, pp. 187-220.

CHAPTER TWO

The Meaning for Old Testament Canon

In the preceding chapter, we have studied the significance of the Dead Sea Scrolls for the three divisions of the Hebrew Bible: Law, Prophets, and Sacred Writings. This is the canon (or authoritative literary standard) by which faith and life are to be measured according to Rabbinic Judaism. The same books (though in a different order) make up the Old Testament "measuring stick" (Greek, *kanón*) of the Evangelical churches. The Roman Catholic Old Testament contains additional books, sometimes printed in Protestant Bibles in a separate section called the Apocrypha. There is a certain logic in favor of the Christian Old Testament being more inclusive than the Jewish Bible; for when the Rabbinical scholars gathered at the Council of Jamnia in A.D. 95 and gave their final definition to the Hebrew canon, the Christian Church had already been employing a wider range of Jewish literature and had been profoundly influenced by it. Had it not been for the Church, the Pharisaic Jews might not have been quite so zealous in their insistence that divine inspiration had come to an end with the writings of Ezra and Malachi.

At the Council of Jamnia there was debate among the Rabbis as to whether such books as Esther, Song of Songs, and Ecclesiastes were worthy of recognition as Holy Writ. Some Rabbis even wished to eject the Book of Ezekiel from the Prophets, on the ground that the priestly program of its last nine chapters conflicts with the Pentateuch. This surely indicates that the canon as a whole was examined and discussed, even though the final decision in the case of the first two divisions of the canon was probably the reassertion of a position of several centuries standing. Thus the Prophetic canon was treated as closed, according to a definition it had received no later than the third century B.C.; but the later Book of Daniel was saved by including it among the Sacred Writings.

Perhaps uniformity with regard to the canon was not achieved immediately, but the second century A.D. seems to have seen the determined effort of Pharisaic Judaism to consign to burial and oblivion all Jewish literature except the canonical books. The Pharisees did believe also in the Oral Law, with its system of legal interpretation based mainly upon the Pentateuch. This was now codified in the Mishnah by Rabbi Judah. In the synagogues the reading of the Hebrew Bible was still accompanied by free, oral Aramaic translation (Targum) following a text which had been largely fixed by tradition. Its transmission continued to be mainly by oral tradition rather than by manuscript for several centuries. A great deal of legendary lore concerning the Bible was also transmitted. Soon Biblical commentaries (*midrâshîm*) devoted to casuistic exegesis or to Jewish legends began to appear. Rabbinic colleges further elaborated the Mishnah until its separate tractates were expanded into vast tomes. All this is a colossal literary heritage from ancient Judaism; and it all springs from, or relates to, the Hebrew canon. The only real exception to this is the material relating to the Feast of Dedication (*Hanûkkâh*), which commemorates the cleansing and rededication of the temple after the orthodox Jews regained possession of it in 165 B.C. Had either I or II Maccabees been accepted as canonical books, the tractate of the Talmud dealing with this festival would have included considerable quotation and exposition of this literature as it expounded the meaning and nature of the observance. Since the Books of Maccabees lacked canonical authority, Talmudic regulations concerning *Hanûkkâh* were based rather upon historical tradition.

Concentration upon the orthodox Bible meant that no effort was made to perpetuate other great Jewish literature. The books familiarly known today as the Apocrypha and Pseudepigrapha of the Old Testament were not preserved for posterity by Jews, but by Christians. Even the works of the two greatest Jewish writers of the first century A.D., Philo and Josephus, were not copied and transmitted by the Jews. It was the Church, not the Synagogue, which cherished this literature and preserved it for mankind.

The sister faiths of Judaism and Christianity were both limited by language factors in the heritage which they received and passed down to succeeding generations from their mother, pre-Mishnaic Judaism. The Hebrew Bible would have been lost, except for the Jews; and, equally, the Greek Old Testament (the Septuagint) would have perished except for the Christians. Only such Jewish sectarian literature as had been written or translated into tongues other than Hebrew or Aramaic was preserved at all. This was the work of the Church, whose official languages in the different regions of the world were Greek, Latin, Syriac, Armenian, Coptic, and Ethiopic, but not Hebrew or Jewish Aramaic.

The discovery of old manuscripts in caves near the Dead Sea has brought about the recovery of vast quantities of Jewish literature which had fallen into oblivion. No wonder the Scrolls are so revolutionary and so revelationary in their importance for an understanding of our religious heritage. Yet, the portrait of our ancestral mother will not be complete until we recover the writings of the Sadducees, of John the Baptist's party, or hopefully also of Hebrew- and Aramaic-speaking Christians. The recovery of the Dead Sea Scrolls indicates that such discoveries may no longer be considered impossible. The vicinity of Pella, for example, to which Jewish Christians retired from Jerusalem during the First Jewish Revolt against Rome (A.D. 68–70), needs to be searched for the possible survival of Hebrew and Aramaic Christian literature.

In the above presentation, I have simply made clear that we have today a wealth of Jewish literature which was not preserved by the living tradition of either Judaism or Christianity. It is impossible to say at present how developed a concept of canon was held by the Essenes at Qumrân. The Law, the Prophets, and the Psalms had a primary importance which is clearly seen by the frequency of their quotation and the numerous commentaries relating to them. To this list we should add Job, so often copied in a paleo-Hebrew script, and also provided with a written Targum. Not all of these works were valued equally. Primary in affection were Deuteronomy, Isaiah, other prophets, and the Psalms. The relative importance of a book is indicated by the number of copies found, and also by the frequency with which it is quoted or alluded to in the religious literature. Theoretically, Moses is fundamental, but the Messianic and eschatological outlook of the society directed the sect's interests more to the prophetic literature. Thus the most popular book of the Law was Deuteronomy, whose ethical concerns relate it most closely to Hebrew prophecy. Hence there were definite, though unexpressed, priorities within the received Scriptures at Qumrân. The absence of Esther from the Qumrân manuscripts that have been so far identified doubtless indicates the low esteem with which the book was regarded, even if its absence among the finds is partly accidental. The discovery of an Esther manuscript now, after numerous copies of other Old Testament Books have been found, cannot appreciably change this picture,[1] since this still would not establish that the book was popular at Qumrân.

Were any of the Apocrypha and Pseudepigrapha considered canonical? There is no doubt but that Tobit, Sirach, Enoch, Jubilees, and the Testament of Levi, of which several copies have been found, were close to canonical status in the Qumrân Community. Since Jubilees was fundamental for the solar year of 364 days which was followed at Qumrân, as opposed to the lunar-oriented year of 354 days (twelve moons) observed by the Pharisees, we may infer that it was practically canonical, perhaps fully so.

The calendar of Jubilees is in several respects a perfect calendar. The year was divided into four quarters of ninety-one days each. Each quarter had two months of thirty days followed by another with thirty-one. Since the calendar had an equal number of weeks (fifty-two), every anniversary always fell on the same day of the week, year by year. The only shortcoming of this calendar is that unfortunately it is not *perfectly* solar. Some system of intercalation would be necessary to keep it in accord with the sun's yearly cycles. Whether the Essenes were aware of this problem, we do not know; but it could have been resolved by intercalating an extra week occasionally. So far as I know, this calendar has not been seriously considered by modern advocates of calendar reform. Perhaps, it never will be, for the simple reason that the year must be allowed to deviate as much as seven days from the earth's annual cycle around the sun before intercalation can take place. A better calendar insofar as modern needs are concerned would be a year of thirteen months of exactly four weeks (twenty-eight days) each, with an additional year-end day, not reckoned among the days of the week. However, this kind of calendar could not have been entertained among ancient Jews (some of whom actually knew that the true year consisted of 365 days), for it impinges upon the inviolable seven-day cycle of the week. The holy Sabbath would be desecrated by it. Many Jews, Christians, and Moslems today would object quite

---

1. On the large number of Biblical texts found, see D. Barthélemy and J. T. Milik, *DJD*, I, III, and forthcoming volumes. Meanwhile, see P. Benoit and others, "Le Travail d'édition des fragments manuscrits de Qumrân," *RB*, LXIII, 1956, pp. 49–67, which appears in English translation in *BA*, Vol. XIX, Dec. 1956, pp. 75–96.

strenuously to the proposed calendar revision of rationalistic moderns. Unless society becomes completely secular, which, as God reigns, shall never be, the calendar of Jubilees may be after all the best hope for the kind of convenient calendar which some moderns desire.[2] To return once again to the problem of canon, J. T. Milik has suggested physical criteria for testing the canonicity of books read at Qumrân. He affirms:[3]

> Certain indices permit us to think that at Qumrân Daniel was not considered to be a canonical book. In fact, all the Biblical manuscripts of 1Q, of which it is possible to calculate the format, have columns whose height is double the width, instead of height and width being nearly equal, as here. Moreover, 6Q has yielded an example of Daniel written on papyrus, whereas the numerous fragments of papyrus from 4Q and 6Q contain no canonical book in its original language.

The papyrus criterion was not an absolute one, for as Frank Cross pointed out, later discoveries have yielded canonical books in their original language upon papyrus.[4] Naturally, however, the more highly a book is cherished, the more precious the material upon which it will be written.[5] With regard to the validity of Milik's other observation as to the size and shape of the columns, we shall have to wait and see. Perhaps it is correct, for Daniel was sufficiently recent that it was proba-

2. The occasional intercalation of a whole week between the old and the new year would keep the year roughly solar; but the permitting of the year to slip as much as six days behind the earth's true solar cycle could be an annoyance to farmers who plant their crops by the present, more regular, calendar. A year-end day, which is not reckoned among the days of the week, could be added to the 364-day year which is prescribed by Jubilees; and on leap year two such days could be added. Thus the conveniences of the Jubilees calendar could be kept, without sacrificing close adherence to the earth's solar cycle. A liberal-minded person could reason that the number of the day of the week has a symbolic rather than a literal significance (and with true right); but it is wishful thinking to suppose that all people would accept this point of view. On the calendar of Jubilees, see Miss A. Jaubert, *La Date de la dernière cène, calendrier et liturgie chrétienne*, Paris, Librairie Lecoffre, 1957.
3. *DJD*, I, p. 150.
4. *JBL*, LXXV, 1956, pp. 122f.
5. A book might be cherished for other reasons than canonicity — as shown by the Copper Scroll from Qumrân Cave Three, with its list of buried treasure. See J. T. Milik's French translation and notes in *DJD*, III, 1962, pp. 211–302. Milik has presented an English translation, "The Copper Document from Cave III of Qumran, Translation and Commentary," in the *Annual of the Department of Antiquities of Jordan* (hereafter cited as *ADAJ*), Vols. IV–V, 1960, pp. 137–55. See also his earlier articles in *BA*, XIX, 1956, pp. 60–64, and in *RB*, LXVI, 1959, pp. 321–57. Cf. J. M. Allegro, *The Treasure of the Copper Scroll*, Garden City, New York, Doubleday, 1960.

bly not endowed with the same authority as older Biblical books. Still one cannot carefully study the Qumrân literature without noting the pervasive influence of Daniel upon the thought and language of the sect.[6] Whatever the theory of canonicity, for all practical purposes Daniel was authoritative.

John Allegro has published a leaflet which he has labeled 4Q Testimonia.[7] It contains the following texts: Deuteronomy 5:28-29; 18:18; Numbers 24:15-17; Deut. 33:8-11; and an elaborated version of Josh. 6:26. The other texts are without commentary, so Allegro's indication that this last may be a quotation from a newly found document called provisionally the 4Q Psalms of Joshua at once commends itself. The leaflet seems to be a collection of passages designed to give the principal Biblical grounds for the special form of Messianic expectation which existed in the Community of Qumrân — Moses and Joshua being quoted as the most indisputable sources. The implied authority attached to the Psalms of Joshua strongly suggests their canonicity for the folk of Qumrân.

In Chapter One, we have seen that the Biblical texts among the Qumrân Scrolls are not all of one type, some approximating the Hebrew underlying the Septuagint, others the Samaritan Pentateuch, and still others being remarkably close to what we call the Massoretic text. Such a diversity of text types shows that the concept of canonicity (insofar as really present at Qumrân) had not led to the establishment (or selection) of an officially recognized text. The Psalms of David had such authority that commentaries were written upon them, and yet a Psalm Scroll from Cave Eleven of Qumrân contained compositions of a late date which are lacking in the Book of Psalms as canonized by Rabbinic Judaism. All this suggests that the idea of canonicity was not rigidly applied by the sectaries of the scrolls.[7a]

6. By this I do not mean to assert that the influence of Daniel is stronger than that of certain other Old Testament works, such as Isaiah, Ezekiel, or the Psalms. On 1Q M, see the list of Biblical references cited by J. van der Ploeg, *Le Rouleau de la guerre,* Studies on the Texts of Judah, Vol. II, Leiden, E. J. Brill, 1959, pp. 195-8, with the Danielic references on p. 198. On Daniel's influence on Qumrân Biblical interpretation, see F. F. Bruce, *Biblical Exegesis in the Qumrân Texts,* Grand Rapids, W. B. Eerdmans, 1959, pp. 7-9 (who is somewhat dependent here upon the earlier writings of Karl Elliger and Géza Vermès).

7. "Further Messianic References in Qumrân Literature," *JBL,* Vol. LXXV (Sept. 1956), pp. 174-87, particularly pp. 182ff.

7a. While the present book was in press, there appeared the superb article of I. H. Eybers, "Some Light on the Canon of the Qumran Sect," in *New Light on Some Old Testament Problems* (Papers read at 5th meeting held at the University of South Africa,

In commenting upon the canonicity of the Books of Maccabees, I have written elsewhere:[8]

> For Biblical scholarship, the concept of canon is an irrelevance; for all literature is welcome material of study for the light it can shed upon the Old Testament (as these books upon Daniel) or the New Testament. The Maccabean books are also appreciated for themselves as the religious literature of God's chosen people, wherein great truths often find apt expression or admirable exemplification.

The same may be said of the Qumrân Scrolls. Our Jewish and Christian canons are doubtless a fixed inheritance which will never be changed, but in theory it would be quite possible to accommodate such a work as the Qumrân Society Manual in the Christian Old Testament, for it specifically states that its regulations (though at the present inviolable) are only provisional "until the coming of the Prophet and the Anointed Ones of Aaron and Israel."[9] Jesus as the One through Whom the Messianic hope has been and will be realized antiquates the terms of this expectation by combining in Himself the roles of prophet, priest, and king. If the Manual of Discipline were to be included in the Christian Old Testament it would change no Christian doctrines, for the New Testament would be allowed to speak the final word. It would simply guarantee that the light it sheds upon the meaning of the New Testament would not be neglected by students of the Bible.[10] Incidentally, the columns of this scroll vary considerably in width, some of them are about twice as long as high. Whether this has any significance for canonicity at all is at present uncertain.[11] We

Pretoria, 30 January—2 February 1962), Die Ou Testamentiese Werkemeenskap in Suid-Afrika, [1963], pp. 1–14.

8. *Interpreter's Dictionary of the Bible* (hereafter cited as *IDB*), Nashville, Tenn., Abingdon, 1962, under the entry "Maccabees, Books of," F. "Canonicity," in Vol. K–Q, p. 215.

9. 1Q S ix, 10f. For translations of this document see Brownlee, *The Dead Sea Manual of Discipline, BASOR*, Supplementary Studies Nos. 10–12, 1951; P. Wernberg-Møller, *The Manual of Discipline*, Studies on the Texts of the Desert of Judah (edited by J. van der Ploeg), Vol. I, 1957.

10. See my footnotes to the Manual of Discipline (*op. cit.*), and the generous remarks of A. Dupont-Sommer, *The Jewish Sect of Qumrân and the Essenes, New Studies on the Dead Sea Scrolls* (translated by R. D. Barnett), London, Vallentine, Mitchell, & Co., 1954, p. 152. These parallels have become part and parcel of some articles on the scrolls in relation to the New Testament.

11. My suspicion is that factors other than canonicity enter into the determination of the size of the manuscript upon which a text is copied. Naturally, the Book of Isaiah by reason of the large quantity of its text would require high columns in order

can only say that this relic from the past has attained a lively and well-deserved place in Biblical scholarship.

In conclusion, I wish to stress that the canonical decisions of the Council of Jamnia were in the main good, and that for the establishment of norms of faith and practice the line must be drawn somewhere between the Biblical and the non-Biblical. Yet the student of the Bible should make extensive use of extra-Biblical writings for the fullest possible understanding of ancient Judaism, if he is to attain an adequate understanding of the New Testament.

---

to keep its length from becoming excessive — the twenty-four feet of the well-preserved copy from the first Qumrân cave being about maximum length. The scroll of the Manual of Discipline was prepared to hold a relatively large quantity of text: the Society Manual, the Society Manual Annex, and the Society Blessings. Although the total quantity was considerably less than the Isaiah Scroll, yet a strip of parchment with high columns would appeal to the scribe in preference to a strip with short columns like those of the Habakkuk Commentary.

CHAPTER THREE

The Meaning for Old Testament Geography

A full understanding of Biblical history requires an accurate knowledge of Biblical geography. When armies or merchants travel from city to city, one needs to know their situation and whether there was a highway or natural pass of some kind between them. To see this relationship is to understand history better. Similarly, to know the terrain and climate is often illuminating.

Indications as to direction in the Old Testament differ radically from our own. We employ a compass which indicates the magnetic north pole; when this is not available we navigate with the aid of the north star. Old Testament orientation was toward the rising sun. As one faced the dawn, everything east was "in front" of him; everything west was "behind" him. Objects to the north were "at the left," and anything to the south was "at the right." Sometimes east and west were distinguished as "toward the sunrise" and "toward the sunset." One could also locate a place by saying that it was between certain well-known cities, or by saying it was in the direction of a certain place. In the context of Palestine, "toward the sea" (the Mediterranean) was a suitable designation for west. "Toward the Negeb" meant south, and "toward (Mount) Ṣâfôn" meant north.[1] English versions usually convert these Hebrew expressions into our terminology, but not always. Thus the King James Version says that Moses' vision of the burning bush was at "the back side of the desert"; whereas the Revised Standard Version locates this theophany at "the west side of the wilderness." We shall now see how this terminology is applied in specific cases.

1. Mount Ṣâfôn was the Phoenician holy mountain, which probably figures as the background for Ezekiel's myth of Paradise lost (Ezek. 28:13–19). Cf. Isa. 14:13. The 48th Psalm identifies Mount Zion with the mountain of "the far north," by way of stressing that it is the true abode of God.

BETHEL, AI, AND RAMATH HAZOR

In his migrations, Abram is said to have pitched his tent between Bethel and Ai and to have built an altar to the Lord at that place. This altar was "in front of Bethel"; and conversely, Bethel was "toward the sea" from the altar, whereas Ai was "in front." So literally reads Gen. 12:8. The Genesis Apocryphon from Qumrân (which is an Aramaic version of Genesis) adds still another detail, Ramath Hazor (the Height of Hazor) was "to the left of Bethel."

Before the Qumrân discoveries, archaeologists had already figured out the ancient locations of Bethel and Ai.[2] A primary clue as to their locations has been the retention of names suggestive of the ancient place names. The modern village of Beitîn appears to be a corruption of the earlier Arabic designation Beit Il (House of God), derived from the Biblical *Bêt Êl* (or Bethel). To the east of Bethel stands the site of an ancient city. Similarly Ai (in the Hebrew *hâ-'Ai*) means "The Ruin," and Joshua is even said to have made it "a perpetual, desolate *tel*" (Josh. 8:28). Between these two cities lie two hills, one of which is presumably the place where Abram built his altar. The fact that a good pass connects this area with Jericho fits well the journeys of Joshua and Elisha (Josh. 8:3–9; II Kings 2:15–23; cf. Josh. 16:1).

Such provisory identification required archaeological verification. Excavation has shown that Beitîn was occupied throughout Biblical history and was an important place both before and after this long period. Et-Tel, however, was destroyed about 2200 B.C. and was never rebuilt. This suits very well the Genesis story, where the name *hâ-'Ai* would serve as an appropriate designation for an erstwhile city even as early as the time of Abram (probably nineteenth century B.C.). The attribution of the destruction of the city to Joshua (Josh. 8) is unsuitable, however, for there is no evidence of the occupation of the place in the thirteenth century B.C. Beitîn (presumably Bethel) was

2. On Bethel, see J. L. Kelso in *IDB*, Vol. A–D, pp. 391–3; and his accounts of more recent discoveries in the *BASOR*, No. 164 (Dec. 1961), pp. 5–19, and in *Bible et Terre Sainte*, No. 47 (May 1962), pp. 8–15. On Ai, see S. Cohen in *IDB*, Vol. A–D, pp. 72f. and bibliography cited there. The following discussion is based upon the usual critical views. However, J. M. Grintz, " 'Ai which is Beside Beth-Aven,' a Re-examination of the Identity of Ai," *Biblica*, XLII, 1961, pp. 201–16, argues persuasively that et-Tel may be Beth Aven, and Ai may be some other place nearby. As against the idea that Ai (Heb. hâ-'Ai = "the Ruin") is unsuitable as the name of an occupied site, one may observe that the similar Arabic name et-Tel is the designation of a modern Syrian village lying between Damascus and Seydnaya.

destroyed in the thirteenth century B.C., apparently by Joshua's army; so it is not without reason that W. F. Albright has suggested that the story in Joshua (with its parallel in Judges 1:22–26) really describes the destruction of Bethel, but at a late date the story was transferred to the nearby ruin of Ai in order to explain the long standing name "The Ruin," or "the Tel," a name which still stands today.

The note in this Aramaic Genesis that Ramath Hazor is to the left, or north, of Bethel serves to reinforce the identification of Beitîn with Bethel, for just five miles north-northeast of Beitîn rises Jebel el-'Aṣûr (Mount 'Aṣûr), also known as Tel 'Aṣûr. This place had previously been identified with Baal Hazor where Absalom feasted his royal brothers (II Sam. 13:23ff.). According to an emended text of I Macc. 9:15, it was at Mount Hazor that Judas Maccabaeus died in battle, presumably this same place.[3]

It is not simply that Ramath Hazor is north of Bethel, but the attribution to Abram of a spectacular view of the Promised Land from this point seems to make Jebel el-'Aṣûr's identification with Hazor unmistakable:

> I went up on the morrow to Ramath Hazor and I viewed the land from that eminence: from the River of Egypt to Lebanon and Shenir and from the Great Sea to Hauran and all the land of Gebal unto Kadesh and all the Great Wilderness east of Hauran and Shenir unto the Euphrates.

The extent of this view, like that of Moses from Mt. Nebo (Deut. 34:1–3), is exaggerated, for wishful thinking can imagine anything in the distant haze; yet Jebel el-'Aṣûr is the highest point of elevation west of the Jordan and south of northern Galilee until one reaches the hills just north of Hebron. When atmospheric conditions are right, one can see from there both the Mediterranean and the Dead Sea. One can survey the Plain of the Jordan and the hills of Ammon and Moab. In the southern horizon one can glimpse the hills above Hebron, and to the north one can make out Mounts Gerizim and Ebal. The elevation of Jebel el-'Aṣûr is actually about 3,333 feet above sea level, whereas Ebal and Gerizim are only 2,890 feet and 3,085 feet, respectively. There seems no room for doubt that Jebel el-'Aṣûr is Ramath Hazor of the Genesis Aprocryphon, a conclusion which in turn reinforces the identity of Beitîn with Bethel.

3. F. M. Abel, *Géographie de la Palestine*, Études Bibliques, Paris, Librairie Lecoffre, 1933, I, p. 372.

With such an amazing panoramic view nearby at Ramath Hazor, one may wonder why the Biblical author has Abram view the land from the lower summit east of Bethel. He may even speculate that the earliest form of the story must have located the incident where the Qumrân Scroll places it, for the view from the hills east of Bethel is nothing like so spectacular. The reason for this shift of vantage point (underscored in the Bible by the words "look from the place where you are" — in the Septuagint, "where you *now* are") is probably theological and cultic; for the oldest name of Ramath Hazor is Baal Hazor. Evidently there was a Baalistic sanctuary there in early times and this made it an unsuitable place for the divine promise to have been made to Abram. The Biblical story in the light of geography and cult seems to say that *Yahweh* (the LORD) rather than the Canaanite Baal gave the land to the Hebrews.[4] Hundreds of years later, when Baalism had been exterminated, the word Ramath (Height of) replaced that of Baal. Therefore, the author of the Genesis Apocryphon could shift the scene of the divine promise back again to Hazor in order to give the patriarch the best view possible in the neighborhood of Bethel.

THE BOUNDS OF THE PROMISED LAND

The extent of Abram's view from Ramath Hazor as described in the scroll was not determined by what is clearly visible to the eyes, but by Messianic dreams of an ideal Holy Land. Abram is commanded, as in Gen. 13:17: "Arise, walk through the length and the breadth of the Land, for I will give it to you." To the concluding promise, the scroll adds: "and to thy seed for ever." Abram's performance of this mission is described as follows:

> And I, Abram, went forth to journey around the land and to view it. I began my circuit at the River Gihon and I came to the shore of the sea until I reached Mount Tôr. Then I turned inward from the shore of this Great Salt Sea and went along Mount Tôr eastward to traverse the breadth of the land, till I reached the River Euphrates. Then I turned along the Euphrates till I reached the Red Sea in the east. Then I followed along the Red Sea till I reached the Reed Sea, which goes out from the Red Sea. Then I turned southward till I came to the River Gihon.

4. On the sanctuary's being situated at the initial and middle point of creation, see Mircea Eliade, *The Sacred and the Profane* (translated by Wm. R. Trask), New York, Harcourt, Brace, 1959, Chapter I. The land derives its meaning as a divine gift from this cultic center.

The River Gihon appears to be one of the tributaries of the upper Nile. From there Abram began to circle the promised land, by way of staking off his claim to the divine promise. He went north to the Great Salt Sea, which is the Mediterranean. He followed the eastern shore line until he was as far north as Mount Tôr. He then turned in order to explore the breadth of the land by crossing these mountains and meandering along the Euphrates which flows southeast into the Indian Ocean (if we include the Persian Gulf as a part of it), which is here called the Red Sea. He then turned back westward in order to encompass the Arabian Peninsula until he reached the Reed Sea, which apparently embraced the Gulf of Aqaba and the Gulf of Suez. By the time he reached the upper end of the latter, he would have gone considerably north, so it was necessary for him to turn south in order to reach his starting point at one of the sources of the Nile — the River Gihon. Enclosed within this vast territory is the major part of the Near East! Such a definition of the Promised Land contrasts sharply with all Old Testament descriptions, unless it be that of the Messianic hope (Zech. 9:10c):

> His dominion shall be from sea to sea,
> and from the River to the ends of the earth.

With this language one may compare Micah 7:12, which was probably also in the mind of the author of the Aramaic Genesis:

> In that day they will come to you,
> from Assyria to Egypt,
> And from Egypt to the River,
> from sea to sea and from mountain to mountain.

These Old Testament passages account for the extensiveness of the domain promised Abram in the scroll, for the land pledged to the patriarch *and his seed* could be no less than that assigned to the Messianic kingdom.

Now examining the details of the passages just quoted, it is clear that "from sea to sea" is interpreted to mean from "the Great Salt Sea" to the "Red Sea," i.e. from the Mediterranean to the Indian Ocean. "From Egypt to the River" is interpreted as meaning from the River Gihon to the Euphrates. The interpretation of "the River" as the Euphrates is certainly correct, and it is noteworthy that the domains of David and Solomon extended that far. The introduction of the name Gihon, instead of the Nile, even if the rivers be identified, was influenced, I believe, by the description of Paradise in Gen. 2:10–14. In other words, the Messianic kingdom is to be bounded by two of the rivers of the Garden of God: the Gihon and the Euphrates. This association of Messianism with the promises made to Abram indicates that Paul was not without precedent in ascribing Messianic significance to the promises that God made Abram.

Mount Tôr, Red Sea, and Reed Sea

From this Messianic geography we may turn to a few points of terminology of practical geographical interest. Mount Tôr, or Mount Bull, is etymologically identical with the Greek Mount Taurus; *tôr* being the Aramaic word for bull, and *taurus,* the Greek. For the first time in a Semitic source we find the name "Red Sea" (*Yammâ' Simmûqâ'*); and as in Herodotus' writing, it refers to the Indian Ocean! [5] In the Old Testament we never find the designation "Red Sea," but the Septuagint version translated *Yam Sûf* (Reed Sea) as *Eruthra Thalassa* (Red Sea). Now the Reed Sea which the Hebrews crossed is commonly believed to be a large inland lake growing up with reeds, east of Baalzephon (Ex. 14:1); though it may have been an extension of the Gulf of Suez. However, the same name is employed for the Gulf of Aqaba at Elath (alias, Ezion Geber), so it is quite apparent that whatever the *Yam Sûf* referred to originally, the later Hebrew writers used this term to refer to the double-branched body of water which includes the Gulf of Suez and the Gulf of Aqaba. With this understanding, the "Seventy" showed their agreement by translating *Yam Sûf* (Reed Sea) as *Eruthra Thalassa* (Red Sea); for this implies that the Gulfs of Suez and Aqaba are an extension of the Indian Ocean which is the Red Sea proper. Likewise, the Genesis Aprocryphon from Qumrân refers to the Reed Sea as a "tongue . . . going out from the Red Sea." This tongue, interestingly, is double pronged, like a serpent's tongue.

The Valley of Shaveh

The meeting place of Melchizedek, king of Salem, with Abram and the king of Sodom was, according to Gen. 14:17, the Valley of Shaveh, which was also the same as the King's Valley, where in later history

---

5. Nahman Avigad and Yigael Yadin, *A Genesis Apocryphon, A Scroll from the Wilderness of Judaea* (English translation by Sulamith Schwartz Nardi), Jerusalem, The Magnes Press of the Hebrew University and *Heikhal ha-Sefer,* 1956, p. 31.

Absalom built himself a monument (II Sam. 18:18). This equation has been of little help in the location of the valley, except that obviously it must be in the vicinity of Salem, a shorter form of the name Jerusalem. One modern identification of this valley has been with the fertile area immediately south of the Davidic Jerusalem (the Hill of Ophel), at the confluence of the Kidron, Tyropaean, and Hinnom valleys. This view seemed to be as likely as any until the Aramaic Genesis Scroll was opened. Here the passage of Genesis is expanded in order to make explicit the identification of Salem with Jerusalem, and the Valley of Shaveh is further defined as the same as the Plain of *Bêt hak-Kerem* (Plain of the Vineyard House).[6]

Now *Bêt hak-Kerem* (Beth-haccherem in the RSV) according to Jer. 6:1 was an important lookout point from which a warning fire signal might be relayed to Jerusalem from Tekoa.[7] Such a dominant point would be somewhere south of Jerusalem, and according to the newly found scroll must certainly lie close to the Holy City. The Israeli archaeologist, Y. Aharony, has excavated a place halfway between Jerusalem and Bethlehem, where the modern Jewish colony of *Râmat Râhêl* (Height of Rachel) is located. There he has uncovered at the earliest level of occupation important royal buildings, dating back to the ninth or even tenth centuries B.C.[8] The Jewish colony has a viewing balcony on top of one of its buildings from which tourist guides point out the church spires of Bethlehem or indicate the location of Tekoa. To the north of this balcony one can see Jerusalem, and in between the two is a nearly level, gently sloping basin. If Aharoni is correct in identifying these ancient ruins with *Bêt hak-Kerem,* then the Plain of *Bêt hak-Kerem* would be the level land to the north of it. The royal constructions at this place make it appear reasonable that this plain was indeed the King's Valley. It is also a most suitable place for the armies of Abram and the king of Sodom to encamp. The very name Valley of Shaveh, which means Valley of the Flat, agrees exactly with the landscape. In the Copper Scroll, an account of buried treasure, found in Cave Three, the valley is called simply "the Flat." *Bêt hak-*

6. Avigad and Yadin.
7. On previous identifications of the place, see James Philip Hyatt, on Jer. 6:1, in *IB*, Vol. 5, p. 857.
8. See Y. Aharony, "Excavations at Ramath Rahel," *Israel Exploration Journal* (hereafter cited as *IEJ*), Vol. VI, 1956, pp. 152ff.; "Excavations at Ramet Rahel," *BA*, XXIV, 1961, pp. 98–118; "Ramat Rachel," *Bible et Terre Sainte*, No. 47 (May 1962), pp. 16f.

Kerem is also mentioned there, but not in such a way as to indicate its relationship with "the Flat." [9]

THE WILDERNESS PROVINCE OF JUDEA

The excavation of Khirbet Qumrân indicated that the foundations of the main rectangle were laid in the eighth (or ninth) century B.C. and that the large round cistern to the west of this was probably pre-Exilic also. This recalled a theory of Martin Noth which had identified Khirbet Qumrân with the ancient Salt City mentioned in Josh. 15:61f.: "In the Wilderness were Beth-arabah, Middin, Secacah, Nibshan, Salt City, and En-gedi: six cities with their villages." Beth-arabah was believed to lie northwest of the Dead Sea, and En-gedi had long been incontestibly equated with 'Ain Jidî, an oasis more than a third of the way down on the western shore of the sea. If Salt City were to be identified with Khirbet Qumrân, so named by reason of its proximity to the Salt Sea (a common Old Testament designation of this lake), only Middin, Secacah, and Nibshan would be left unidentified.

Frank M. Cross and J. T. Milik, accordingly, in August 1955, explored the basin of the plateau above the cliff of Qumrân, where ruins of ancient sites had been previously observed.[10] This basin, known today as the Buqê'ah, is believed to be the Biblical Valley of Achor (Josh. 7:26). Here they examined the mounds of three fortresslike settlements. The pottery recovered from trial trenches indicated that these places were settled during one period only, that of the Hebrew monarchy, beginning perhaps in the ninth century B.C. They were evidently destroyed by the Chaldeans in the early sixth century, when Judah was scourged twice and captives were taken to Babylonia. A later Israeli expedition showed that a similar fortress settlement existed near 'Ain Jidî during the same period. Putting these facts together, Cross and Milik identified the three sites in the Buqê'ah with the Biblical places: Middin, Secacah, and Nibshan—identifying the places from north to south, according to the Biblical order.

John Allegro has objected to these identifications, arguing that more logically the entire list of six cities should be arranged in sequence from north to south. According to him, Khirbet Qumrân is to be identified

---

9. The Flat *hash-shô'* figures in viii, 10–16 (sections 38–9); but *Bêt hak-Kerem* appears later at x, 5 (section 48).

10. Frank M. Cross, Jr., and J. T. Milik, "Explorations in the Judaean Buqê'ah," *BASOR*, No. 142 (April 1956), pp. 5–17.

with Secacah, for reasons to be explained below. Between Beth-arabah and Secacah should appear Middin, i.e. to the north of Khirbet Qumrân. Nibshan and Salt City should appear between Secacah and En-gedi, i.e. to the south of Khirbet Qumrân. In order to sustain this theory, however, Allegro will have to discover rival locations. There is no evidence, as yet, that these other sites exist. Regardless of the identity of the cities of the Wilderness, they still illustrate full well the Chronicler's remark (II Chron. 26:10) concerning King Uzziah (who reigned from 783–742 B.C.): "And he built towers in the Wilderness." Frank Cross and G. E. Wright believe that these little citadels were built previously under the reign of Jehoshaphat (who reigned from 873–849 B.C.).[11] II Chron. 17:12 says of him: "He built in Judah fortresses and store-cities." Although the latter reference suggests the possibility of this work having been initiated by Jehoshaphat, only the statement concerning Uzziah refers explicitly to the Wilderness. The preference for Jehoshaphat is determined largely by the theory that the town lists of the Judean provinces as outlined in Joshua were composed no later than the ninth century B.C. It is not yet clear from the limited excavations conducted, however, that these places were not first built during the reign of Uzziah.

Secacah, which is mentioned only once in the Old Testament, appears four times in the text of the Copper Scroll with its lists of buried treasure:

> In the tumulus, which is in the Vale of ha-Secacah ["the Shelter"], dig . . . cubits: 12 talents of silver. At the beginning of the aqueduct which is at Secacah, on the north side, under the large stone dig . . . cubits: 7 talents of silver. In the cleft which is in Secacah, to the east of Solomon's Pool: vases of aromatic spices. And near there, from above the Canal of Solomon in the direction of the large block of stone (count off) sixty cubits, dig three cubits: 25 talents of silver. In the tomb situated in the torrent ha-Kippa, coming from Jericho to Secacah, dig seven cubits: 32 talents.[12]

According to both Milik and Allegro, "the Vale of ha-Secacah" is the lower course of Wady Qumrân, the stretch of this wash which opens into the lowland by the Dead Sea, where the Essenes engaged in

11. "The Boundary and Province Lists of the Kingdom of Judah," *JBL*, LXXV, 1956, pp. 202–26, with reference here to p. 224.
12. J. T. Milik's translation of iv, 13 — v, 14 (sections 22–26), in the *ADAJ*, IV–V, 1960, p. 140.

agriculture.[13] The aqueduct at Secacah is reasonably identified with that descending from the waterfall of the wady to Khirbet Qumrân — as both Milik and Allegro agree. There is accord even on the fact that the so-called Solomon's Pool and the Canal of Solomon are to be sought at Khirbet Qumrân. From this scroll passage one could readily conclude that Secacah is Khirbet Qumrân, so strongly is this name attached to the locality. Milik believes, nevertheless, that Secacah is to be identified with Khirbet es-Samra, the largest of the three ancient citadels up in the *Buqê'ah* above Qumrân, holding that the wady received its name in ancient times because one of its principal tributaries flowed past Secacah. Assuming this to be true (since Khirbet Qumrân with its prospect upon the Salt Sea is the most likely location of Salt City), it is not at all improbable that centuries after these pre-Exilic sites lay in ruins and their identities were forgotten, the name Secacah which had attached itself to the wady was then reapplied to the Essene settlement at Qumrân. According to this suggestion, both Milik and Allegro would be correct.

Many other places of Biblical history are referred to in the Copper Scroll. Important light upon the topography of Roman Jerusalem seems especially to be indicated. A discussion of this would not only take us away from the area of Old Testament studies, which we are dealing with here, but it would also bring us into the area of greatest controversy between Milik and Allegro.

TEMA, OR TEMAN

The Old Testament contains two similar place names, Tema and Teman. Both are translated as Thaiman in the Septuagint, and so some have concluded that they are variant spellings of the same place.[14] It would be possible to argue that the Prayer of Nabonidus (discussed above) attests the correctness of this theory; for it locates King Nabonidus at Teman, whereas the monuments place him at Tema.

The internal evidence of the Old Testament justifies a distinction between the two places. Teman is associated with Edom, rather than

---

13. Milik, in *ADAJ*, IV–V, 1960, p. 146; Allegro, *The Treasure of the Copper Scroll*, pp. 69ff. On the agricultural development of this area, see R. de Vaux, "Excavations at 'Ain Feshkha," *ADAJ*, IV–V, pp. 7–11.

14. This is not a commonly held view, and I am at a loss to discover at the present time the supporters of this position, which my notes indicate has been advanced. It is worth discussing, however, lest anyone should think the evidence of the Septuagint plus that of the scroll fragment support the identity of Tema and Teman.

Arabia where Tema is located.[15] Although this location of Teman might be explained as due to inexact geographical knowledge, such an explanation appears dubious when one reckons with the divergent genealogical relationships. According to Genesis, Teman was a son of Eliphaz, the son of Esau; but Tema was the ninth of the twelve sons of Ishmael.[16] Ishmael was a son of Abraham and Hagar; whereas Esau was a son of Isaac and Rebecca. Now encroachments from Arabia pressed in upon Edom in post-Exilic times. These began in the sixth century B.C., but the Edomites had not yet been fully dispossessed in the time of Malachi (about 480 B.C.). By the time Alexander the Great conquered Syria-Palestine, in 332 B.C., the Edomites had already become resettled in southern Judah. Their territory was known as Idumea. The Arabs who took over Seir, the ancient mountain area of Edom, established the kingdom called Nabatea, which retained its autonomy until the second century A.D. It seems probable to me that the Edomite city of Teman was destroyed by the Arabs and was never again rebuilt, at least not under this name.[17] Henceforth there remained only the Arabian oasis city of Tema, which Jews readily confused with the Biblical Teman, which no longer existed.

15. On Teman, see Josh. 12:3, 4; Amos 1:12; Ob. 9; Jer. 49:7, 20; Ezek. 25:13; Hab. 3:3. See, likewise, "Eliphaz the Temanite" in Job 2:11; 4:1; 15:1; 42:7, 9, and "the land of the Temanites" in Gen. 36:24. On Tema, see Isa. 21:14; Jer. 25:23; Job 6:19; I Chron. 1:30.

16. Gen. 36:15; 25:15.

17. If, as G. E. Wright suggests, Teman was the capital of Edom, and Sela the fortress to which the Edomites retired for safety, it would seem not improbable that Petra (although a translation of Sela, rock) was the successor to Teman. See Wright, *The Westminister Historical Atlas,* Philadelphia, The Westminster Press, 1956, p. 70b. However, this conclusion is rendered uncertain by references in Byzantine times to a military post at Teman, which was located variously at either fifteen or five miles from Petra. See Abel, *op. cit.,* I, p. 285; Nelson Glueck, *Explorations in Eastern Palestine,* II, *Annual of the American Schools of Oriental Research* (hereafter cited as *AASOR*), Vol. 15 (1934–35), pp. 82f. Perhaps the tradition of the name Teman clung to the vicinity for many centuries after the destruction of the place, but it was of no significance until a Roman fort was placed there. Names can sometimes wander a few miles from the original location, or even reappear after being suppressed for a time.

CHAPTER FOUR

The Meaning for Old Testament Interpretation

The Qumrân Scrolls open up many new sources for the Old Testament interpreter. These are rich and varied. They include: (1) Old Testament commentaries; (2) Targums, paraphrases, and expansion — a sort of rewriting of Biblical books; (3) Old Testament quotations, directly cited and interpreted; (4) interpretations implied in indirect quotations; (5) clues as to meaning from Qumrân usage of Old Testament words; (6) textual variants in Biblical manuscripts. All these are of interest for the history of Old Testament interpretation. Sometimes the scrolls even present us with interpretations which bring us closer to the original meaning of a passage. In the present chapter we shall discuss only the first five aids to Biblical interpretation, for we have already treated the sixth somewhat in Chapter Three, above. It will also be abundantly illustrated in Part II, which will be devoted entirely to the large Isaiah Scroll (1Q Isaᵃ). However, in connection with other points of this chapter, attention will be directed to significant textual variants.

I. COMMENTARIES

The discovery of the Qumrân Scrolls has brought to light for the first time Biblical commentaries from the time before Christ. Their point of view, unlike that of modern commentaries, is not historical, critical, or even devotional. Nor is their great concern the same as that of the Rabbinic *midrâshîm* (anglicized as "midrashim"). Rabbinic Judaism knows two types of *midrâsh: midrash haggâdâh* and *midrash hᵃlâkhâh* (anglicized as "midrash," "midrash haggada[h]," and "midrash halakah"). In the former the theological and the inspirational are major, and they are conveyed through imaginative story, especially through legends developed from the Biblical narrative. In the latter, the application of the Law to daily life is primary, and fanciful methods of extorting desired meanings from the Biblical text are employed. This cunning exegesis is dedicated to the proposition that the legal system of the Oral Law of Pharisaic Judaism is really implicit within the written text of the Pentateuch. Demonstration of this was one way of asserting that the Oral Law really went back to Moses himself. The detailed proofs often quote the opinions of famous Rabbis from the last two pre-Christian centuries and the first two Christian centuries (and even later). Though the Rabbinic commentators cite the text verse by verse, they also quote all other parts of the Scriptures, with the flow of the commentary being determined largely by the direction the discussion happens to take by reason of someone's objection to or approbation of a given interpretation.

The newly found commentaries are devoted to the Prophets and the Psalms rather than to the Pentateuch, to predictive prophecy rather than to the Law. The same forced interpretative methods are used to extort desired meanings from the text as were used in Rabbinic exegesis; but they are mainly implicit, rather than explicit. The motivation for such exegesis is mostly a prophetic, rather than a legal interest. A great leader, called the Righteous Teacher, appeared as the reformer of the true Israel and as the herald of the last days. Spiritual foes attacked the new society which he founded. The principal opponents were the Wicked Priest and the Man of Lies (or false prophet). Possibly these much castigated men are one and the same person. In any case, the Wicked Priest is the Chief Priest; for the former title (hak-kôhên hâ-râshâ') is an opprobrious pun upon the latter (hak-kôhên hâ-rô'sh).[1] The conflict between the Righteous Teacher and the Wicked Priest had been predicted in Scripture, according to the Qumrân commentaries. Likewise, the prophets had foretold the wars and political dissensions of the last two centuries B.C., including the invasion of the Near East by the Romans. The methods of adducing Biblical proofs for these predictions are as fanciful as those of midrash halakah. The orientation, however, instead of being directed toward textual support of the Oral Law, is aimed at the clarification of recent and contemporary history as it relates to the religious life of the Jews. No wealth of Rabbinic authorities is presented in proof of interpretations, but only the inspired authority of the Righteous (and Authentic) Teacher. He is not quoted directly; but implicitly his authority stands

1. So rightly observes Karl Elliger, *Studien zum Habakkuk-kommentar vom Toten Meer*, Beiträge zur historischen Theologie (edited by Gerhard Ebeling), Tübingen, J. C. B. Mohr, 1953, p. 266. I had independently arrived at the same conclusion.

back of these sectarian commentaries, for it is to him explicitly that "God revealed all the mysteries of the words of His ambassadors the prophets." [2] Brief passages (ranging from a single clause to three verses in length) are quoted and immediately interpreted. The passage quoted is called a *dâvâr* ("a word"),[3] and its prophetic interpretation is called its *pêsher*. I have suggested that this type of commentary be classified as midrash in order to indicate its affinities in exegetical method with other ancient Jewish commentaries, but that it be qualified as midrash pesher by way of distinguishing it from the other types of Jewish midrash.[4] Most scholars, however, call it simply *pêsher* (anglicized as "pesher").

Actually the Qumrân examples of midrash pesher are earlier than the Rabbinic midrashim — the earliest of which was Mekilta, a commentary upon Exodus written in the second century A.D. In point of time the Essene commentaries come from a period when Targum was flourishing. Targum was the Aramaic free translation delivered orally in the synagogue when the Hebrew Scriptures were read. After the reading of each verse of the Law, the Aramaic interpretation followed; and after the reading of three verses of the Prophets, an explication was given. The regular alternating of text and interpretation in the Qumrân Scrolls is probably derived from Targum — only the interpretative material of the scrolls is in Hebrew. Quotations and interpretations are introduced, moreover, by exegetical formulas, such as the following: "And when it says . . . its meaning concerns . . ." As in Targum, the exegetical rules by which an interpretation was deduced are implicit, rather than explicit. Another striking likeness is that both find in the Prophets predictions of historical events as recent as the interpreter himself,[5] although these seem to be focused largely upon

2. 1Q p Hab vii, 4f.
3. This use of *dâvâr* for a prophetic passage may stem from the headings of oracles, like those found in Ezekiel which begin: "The *word* of the Lord came to me, saying." Prof. James M. Robinson of the Southern California School of Theology at Claremont suggests the parallel usage in the tradition concerning Matthew's *logia*.
4. I first proposed this in *The Dead Sea Habakkuk Midrash and the Targum of Jonathan*, a mimeographed publication (no longer available) which I issued at Duke University in February 1953. My suggested new classification, *midrash pêsher*, was embraced by Krister Stendahl in his book, *The School of St. Matthew*, Lund, C. W. Gleerup, 1954, pp. 184, 193. See note 6 below.
5. In the Song of Hannah, for example, the Targum finds a whole series of historical allusions leading down into subsequent history until the Messianic Age. In Hab. 3, the Targum finds among other predictions a prophecy of the oppressive tax system of the Romans.

the period of the Teacher, in the case of midrash pesher. The actual interpretations of the prophetic Targum strongly influenced those of the Habakkuk Commentary, as I have shown elsewhere.[6] All these facts indicate the strong affinity between midrash pesher and Targum, but the former is distinguished from the latter by format and language. Targum as paraphrastic translation also follows the Hebrew text much more closely.

The term *pêsher* (Aramaic *pashâr*) is drawn from Daniel, who was the inspired interpreter of dreams, of the enigmatic handwriting on the wall, and even of the Old Testament itself. The meaning was always a hidden meaning which other wise men and astrologers were unable to divine. The meaning also frequently related to the last days, as in the cases of Nebuchadnezzar's dream image (Chap. 2) and Daniel's own vision of "one like a son of man" (Chap. 7). The second half of the book is filled with literary allusions which implicitly interpret the writings of earlier prophets. Explicitly, Daniel (9:2) says:

> In the first year of his [Darius'] reign, I, Daniel, perceived in the books the number of years which, according to the word of the LORD to Jeremiah the prophet, must pass before the end of the desolations of Jerusalem, namely, seventy years. (RSV)

In Daniel's charismatic exegesis, the seventy years of Jer. 25:11f. and 29:10 become seventy weeks of years — i.e. 490 years. The real ground for this reinterpretation was nothing obscure in the text of Jeremiah, but rather the recognition that the Messianic hopes of the prophets were not fulfilled within seventy literal years. The author of Daniel used the geometrical extension of seventy to express his faith that the new age of the Kingdom of God was on the verge of breaking into history in his day. With an inaccurate knowledge of chronology (or with only a symbolic meaning for chronology), he expected the consummation to come in 165 or 164 B.C. Later Jews reinterpreted Daniel to refer to the coming of God's reign in the Roman era. Among these were the people of Qumrân, who apparently referred to the Romans as Kittim.

---

6. "The Habakkuk Midrash and the Targum of Jonathan," *The Journal of Jewish Studies* (hereafter cited as *JJS*), Vol. VII, nos. 3 and 4, 1955, pp. 169–86. This removed the necessity of keeping in print my earlier mimeographed publication (see note 4 above); but it did not reproduce all its contents, such as my reasons for introducing the new terminology *midrash pêsher* and the views cited by Stendahl on p. 192, n. 1 of his work.

The most extensive midrash pesher so far published is that of the Prophet of Habakkuk. No treatment of its midrashic exegesis need be given here for that has been done elsewhere.[7] Rather, let us point out that this document, though primarily of interest for the history of Biblical interpretation, is not without some interest for understanding the message of the original prophet. We have seen this already in connection with the text-critical value of its Biblical quotations; but more than this, something of the thought of the original prophet does come through in the commentary itself. Insofar as this is true, it may be regarded as an existential application of the prophet's message to a later age. The following major teachings of the prophet come through unobscured:

(1) Internal dissension and godlessness within Judea cannot be for ever overlooked by God, but must be scourged by Him.

This interpretation stands related to the reading "O traitors" at 1:5 for "among the nations" of the Massoretic text; but the idea is developed much more extensively in the scroll. The Judean situation, of course, is not that of the seventh century b.c.

(2) The Lord, as the God of history, will use a great foreign power to scourge his people.

In Habakkuk, it is the Chaldeans whom God uses. In the scroll, it is the Romans.[8]

(3) The only recourse of the righteous is to await patiently the fulfillment of God's purposes in history.

This means the maintenance of hope through an undiscourageable faith, even when the prophecies seem to be delayed in fulfillment. It also means faithfulness to God, in humble submission to His will.

(4) The righteous by their faith and faithfulness shall survive as those whose final triumph God will bring.

7. "Biblical Interpretation among the Sectaries of the Dead Sea Scrolls," *BA*, Sept. 1951. In my mimeographed publication of 1953 (see note 4 above), I retracted hermeneutic principle no. 13, on the ground that I could now explain the alleged examples of this principle on the basis of the Targum. See also L. H. Silberman, "Unriddling the Riddle, a Study in the Structure and Language of the Habakkuk Pesher," *RQ*, No. 11 (Nov. 1961), pp. 323–64.
8. The best article on this subject is still Roger Goosens, "Les Kittim du Commentaire d'Habacuc," *La Nouvelle Clio*, 1952, pp. 137–70.

In the original prophecy, this calls for adherence to the prophetic interpretation of God's ethical demands. In the pesher, it means loyalty to the Righteous Teacher as God's spokesman at the brink of the last days.

(5) Tyranny is seen as suicide, when history is allowed to run its full course.

In Habakkuk, this truth was set forth with regard to Assyria as an ominous example of what Chaldea should expect. In the Commentary, it is the Jewish Kingdom of the Maccabees whose doom at the hand of the Romans is foretold. At this point it may be noted that some Old Testament interpreters believe that the series of woes beginning with 2:6*b* are directed toward a Judean ruler, perhaps Jehoiakim.[9]

(6) The whole world is subject to the eschatological judgment of God.

This eschatological outlook probably does not belong to the original composition of Habakkuk; but his book was edited in succeeding centuries, and as it now comes to us in the Bible, this element is a vital part of the book.

Two universalistic statements of the earlier prophets were inserted editorially into Habakkuk (2:13–14):

Are not these pronouncements from the LORD of hosts:

"Peoples labor only for fire,
  and nations weary themselves for naught";

"For the earth will be filled
  with the knowledge of the LORD's glory
  as water covers the sea"?

The first quotation is from Jer. 51:58, where it relates to Chaldea in a non-eschatological sense. This is the principle by which God rules all heathen nations. In Habakkuk, however, this pronouncement is linked with the Messianic promise of the second quotation (Isa. 11:9), so that the passage appears to be eschatological. These two universal statements were coupled in order to set forth the prospect of universal judgment and the inevitable triumph of the knowledge of the Lord's

9. See Friedrich Horst in Th. H. Robinson and F. Horst, *Die Zwölf Kleinen Propheten,* Handbuch zum Alten Testament, erste Reihe 14, Tubingen, J. C. B. Mohr. 1954, pp. 182f.

glory. It is not merely that the world may choose between the one or the other, but when universal judgment is complete the worship of the Lord alone will ensue. The author of the Habakkuk midrash saw this clearly. He even interpreted the "fire" as the brimstone with which God would scourge both apostate Jews and idolatrous nations. After the sway of falsehood is brought to an end, the knowledge of the Lord will flood the earth as the water does the sea.

Some Old Testament critics have noticed the ominous character of Hab. 2:20:

> But the LORD is in His holy temple;
> let all the earth keep silence before Him.   (RSV)

They have thought that this verse, following as it does the condemnation of idolatry, implies a threat. They are reminded of the first chapter of Micah, wherein the Lord is presented as descending from His heavenly temple in order to wreak judgment upon Samaria and Jerusalem. In Habakkuk the whole world stands under the judgment of God. We are prepared for a theophany; and although chapter 3 of Habakkuk was probably not a part of the original text of the book, still it was fitting that this ancient hymn traditionally ascribed to Habakkuk should have been inserted at this point, for this chapter provides us with a coming of God in judgment.[10] Instead of being from God's heavenly temple as required by Hab. 2:20, the coming is from Sinai, and so this psalm was not at all composed for its present position. Yet it fits in admirably here, by way of emphasizing the eschatological role of Yahweh as the universal judge. This awesome prospect of judgment is the interpretation drawn by the scroll from Hab. 2:18–20:

> Its prophetic meaning concerns all the nations who worship stone and wood; but on the Day of Judgment, God will destroy all worshippers of idols and the wicked from off the earth.

When this has been fulfilled, the whole earth will be awed to silence before the majesty of the Eternal. The eschatological interpretation of Hab. 2:20 seems to be valid, despite the elaboration given it in terms of later apocalyptic thought. The fundamental error of the pesher is that it seeks to read the entire book of Habakkuk as eschatological, as though Habakkuk were not speaking of the Chaldeans (or Assyrians) of the late seventh century B.C. at all! Still the eschatological applica-

---

10. See Paul Humbert, *Problèmes du livre d'Habacuc*, Neuchâtel, 1944.

tion of the prophecy was prepared for by the latest additions to the Biblical book.[11]

2. THE BIBLE REWRITTEN

A. *Chronicles*

The Old Testament itself gives us illustrations of earlier literature being rewritten for the sake of fresh interpretation. The outstanding example of this is the Chronicler's rewriting of Samuel and Kings. In his revisions, he sometimes enriched his work by utilizing additional sources; but many of the changes are theologically inspired and represent deliberate changes unrelated to new historical information. Thus when the Chronicler says that Satan tempted David to take the military census of Israel, he was utilizing later theology to correct the earlier statement in Samuel that the Lord had tempted David (I Chron. 21:1; II Sam. 24:1).[12] Sometimes the substitution of a synonym clarifies the meaning of a word. It may even suggest to us an historical inference. Thus Aubrey R. Johnson has called attention to the Chronicler's wording "priests and Levites" (II Chron. 34:30) for "priests and prophets" in II Kings 23:2. Johnson has used this clue in developing his thesis that the prophetic guilds of pre-Exilic times, with their hymn-composing proclivities, were included among the Levitical guilds of post-Exilic Judaism.[13] The Chronicler constantly ascribes the development of temple music and psalmody to certain Levitical guilds whose names appear at the heading of many a psalm. He also refers repeatedly to the composition or rendering of a psalm as prophecy.[14] Hence the

11. One may retort at this point, "But it is not simply Habakkuk, but all the prophets (including the psalmists) who are transformed into eschatologists." This is true, but the argument may be broadened. Just as Trito-Isaiah, Deutero-Zechariah, Joel, Ezek. 38–39, and Daniel 7–12 reapply certain prophecies of the earlier prophets to their own apocalyptic expectation, so prophecy as a whole was later reapplied in an apocalyptic and/or eschatological manner in the Qumrân literature. The argument is not textual, but historical, the Qumrân Community continuing and developing the ideas of the last Old Testament prophets.

12. Of course, the passages are readily harmonized by allowing that even Satan cannot do anything which the Lord does not permit, an idea which may be supported by the Book of Job. Even so, the earlier author felt no necessity of introducing a devil to relieve the Lord of direct responsibility.

13. Aubrey R. Johnson, *The Cultic Prophets in Ancient Israel,* Cardiff, University of Wales, 1944.

14. I Chron. 25:1–3. Seer, as a synonym of prophet, is used to designate the founders of the Levitical guilds in I Chron. 25:5; II Chron. 29:30; 35:15. The term "man of God" applied to David (II Chron. 8:14; Neh. 12:24, 36) probably refers to him as a

association of prophet and Levite is much broader than a single text. On the other hand, it was an anachronism on the part of the Chronicler to call these cultic prophets Levites, for in pre-Exilic times Levite was merely a synonym for priest. Hence the author of Deuteronomy speaks repeatedly of "the priests, the Levites," whereas post-Exilic authors (including the Chronicler) speak of "the priests and Levites," with the latter serving in various capacities as assistants to the priests.

Still another inference may be developed from the association of prophet with psalmist, the close relationship between psalmody and prophecy — an aspect of the subject not developed by Johnson. This relationship is to be reinforced from literature older than Chronicles. The prophetess Miriam took timbrel in hand and sang a psalm after the miraculous crossing of the Reed Sea. Likewise, the prophetess Deborah has left as the only sample of her prophecy the song of Judges 5. Of course, her prophetic role included also her statesmanlike leadership of Israel. In the time of Samuel there were cultic prophets who prophesied to "harp, tambourine, flute, and lyre" (I Sam. 10:5). This was doubtless inspired singing, not merely ecstatic utterance. Saul himself was caught up into this prophesying (I Sam. 10:10). On a later occasion he stripped himself naked and lay in a trance (I Sam. 19:24). A popular reproach for Saul thereafter was: "Is Saul also among the prophets?" In the time of Jehoshaphat, Elisha required a minstrel before he could prophesy; but as the minstrel played, he indited not a hymn, but an oracle (II Kings 3:14–19). Since traces of oracular speech are found in the Psalms, this is not to be regarded as a radical departure from the sphere of psalmody. In fact, one of David's psalms is explicitly defined as an oracle (II Sam. 23:1–7). This passage is contained in the psalter of 11Q Ps^a.

From the circumstance that both oracles and hymns flow from prophecy, I infer that there are two branches of prophecy in the Old Testament, psalmody and oracular preaching. They spring from a common root, cultic music.[15] However, as early as Amos, oracular

---

prophet. Cf. I Chron. 23:14; II Chron. 30:16; Ezra 3:2; II Chron. 25:7. David was a prophet in his function of cult-founder and psalmist.

15. To be sure I Sam. 9:9 states, "he who is now called a prophet was formerly [in Samuel's time] called a seer." When Samuel functioned as an ecstatic prophet at the high place, this was indeed different from his functioning as a seer. Yet the oracular function was not alien to such prophetic frenzies, as is clear from the much earlier account of the possessed youth described by Wen-Amon. See the translation of John A. Wilson in James B. Pritchard, *Ancient Near Eastern Texts relating to the Old Testa-*

preaching rose to the height of criticizing the cult, and thereafter it seems often to have stood outside it. Yet the books of Amos and Isaiah do have their hymnic sections; and the prophetess whom Isaiah married (Isa. 8:3) was probably a temple singer.[16] Isaiah's own prophetic call had been received within the temple (Chap. 6). Separation of the great preaching prophets from the cult was not therefore absolute.

The thought of divine inspiration belonged equally to psalmody and oracular speech — the one being inspired praise, the other being inspired preaching. Both were originally in poetic form, and probably both were chanted. There is probably more than simile involved when Ezekiel speaks of people listening to him for the beauty of his voice, as to a chanter of love songs (Ezek. 33:30–32).[17] Some have marveled that the Old Testament which contains so much poetry has no word for poet; yet it does have such a word; it is "prophet" (*nâvî'*)! Just as the coming of the muse was implored by poets of the Greco-Roman world so that they might utter poetry, so the gift of the Spirit of God was necessary for the utterance of Biblical prophecy. Such inspired poetry includes hymnody, which is still referred to as prophecy as late as the New Testament! [18]

All this is no mere digression. It has its point for the Dead Sea Scrolls. Not only does it illustrate how the rewriting of earlier history may set one on the trail of a deeper understanding of the Bible, but it also adds to the prophetic stature of the Qumrân Righteous Teacher.

---

ment, Princeton, Princeton University Press, 1955, p. 26b. However, the fact that so prominent a man as Samuel could be both a seer and an ecstatic prophet probably strengthened the tendency toward oracular functioning among ecstatic prophets, so that the time came when prophets and seers were scarcely distinguishable. See D. N. Napier, "Prophets, Prophetism," in *IDB*, Vol. K–Q, p. 898. For the association of poetry and hymnody with early Hebrew prophetism, see Walther Eichrodt, *Theology of the Old Testament* (translated from the German by J. A. Baker), Philadelphia, Westminster Press, 1961, pp. 312, 322f.

16. Cf. Norman K. Gottwald, "Immanuel as the Prophet's Son," *Vetus Testamentum* (hereafter cited as *VT*), Vol. VIII, No. 1 (Jan. 1958), pp. 36–47, especially, pp. 43–5. This suggestion of Gottwald is a good one; but it need not be related to the problem of identifying the mother of Immanuel.

17. In the editorial arrangement of the book, Ezekiel gains a reputation for eloquence immediately after his release from dumbness, following the destruction of Jerusalem (33:21–22). However, in 33:30–32 the doom of Jerusalem is yet to come. Here is an interesting indication that the dumbness of the prophet must not be dated back to the beginning of his career (3:25–26), but that it must be limited to a brief time before the destruction of the temple (24:15–27). Cf. below, p. 252.

18. See Appendix B.

Already we have seen how he was endowed with the gift of inspired interpretation of Old Testament prophecy. In addition to this, he had also the charismatic gift of hymn writing, and it is precisely in the hymns that he lays claim to the gift of the Holy Spirit.[19]

B. *Jubilees*

The Book of Jubilees is a rewriting of Genesis for the sake of improving its orthodoxy and also by way of smoothing out many a thorny problem. Prior to the scroll discoveries, its text was fully preserved only in Ethiopic translation. Now fragments of the original Hebrew text have appeared at Qumrân.

Jubilees answers practically every question any skeptic has put to the Book of Genesis, and for this reason it was cherished at Qumrân, where it was received, not as a substitute for Genesis, but as a helpful companion. These questions are not explicitly raised; but they are all carefully answered. If Moses wrote Genesis, where did he get his information? Answer: He received it by revelation at Mount Sinai and wrote it down at the dictation of "the angel of the presence." When did God create the angels? Answer: On the first day. When did God make Eden? How does this story of creation in chapter 2 of Genesis fit into the account of chapter 1? Answer: Eden was made on the third day. Why does Gen. 1 represent the creation of the human race, both male and female, taking place on the sixth day, whereas Gen. 2 indicates that Adam lived for a time without a wife? Surely he did not have time to get very lonesome, if she was made on the same day as he! Answer: She was made on the sixth day of the second week! This also explains why a mother is ceremonially unclean one week longer after giving birth to a daughter than to a son (Lev. 12:2–5). To whom was God speaking when he said, "Let us make"? Answer: To the angels. Why did not Adam and Eve die on the day they ate of the forbidden fruit, as the Lord said they would? Answer: They did! A "day" here means a thousand years. As a consequence of their sin, they and their descendants have all died before they were one day old. Where did Cain get his wife? Answer: Naturally, he

19. 1Q H vii, 6f.; xiii, 18f.; xiv, 25; xvii, 26. On the probability that the Teacher came to be identified with the eschatological Prophet of Deut. 18:15ff., see A. S. van der Woude, "Le Maître de Justice et les deux messies de la communauté de Qumrân," in *La Secte de Qumrân et les origines du christianisme,* Recherches Bibliques IV (hereafter referred to as *Rech. Bib. IV*), Brussels, Desclee de Brouwer, 1959, pp. 121–34.

married his sister! She was born to Adam and Eve in the second year-week after Cain. Her name was Awan. How could anyone be righteous before the giving of the Law at Sinai, as, for example, the Patriarchs? Answer: The essential outlines of the Law had been revealed by God in the beginning. Even Adam and Abraham observed the orthodox calendar with all its religious festivals, its sabbatical years, and its jubilees (a jubilee being a Sabbath of sabbatical years).[20] Why then did God need to reveal the Law to Moses at Sinai? Answer: The Hebrews forgot it during their sojourn in Egypt.

Let the above illustrations suffice to demonstrate what an excellent rewriting job the author of Jubilees has done. All questions are so neatly answered, one does not even think to raise them! What wonderful Scripture this would be for answering skeptics concerning the historical problems of Genesis, if only one believed in the inspiration of Jubilees! However, it can render an even greater service by showing that the inconsistencies pointed out by reverent (and irreverent) literary critics of Genesis are really there. If there is no problem, why does Jubilees seek to integrate the two stories of creation?

Jubilees sometimes follows the text of Genesis quite closely. In these places it is of interest to the textual critic. It may even help to give us a more accurate text of Genesis at certain points, especially when the newly found Hebrew text is published. It is reported to be in close agreement with the Ethiopic version.

c. The Genesis Apocryphon

This scroll, which we have already examined in connection with Biblical geography, resorts to another device in order to rewrite Genesis. Each major character is allowed to tell his own story in the first person. This allows for intimacies of detail omitted in the Old Testament Genesis. Although it is written in Aramaic, it follows the Hebrew text so closely at certain points that it will be of value for textual criticism. The fact that it is written in Aramaic will also assist in determining the meaning of certain Hebrew words. Like Jubilees, also, it eliminates inconsistencies from the stories of Genesis.

There are two stories in Genesis of Abram (or Abraham) lying about his wife. One story is laid in Egypt (12:10–20); the other, in Palestine (20:1–18). In both accounts Sarai (or Sarah), following her husband's

20. Lev. 25.

advice, claims to be his sister.[21] This ruse was to prevent any one who saw the beauty of Sarah from killing Abraham in order to take away his wife. Since they were childless, the claim would be readily believed. Only in the second story is the excuse given that she was indeed his half-sister, the daughter of his father, but not of his mother. The ruse worked. In each story the king took Sarai — without killing Abram! In both accounts she was introduced into the harem. The implication of the first account is that the Pharaoh actually did cohabit with her. This unwitting sin was punished by a plague, which in some unexplained manner led the Pharaoh to discover the source of divine displeasure. He released Sarai, and expelled Abram and his wife for their untruthfulness. In the parallel account of Gen. 20, King Abimelech was prevented from violating her by a timely dream in which God revealed to him the true identity of Sarah. This does not make sense, however; for if she were so ravishingly beautiful that the king sent for her and removed her by force, he would not wait many nights in order to cohabit with her — even if he did have a large harem! Still this same version of the incident ends with Abraham praying for the healing of Abimelech and the women of his household who, as a result of Sarah's abduction, had been divinely plagued with barrenness. It would take months, if not years, for the king to discover that his whole harem was barren! In both narratives, the great patriarch was loaded with gifts from the king. In the first, they were either the bride's purchase price or benefactions of honor and esteem for Sarai's brother. They were given soon after Sarai had been taken. In the second, they served as reparations (or atonement) for the abduction of the patriarch's wife, and they were not given until her release to her real husband.

A new form of the story appears in the Genesis Apocryphon.[22] The scene is located in Egypt, during the reign of Pharaoh Zoan. One of his princes, by the name of Hyrcanus,[23] saw Sarai and reported her

21. In Gen. 12, the names of the Patriarch and his wife are Abram and Sarai; but in Gen. 20, they are Abraham and Sarah. According to Gen. 17:5, 15, the earlier names Abram and Sarai were later changed by God to Abraham and Sarah. This is probably a harmonizing account which was intended to explain the different forms of the names in the Judean (J) and the Ephraimite (E) traditions. In the present story, the Genesis Apocryphon employs the earlier forms found in Gen. 12. In the following discussion, I shall use the spelling which happens to occur in the source quoted.

22. 1Q Gen[apoc] xx. See Avigad and Yadin, op. cit., pp. 23–7, 45–6.

23. The word is not vocalized by Miss Nardi (in Avigad and Yadin), but it is simply transliterated. Despite the ambiguity of the last letter (equivalent to either $\acute{s}$ or $\check{s}$),

beauty to the Pharaoh by exclaiming over every aspect of her body: "How lovely! How perfectly beautiful!" He also reported that her wisdom equaled her beauty. The king sent for her and had her brought into his presence; and he was so enamored by her charm, that he actually ordered that Abram be put to death so that he might have Sarai as his wife. Then it was that Sarai told the king that Abram was her brother. This state of affairs had been foreseen by Abram in a dream which he had shared with his wife. Her lie was therefore a part of the divine plan and was not resorted to until Abram's life was really threatened. After Sarai was taken from him, Abram and his nephew Lot spent the first night in prayer in order that Sarai's chastity might not be violated. The prayer was answered, for God sent an evil spirit to afflict the king so that he was prevented from approaching her.[24] The plague afflicted also his entire household. This situation lasted for two years, so Sarai retained her chastity unscathed. At the end of that time a search was made for every possible wizard or physician who might heal the king and his household. These occult scientists were unable to come, first of all because the plague had attacked even them, and again because the evil spirit drove them from Egypt. In his quest for physicians, Hyrcanus came to call Abram. Since his uncle was absorbed in a heavenly dream, Lot did not awaken him, but received the call himself.[25] He informed Hyrcanus that Sarai was Abram's wife and that her abduction had brought the affliction from which the king and his household were suffering. Hyrcanus lost no time in reporting this. The Pharaoh summoned Abram, rebuked him for the trouble he had caused him in the case of Sarai, and ordered both of them to clear out of Egypt, but requested that first of all he pray for him so that the pestilential spirit might be removed. Abram acceded, he prayed for the Pharaoh and laid his hand upon him; and immediately he recovered his health and the evil spirit departed. The

it seems to me that the termination of the word is the *os* of the Greek nominative. For possible historical significance of the name, see J. Coppens, "Allusions historiques dans la Genèse apocryphe," in *Rech. Bib. IV*, pp. 109–12.

24. 1Q Gen^apoc xx, 16. Avigad and Yadin translate (p. 43) "a pestilential wind"; but the words wind and spirit are identical and both ideas fit the context, so that one might render *rûaḥ* as "spirit-wind."

25. Unfortunately there is a lacuna in the text at this point (line 22), but a very small one. I read: "But [I was] in a dream, and Lot said to him," restoring *HWYT*. This explains the sudden change of speaker from Abram to Lot. Abram could not be awakened while dreaming, for this would interrupt a divine disclosure to him; for the sleep of Abram was not accompanied by ordinary dreams, but by visions of divine significance.

monarch then bestowed upon him many bountiful gifts, including Hagar, who became Abram's servant wife.

This new form of the story begins in close accord with Gen. 12. The scene is located in Egypt rather than Palestine, and the names are Abram and Sarai rather than Abraham and Sarah. Sarai's chastity was preserved as in Gen. 20, but only because the plague mentioned in Gen. 12 had attacked the king on the first night after his marriage to her. The plague lasted for two years, a duration quite suitable to the context of Gen. 20, where a considerable length of time would be required to demonstrate the barrenness of the king's consorts. In the setting of the scroll, however, this long duration appears inexplicable. Naturally the king's wives could not conceive, if he was completely impotent; and why did he apparently wait so long to call his physicians? The explanation for this incongruity is that the two years was borrowed from the account in Jubilees, where the author may very well have been influenced by Gen. 20. The request that Abram should pray for the Pharaoh in order that he and his household should be healed is also borrowed from Gen. 20. The king bestowed his gifts upon Abram only after the whole affair was resolved — again as in the second Genesis account.

Unfortunately, the portion of the Genesis Apocryphon which would tell of Abram's similar experience with Abimelech (Gen. 20) is no longer preserved; but I believe it quite certain that this incident was omitted. There are two compelling reasons for this conclusion: (1) The story of Abram in Egypt has already combined elements from the two parallel stories. (2) The Book of Jubilees (whose brief account the author of the scroll was following in addition to Genesis) also omits the Abimelech affair. Here is another demonstration, therefore, that the recognition of the two accounts of Genesis as really variant forms of the same episode is not a cunningly devised theory of modern higher critics, with an alleged hostility toward the truth of the Bible. We moderns may think the ancient Jews were naïve; but the way they rewrote Genesis shows that they recognized most of the problems of modern literary criticism and undertook a reinterpretation with a freedom which is shocking to the present-day Fundamentalist.

Jubilees and the Aramaic Genesis from Qumrân make us grateful to God that the ancient Hebrew editors of the Pentateuch did not efface all parallel stories by a neat job of rewriting, but alternated stories from different sources. Sometimes they combined more than one version into a single narrative, in full recognition that they were handling variant accounts of the same event; but frequently also they set down both accounts as if they referred to different episodes. Even where they combined narratives, it was by a literary interweaving which enables higher critics to reconstruct in large measure the separate accounts before they were combined.[26] Because the Biblical editors so handled their sources, we have received a much richer heritage of Hebrew lore — receiving two or even three forms of the same story,[27] instead of only one imaginatively rewritten account. We Christians may even be more grateful that the Church canonized our four Gospels rather than the later interwoven account, Tatian's *Diatessaron*.[28]

Comparison of several versions of an event may not only help us to arrive at greater historical probability (or at least the most primitive form of a story), but also enable us to trace the development of ethical consciousness or increased apprehension of divine truth. This may be seen in the different accounts of the abduction of Sarai (or Sarah) the wife of Abram (or Abraham). In Gen. 12, no excuse for Abram's lie was felt to be necessary, except that his own life was endangered. This meant the sacrifice for a time of Sarai's chastity; but this was a necessary sacrifice of the woman for the sake of the man, a practice which finds other illustrations in the Old Testament.[29] This form of

26. An outstanding example of this is the selling of Joseph into Egypt (Gen. 37:12–36; 39:1). According to the E. story, Reuben saved the life of Joseph by suggesting that he be thrown into a pit, thinking that he would return later to release him; but, unfortunately, Midianite traders came by, kidnapped him, and took him to Egypt where they sold him to Potiphar. The story in the Koran is similar to this. According to the J story, Judah saved Joseph's life by suggesting that they sell him as a slave to the Ishmaelites, who for their part sold him to Potiphar in Egypt. In the combined story, Judah's suggestion comes after Joseph has already been put into the pit; and "Ishmaelites" and "Midianites" are treated as synonyms, so that the ordinary reader fails to notice what has happened in the compilation of the narrative. In separating the two stories, 37:27 should be joined to the following verse in this fashion: "And his brothers heeded him, / and sold him to the Ishmaelites . . ." Likewise, 37:24b should be joined with 37:28 as follows: "The pit was empty, there was no water in it. / Then Midianite traders passed by; and they drew Joseph up and lifted him out of the pit, and took him to Egypt." The wording of the last clause is uncertain, because in one form or another it belonged to both accounts.

27. An outstanding book in making clear to laymen what is involved in Pentateuchal criticism is E. Trattner, *Unravelling the Book of Books*, New York, Scribner's, 1929. The new form-critical approach is well represented by Aage Bentzen, *Introduction to the Old Testament*, Copenhagen, G. E. C. Gad, 2nd ed., 1952, Vols. I and II. See also D. N. Napier, *From Faith to Faith*, New York, Harper, 1955.

28. On this Gospel harmony, see Bruce, *The Books and the Parchments*, pp. 185–8.

29. See Gen. 19:8; Jud. 19:22–26.

the story is believed to have been written by a Judean who drew upon oral tradition in the ninth, or possibly tenth century B.C. Recent scholarship favors the earlier date. In Gen. 20, Sarah has become Abraham's half-sister, because it was felt that no prophet of God could tell a complete lie, even if his life was imperiled. Thus the patriarch told the truth, but not the whole truth. Sarah's chastity was also preserved, for it was unthinkable that God would allow her virtue to be impaired. This form of the story is believed to have been written in the Northern Kingdom of Israel, either in the eighth or ninth century B.C. The Aramaic version of the Genesis Apocryphon portrays an even greater ethical concern. Even the telling of a half-truth is not allowed to Abram or his wife until the threat to his life has become real, rather than merely potential. Abram did not lightly abandon his wife to the Pharaoh; she was removed by force. He and Lot, moreover, devoted themselves to earnest prayer for the safeguarding of Sarai's purity; for it is unthinkable that any saint could really acquiesce to the sacrifice of his wife in order to save his own life.

In the scroll's version of the story, adultery has become so serious that even an innocent, unwilling partner to adultery cannot be received back by her husband. This belief is indicated by the wording of Abram's prayer: "May he not defile my wife *away from me.*" [30] This view was probably derived from a stringent interpretation of Deut. 24:1–4, whereby a divorced woman cannot be received back after she has become another man's wife and has been "defiled" by him. According to Rabbinic exegesis, marriage was not really consummated until a man had "defiled" his wife through sexual intercourse. Conversely, sexual intercourse with a woman, even without the payment of a dowry, was one real (though irregular) method of acquiring a wife.[31] Essene thought seems to have carried the idea even further. The forcible removal of Sarai from Abram was divorce, and her rape by the king would be remarriage. Such an event would so "defile her" (despite the fact that both Abram and Sarai were morally innocent) that her return to Abram would be forever excluded.

Prophetic texts lent support to this interpretation. One of these was Jeremiah 3:1:

30. This phrase is not represented in the English translation of Miss Nardi, but it does appear in the Hebrew translation of Avigad and Yadin, *op. cit.,* pp. 43 and *LW.*
31. See the Babylonian Talmud, Seder Nashim, Tractate Kiddushim 4b, 5a, 9b. In Sotah V, 1, a woman suspected of adultery is forbidden to her husband.

"If a man divorces his wife
and she goes from him
and becomes another man's wife,
will he return to her?
Would not that land be greatly polluted?

"You have played the harlot with many lovers;
and would you return to me?"
        says the LORD   (RSV)

Here the legal norm of Deuteronomy is already applied to the case
of an immoral wife (Israel), even though her husband (the Lord)
had not divorced her. In actual life, there is the story of Hosea's faithless wife, whom the prophet received back into his household but not
into the intimate relationship of married life. He strictly charged her,
according to Hos. 3:3:

"Many days you must dwell as mine; you must not play the harlot,
nor have a husband; nor will I myself come near you." (*An American
Translation*) [32]

Still another text would lend even greater strength to Essene stringency
in its interpretation of Deuteronomy. King David never again co-
habited with the women of his harem whom his son Absalom had ap-
propriated when he forcibly took over the kingdom from his father

32. The American Standard Version (hereafter cited as ASV) also sets forth this interpretation. The RSV, unfortunately, departed from the excellent example of correct
understanding on the part of earlier translators. Actually, I do not believe that chapter
3 is authentic to the prophet Hosea, but that it represents a contribution and experience
of a disciple of his who found a haven in Judah after the destruction of Samaria in
721 B.C. See my article on Hosea in *Harper's Biographical Dictionary of the Bible.*
  Some scholars (including J. D. Smart in *IDB,* Vol. E–J, p. 651) assign chapter 3
to the prophet Hosea and attribute chapter 1 to an editor, which is just the opposite
of my position. Hosea's practice elsewhere, however, is to refer to himself in the third
person (as in 9:7–8). Chapter 1 contains two editorial additions (the superscription
[v. 1] and the note of hope which reverses the prophet's message of doom [vv. 10–11;
in Heb. 2:1–2]) — both of which betray the later editorial concern with Judah. These
portions can be omitted and still leave intact the autobiographical part of Hosea. Chapter
3, however, is an indivisible whole which betrays not only the later standpoint of the
hope editor but also his concern with Judah. Note the reference to the restored Davidic
king in 3:5, which would be without meaning for Israel. Chapter 3 might be wholly
fictional and solely of an allegorical character; but in favor of a literal interpretation is
the purchase price of the woman, the details of which have no obvious allegorical
meaning.

(II Sam. 16:21f.; 20:3). In the language of Qumrân, one could say that Absalom had *defiled* these concubines *away from* David.[33]

According to Josephus, celibate Essenes abstained from marriage because they believed that no woman is faithful to only one man.[34] I have doubted the accuracy of this explanation, yet one has to admit that if one believed that the fidelity of women was not to be relied upon, the logic of the above moral point of view would be abstinence from marriage in the first place. Such skepticism of womanhood may even have appealed to the experience of the author of Ecclesiastes (7:28): "One man among a thousand I found, but a woman among all these I have not found." (RSV)

The real reason for Essene asceticism, I believe, is related to the idea that sexual intercourse is defiling. Unlike the defilement caused by violation of the Law, such as eating unclean food and commiting adultery, this particular defilement is not only minor, but it is an inescapable duty of anyone who would fulfill the divine obligation of propagating the human race. A few Essenes, according to Josephus, married, doing so out of this sense of duty.[35] Nevertheless, according to the Old Testament, he who would be cultically clean for participation in rites and festivals or for close contact with the numinous or holy must be free from this defilement. Purifying baths and refraining from the conjugal relationship were necessary preparation on the part of the men of Israel at the foot of the Mount of God (Ex. 19:10–15). Similarly David's men were given the sacred bread at the santuary of Nob only on condition they had kept aloof from women (I Sam. 21:4–6). Pharisaic tradition explains that the complaint of Miriam and Aaron against Moses concerning his Cushite wife (Num. 12:1–2) was that he had not been fulfilling the obligation of a husband to her. The reason for such strange asceticism on the part of Moses was that he had had to maintain ritual purity in the presence of God

---

33. Here is a story which shows that this idea of the people of Qumrân has extremely ancient roots. I wonder if there are parallels among other nations of the ancient Near East which would explain this revulsion against taking back a woman who had been defiled by another. However, the proscription may rather have arisen as a reaction against an ancient custom of hospitality in sharing one's wife with an honored guest. Deut. 24:2–4 makes this illegal, even if the husband provides a written divorce for the occasion.

34. Jewish Wars (hereafter abbreviated as J.W.) II, viii, 2 (¶ 121).

35. J.W. II, viii, 13 (¶ 160f.). See also his treatise Against Apion, II, 24, where this point of view is represented as characteristic of Judaism generally.

with Whom he was in daily communication.[36] Non-marrying Essenes probably believed that in their daily assemblies and sacred repasts their association with the holy was so great that marriage would interfere with their ceremonial fitness.[37]

D. *Targums*

The interpretations of the Habakkuk Commentary show the strong influence of the Jewish Targum to the Prophets (the so-called Targum of Jonathan). Insofar as Targum is *free* Aramaic translation, it amounts to a minor rewriting of the Old Testament. It was probably mainly oral in the period prior to the destruction of Qumrân. Nevertheless, there is a Targum of Job among the manuscripts of the Eleventh Qumrân Cave. It by no means agrees with the already known medieval edition of the Rabbinic Targum; but it represents an independent tradition which follows the Hebrew rather closely.[38] It is important for textual study, therefore, as well as for Biblical interpretation.[39]

E. *The Aaronic Benediction*

The benediction given Aaron and his sons with which to bless the people Israel is given in Num. 6:24–26, as follows:

36. Midrash Rabba, Ex. Rab. xix, 3; Deut. Rab. xi, 10; also the Babylonian Talmud, Shabbath 87a, Yebamah 62.

37. When I prepared my translation of the Manual of Discipline, it was not yet clear that other fragments of this scroll should be treated as separate literary compositions. After only cursory examination of these as yet unpublished texts, I used them for a restoration of the first line of the first column of 1Q S, which involved the mention of women and children. Later study revealed that this was a manifest error. The Society Manual (1Q S) was apparently the book of faith and order for non-marrying Essenes, whereas the Society Manual Annex (1Q Sa) set forth the practices and expectations of the marrying Essenes. Both groups stood related somehow to the Community Center at Khirbet Qumrân, in the outlying cemeteries of which are to be found the skeletons of women and children as well as men, whereas the main central cemetery (insofar as at present determined) contained the skeletons of males only. Probably only the male members of the marrying Essenes were permitted to visit the Community Center, and that only after engaging in certain lustrations.

38. On the Targum of Job, see the Babylonian Talmud, Shabbath 115a, and my discussion of this in *JJS*, VII, nos. 3 & 4, 1956, pp. 182f. Two Dutch scholars, Profs. J. van der Ploeg and Adam van der Woude opened and studied this scroll for the first time in Jerusalem, Jordan, March, 1962. I was privileged to hear Dr. van der Woude's first lecture on this scroll at the American School of Oriental Research in Jerusalem shortly before his return to the Netherlands.

39. The Genesis Apocryphon might be described as a sort of Targum, except for the fact that each major character speaks in the first person. See Matthew Black, *The Scrolls and Christian Origins*, New York, Scribner's, 1961, pp. 192–8.

The Lᴏʀᴅ bless you and keep you:
The Lᴏʀᴅ make his face to shine upon you,
    and be gracious to you:
The Lᴏʀᴅ lift up his countenance upon you,
    and give you peace.   (ʀsv)

In a covenant ceremony practiced at Qumrân this text was expanded
with spiritually moving language. The Essene additions to the text are
italicized in the rendering given here:

May He bless you *with every good,*
    and keep you *from every evil.*
May He shine *into your heart with life-giving wisdom*
    and graciously grant you *eternal knowledge.*
May He lift up his *merciful* face toward you
    for your *eternal* peace.[40]

This beautiful rewriting in the Qumrân Society Manual not only en-
riches the meaning of the benediction, but it guarantees a highly
spiritual interpretation. At least one Biblical passage has influenced the
language: "The Lᴏʀᴅ will keep you from every evil" (Ps. 121:7a).[41]
This may have suggested also the antithesis "with every good." "Good"
and "evil" relate to physical benefit and harm, but not exclusively. In
the context of Qumrân, the reference is also to spiritual benefit and
harm, and likewise to moral good and evil. In the annual covenant
ceremony one vowed "to keep far from every evil and to cling to
every good deed." The notion that the light which beams from God's
face should impart wisdom and knowledge is distinctively Essene.
This wisdom is described as "life-giving" and "eternal" by way of
emphasizing that it is more than earthly shrewdness. It concerns not
merely successful earthly existence, but also (and especially) triumphal
life with God through all eternity. God's face (or countenance) is
characterized as "merciful," because contrariwise He shows an "angry
face" toward His foes, and because moral achievement is impossible
apart from God's mercy. The word translated "peace" may in both
forms of the benediction be best rendered "welfare" or "well-being."
There are many different possible levels of interpreting Hebrew
shâlôm. Theophile J. Meek's rendering (in *An American Translation*)
"make you prosper" for "give you peace" seems to be a deliberate

40. 1Q S ii, 2–4.
41. Cf. the Midrash Rabbah on Num. 6:22–27, especially Num. Rab. xi, 5.

choice of a purely materialistic level of understanding. Perhaps this did represent the idea of the benediction in the earliest stage of its use; but it is the genius of the Hebrew original that a single word may come to be interpreted at a much higher level than it was at first. In a deeply religious community the "well-being" which one desires above all others is not wealth or health, but a soul in true accord with the will of God. To guarantee this highest level of understanding, the word "eternal" was inserted in the expanded form of the benediction. The divine name Yahweh (LORD) was omitted at Qumrân through the belief that this name is so awesome that one dare not utter it.

3. OLD TESTAMENT QUOTATIONS

A. *Textual Support of Essene Life*

The Old Testament is quoted by the Qumrân sect in order to justify its manner of life and its Messianic expectation. These two ideas may be closely blended, or they may be largely separate. Both are present in the sect's interpretation of Isa. 40:3 in its book of discipline: [42]

> When these become a community in Israel, according to these rules, they will separate themselves from the midst of the habitation of perverse men to go to the Wilderness to clear there the way of HUHA, as it is written:
>
> In the Wilderness clear the way of . . . . ; [43]
> Level in the Arabah a highway for our God.

That means studying the Tôrâh which He commanded through Moses, so as to do according to all that was revealed time after time and according to that which the prophets revealed through His Holy Spirit.

42. 1Q S viii, 12–16.
43. Four dots are employed for the sacred Tetragrammaton (*YHWH* = *Yahwèh*, or possibly *Yâhwêh*) which for this scribe was too sacred to write. In the line above, he introduced a surrogate, which I have explained as an abbreviation of the phrase "He is the God." See my treatment in Supplementary Studies 10–12 of the *BASOR*, p. 33, n. 29. Max Reisel, *Observations on 'HYH 'ŠR 'HYH (Ex. iii:14), HW'H' (DSD viii:13)and ŠM HMPWRŠ*, Assen, Van Gorcum and Company, 1957, has argued that *Hú'hâ'* of 1Q S is derived from an original pronunciation of the Tetragrammaton as *Yahúah*. If this be so, then we should interpret the Qumrân variant as a deliberate defacement of the word in order to avoid its true pronunciation. This may have been influenced by the frequent Deutero-Isaiah declaration: "I am He (*"nî hú'ah*)." Although Reisel presents his case with great skill and erudition, I am not convinced. For the pronunciation and meaning of the Tetragrammaton, see Appendix E.

As E. F. Sutcliffe has convincingly shown, this passage belongs to a portion of the Society Manual which was composed by the Righteous Teacher as the constitution of the founding group of fifteen men who first went to the Wilderness of Judea.[44] In this case, the interpretation of Isa. 40:3 lay at the roots of the Essene way of life and was not merely an afterthought for vindicating their strange exclusiveness. From the archaeological context of the scrolls and the Qumrân Community, one can see that the Wilderness referred to is a specific one located in the Arabah (*^{a}râvâh*), which geologists call the Great Rift. Even today the Ta'amireh Bedouins refer to the wild arid region west of the Dead Sea as the Wilderness. This specific, geographical interpretation was not without precedent within the Book of Isaiah, for in chapter 35 the threat of the previous chapter that Edom will become "waste and void" (with allusion to Gen. 1:2) is reversed by the paradisic description of what will happen to the Wilderness. The latter is undoubtedly the arid region of Judah which in contrast with Edom will become fertile and fruitful. I do not think that this was the original meaning of 40:3, where initally the allusion was rather to a new deliverance from the Babylonian Exile, likened to the Exodus from Egypt. Nevertheless, by interpreting the nouns *midbâr* (grazing land) and *^{a}râvâh* (arid steppe) as proper nouns, the Essenes located themselves in the desert of Judea. "Clearing the way" and "leveling the highway" meant the study and practice of God's will as revealed in the Holy Scriptures. The implication is that when this highway has been properly erected, God will manifest himself by bringing in the Messianic Age.

The above discussion is of interest for the history of Biblical interpretation; but one incidental by-product of the quotation is the evidence it affords for Biblical punctuation. The tradition associated with John the Baptist punctuates differently. It divides the clauses as follows:

> A voice cries in the Wilderness:
> "Clear the way of the LORD;
> level in the Arabah a highway for our God." [45]

44. *The Monks of Qumrân as Depicted in the Dead Sea Scrolls with Translations in English,* Westminster, Maryland, The Newman Press, 1960, pp. 152–155.

45. Matth. 3:3; Mark 1:3; Luke 3:4; John 1:23 — where, however, the Gospels follow the Septuagint in translating "a voice *of one* crying in the Wilderness," which is a possible rendering of the Hebrew. C. C. Torrey punctuates as here, on the basis of his understanding of Hebrew metrics. See his *The Second Isaiah, A New Interpretation,* Edinburgh, T. and T. Clark, 1938, pp. 225, 304.

As the passage is quoted in the Manual of Discipline, reference to the "voice" is omitted, evidently because it was regarded as introductory and without prophetic significance. According to this view, the passage should be punctuated:

> A voice cries:
> In the Wilderness clear the way of the LORD;
> level in the Arabah a highway for our God.

Poetic parallelism is better in the latter form of quotation, which is supported by the Manual. The variant punctuation of the New Testament was occasioned by the desire of interpreting the Baptist as the "voice." This was not based upon ignorance of Hebrew parallelism, for other Jews paid no attention to this when a desired interpretation could be obtained by ignoring it. It rests rather upon a theological difference between John and the Essenes. In contrast with them, he was not content to live in complete isolation. He would so preach that multitudes would flock to him from the populous cities to hear his call to repentance.

There are numerous examples in the Damascus Covenant (or Damascus Document) of deriving rules of conduct by ingenious Biblical interpretation. When this composition was first published by Solomon Schechter in 1910, he called it "a Zadokite Work." [46] Although he had found it in 1896 in the storage room of an old medieval synagogue in Cairo along with other late medieval manuscripts, he argued that the composition was the work of an ancient sect called the Zadokites. The basis of this identification was twofold: (1) The composition seems to refer to the members of the sect as "sons of Zadok." (2) Certain references in ancient Rabbinic literature refer to "Zadokites" in language appropriate to these so-called "sons of Zadok." Scholars of Rabbinic literature had previously tried to identify

---

46. *Documents of Jewish Sectaries,* Vol. I: *Fragments of a Zadokite Work,* Cambridge, 1910. Other editions of the text are Leonard Rost, *Die Damaskusschrift neu bearbeitet,* Berlin, 1933; C. Rabin, *The Zadokite Documents,* Oxford, Clarendon Press, 1954. My method of reference to this work is to employ the letters CDC (abbreviating the title Cairo Fragments of a Damascus Covenant). Page and line of the Hebrew text are cited, with the Roman numeral referring to the page number assigned the text by Schechter; but these are followed in parentheses by the chapter and verse numbers given by R. H. Charles, *Apocrypha and Pseudepigrapha of the Old Testament,* Oxford, Clarendon Press, 1913, Vol. II, pp. 799–834. Chapter numbers are indicated by Arabic numbers, as also verse and line numbers (the last, of course, appearing only after page numbers).

the term "Zadokite" (Heb. *Ṣədûqî'*) with the New Testament "Sadducee." According to Schechter's thesis, the "Zadokite" of Rabbinic literature is sometimes the Sadducee, but at other times a member of a wholly different sect. Thus he believed that he had discovered fragments of the lost literature of this previously unrecognized sect. He may possibly have been right in this thesis; but if so, this does not exclude the close kinship (or even identity) of the sect with the Essenes. The very title Zadokite Work which he introduced was intended to convey his identification of the sect. Most scholars have preferred the noncommittal title Damascus Covenant, a designation derived from the fact that the work refers to a covenant entered into by the sect "in the land of Damascus."

Prior to the discovery of the Qumrân Scrolls, a few scholars contested the antiquity of the Damascus Covenant on two grounds: (1) the lateness of the manuscripts in which it is contained, and (2) alleged affinities with a medieval Jewish sect known as Karaites. The discovery of the scrolls at once confirmed the antiquity of the Damascus Covenant; for there were pervasive similarities of language and terminology between this composition and the ancient non-Biblical scrolls of Qumrân. Even the same persons appear in both bodies of literature, the Teacher of Righteousness and the Man of Lies. Finally fragments of the Damascus Covenant were discovered among the ancient manuscripts of Caves Four and Six.[47] This proves beyond all cavil both the antiquity of the Zadokite work and its relatedness to the Qumrân sect.[48]

The practice of monogamy set forth in Chap. VII of the Damascus Covenant was supported by appeal to various Scriptures. One Biblical text was Gen. 2:27b: "A male and a female he created them."[49] Gen. 7:9 was appealed to as support of the idea that "*a male and a female*" should not be reduced to the idea of "male and female" (RSV), for side by side with this expression it states that the animals entered the ark "two and two." Even the prohibition that a king should not multiply wives for himself (Deut. 17:17) was introduced as textual rein-

---

47. See *DJD*, III, pp. 128–31.
48. To my knowledge, only Solomon Zeitlin opposes the antiquity of the Damascus Covenant; but he also rejects the views of the archeologists and paleographers regarding the date of the scrolls. See his numerous articles in *The Jewish Quarterly Review* (hereafter abbreviated as *JQR*), beginning in 1948, also his book *The Dead Sea Scrolls and Modern Scholarship*, *JQR* Monograph Series, III, Philadelphia, Dropsie College, 1956.
49. Cf. Matth. 19:4; Mark 10:6 — where Jesus employs the same text on behalf of monogamy.

forcement for monogamy, although it is not clear from the Biblical context how many wives would represent multiplicity. Perhaps, the Damascus community would argue that taking a second wife during the lifetime of the first was multiplying by two! Even David violated this rule, but the Book of the Law was at that time sealed up in the ark of the covenant until Zadok took office, so that his polygamy was due to his ignorance. Actually Zadok figures earlier (along with Abiathar, or his son Ahimelech) in the histories of Samuel and Chronicles; yet according to I Chron. 29:22b, Zadok was not anointed as Chief Priest until Solomon was anointed king.[50] Apparently the Damascus folk followed the Chronicler as to the time that Zadok took office. One may, of course, introduce a caveat here, that Zadok's opening of the Law Book made no difference in the conduct of David's son Solomon. However, even in the Old Testament, Solomon is regarded as a sinner with his vast multiplicity of consorts, so the folk of the Damascus migration probably believed that the excuse of ignorance which they extended to David could not be proffered to Solomon.

Another example of Biblical quotation in support of Essene rules for daily conduct is the prohibition of receiving from an outsider anything without payment:[51]

> Moreover, he may not eat anything of theirs, nor drink, nor take from their hand anything whatsoever except for a price, as it is written:

> "Cease ye from man whose breath is in his nostrils,
> for of what value is he to be reckoned?"

> For all who are not reckoned in His covenant are to be separated, both they and all they have; and the holy men may not rely upon any of the deeds of vanity. For vain are all who do not recognize His covenant; and all who despise His word He will destroy from the world, since all their deeds are uncleanness before him and uncleanness is in all their property.

The quotation of Isa. 2:22 served to suggest the idea of a separated life. The idea of human vanity in the verse was restricted by them to those who refused to enter their special covenant with God. Separation, there-

50. This reminds one of the two anointed ones (a priest and a king) who are to have pre-eminence in the Messianic Age according to the Qumrân literature. Cf. Kurt Schubert, *The Dead Sea Community: Its Origin and Teachings*, New York, Harper, 1959, pp. 113–21.
51. 1Q S v, 16–20.

fore, must be from outsiders alone, not from "the holy men" of the community. The verb "reckoned" suggested in some obscure manner the idea that the property (or "filthy lucre") of one outside the community ceased to be filthy once it was acquired by purchase; for by honest bargaining it had become a part of the community holdings which were consecrated to God. Separatism was therefore maintained in a manner which made possible commercial relations with the outside world.

B. *Textual Support of Messianic Hope*

Another scroll from Qumrân Cave Four has been named by John Allegro 4Q Midrashim, because it contains a series of Biblical quotations, each of which is followed by an interpretation, or midrash.[52] I quote here only four lines which are "mainly concerned with the reestablishment of the House of David in the last days." [53]

> ["Moreover] the LORD [de]clares to you that He will build you a house: *'And I will raise up* your son after you, and I will establish the throne of his kingdom for ever. I [will be] his father and he shall be My son.'" [II Sam. 7:11b–14a]. He is David's "Branch," who will take office with the Interpreter of the Law who [will reside] in Zi[on in the l]ast days; as it is written: *"And I will raise up* the booth of David that is fallen." [Amos 9:11]. It is "the booth of David that is fallen"; [and a]fterward, he will take office to save Israel.

First of all, the quotations from the Bible in this scroll passage may be examined for their textual value. The quotation of II Sam. 7 omits several clauses, but this seems to have been occasioned by the desire for brevity in a rather repetitious text. The reading *"He* will *build* you a house" for *"The* LORD will *make* you a house" is of doubtful significance. The quotation from Amos 9:11 reads *WHQYMWTY ("And* I will raise up") instead of the Massoretic *'QYM* ("I will raise up"); yet this same form of the quotation appears in the Damascus Covenant (at vii, 16 = 9:6). Interestingly, as Chaim Rabin observes, this reading corresponds with the fuller quotation of Acts 15:16: [54]

---

52. Allegro named the document provisionally 4Q Florilegium in *JBL,* LXXV, 1956, p. 176, and perhaps he still retains it; but his fuller publication, "Fragments of a Qumrân Scroll of Eschatological Midrashim," *JBL,* LXXVII, 1958, pp. 350–4, seems to suggest the new name 4Q Midrashim. In any case, this would be in keeping with the general preference of finding an appropriate Semitic name for each book.
53. The RSV is followed here, except that it is modified where the readings of the scroll diverge.
54. *Op. cit.,* p. 29.

> After these things I will return,
> and I will build again the tabernacle
> of David which is fallen. (ASV)

Luke, the author of Acts, did not at this point draw upon the Septuagint, which is here in full accord with the Massoretic text:

> In that day I will raise up
> the tabernacle [or booth] of David that is fallen. (ASV)

Since it is unlikely that "and" stood after the phrase "In that day," the implication is that the same Hebrew manuscript tradition which read "*and* I will raise up" also read the preceding clause "After these things I will return." Here is important evidence that probably also in some of the other erratic forms of Old Testament quotation in the New Testament, Hebrew manuscripts were followed which diverged from the Massoretic text. Even a general, though inexact, agreement with the Setuagint need not point to dependence upon that Greek version, but it may represent independent resort to the Hebrew tradition underlying the Septuagint.[55]

Secondly, we may note the interpretations that are associated with the Biblical quotations in 4Q Midrashim (as we return to the scroll passage with which the present discussion began). The fact that the Lord's promise in each case began with the same expression "And I will raise up" (in italics above) assisted the inference that each was concerned with a restoration, with a raising up *again* in Messianic times. This was probably the original intent of Amos 9:11; but it is not at all the case for II Sam. 7:11b, which referred originally to Solomon who immediately succeeded David. Yet in the interpretation of 4Q Midrashim, David's promised son is the future Messianic "Branch" foretold by Jeremiah (23:6; 33:15) and Zechariah (3:8; 6:12).[56] One interesting aspect of the exposition of Amos is that a literal interpretation is indicated by the tautologous statement: "It is the booth of David that is fallen." If no scribal omission occurred here, "the booth [or tabernacle][57] of David" refers to a renewed and purified temple and cult, in which the Messianic priest (called the Interpreter of the Law) will minister. After this has been achieved, the Messianic King of Davidic lineage

---

55. Cf. the citation of Deut. 32:43 in Heb. 1:6, which is discussed above, pp. 9f.
56. In the prophecies of Zechariah, Zerubbabel was expected to fulfill the role of the Branch; but after this hope failed, the expectation of the Branch continued.
57. Instead of translating "booth," the older versions render "tabernacle" — a meaning most appropriate in the present context, since allusion seems to be to the temple as a royal sanctuary.

will take office. I suspect that some phrase (or clause) has accidentally been omitted by an ancient scribe, or the passage would not be quite so tautologous. Even so, this was probably the basic idea of the passage.

Considerable interest attaches to a document which John Allegro has named 4Q Patriarchal Blessings because it is concerned with the prophetic interpretation of Jacob's blessing in Gen. 49. In verse 10, the role of dominance is assigned to Judah; and allusion is doubtless made to the greatness of the kingdom of Israel to be achieved under the sovereignty of David and Solomon. After the power of the Kingdom of Judah was broken, faith in the eternal validity of Jacob's blessing was not destroyed; but in the understanding of the devout it became a prediction of a new David to arise in the last days. The published portion of this scroll reads as follows: [58]

> *"A ruler shall [not] depart from the tribe (shêvet) of Judah."* When dominion becomes a reality for Israel, David's enthroned (descendant) [shall not] be cut off; for *"the ruler's staff"* is the covenant of kingship, [and the cla]ns of Israel are the *"feet."* "Until the true Messiah come," namely, David's "Branch," for *"to him"* and to his seed has been given the covenant of kingship over His people for perpetual generations. When He has kept the [covenant with him, God will raise up the "Branch of David" and the Interpreter of] [59] the Law with the men of the community; for [*"the gathering* of the peoples"] is the assembly of the men of . . .

With this one may compare both the King James and the Revised Standard Versions of Gen. 49:10:

> The sceptre (shêvet) shall not depart from Judah,
>   nor a lawgiver from between his feet,
> until Shiloh come;
>   and unto him shall the gathering of the people be. (KJV)

> The scepter shall not depart from Judah,
>   nor the ruler's staff from between his feet,
> until he comes to whom it belongs;
>   and to him shall be the obedience of the peoples. (RSV)

One of the most notable features of the Biblical text as quoted in the above scroll passage (the italicized portion) is its free departure from the Hebrew text which underlies the King James and the Revised

58. *Op. cit.*, p. 174–6.
59. With my restoration, cf. 4Q Midrashim i, 11 (*JBL*, Dec. 1958, p. 353).

Standard versions. Apparently its variant text of Gen. 49:10 reads as follows:

> A ruler shall not depart from the tribe of Judah,
> nor the ruler's staff from between his feet
> until the true Messiah come, to whom it belongs;
> and to him shall be the gathering of the peoples.

There is no chance that this enlarged text is original, for obviously it is an expanded rewriting of the Biblical passage. It represents the sort of paraphrastic enlargement found in the Jewish Aramaic Targums and is probably quoted from such a work.[60] We thus have two layers of interpretation here: one in that of the Biblical quotation itself, the other in the commentary upon it!

In the first layer of interpretation, the word *shêveṭ* (scepter) was taken in two senses: as a poetic figure for "ruler" (*shallîṭ*), and as "tribe" (an alternative meaning of *shêveṭ*).[61] The word *Shîlôh* was also taken in two senses: as a designation of "the true Messiah," and as the phrase "to whom [or, to him] it belongs." [62] Thus the possible, alternative renderings, which the King James Version and the Revised Standard Version display by their differing translations, were both kept at Qumrân!

In the second layer of interpretation, "the ruler's staff" is interpreted as "the covenant of kingship" God made with David as to the perpetuity of his dynasty.[63] Likewise, the commentary indicates that the word *yiqqəhath* is interpreted as "gathering" (to be derived from the Hebrew root *qâwâh* II), rather than "obedience" (to be derived from the theoretical Hebrew root *yâqah*, as in Arabic).[64] The interpretation, like the commentary upon II Sam. 7 (already discussed, immediately above), also looks forward to two Messianic figures: the Interpreter of the Law and David's "Branch." These seem to be variant titles, re-

60. This is in Hebrew rather than Aramaic, yet if the Genesis Apocryphon were wholly preserved, there might be some interesting comparisons at this point.
61. In the Targum of Onkelos, one reads similarly: "One to exercise rulership shall not depart from the house of Judah."
62. The former interpretation tends to confirm the view of Sigmund Mowinckel (*He That Cometh* [translated by G. W. Anderson], Nashville, Abingdon, 1954, p. 13, n. 2) that the word *shîlôh* is a poetical word borrowed from Accadian, meaning "his ruler."
63. Cf. II Sam. 7:15–17; Ps. 89:20–37; Isa. 55:3.
64. In this the scroll's interpretation agrees with the King James Version (hereafter abbreviated as KJV), as against the RSV, but the latter is supported by the Targum of Onkelos.

spectively, for "the Priest" and "the Messiah of Israel" mentioned in the Society Manual Annex,[65] where these men are to participate in the community banquet of bread and wine. The assurance that "David's enthroned descendant shall not be cut off" corresponds exactly with the popular objection to a martyred Messiah mentioned in John 12:34: "Our Law teaches us that the Messiah continues for ever." [66] The scroll passage shows us that such teaching was derived from the Law.[67]

4. INDIRECT QUOTATIONS

All the manifold uses of direct Biblical quotation are employed in the indirect quotations of the Old Testament. The handling of these Biblical allusions implies interpretations which are the basis of Essene life and faith. Sometimes their interest is solely for the history of Old Testament exegesis. Occasionally they may point the way to a better understanding of the Old Testament in its original intention.

A. Biblical Roots of Essene Practice

In the Society Manual Annex, there is a projection into Messianic times of rules and ordinances which will govern the society. When a youth is twenty years old, he may marry, for this is the age "when he knows good and evil." [68] It appears doubtful that this ordinance was postponed until the indefinite future. Surely the noncelibate Essenes would have begun this practice already, since they lived on the brink of Messianic times. They probably also observed the accompanying rule that boys should receive ten years of schooling.

Considerable attention has been given to the expression "when he knows good and evil." According to one view it means moral maturity.[69] According to another, it means the age of sexual awareness, with all its potentialities for weal or woe.[70] Either understanding is apropos as a requirement for marriage. In a society where double

65. 1Q Sa ii, 11ff. For a translation of this material, see Millar Burrows, *More Light on the Dead Sea Scrolls*, p. 395.
66. This passage does not rule out the doctrine of a suffering Messiah, as long as his suffering is not mortal.
67. This is true in the strictest and narrowest sense of the word Law, the Pentateuch. Contrast Marcus Dods in *The Expositor's Greek Testament*, Grand Rapids, Michigan, Wm. B. Eerdmans (undated), Vol. I, p. 811.
68. 1Q Sa i 10f. See Burrows, *op. cit.*, p. 394.
69. G. S. Buchanan, "The Old Testament Meaning of the Knowledge of Good and Evil," *JBL*, LXXV (June 1956), pp. 114–20.
70. Bo Reicke, "The Knowledge Hidden in the Tree of Paradise," *Journal of Semitic Studies* (hereafter cited as *JSS*), III (July 1956), pp. 193–201; R. Gordis, "The Knowl-

meanings in Scriptural exposition abound, we must certainly entertain the possibility that both understandings of the expression were held. On the side of the sexual interpretation, it has been pointed out that the serpent's promise that the eyes of Adam and Eve would be opened so that they would know good and evil when they ate of the forbidden fruit was fulfilled in their knowing that they were naked (Gen. 3:1–7). The generation of Israelites which emerged from the Wilderness to conquer the Promised Land were those who had been too young to know good and evil when the spies brought a discouraging report to the Hebrews at Kadesh Barnea (Deut. 1:39). Barzilai, an octogenarian, described himself in II Sam. 19:35 (KJV) as too old to "discern between good and evil," to "taste what I eat or what I drink," "to hear any more the voice of singing men and singing women." This is clearly in the realm of the sensual, so that the suggestion of a sexual reference in "good and evil" is not wholly irrelevant. Since one could be either too young or too old for this knowledge, the sexual interpretation seems to be strongly supported. It has even been claimed that this interpretation sheds light upon Isaiah's prophecy that before the child Immanuel "knows how to refuse the evil and choose the good" Assyria will overrun Syria and Israel, the foes of Judah (Isa. 7:14–16).[71] This prophecy was delivered in 734 B.C. In 732, Assyria took Gilead and Galilee and deported their Israelite inhabitants, but it was not until 721 B.C. that Samaria fell and its inhabitants were deported. If Immanuel was born in 734 B.C., he would have been only thirteen years old, and Isaiah's prophecy would have been fulfilled with exactitude, when the child was just about to reach the age of puberty at which time full sexual awareness would come upon him. According to this interpretation, the Society Manuel Annex unduly postponed this age until twenty; but surely this indicates that something more than the age of puberty was involved in their thinking. According to Midrash Rabbah, Gen. XIV, 7, Adam and Eve were created fully grown, at the age of twenty.

Against the sexual interpretation of "knowing good and evil," one may argue that the serpent's promise set forth the temptation of self-deification, of becoming like God, in knowing good and evil.[72] At a

edge of Good and Evil in the Old Testament and the Qumrân Scrolls," *JBL*, LXXVI (June 1957), pp. 123–38. For a criticism of their views, see Harold S. Stern, "The Knowledge of Good and Evil," *VT*, VIII (Oct. 1958), pp. 405–18.

71. For further discussion of this passage see Appendix C.

72. Self-deification is the cause of man's fall in the mythological story alluded to in Ezek. 28 and Isa. 14:12–14. This is the cardinal sin in the Book of Daniel and finds

primitive stage of religion, sexuality may have been regarded as an attribute of the gods, but within the total scope of the Old Testament such an interpretation is unthinkable. Robert Gordis has argued that the choice set before Adam and Eve was personal immortality through obedience to God, or vicarious immortality through descendants, and that Adam and Eve in choosing procreation had spurned the grace of the Creator who otherwise would have made them immortal. This interpretation would probably be valid for Gen. 3 at a primitive stage; but it could not have been maintained after it was brought into juxtaposition with Gen. 1, where man when first created was blessed by his Maker with the injunction that he should be fruitful and multiply.

The curse of Eve, then, was not childbearing, but the suffering which would attend it. Knowing good and evil, it could be claimed, means possessing complete knowledge; [73] for when David saw through the cunning pretense of the wise woman from Tekoa, she flattered him by saying that "the king is like the angel of God to discern good and evil." If this interpretation be applied to Gen. 3, the serpent promised full and complete knowledge like that of God, but Adam and Eve were cheated. All they got was a sense of shame which made them aware

---

its classic example in Antiochus Epiphanes (Dan. 11:36; II Macc. 9). To all this, Christ is the complete antithesis by forsaking the prerogatives of divinity for full humanity (Phil. 2:5–11), a doctrine without mythological parallel in the ancient world.

73. One must recall here that good and evil are not necessarily ethical terms; yet cf. II Sam. 14:17 cited below.

The present presentation will appear overly simplified to scholars who have followed the whole range of literature and interpretation of the last fifty years; but I confine myself here to a summary of the literature and ideas that have been brought into play in connection with the Qumrân Scrolls. Other studies of importance include the following: H. D. A. Major, "The Tree of Knowledge of Good and Evil," *The Expositor*, 8th Series, XII, 1916, pp. 259–85; H. T. Obbink, *Het bijbelsch Paradijsverhaal en de Babylonische bronnen*, 1917; N. P. Williams, *The Ideas of the Fall and of Original Sin*, London, Longmans Green, 1927; J. Begrich, "Die Paradieserzählung," *ZAW*, L, 1932; K. Budde, *Die biblische Paradiesgeschichte*, Giessen, Topelmann, 1932; T. C. Vriezen, *Onderzoek naar de paradijsvoorstelling bij de oude Semietische Volken*, 1937. P. Humbert, *Études sur le récit du paradis et de la chute dans la Genèse*, Neuchâtel, 1940. J. Coppens, *La Connaissance du bien et mal et la péché du Paradis*, 1948; Martin Buber, *Good and Evil, Two Interpretations*, New York, Scribner's, 1953; G. Lambert, "Le drame du jardin d'Eden," *NRTh*, Nov.–Dec. 1954, pp. 3–63 (917–1072); I. Engnell, "Knowledge and Life in the Creation Story," *Supplements to Vetus Testamentum* (hereafter cited as *SVT*), III, 1955, pp. 103–19; Susumu Jozaki, "The Tree of Knowledge of Good and Evil," *Kwansei Gakun University Annual Studies*, VIII, 1959; pp. 1–18. One should also consult commentaries upon Genesis, such as: S. H. Hooke, *In the Beginning*, Oxford, Clarendon Press, 1948; Gerhard von Rad, *Genesis, a Commentary* (translated from the German by John H. Marks), Philadelphia, Westminster, 1961.

of their nakedness. From henceforth, also, they would know through experience evil as well as good. Omniscience is certainly out of the question as a prerequisite for marriage, so that an attenuated meaning of ethical maturity would seem to be a more relevant understanding in the context of the scroll.

Whatever the scroll means by knowing good and evil, it is clear why the age was set at twenty. This was done by comparing Scripture with Scripture. Num. 14:29 had indicated that only those under twenty would be admitted to the Holy Land after the nation had been panicked by reports delivered by the spies. The older generation had to die off and the younger grow up before the conquest could begin. When the story is retold in Deuteronomy, it is those who were too young to know good and evil to whom the land of Canaan is promised (Deut. 1:39). Putting these two passages together, the Essene Congregation set the age of knowing good and evil at twenty. It is their linking of this expression with the requirement for marriage which suggests that tradition had preserved a sexual connotation for this term from primitive times, but their understanding of twenty as the age of moral maturity would not be excluded.

Another example of implicit Biblical interpretation was the Essene denial of the validity of cleansing for the unrepentant. In discussing this, the Society Manual declares: "Unclean, unclean shall he be as long as he rejects God's laws so as not to be instructed by the community of His counsel." [74] "Unclean! Unclean!" was the cry prescribed for the leper in Leviticus 13:45. He was to be isolated from society until he was pronounced clean by the priest. In its use of the same language, the Qumrân society indicated that it believed that there were moral lepers who should be treated in the same way as physical lepers.

B. *Biblical Roots of Essene Doctrine*

The Manual of Discipline contains a section devoted to its doctrine of ethical dualism.[75] When God created the world He created two spirits, who may be variously called the Spirit of Truth and the Spirit of Perversity, or the Angel of Light and the Angel of Darkness. Humanity is subject to the contesting sway of these two spirits. The children of light are those who follow the Angel of Light, yet they are

74. 1Q S iii, 6.
75. 1Q S iii, 13 — iv, 26.

sometimes "tripped up" by the Angel of Darkness. The children of darkness are wholly under the control of the Angel of Darkness and follow him in their perversity. Thus the two spirits, or two Angels, lead men down two different roads: the way of light and the way of darkness. The former is marked by growth in moral and spiritual sensitivity; the latter is characterized by increased wickedness and obduracy. The end of the former is immortality in the splendor of eternal light; the end of the latter is "bitter misfortune amid the calamities of darkness until their destruction, without remnant or survivor."

A strong Zoroastrian influence pervades this dualism,[76] but the thought of the sect was not derived directly from that source. Biblical roots for this doctrine must surely be sought.[77] Insofar as the two angels are concerned, there are Old Testament passages upon which this doctrine could be readily founded. In Zechariah 3, High Priest Joshua stood before the angel of the Lord, and "the Satan" was standing by in order to accuse him; but the Lord's angel interceded for Joshua. The terminology is different, and "*the* Satan" does not appear as a tempter, but only as the Lord's prosecuting attorney whose duty it is to accuse the evildoer. Yet, in later theological speculation, he did develop into the demonic tempter, so that by the time the Qumrân Scrolls were written he had long been recognized as a fallen angel. From that perspective, the dualism of Zech. 3 would be complete. Similarly in Job, the notable saint was accused (this time falsely) of a sham righteousness, and the Lord allowed "the Satan" to test Job. Poor Job seems never to have been aware of the source of his suffering which ensued; but at certain points of his long-winded debates and soliloquies, he rose to the faith that he had a heavenly mediator or redeemer. These two are implicitly opposed to one another, the heavenly accuser and the heavenly intercessor. The role of the latter is further developed in the Elihu interlude:

> His soul draws near the Pit,
> and his life to those who bring death.

---

76. A. Dupont-Sommer, "L'instruction sur les deux esprits dans le 'Manuel de Discipline,' " *RHR*, CXLII, 1952, pp. 5–35; K. G. Kuhn, "Die Sektenschrift und die iranische Religion," *Zeitschrift für Theologie und Kirche*, XLIX, 1952, pp. 296–316.
77. See the studies of O. J. F. Seitz, "Two Spirits in Man: an Essay in Biblical Exegesis," *New Testament Studies* (abbreviated as *NTS*), VI, 1959–60, pp. 82–95; F. Nötscher, "Voies divines et humaines selon la Bible et Qumrân," in *Rech. Bib. IV*, pp. 135–48; Herbert G. May, "Cosmological Reference in the Qumran Doctrine of the Two Spirits and in Old Testament Imagery," *JBL*, LXXXII, 1963, pp. 1–14.

If there be for him an angel,
a mediator, one of the thousand,
to declare to man what is right for him;
and he is gracious to him, and says,

"Deliver him from going down into the Pit,
I have found a ransom;
Let his flesh become fresh with youth;
let him return to the days of his youthful vigor."

Then man prays to God, and he accepts him,
he comes into his presence with joy.
He recounts to men his salvation,
and he sings before men and says:

"I have sinned and perverted what was right,
and it was not requited to me.
He has redeemed my soul from going down into the Pit,
and my life shall see the light." (Job 33:22–28. RSV)

The angelic mediator contemplated here is more than an intercessor. He is also a moral guide "to declare to man what is right for him." Similarly, in I Chron. 21:1, Satan emerges as a tempter, rather than an angelic accuser. The roles of intercessor and accuser are entirely absent in the dualistic passage of the Qumrân Manual of Discipline; yet the roots of the dualism go back to Zechariah and Job. Under the influence of Zoroastrianism, Satan became the enemy of the intercessory angel and both became tempters: one tempting people into the way of sin, the other alluring men into the way of righteousness.

According to the earliest form of Zoroastrian faith, light and darkness were created by the supreme God, Ahura Mazda. Later faith tended to regard light and darkness as both eternal and as co-existent. The Exilic prophet who wrote Isa. 40—55 claimed for Yahweh (the LORD) what the Iranian claimed for Ahura Mazda: [78]

I form light and create darkness,
I make weal and create woe.
I am the LORD, who do all these things. (45:7. RSV)

[78]. Some of the nineteenth-century commentators suggested that the passage was directed against Zoroastrian dualism. However, primitive Zoroastrianism was monotheistic; and its tendencies toward dualism were not developed until after the time of Second Isaiah (author of Isa. 40—55). If a polemic is involved, it might be against Babylonian dualism, with Marduk its god of light and Tiamat its goddess of darkness.

This rival claim made for the Lord proved to be an entering wedge of a fully developed dualism for the folk at Qumrân, in whose view the God of Israel created the angel of light and the angel of darkness, and then placed humanity within the moral struggle between these two angels. The idea of the two ways was also easily drawn from the Old Testament, where it appears in embryonic form.[79]

c. Biblical Roots of Essene Messianism

We have already seen the use of direct Biblical quotation in the exposition of Messianic expectations. Here we shall examine Biblical allusions and implicit interpretations of the Scriptures. Under this heading we shall also include the document called 4Q Testimonia, which indeed contains full quotations, but in which the texts have no accompanying interpretation. One reason for this grouping is that its contents must be correlated to the expectation of the Society Manual, to which we now turn.

Of utmost importance for the general understanding of Essene Messianic thought is the statement of this Manual that the rules of the community were to continue in force "until the coming of the Prophet and the Anointed Ones of Aaron and Israel." [80] It is now clear that this comment refers to three eschatological figures; the Prophet, the Messiah of Aaron (an anointed priest of Aaronic descent), and the Messiah of Israel (an anointed king of Davidic descent). We have become so accustomed to think in terms of a single Messianic figure that the doctrine of three sounds strange to us.[81] The New Testament does recognize John the Baptist as a prophetic forerunner; but the three Messianic offices of prophet, priest, and king are there, with Jesus, combined in a single person.

It was immediately clear that the title "prophet" was drawn from Deut. 18:15, where Moses predicted that the Lord would raise up a prophet like himself. The Biblical roots for belief in a Davidic Messiah are extensive and are well known; but the idea of a priestly Messiah to

---

79. Deut. 30:15–20; Jer. 21:8; Ps. 1; and Prov. 2:13; 7:8, 27; 8:20.
80. 1Q S ix, 11.
81. The title Messiah (or anointed) of Aaron does not occur in the published Qumrân literature, but it is implicit in the above quotation. Even if this nomenclature was never used at all in the singular, it becomes a helpful terminology for us — just as the word Messiah gives us a useful term in discussing certain Old Testament prophecies at a time prior to its technical usage. The earlier royal association of this title is indicated by the fact that "the Messiah" in the Qumrân literature is always unambiguously the ideal Davidic king of the last days.

stand alongside the Davidic Messiah is largely new to Biblical scholarship. In the Testaments of the Twelve Patriarchs, whose sources were composed very largely in the period between the Old and New Testaments,[82] there are prophecies concerning both a priestly and a Davidic Messiah. Most critics prior to the study of the Dead Sea Scrolls had argued that the original text of this work presented only a priestly Messiah, although the contrary opinion, that it set forth originally the doctrine of a Davidic Messiah alone, was not without its advocate. That both were integral to the original text was seldom recognized,[83] but this is the position which now appears probable.

If we go back to the first known Messianic movement, we discover that the two leaders of the early post-Exilic community of Jews were Zerubbabel, the governor, and Jeshua, the high priest. The former was a descendant of King Jehoiachin, who had been taken into exile in 597 b.c. As a Davidic scion, he drew to himself hopes of a revived kingdom; but these hopes did not omit a prominent place for the high priest. In Zechariah's vision of the two olive trees and the candelabrum, the trees are identified with Zerubbabel and Jeshua, "the two sons of oil who stand by the LORD of the whole earth." [84] "Two sons of oil" is the literal expression which is correctly translated in the Bible as "the two anointed"; but it does not give us verbal agreement with the language of the Manual of Discipline. Of course, a study of Old Testament usage of the word "anointed" will show that priests, as well as kings, were anointed, so that there is no serious disparity. Nevertheless, even this minor discrepancy is bridged by the statement of I Chron. 29:22: "They *anointed* him [Solomon] as prince for the LORD, and Zadok as priest." [85] Here the two anointed stand side by side, the representatives of state and church. Messianism in Hebrew faith involved a restoration of her idyllic past, a return to the days of David and

82. On manuscript fragments of the Testaments of the Twelve Patriarchs, see R. H. Charles, *op. cit.* Vol. II, p. 290; J. T. Milik in *DJD*, I, pp. 87–91; "Le Testament de Levi en Araméen; fragment de la grotte 4 de Qumrân," *RB*, LXII, 1955, pp. 398–406; M. de Jonge, *The Testaments of the Twelve Patriarchs, A Study of Their Text, Composition and Origin*, Assen, 1953 (reviewed by J. T. Milik in *RB*, 1955, pp. 297ff.).
83. See G. R. Beasley-Murray, "The Two Messiahs in the Testaments of the Twelve Patriarchs," *Journal of Theological Studies* (hereafter abbreviated as *JThS*), Vol. 48, 1947, pp. 1–12; T. W. Manson, "Miscellanea Apocalyptica III," *JThS*, Vol. 48, 1947, pp. 59–61.
84. Zech. 4:14.
85. Cf. my comments in *JBL*, LXXX, 1961, pp. 278f. In this same issue, see W. F. Stinespring, "Eschatology in Chronicles," pp. 209–19.

Solomon. The Messianic kingdom would have new splendors of its own, but the portrait of the two anointed which belonged to the past would also belong to the future. We have already seen these companion figures in other scroll passages, where they are called "David's Branch" and the "Interpreter of the Law." [86]

The document that John Allegro has entitled 4Q Testimonia contains a list of Messianic prooftexts unaccompanied by interpretation.[87] The first two references relate to Moses (Deut. 5:28–29) and the prophet like Moses (Deut. 18:18–19). These two were probably grouped together with the idea that one must know Moses before he can know the one like him; or even better, he must learn to obey Moses if he is to be prepared to obey his successor.[88] Some Biblical scholars have interpreted Deut. 18 as referring to Old Testament prophets in general rather than to a Messianic figure. It is possible that such an interpretation may have adhered to the passage when the Book of Deuteronomy was first written; but when the final editors of the Pentateuch (perhaps of the fifth century B.C.) stated, "There has not arisen a prophet since in Israel like Moses," they automatically projected the fulfillment of the promise of Deut. 18 into the future.[89] In the days of the Maccabees, expectation of the Prophet figured prominently. New Testament writers identified him with Jesus.

The next passage of 4Q Testimonia is an excerpt from the prophecy of Balaam (Numbers 24:15–17). The significant portion of this prophecy is its climax:

> A star shall come forth out of Jacob,
>   and a scepter shall rise out of Israel;
> It shall crush the forehead of Moab,
>   and break down all the sons of Sheth.

When originally composed, both the "star" and the "scepter" (or "comet") referred to David, whose conquests would extend to Moab; but the synonymous parallelism was ignored in the Damascus Covenant, where "the star" was explained as "the Interpreter of the Law" (the priestly Messiah) and "the scepter" was identified with "the

---

86. Above, pp. 88, 90.
87. *JBL,* LXXV, 1956, pp. 182–7.
88. Cf. Luke 16:29–31.
89. For the relationship of Messianic thought to the figure and accomplishments of Moses, see Joseph Klausner, *The Messianic Idea in Israel* (translated by W. F. Stinespring), New York, Macmillan, 1955, Chaps. 2 and 3.

Prince of all the Congregation" (the royal Messiah).[90] The Damascus Covenant refers to the coming of "the Interpreter of the Law" to Damascus; but it is not clear whether this event has already happened or whether it lies in the future.[91]

The next quotation in 4Q Testimonia is Deut. 33:8–11, a passage which glorifies the tribe of Levi as the priestly tribe possessing Urim and Thummim. Until a commentary is found upon this passage, we may not be sure whether this was cited by way of emphasizing the importance of the priesthood for all times to come, or whether this was thought of as referring in some specific ways to the Righteous Teacher and/or the Messiah of Aaron. The fact that both are priests complicates the possible applications. Two identical verses of Ezra (2:63) and Nehemiah (7:65) mention a post-Exilic waiting "until a priest with Urim and Thummim takes office." This sounds so similar to the expectant awaiting of the Prophet in I Maccabees,[92] one wonders whether this passage really does look forward to the coming of a priestly Messiah, and whether Deut. 33:8–11 was included in 4Q Testimonia because of its parallel mention of the Urim and Thummim.

The final quotation of 4Q Testimonia has moved from Pentateuchal materials to an excerpt from the supposed Psalms of Joshua, which reads as follows:[93]

At the time when Joshua finished praising and giving thanks in his psalms, he said:

"Cursed be the man who builds this city.
At the cost of his firstborn shall he lay its foundation,
and at the cost of his youngest son shall he lay its gates.

"Behold, an accursed man,
a diabolical man shall take office
To become 'the fowler's snare' to his people,
and destruction to all his neighbors.

"When he takes office . . .

90. The Cairo Fragments of the Damascus Covenant (abbreviated as CDC) vii, 18f. (9:8f.).
91. See the translation of Chaim Rabin, *op. cit.*, p. 30, also that of van der Woude, *op. cit.*, p. 132.
92. 4:46; 14:41.
93. For the text, see Allegro, *op. cit.*, pp. 185ff. The translation given here is my own.

[so] that the two of them may be instruments of violence. And they shall build again the . . . [and will] establish for it a wall and towers, to provide a refuge of wickedness . . . in Israel, and a horrible thing in Ephraim, and in Judah . . . and they shall cause pollution in the land, and great contempt among the sons of . . . [bl]ood like water on the rampart of Lady Zion and in the boundary of Jerusalem."

The first stanza of Joshua's curse is borrowed from Josh. 6:26 where its omission of the reference to Jericho agrees with the Septuagint text. This reading may have made possible a transfer of the bearing of the curse from Jericho to Jerusalem. Presumably the passage continued its poetic parallelism to the very end, but the text is too broken toward the last to make possible such an arrangement.

There is little room to doubt that this passage was believed to refer to the principal Wicked Priest and two of his sons. In Allegro's theory, the reference is to Alexander Jannaeus (Jewish ruler from 103–76 B.C.) and his two sons, Hyrcanus II and Aristobulus II, who vied for authority in Jerusalem after the demise of their mother (who ruled from 76–67 B.C.). Caesar, according to Josephus, gave permission to Hyrcanus II to rebuild the walls of Jerusalem in 47 B.C. The weakness of this theory is that there is no suggestion of rivalry between the sons in the references to them in 4Q Testimonia. Neither does it deal with the historical allusions as a whole.

In the theory of Frank Cross, the Wicked Priest is Simon (who ruled from 143–135 B.C.) and the reference is therefore to his two sons Judas and Mattathias, who together with their father were assassinated in the fortress called Doq on a hill northwest of Jericho.[94] Thus, despite the variant reading of Josh. 6:26, the passage was really applied to Jericho. The blood bath of Jerusalem mentioned at the end of the passage refers to the attack upon the city by Antiochus VI in 134–132 B.C. immediately following Simon's death. The strength of this theory is that it combines so many historical details, including both Jericho and Jerusalem. Its greatest weakness is that, in all probability, John Hyrcanus rather than Judas was Simon's oldest son.[95]

94. *The Ancient Library of Qumrân*, pp. 112f.
95. The three sons of Simon are introduced to us by I Maccabees in the order of their age: John (I Macc. 13:53), Judas (I Macc. 16:2), and Mattathias (16:14). In each of the last two passages, however, two sons are mentioned with a curious reversal of the true chronological order, which is to be explained as a matter of giving precedence in both cases to the previously unmentioned son. The fact that John was made com-

A third possibility is that the Wicked Priest was John Hyrcanus I (who ruled from 135–105 B.C.) and that his two sons are Aristobulus I (who ruled in 104 B.C.) and Alexander Jannaeus, who succeeded him. Aristobulus was the eldest son and Alexander was the third in line of five sons. The latter was therefore not the youngest son, but the youngest to succeed his father. The blood bath at Jerusalem will then refer to blood spilled by these priests in Jerusalem. This is particularly apropos of Alexander Jannaeus, who crucified eight hundred Pharisees. One strength of this theory is that each of the sons actually succeeded his father as priest-king. Another is that John Hyrcanus fits so admirably other historical allusions of the scrolls. He is most probably the Wicked Priest whose rule was at first popular but later fell into disrepute. No other priest fits so well here as Hyrcanus, who broke with the Pharisees and presumably with other Hasidic groups during his reign.[96] When Hyrcanus turned Sadducee, he may well have been dubbed the Man of Lies, or the Prophet of Lies, which could be another term of opprobrium for the same man. In any case, Josephus records of Hyrcanus alone that he was reputed to have the gift of prophecy.[97] The Prophet of Lies, according to the Habakkuk Commentary "misled many into building his city of vanity through bloodshed" — a datum which fits admirably the 4Q Testimonia.[98] The role of "the fowler's snare" attributed to the "accursed man" in the Testimonia is ascribed by Hosea 9:8 to the faithless prophets of Israel. It could therefore be aptly applied to Hyrcanus. When it comes to being a source of "destruction to all his neighbors," Hyrcanus' conquests abundantly qualify him.[99] Both of Hyrcanus' sons died in great agony, according to Josephus, and their deaths seem to be referred to in the Habakkuk Commentary, where they are said to have paid for their evil deeds by the manner in

mander of all Simon's forces and stationed in the disturbed coastal area (13:53) is explained by his now having become a man (Greek *hoti anêr estin*), with the implication that he was the first of Simon's sons to reach manhood. In 16:4ff. he seems to be in charge of the army; and he did not attend the banquet held at Doq because of his heavy responsibilities.

96. Jewish Antiquities (abbreviated as J.A.), XIII, x, 5–6 (¶ 288–98); J.W., I, ii, 8 (¶ 67). The latter passage speaks of a discontent with Hyrcanus which ended in open, but unsuccessful, war. In J.A., ¶ 296, Hyrcanus punishes those who follow Pharisaic, rather than Sadducean, interpretation of the Law. Earlier Hasmonean priests had taken punitive measures against the Hellenizers; but John Hyrcanus appears to have been the first Hasmonean to persecute other groups.

97. J.A., XIII, x, 3 (¶ 282–3); XIII, x, 7 (¶ 300); J.W., I, ii, 8 (¶ 68–9).

98. 1Q pHab x, 9f.

99. See Josephus, J.A., XIII, ix, 1 & x, 2–3. (¶ 254–8, 275–81).

which they died.[100] Although there is no obvious interpretation of the last passage of 4Q Testimonia, it fits best of all John Hyrcanus and his two sons as the persecuting Wicked Priests.

5. Word Usage

The way the Qumrân Scrolls use Biblical words in new contexts sometimes points to a later meaning. This seems probable to me in the case of *qêṣ,* in the sense of "period of time" rather than "end." The same is probably true of *yaḥad,* used in the sense of "community" (a togetherness) rather than as the adverb "together." In each case, however, scholars have suggested Old Testament passages in which they believed that these meanings were suitable.[101] In the present study, I shall limit myself to three terms found in the Manual of Discipline which may provide us with an important clue as to the original meaning of the Old Testament.

A. *Maśḳîl (Cantor)*

The Qumrân Scrolls speak of an official called the *maśḳîl* whose duty it is to instruct and to bless the varied members of the people of God. His name appears mostly in the headings which begin, *"For [the use of] the maśḳîl."* [102] Translators of the Old Testament have debated the question as to whether this word means "the wise" or "the teacher," but the prevalent translation is "the wise." Qumrân usage suggests that a special class of persons bore this title; and since the functions of teaching and blessing are elsewhere in the scrolls assigned to priests, the *maśḳîl* apparently should be a priest. The possibility that a Levite could function in this capacity is suggested by II Chron. 30:22: "And Hezekiah spake comfortably unto all the Levites *that taught (hammaśḳîlîm)* the good knowledge of the Lord"(KJV — italics my own). The preceding verse says that both Levites and priests devoted themselves day after day to the enthusiastic praise of God. Verse 22 inter-

100. Aristobulus' death is referred to in 1Q pHab ix, 1ff. See Josephus, J.A., XIII, xi, 2 (¶ 311) and J.W., I, iii, 5 (¶ 79–80), and my discussion in "The Historical Allusions of the Dead Sea Habakkuk Midrash," *BASOR,* No. 126, pp. 10–20, with attention here to pp. 13 and 18. The death of Alexander Jannaeus is alluded to in 1Q pHab xi, 8–15 in accordance with J.A., XIII, xv, 5 (¶ 398). See my discussion, *op. cit.,* p. 15.
101. E. L. Sukenik, *Məgillôt Gənûzôt,* I, Jerusalem, Israel: Bialik Foundation, 1948, pp. 22f.; S. Talmon, "The Sectarian *YḤD*—a Biblical Noun," *VT,* III, 1953, pp. 133–40.
102. 1Q S iii, 13; 1Q Sb i, 1; iii, 23; v, 20. The function of the *maśḳîl* as a teacher stands outside this formula in 1Q S ix, 12, 21, which should be examined in the light of ix, 12–26, concerning which see below at n. 108.

preted in the light of this sequence indicates that the Levites had done nothing different from that of the priests, but that Hezekiah singled them out for special encouragement.

It is this context which led to revision in the later English versions of II Chron. 30:22. The American Standard Version renders the verse: "And Hezekiah spake comfortably unto all the Levites that had good understanding *in the service* of Jehovah." The forced character of the translation is indicated by the ASV italics which were employed for interpolated words; yet the Revised Standard Version has followed this rendering with but minor revision, including the elimination of the italics. This was done because the reference to singing seemed to eliminate the thought of teaching. It was ill-conceived, however, for there is one class of didactic psalm in the Old Testament which is entitled *maśkîl* ("that which teaches").[103] Since both hymn and sermon were chanted originally,[104] the musical context by no means eliminates the possibility that the Levites and priests "taught the good knowledge of the Lord" in song. "Knowledge of the Lord," moreover, was taught by recounting His saving acts in history, and this was most frequently done in song. The hymns of Miriam and Deborah, as well as many other psalms, illustrate this point. Prior to the writing of the Pentateuch (or its sources), the varied traditions which are found there were probably transmitted by bards.

The Book of Daniel contains other references to the *maśkîl*, always in the plural and preceded with the definite article (*ham-maśkîlîm*).[105] The American Standard Version follows the King James Version in its translation "the wise," but it gives as a marginal suggestion "the teachers." The latter rendering is especially suggested by Dan. 12:3, which in a rather literal translation may be rendered:

> Those who *make wise* shall shine
> as the brightness of the sky;
> Those who *make* the many *righteous,*
> as the stars for ever and ever.

---

103. Or, perhaps, "that which ponders." Cf. Francis Brown, S. R. Driver, and Charles A. Briggs, *A Hebrew and English Lexicon of the Old Testament with an Appendix Containing the Biblical Aramaic, Based on the Lexicon of William Gesenius, as Translated by Edward Robinson,* Oxford, The Clarendon Press, 1907, 1952, p. 968b. Ps. 47:8 (English 47:7) uses the term in the body of a psalm.
104. Cf. above, pp. 88ff.
105. Dan. 11:35; 12:3, 10.

The word *maśkîl* is a causative participle in Hebrew; and therefore its earliest, unattenuated meaning should be "make wise." The parallelism with "make righteous" in the above verse surely indicates that the rendering given here is superior to the usual translation, "Those who are wise shall shine." Two roles of the teacher are stressed by this verse: (1) to indoctrinate by "making wise" and (2) to mould character by "making righteous." [106] In Hebraic thought these are inseparable aspects of the same thing; but it is the former expression which seems to have become a fixed term for "teacher," for it alone is used absolutely and without an object in Daniel and the Qumrân Scrolls.

Now Daniel is believed to have been written by a member of the Hasideans (or Hasidim) who are mentioned in I and II Maccabees. These zealots for the observance of God's covenant joined the Maccabean uprising against the Syrian king Antiochus Epiphanes in 168 B.C. After religious freedom was obtained, they showed little interest in the political objectives of the Maccabean (or Hasmonean) rulers, and eventually they broke with these priest-monarchs.[107] Both Pharisees and Essenes were included in this falling away, and probably both parties were derived from the Hasidim. The Qumrân literature stands so close to the Hasidic tradition, it is entirely probable that the Hasidic use of *maśkîl* as a title for "teacher" was transmitted into its community life directly, quite apart from the influence of Daniel. This means that the Qumrân usage of the term must be taken seriously as pointing to a special class of person, if not more specifically to a particular official of this title. We must take this into consideration in any future translations of the Old Testament. In the case of II Chron. 30:22, the best rendition would probably be: "And Hezekiah spoke encouragingly to all the Levites *who taught through song* the good knowledge of the LORD." If the Chronicler's usage be stressed, we might even conclude that "cantor" would be a better rendering in Daniel than "teacher." The Qumrân Society Manual at iii, 13 might even be rendered, "For the cantor's use, that he might instruct and teach all the sons of light." This suggestion may be reinforced by the *maśkîl's* function of blessing, for here is a literary type wholly compati-

---

106. Only formally does this distinction exist, for this is synonymous parallelism. See my article, "The Priestly Character of the Church in the Apocalypse," *NTS*, V, 1959, pp. 224f.

107. Cf. what I have written concerning the authorship and date of I Maccabees in *IDB*, Vol. K–Q, "Maccabees, Books of," B. 8, pp. 205*b*f.

ble with cantilation.[108] Yet the cantor of the synagogue chants all parts
of the Scriptures.

B. 'Ahᵃvat ḥesed (Devoted Love)

There are several indirect quotations of Micah 6:8 which could
logically have been included under the use of Biblical allusions in our
earlier discussion, but we shall restrict ourselves here to the meaning
attached to the single Hebrew phrase 'ahᵃvat ḥesed. In my translation
of the Society Manual, I observed that the contexts in which these words
appear do not support the meaning "to love kindness," but rather, "a
kindly love" — or better still, "a devoted love." The actual expression
which I chose to translate the phrase was "loving devotion," [109] because
in idiomatic English this wording suited best the sentences where it is
found, especially in ii, 24f.: "for they all shall live in true Unity and
good humility and *loving devotion* and righteous purpose, *each toward
his fellow* in the holy Council." This quotation shows that the phrase
borrowed from Micah is set in the context of other nominal phrases in
which a virtue is enhanced by an appropriate attribute: true, good,
and righteous. In each case the attributive idea is expressed by the
genitive (or construct) relationship in the Hebrew: "in unity of truth,
and humility of goodness, and love of devotion, and purpose of righteousness."

Taken by itself, "love of devotion" could mean "a love *for* devotion
(or kindness)," and it is so interpreted in our English translations. This
seemed to be the obvious syntactical relationship in Micah 6:8 where
it was evidently grouped in a series of infinitives:

> He has showed you, O man, what is good;
> and what does the LORD require of you
> But to do justice, and *to love kindness,*
> and to walk humbly with your God   (RSV)

108. In the Society Blessings, the leaders of the Messianic Age are to be blessed; but in
the Society Manual (ix, 12–26), the discussion of the duties of the *maśkíl* flow into a
hymn blessing God. It was this awareness of continuity, despite the different literary
character which led me to group under a single heading the whole of ix, 12—xi, 22 in
my "Analytical Table of Contents of *DSB*," *BASOR*, Supplementary Studies, 10–12,
1951, Appendix I, pp. 56f. Since writing the present chapter, I have discovered that
J. Strugnell, "The Angelic Liturgy at Qumrân, 4Q *Serek Širôt 'Ôlat Haššabāt*," *SVT*,
VII, 1960, pp. 318–45, has disclosed evidence that a *maśkíl* was to compose hymnic
liturgies for use in Sabbath worship at Qumrân.
109. This turning of the phrase was criticized by Philip Hyatt in his article, "On the
Meaning and Origin of Micah 6:8," *Anglican Theological Review*, Vol. XXXIV (Oct.
1952), No. 4, pp. 232–9.

This syntax is not necessarily correct. The second half of the verse may list a series of the objects of the verb *"to do"*: "justice, devoted love, and humbly walking with your God." It is precisely this which happens in the Manual's usage at viii, 2: "through *doing* [or, practicing] truth and righteousness, and *justice and devoted love, and humble walking* each with his fellow." According to the scroll, then, the passage should be translated:

> He has showed you, O man, what is good;
> and what does the LORD require of you
> but to practice justice and devoted love
> and humble walking with your God?

Either construction of Micah 6:8 is theoretically possible, but there is one awkward aspect of the older syntactical understanding which is brought out in the RSV margin: "and to love steadfast love." One scarcely thinks of loving love, so the Standard Bible Committee avoided this tautology by retaining "kindness" of the American Standard Version at this place — despite the general rule that *ḥesed* was to be rendered "steadfast love." *Ḥesed* combines love and loyalty in its meaning, hence the RSV rendering with two words. *Devotion* is an English word which shares the twofold character of "steadfast love" and which may serve as appropriate translation of *ḥesed*. By "a love of *ḥesed*," it seems entirely probable that Micah meant "a love of the *ḥesed* type" — a *devoted* love. It is because the Essene Community believed that the practice of Micah 6:8 was facilitated by their community life, in which their walk with God was also a walk with one another, that they so often used the language of this passage. In so doing, they apparently picked up from the then living Hebraic tradition the correct understanding of *'aháhvat ḥesed*.[110]

c. *yêṣer sâmûkh* (*the Steadfast Mind*)

The Society Manual also clarifies a difficult phrase in Isa. 26:3, which in the King James Version is rendered: "Thou wilt keep *him* in perfect peace, *whose* mind *is* stayed *on thee*." The italics of this version indicate the amount of interpretation that was introduced into the text in order to make sense of the two words *yêṣer sâmûkh* ("mind stayed"). This rendering was largely imitated in the Revised Standard Version, except for the removal of italics. Now the Manual of Discipline employs

110. Cf. Philip Hyatt, *ibid*.

the phrase *yêṣer sâmûḵh* several times with the contextual indication that what it means is simply "the staid [or steadfast] mind," so that the rendering of Alexander R. Gordon in *An American Translation* is fully substantiated:

> The steadfast mind Thou keepest in perfect peace,
> for it trusts in Thee.

The RSV rightly introduces a tristich; but it errs in conforming its language to the phrasing of the KJV, whereas the Hebrew sequence yields the following:

> The mind that is steadfast
> Thou dost keep in perfect peace,
> for it trusts in Thee.

Perhaps the Standard Bible Committee was too bewitched by the beauty of the King James language to follow the lead of Gordon, but thereby they perpetuated a mistranslation.[111]

Word studies of this kind may be multiplied by drawing upon all the scrolls. The meanings which words receive in this vast body of literature are not necessarily original, but in special cases they convey the original meaning which rectifies our understanding of the Old Testament.

111. In this presentation of Isa. 26:3 I am reproducing in revised form material first published in *The Duke Divinity School Bulletin*, XVII, 3 (Nov. 1952), pp. 70f.

CHAPTER FIVE

The Meaning of the Scrolls for the New Testament

The original title of this lecture was "The Dead Sea Scrolls and Christianity." Such a caption implies a possible connection between that dynamic world-conquering movement known as Christianity and an isolated community of Jewish sectaries living in retirement near the Dead Sea. It suggests that those who heard their Lord's commission to go forth into all the world and make disciples of all nations had at least an important background in the sectarian Judaism as represented by the Dead Sea Scrolls. In this chapter I wish to stress the uniqueness of Christianity, while giving full recognition to the religious soil from which the religion of Jesus and the Apostles sprang. This soil was Pharisaic as well as sectarian (or Essene), but it is to the latter to which we shall give our attention here.[1]

The scrolls make us aware of a Messianic expectation centered in the desert — not just any desert, but specifically the Wilderness of Judea. In Matthew 24:24, we have the caution against seduction by false messiahs in the warning: "If they say to you, 'Lo, he is in the Wilderness,' do not go out." The Qumrân manuscripts show us that this was a rather common idea, and a very important one for New Testament background. One will recall the ministry of John the Baptist in the Wilderness, concerning which all four Gospels quote Isaiah 40:3:

> A voice of one crying in the Wilderness,
> Clear the way of the Lord,
> Level in the Desert a highway for our God.

---

1. One must not forget significant work done in exploring Rabbinic parallels to the New Testament, such as W. D. Davies, *Paul and Rabbinic Judaism*, London, S. P. C. K., 2nd ed., 1955; Morton Smith, *Tannaitic Parallels to the Gospels*, JBL Monograph Series, VI, 1951; and especially, Paul Billerbeck and H. L. Strack, *Kommentar zum Neuen Testament aus Talmud und Midrasch*, Munich, Beck, 1922–56 (5 vols.).

The same verse was utilized by the Essenes, in explaining their withdrawal into the Wilderness, in a passage already discussed above.[2] The barren wild to which one must retire in order to clear the way for the inbreaking of the Messianic Age was interpreted by the scroll folk as that part of Judea near the northwestern shore of the Dead Sea. We know this because they built here their large community center, with its buildings for study, worship, communal meals, and manuscript copying.[3] Their Manual of Discipline (or Society Manual), which was discovered in a nearby cave, describes their practices in such close agreement with ancient descriptions of the Essenes that most scholars today recognize that the people who wrote this literature belonged to the Essene movement, and that their community center at Khirbet Qumrân may have been the headquarters of Essenism.[4] Why were these people and their scrolls in this religion? The only key to their presence here is the quotation of Isaiah which their Manual of Discipline shares with all four Gospels of the New Testament in their explanation of the Wilderness ministry of John.

The centering of Messianic hope upon the Judean Wilderness was not original with the Essenes, for careful study of the Old Testament reveals the myth of Paradise Lost and Paradise Regained associated with this very region. Abram and Lot, in scanning the land of Canaan from a high vantage point, noticed that "the Jordan valley was well

2. Pp. 83ff. Cf. p. 136.
3. R. de Vaux, *L'Archéologie et les Manuscrits de la Mer Morte*, London, British Academy, Oxford University Press, 1961. J. van der Ploeg, *The Excavation at Qumrân, a Survey of the Judean Brotherhood and its Ideas* (translated by Kevin Smyth), London and New York, Longmans, Green, 1958. A. D. Tushingham, "The Men Who Hid the Dead Sea Scrolls" (illustrated with 8 photographs and maps, and with 5 paintings in color by Peter V. Bianchi), *The National Geographic Magazine*, CXIV, 1958, pp. 784–808. One may consult also R. de Vaux, "Fouilles au Khirbet Qumrân," *RB*, LX, 1953, pp. 83–106; LXI, 1954, pp. 206–36, LXIII, 1956, pp. 533–77; "Excavations at 'Ain Feshkha," *ADAJ*, IV–V, 1960, pp. 7–11.
4. A. Dupont-Sommer, *The Dead Sea Scrolls a Preliminary Survey* (translated from the French by E. Margaret Rowley), Oxford, Basil Blackwell, 1952; *The Jewish Sect of Qumran and the Essenes;* Charles T. Fritsch, *The Qumrân Community, Its History and Scrolls*, New York, Macmillan, 1956; J. T. Milik, *Ten Years of Discovery in the Wilderness of Judaea* (translated by John Strugnell), Studies in Biblical Theology, No. 26, Naperville, Ill., Alec R. Allenson, 1959; Edmund F. Sutcliffe, *op. cit.;* Matthew Black, *op. cit.*, pp. 173–91. My own studies ("A Comparison of the Covenanters of the Dead Sea Scrolls with Pre-Christian Jewish Sects," *BA*, XIII, 1950, pp. 50–72; *The Dead Sea Manual of Discipline, Translation and Notes, BASOR*, SS. Nos. 10–12, 1951) were written prior to the publication of the preliminary reports on the excavations, being based upon the texts alone.

watered everywhere like the garden of the Lord."[5] Into this Eden, Lot moved, finally settling at Sodom; but, because of the wickedness of the people of Sodom and of nearby Gomorrah, this earthly paradise was destroyed. Hence for all future time this region of Palestine was doomed to be waste and unproductive. However, the latter prophets visualized Paradise restored taking place in this very region. Ezekiel 47 tells of a spring arising beneath the altar of the temple at Jerusalem which will flow down to the Dead Sea and fructify the entire region. The trees which grow on either side of this stream, which produce monthly, and whose leaves are a source of healing, doubtless include the Tree of Life.[6] When the stream reaches the Dead Sea it will transform the lethal waters of that salty lake into a body of living water swarming with fish like the Mediterranean.[7]

Another variation of this theme of Paradise lost and regained is to be found in the books of Joshua and Hosea. Achan, who broke the religious ban against the plundering of Jericho, was taken along with his whole household to a basin in the plateau just west of Khirbet Qumrân, to a place called the "Valley of Achor," i.e. "the Valley of Trouble." There Joshua put them to death, saying: "Why did you bring *trouble* upon us?" Doubtless there is in this story of the Valley of Trouble an etiological association with the desolateness of this area; but Hosea envisages precisely here Paradise regained, when he predicts that the Lord will take Israel out into the Wilderness and, after winning her affection, "will make the Valley of Achor a door of hope."[8] Near this "door of hope," then, the Essenes retired, with the Biblical faith that the New Eden would appear just here, in the most wild, most arid, and least accessible of all the regions of Palestine.

Against this background we know how to interpret John the Baptist's ministry.[9] We know what Luke meant when he said: "The child grew and became strong in spirit, and he was *in the Wilderness* till the

---

5. Gen. 13:10.
6. Rev. 22:2 interprets correctly here.
7. Certain lagoons were to be preserved as a source of salt (Ezek. 47:10–11). Cf. W. R. Farmer, "The Geography of Ezekiel's River of Life," *BA,* XIX, 1956, pp. 17–22.
8. Josh. 7:24–26; Hos. 2:14–15. On Hosea as a Second Joshua, see my article on Hosea in *Harper's Biographical Dictionary of the Bible.*
9. Brownlee, "John the Baptist in the New Light of Ancient Scrolls," in Krister Stendahl, *The Scrolls and the New Testament,* Chap. III, pp. 33–53; J. A. T. Robinson, "The Baptism of John and the Qumrân Community," *Harvard Theological Review* (hereafter cited as *HTR*), Vol. 50, 1957, pp. 175–92; "Elijah, John, and Jesus: an Essay in Detection," *NTS,* IV, 1958, pp. 175–91. Jean Steinmann, *John the Baptist and the Desert*

day of his manifestation to Israel." [10] Being "in the Wilderness" meant participation in the expectation of the Messianic Age which would first dawn in the Judean Desert. The fact that he entered here as a lad prior to his call to be a prophet has created problems for critical historians. How did he live out there? Who took care of him? How could he receive there proper training for his prophetic ministry? One scholar has branded this detail as "intrinsically improbable" and as serving "largely to fill a blank period in earlier accounts of his life." [11] In so judging, he was giving expression to the usual critical point of view. Yet the ideas of John's later preaching have so much kinship with Essene thought as to suggest that he lived among the Essenes as a boy — not necessarily, of course, at Khirbet Qumrân, but possibly. [12] One is reminded also of the description which the ancient Jewish historian Josephus gives of non-marrying Essenes:

> Marriage they disdain, but they adopt other men's children, while yet pliable and docile, and regard them as their kin and mould them in accordance with their own principles. [13]

While I think it intrinsically probable that John had been reared by the Essenes and that Luke 1:80 embodies a true tradition with regard to his childhood, John could not be entirely confined by the Essene mould.

Through the moving of God's spirit, the soul of John the son of Zechariah became dissatisfied. The Essenes had believed that if they were good enough, God would honor them by sending them three great Messianic leaders: a prophet, a priest, and a king. [14] In order to

Tradition (translated by Michael Boyes), New York and London, Harper, Longmans, 1958. J. Gnilka, "Die essenischen Tauchbader und die Johannestaufe," *RQ*, 1961, pp. 185–208.

10. Luke 1:80.

11. C. H. Kraeling, *John the Baptist*, New York, Scribner's, 1951, p. 7.

12. There may have been some other center of Essenism to which John was attached in his youth; therefore, I have never located him specifically at Qumrân. See further, A. S. Geyser, "The Youth of John the Baptist, a Deduction from the Break in the Parallel Account of the Lucan Infancy Story," *Novum Testamentum* (hereafter abbreviated as *Nov. Test.*), I, 1956, pp. 70–75; P. Benoit, "L' enfance de Jean Baptiste selon Luc," *NTS*, III, 1957, pp. 169–94.

13. J.W., II, viii, 2 (¶ 120), translation that of H. St. J. Thackeray, in the Loeb Classical Library.

14. Cf. 1Q S ix, 11 and what has been written above, pp. 98–101. See also A. S. van der Woude, *Die messianischen Vorstellungen der Gemeinde von Qumrân*, Assen, van Gorcum & Co., 1957. It seems probable that by the time of John the expectation of two

achieve this perfection, they forsook the contamination of an evil society and laid down stringent rules against disputing with the "men of the pit." In their separatism they were preparing only themselves for the coming of the Kingdom of God. John found significance in the "voice" of Isa. 40:3, which the Essenes ignored. He exclaimed, as reported in the Fourth Gospel:

> I am the Voice of one crying in the Wilderness,
> Clear the way of the Lord, as the prophet Isaiah said.[15]

Since the Essenes used this Scripture of themselves, there is no need to doubt that John used it of himself. The only difference is that John identified himself with the Voice. As he read the text, it was not enough that men in sequestered life should prepare only themselves for the coming Kingdom of God. It was necessary to become a *voice* awakening the nation to repentance. Through an ingenious tactic, he found it possible to become that voice himself — and still remain in the desert! He went to the crossroads of the Jordan, where commerce passed between Perea and Judea, and where pilgrims came and went in their journeys to and from Jerusalem. There he was still in the desert, but he met people, preached to them, and did what the Essenes were forbidden to do, he "disputed with men of the pit," i.e. with hellbound sinners. Like the Essenes he expected the damned to be baptized into an eschatological river of fire (an idea derived from Zoroastrianism), but the redeemed to be baptized with the Holy Spirit. The time was short. God's mighty Messiah would soon arrive and administer these baptisms. Men must repent and submit to a baptism for remission of sins that they might experience the spiritual and blessed baptism of the Messiah, or else expect the woes of the damned.

John, according to Josephus, invited men "to come *together* in baptism," [16] evidently beckoning them into the society of the New Israel which God was already creating for the coming Messiah. Similarly, the Essenes, after successfully passing two years' probation, were allowed to enter the baptismal water in order to attain the society of the holy. The Essene washing may have been re-enacted frequently, and there

---

Messiahs had been changed to only one, at least in some Essene circles. See Brownlee in Stendahl, *op. cit.,* p. 45; John F. Priest, "*Mebaqqer, Paqid,* and the Messiah," *JBL,* LXXXI, 1962, pp. 55–61.
15. John 1:23. Cf. above, pp. 83ff.
16. J.A., XVIII, v, 2. The expression "come together" reminds one of the verb "to unite with" (or "form a community") in 1Q S i, 8; v, 14, 20; ix, 6.

were doubtless other differences; but, fundamentally, the rite of lustration was the decisive act in joining the "Community of God."[17]

The Essenes had regarded themselves as the new elect with whom God would renew His covenant by sending them a prophet like Moses to lead them. This prophet is called in one passage "the faithful shepherd," an ancient title for Moses.[18] They also thought of themselves as the Suffering Servant of the Lord depicted in Second Isaiah, whose function it would be to atone for the land (or earth).[19] By this they did not mean all that we Christians mean by such language applied to Jesus. Nevertheless, they were to be a redemptive community which must pass through the refining furnace of suffering. The author of the Qumrân Hymns believed that out of his own travail was to be born a new community fulfilling the Messianic function of the "Wonderful Counselor" of Isa. 9:6.[20] This application seemed appropriate, since the community was itself eventually to give birth to the royal Messiah of the house of David, who, together with the expected priestly Messiah, would lead the children of light in a forty-year war whereby the children of darkness would be subdued and the children of light would rule the world.[21]

All these hopes in one way or another were centered upon the Wilderness of Judea, when down to the Jordan came a youth from Galilee, a Nazarene of expectant faith, wishing to identify Himself with the New Israel which God through John was calling into being. When He submitted to John's baptism, He saw the Holy Spirit descending upon Him in a bodily form, as a dove. He heard a voice calling from heaven, "Thou art my beloved son, in whom I am well pleased." This

17. See Brownlee, in Stendahl, *op. cit.*, pp. 39f.; O. Betz, "Die Proselytentaufe der Qumrânsekte und die Taufe in Neuen Testament," *RQ*, I, 1959, pp. 213ff.

18. In *DJD*, I, document no. 34 (on pp. 136, 152–5), ii, 5–8. For an English translation, see Theodor H. Gaster, *The Dead Sea Scriptures in English Translation*, Garden City, New York, Doubleday, 1956, pp. 311f., under the title "The New Covenant." In a note on p. 321, Gaster observes: "The lawgiver was known in later Jewish literature as 'the faithful shepherd'; cf. Ex. 3:1. Cf. also John 10:14." See also Isa. 63:11 where Moses and Aaron are both called "shepherds of the flock"; and this passage in its Septuagint form is applied to Jesus the leader of the Second Exodus in Heb. 13:10 (where the realm of the dead replaces the sea in Jesus' victory). See also the expression "faithful prophet" in I Macc. 14:41.

19. Brownlee, "The Servant of the Lord in the Qumrân Scrolls," *BASOR*, No. 132 (Dec. 1953), pp. 8–15; No. 135 (Oct. 1954), pp. 33–8. In the latter, please correct the misprint of "external planting" to "eternal planting" in the quotation of 1Q S viii, 5, on p. 34.

20. Concerning this passage, see Appendix C.

21. I refer here to the Military Manual, 1Q M.

language suggests that Jesus is the royal Son of God described in Psalm 2 and the Lord's Ambassador upon whom God's good pleasure rests.[22] In Jesus, there has arrived the Messianic leader of God's elect, Who ever increasingly in Himself must assume the redemptive role of the Servant until at last He dies upon Golgotha to save mankind. Here is "the lamb of God Who bears away the sin of the world." [23]

This is the historical setting in which is to be placed the ministry of Jesus, who united in Himself all categories of Messianic hope. Here is a prophet like Moses, but One Who had a way of making everything else secondary to love of God and love of neighbor.[24] Here is one excelling in healing power the reputation of Elijah and Elisha. Here is the Faithful Shepherd, Who does not abandon the sheep when He sees the wolf coming, but lays down His life for them. Here is One Who, though of royal lineage, did flee at the suggestion of a crown, slipping away into the solitude of night.[25] Still, He died upon a cross which bore the inscription "the King of the Jews." Here is One Who, though not of Aaronic lineage, nor ever donning priestly robes, became the high priestly Redeemer of God's elect, the creator of that New Israel which burst both the bonds and the bounds of the Old Israel and became *hê ekklêsia tou theou,* the "elect from every nation, yet one o'er all the earth."

In the process of fulfillment there emerges one figure, not three as the Essenes expected; and as all Messianic categories meet in Him, they are all modified and ennobled. As for His prophetic office, no man ever so spoke of the Kingdom of God in such a strongly ethical and morally compelling manner. As for His royal office, here is not a king who "tramples peoples like the mire of the streets," [26] as one scroll passage describes the Davidic Messiah, but One Who won men's hearts by enduring the mockery of a crown of thorns, and Who by His Spirit marshals His disciples as a spiritual army against the principalities and powers of the spirit world which seek to dominate the society of men.

22. For "Thou art my son," see Ps. 2:7; for "in whom I am well pleased," see Isa. 42:1. The Hebrew word *'eved* means "servant" in widely variant senses such as slave, worshipper, and ambassador. See Curt Lindhagen, *The Servant Motif in the Old Testament,* Uppsala, Lundequistska bokhandeln, 1950. In the Servant Songs, some such translation as "legate" or "ambassador" seems preferable.
23. John 1:29. The Greek *ho airōn* means not simply "who takes away," but "who takes away by bearing it."
24. Matth. 22:37–38, and the whole tenor of His teaching elsewhere.
25. John 10:12–15; 6:15.
26. 1Q Sb v, 28.

By His death and resurrection He dethrones the Devil and becomes enthroned Himself in the hearts of those who identify themselves with His suffering and compassionate mission of saving the world from sin and death.[27] Here is a Priest Who offers Himself as a holocaust, a sympathetic High Priest "who was tempted in all points like as we are," Who learned the cost of obedience through suffering, and Who is "able to succor all those who draw nigh to God through Him." [28]

As one views this great drama of redemption presented to us within the pages of the New Testament, and sees the figure of the Christ etched in blood and glory against the darkening horizon of the Old Israel, he is not at all alarmed by the statement of Edmund Wilson that Christianity in the light of the scrolls becomes "simply an episode of human history." [29] Wilson, unfortunately, did not perceive that Christianity's uniqueness lies not in any claim that its revelation came initially in the form of never-before promulgated dogma, but rather in the evidence of God's self-disclosure in an historical process which reached its climax in Christ and is moving toward its ultimate goal only through Him.[30] Not only does Biblical scholarship accept this historical development but one of its self-imposed and ever continuing tasks has been to learn more about God's progressive revelation in its relationship to history and culture. An important new link between the Old and New Testaments has been provided; but this new link strengthens rather than weakens the claim that Christ is the true fulfillment of Judaism and the key to history. Divine revelation in the Hebrew-Christian faith is pre-eminently human experience with a divine meaning. Comprehended within this experience are episodes of eternal significance — world-shaking and world-shaping incidents, the greatest of which is God's word to men in Christ.

For the understanding of this word, the scrolls provide brilliant illumination. Let us now discuss the ways in which this elucidation manifests itself.

27. All the Gospels represent Jesus as engaged in battle with Satanic power; but this is focused upon the cross by John 12:31; 14:30; 16:11. Cf. Col. 2:10–15; Heb. 2:14. For the atonement as a defeat of diabolical forces, see G. E. H. Aulen, *Christus Victor*, New York, Macmillan, 1956. This transformation of the holy war motif of the Old Testament was prepared for by notions of Satanic conflict in the circles of apocalyptic Judaism.
28. Heb. 4:15–16; 5:9. Cf. Brownlee in *NTS*, III, 1956, p. 30.
29. Edmund Wilson, *The Scrolls from the Dead Sea*, New York, Oxford University Press, 1955, p. 108.
30. Cf. the reply of Frank M. Cross, Jr., in *CC*, August 3, 1955, pp. 889f.

Think of the fresh light upon the linguistic background of the New Testament. For the first time we are able to supplement the material of Daniel for pre-Christian Jewish Aramaic. The Aramaic scroll materials include a paraphrase of Genesis in which legendary and interpretative lore are combined; also, a document describing the New Jerusalem in a very terrestrial manner, portions of the Testament of Levi, and fragments of an Aramaic Tobit (of which there are also fragments in Hebrew). Most sensationally, in the eleventh scroll cave found in January 1956, there has been identified a copy of the Targum of Job, i.e. an Aramaic translation of Job. It had already been shown that the Essene commentary upon Habakkuk had been dependent upon the Jewish Targum to the prophets.[31] This is tremendously important, for it proves that in the future we should pay as much attention to Targum as to Septuagint in the study of the background of the New Testament. This is a largely neglected field of New Testament scholarship.

We must reckon not only with an Aramaic background, but also with a Hebrew background, for the scrolls show that in the area of religious literature Hebrew was not a dead language. The tradition that Matthew wrote his *logia*, divine oracles, in Hebrew should not be explained away by saying that Hebrew is an error for Aramaic. We do not know precisely the contents of the Hebrew Matthew, but they were doubtless embodied in some manner in the Greek Gospel which we know. In the case of Matthew 13:17, there is a curious difference of text from its parallel in Luke 10:24, which is easily explained as a misreading of the Hebrew, "prophets and kings" for "prophets and righteous men." Back of these differences lies a simple confusion, almost identical with a misreading by me in the first translation of the Habakkuk Commentary.[32]

31. "The Habakkuk Midrash and the Targum of Jonathan," *JJS*, VII, 1956–57, pp. 169–86. Cf. A. Diez Macho, "The Recently Discovered Palestinian Targum: Its Antiquity and the Relationship with the Other Targums," *SVT*, VII, pp. 222–45. For the use of the Targums to interpret the New Testament, see A. T. Olmstead, "Could an Aramaic Gospel Be Written?" *JNES*, I, 1942, pp. 64f.; Paul Winter, "Lc 2:49 and Targum Yerushalmi," *ZNTW*, 1954, pp. 145–79; M. E. Boismard, "Les citations targumiques du quatrième évangile," *RB*, LXVI, 1959, pp. 374–8; R. le Deaut, "Traditions targumiques dans le corpus Paulinien? (Hebr. 11, 4 et 12, 24; Gal. 4, 29–30; II Cor. 3, 16)," *Biblica*, XLII, 1961, pp. 28–48.
32. "The Jerusalem Habakkuk Scroll," *BASOR*, No. 112 (Dec. 1948), pp. 8–18, reading "righteous kings" (*MLKYM YŠRYM*) instead of "kings and princes" (*MLKYM WŚRYM*) at iv, 3 on p. 11. This was corrected in *BASOR*, No. 116 (Dec. 1949), p. 16. On Matth. 13:17 in relation to Luke 10:24, cf. T. W. Manson, *The Teaching of Jesus*, Cambridge, The University Press, 1935, p. 32, n. 3. For Luke's possible use of a Hebrew source,

There is a theory that Matthew's *logia* were a list of Old Testament prooftexts embodied in the Gospel according to Matthew. This theory has been used to explain the frequent quotation of particular passages in all the divergent sources of the New Testament — the assumption being that they had access to a common document of *testimonia*.[33] Whether or not this is so, a precedent for such a work is found in the fourth scroll cave in a list of Messianic prooftexts representing their scheme of prophecy.

One of the most important aspects of the scrolls for New Testament background is the discovery of Jewish interpretations of verses quoted in the New Testament. When Jesus said, "Blessed are the meek for they shall inherit the earth," his words embodied a quotation of Psalm 37:11: "The meek shall inherit the land." A fragment of a commentary upon the Psalm from Cave Four declares: "Its meaning concerns the congregation of the poor who accept the season of affliction."[34] It happens that the Hebrew word for "meek" in the Psalm can also mean "poor," "afflicted," "humble," or even "pious." From the scroll literature we also learn the Hebrew original of the phrase "poor in spirit." The Military Manual from the first cave contains the phrases "afflicted of spirit" and "crushed of spirit" which are derived from Isa. 66:2.[35] These "afflicted of spirit" are the same as the "meek" and also the same as the "poor" mentioned in the Lukan form of the Beatitudes. The scrolls show us that we are not to think of different categories of the blessed, but of different descriptions of the same people.

The study of the scrolls is always full of surprises. Some of these enrich our understanding of the Scriptures, others alter it.[36] The Essene belief that a man could no longer cohabit with his wife after she had lived with another seems to be set forth in the Aramaic Genesis Apocryphon.[37] The effect of this is to alter my understanding of

---

see McL. Wilson, "Some Recent Studies in the Lucan Infancy Narratives," *Studia Evangelica*, LXXIII, 1959, pp. 235–53.

33. See C. H. Dodd, *According to the Scriptures, the Sub-structure of New Testament Theology*, London, James Nisbet, 1952, Chap. II, pp. 28–60.

34. 4Q pPs. 37, fragment 1, lines 9f., published by J. M. Allegro, "A Newly Discovered Fragment of a Commentary on Psalm XXXVII from Qumrân," *Palestine Exploration Quarterly*, LXXXVI, 1954, pp. 69–75. Cf. the translation of Millar Burrows, *More Light on the Dead Sea Scrolls*, pp. 401–3, as also that of Gaster, *op. cit.*, pp. 259–61.

35. 1Q M xiv, 7 and xi, 10. Cf. Brownlee in *JBL*, LXXX, 1961, p. 279.

36. Contrast M. Burrows, *The Dead Sea Scrolls*, p. 343: "I do not find my understanding of the New Testament substantially affected. Its Jewish background is clearer and better understood, but its meaning has neither been changed nor significantly clarified."

37. See above, pp. 78ff.

Matthew's supposed permission of divorce in the case of adultery. This is generally supposed to be a laxer standard than that of the Gospel according to Mark, where no such provision is made.[38] Viewed from the standpoint of Qumrân, however, this may be a case of greater stringency in morality — divorce of an immoral wife being mandatory. In this regard, the example of Joseph is not irrelevant. Although he was only betrothed to Mary, the discovery of her pregnancy and apparent unfaithfulness to him led him to resolve as a righteous man to divorce her. He was at the same time a considerate man, and so he planned to do this quietly so as not to subject Mary to public ridicule.[39]

An interesting enrichment of meaning for the Gospels also stems from the Genesis Apocryphon. Jesus' healing by the laying on of hands is paralleled in Abram's healing of the Pharaoh; but most significantly both the scroll and the Gospels speak of the rebuke of the evil spirit in cases of exorcism, but with an important difference. The Pharaoh requested Abram: "Now pray for me and all my house that this evil spirit may be rebuked from us." Abram did as requested, and in his own description of his work, he says: "I prayed . . . and I laid my hand upon his head and the plague departed from him and the evil spirit was rebuked from him and he lived." [40] Now it happens that this word for "rebuke" is employed alike in Hebrew, Aramaic, and Syriac for the rebuking of Satan in Zechariah 3:2: "And the Lord said to Satan, 'The Lord rebuke you, O Satan! The Lord who has chosen Jerusalem rebuke you.'" Except in Hebrew, this appears to be the exclusive example of the use of this verb.[41] We may therefore conclude that when an evil spirit is rebuked from the Pharaoh that this is the technical language

38. It is generally supposed that this is merely permissive, not mandatory, a matter of relaxation on the part of Matthew (5:31f.; 19:9), as against Mark (10:11f.). However, Matthew's Gospel is not one of relaxed morality, but of great moral stringency, as is manifest by the entire Sermon on the Mount (Chaps. 5–7).

39. Matth. 1:18f. Also in Rabbinic Judaism, a woman suspected of adultery is forbidden both to her husband and to her paramour. See Sotah v, 1. Joseph's continence during Mary's pregnancy (Matth. 1:25) agrees not only with Essene piety, but with the rules held by other Jews as well. See Josephus, Against Apion, II, 24 (¶ 203).

40. 1Q Gen^apoc xx, 28f. S. S. Nardi, in Avigad and Yadin, op. cit., translated the word 'TG'RT as "depart" or "be gone"; but this was only a guess based on the context.

41. The Greek verb epitimaô, which is employed in Zech. 3:2 and its parallel Jude 9, is the same verb which is regularly employed when Jesus rebukes demons; and although certain other uses of the verb are attested, some of them are not unrelated, as, for example, Jesus' rebuke of the wind and the sea (Matth. 8:26; Mark 4:39; Luke 8:24), of a fever (Luke 4:39), and of Simon (Mark 8:33). For additional parallels with Jesus' healing ministry, see A. Dupont-Sommer, "Exorcismes et guérisons dans les écrits de Qoumrân," SVT, VII, 1960, pp. 246–61.

of exorcism. Most importantly, the passage does not say that Abram rebuked the pestilential spirit which afflicted the Pharaoh and his household, but that the spirit was rebuked when Abram prayed. In other words, it was the Lord Himself (or His mediating angel) who rebuked (or expelled) the evil spirit.[42] It is precisely at this point where Jesus' exorcisms differ. Jesus Himself as the divine Lord rebukes the demons and they cringe before His personal authority. The rebuking of evil spirits was a divine prerogative which even faithful Abram, the friend of God, did not take upon himself.

Especially in the area of Messianic interpretation of the Old Testament is the background of Jewish interpretation important. It has long been customary on the part of many critics to compare a scholarly interpretation of an Old Testament passage with the New Testament explanation of the same text in order to admire the ingeniousness of the New Testament interpretation, or perhaps to prove its fallaciousness. We are now learning that this was largely anachronistic. Very frequently the passages involved, as proved by the Qumrân literature, had already received either a Messianic or a semi-Messianic interpretation. The New Testament writers in their quotations of the Old Testament were simply saying that the Messianic hopes that had become associated with these verses have now been fulfilled by Christ. Sometimes in the fulfillment the meaning of the prophecy was further enriched, for in the understanding of the devout the meaning of a passage was not static.

Take as an example of a developing interpretation, Habakkuk 2:4, "the just shall live by faith." To the original prophet this meant that the righteous man who persists in his faithfulness to God will survive the Chaldean invasion of Judah. The interpretation found in the Aramaic Targum seems to identify the faith of Hab. 2:4 with faith in the prophet's message.[43] In the ancient commentary upon Habakkuk from Qumrân, this thought is further extended to faith in the Teacher of Righteousness, an early leader of the sect, who was believed to have the charismatic gift of discerning the secret depths of the prophetic message. In Paul this faith is transferred to the Messiah Himself, Who interprets prophecy by fulfilling it and by becoming the world's Redeemer.

The religious thought and terminology of a great deal of the New

---

42. In the narrative of Zechariah and often elsewhere in the Old Testament, the Lord and His angel are not clearly distinguished. Cf. Gen. 16:7–13; Jud. 13:21f.
43. See *JJS*, VII, 1956–57, p. 173.

Testament is so greatly illuminated by the scrolls that the Jewish origin of most of the thought in the New Testament is strongly undergirded. In the case of the Gospel according to John,[44] the writings of the Apostle Paul,[45] and the Epistle to the Hebrews,[46] the results appear to many somewhat revolutionary. Scholars of the New Testament have long been seeking the religious background of its terminology and concepts, for every literary work requires examination in the light of current literature if it is to be fully understood. The closest analogies to much of the language of these New Testament writings have been found in the mystery cults of the Greco-Roman world. Consequently, the Gospel according to John, for example, has been regarded as more Hellenistic than Jewish — in fact the most Greek of the entire New Testament. Ironically, this same Gospel is the one about which there have arisen most frequently theories of original composition in Aramaic,

---

44. K. G. Kuhn, "Die in Palästina gefunden hebraischen Texte und das Neue Testament," *Zeitschrift für Theologie und Kirche*, XLVII, 1950, pp. 192–211; W. Grossouw, "The Dead Sea Scrolls and the New Testament," *Studia Catholica*, 1951, pp. 289–99; F. M. Braun, "L'arrière-fond judaïque du quatrième Évangile et la Communauté de l'Alliance," *RB*, LXII, 1955, pp. 5–44; *Jean le théologien et son Évangile dans l'église ancienne*, Paris, J. Gabalda et Cie, 1959; Lucetta Mowry, "The Dead Sea Scrolls and the Gospel of John," *BA*, 1954, pp. 78–97; Oscar Cullmann, "The Significance of the Qumrân Texts for Research into the Beginnings of Christianity," in Stendahl, *op. cit.*, pp. 18–32; R. E. Brown, "The Qumrân Scrolls and the Johannine Gospel and Epistles," in Stendahl, *op. cit.*, pp. 183–207; F. M. Cross, in *IB*, XII, pp. 660–62; *The Ancient Library of Qumran*, rev. ed., pp. 206–16; I. de la Potterie, "L'arrière-fond du thème johannique de vérité," in *Studia Evangelica*, Band 73, 1959, pp. 277–94; J. A. T. Robinson, "The New Look on the Fourth Gospel," *Studia Evangelica*, Band 73, pp. 338–50. For a defense of critical orthodoxy, see Howard M. Teeple, "Qumrân and the Origin of the Fourth Gospel," *Nov. Test.*, IV, 1960, pp. 6–25.

45. W. Grossouw, "The Dead Sea Scrolls and the New Testament," *Studia Catholica*, 1952, pp. 1–8; Sherman E. Johnson, "Paul and the Manual of Discipline," *HTR*, XLVIII, 1955, pp. 157–65; E. Earle Ellis, "A Note on Pauline Hermeneutics," *NTS*, II, 1955–56, pp. 127ff.; R. E. Murphy, "The Dead Sea Scrolls and New Testament Comparisons," *Catholic Biblical Quarterly* (hereafter cited as *CBQ*), XVII, 1956, pp. 263–72; K. G. Kuhn, "New Light on Temptation, Sin, and Flesh in the New Testament," in Stendahl, *op. cit.*, pp. 94–113; W. D. Davies, "Paul and the Dead Sea Scrolls: Flesh and Spirit," in Stendahl, *op. cit.*, pp. 157–82; Millar Burrows, *The Dead Sea Scrolls*, pp. 333–7; *More Light on the Dead Sea Scrolls*, pp. 119–22; W. Grundmann, "Der Lehrer der Gerechtigkeit von Qumrân und die Frage nach der Glaubensgerechtigkeit in der Theologie des Apostels Paulus," *RQ*, II, 1960, pp. 237ff.

46. Brownlee, "Messianic Motifs," *NTS*, III, 1956–57, pp. 30, 204, n. 2; 206; Yigael Yadin, "The Dead Sea Scrolls and the Epistle to the Hebrews," in *Aspects of the Dead Sea Scrolls*, Scripta Hierosolymitana, Vol. 4, Jerusalem, Israel, Hebrew University, 1957, pp. 36–55; C. Spicq, "L'Épître aux Hébreux, Apollos, Jean-Baptiste, les hellénistes et Qumrân," *RQ*, I, pp. 365ff. On the heavenly temple which figures in the epistle, see J. Strugnell, *op. cit.*, pp. 318–45.

so strong is its Semitic flavor. Other scholars have noted that though much of the terminology is the same as in Greek literature, the meanings of the words and phrases are often quite different. Into this area of uncertainty and ignorance have come the Dead Sea Scrolls as a flash of light, illuminating almost everything. In the Manual of Discipline and in other Essene documents we find in Hebrew form the supposed (and perhaps truly) Hellenistic vocabulary, this time with meanings much closer to the New Testament.[47] To our amazement, this literature is not only Jewish, but Palestinian. Consequently the ultimate sources for the Fourth Gospel must be Palestinian in origin. If the Gospel as we know it was composed elsewhere, we must account for the migration of this thought and vocabulary. Perhaps it was carried by the John-the-Baptist movement, or again by a migration of the Essenes; but the language is associated with a Judean tradition concerning the life of Christ and was most probably transmitted by a disciple of the Lord, whether or not he himself composed the gospel.

A very interesting light upon the New Testament relates to the supermundane character of the Church. The society of the Essenes was regarded as so sacred that holy angels were invisibly present at their meetings. For this reason the ceremonially unclean were excluded.[48] In their Military Manual for the eschatological war, they prescribe that the unclean shall not march forth into battle, and that all excrement and filth must be buried — because the holy angels are marching with them into battle.[49] Most strikingly, Paul in writing to the church at Corinth, urges women to appear veiled in church "because of the angels." Undoubtedly the thought is the same as in the scrolls: angels who attend invisibly the church services and who unite with the saints in the worship of God must not be offended by any indecency.[50] The usual point of view in the New Testament, however, is that man's communion is directly with God Himself in His various personal distinctions of Father, Son, and Holy Spirit.[51] It is especially the prominent

47. See F. M. Braun, "Hermétisme et Johannisme," *Revue Thomiste*, 1954, pp. 548f.; 1955, pp. 22–42; 259–99.

48. 1Q Sa ii, 4–11; 4Q Midrashim i, 4 (in *JBL*, 1958, p. 351).

49. 1Q M vii, 6f.

50. I Cor. 11:10. See J. A. Fitzmyer, "A Feature of Qumrân Angelology and the Angels of I Cor. xi, 10," *NTS*, IV, 1957–58, pp. 48–58. I had independently reached the same conclusions.

51. D. Barthélemy, "La sainteté selon la communauté de Qumrân et selon l'Évangile," *Rech. Bib.* IV, pp. 203–16.

role of the Spirit which relegates the angels to an insignificant place in Christianity.

Finally, there is in the Qumrân literature the great feeling that the ultimate salvation of the people of God depends upon a direct invasion of heavenly power into this earthly scene of human struggle. In the Military Manual, the children of light defeat the children of darkness three times; and three times the children of darkness defeat the children of light. Before the third battle, victory was already assured by God's dispatch of a mighty angel, apparently Michael, into the conflict.[52] No merely human messiahs can lead the army of the children of light to final victory in order that light and truth may banish darkness and error from the world. Heaven itself must intervene. Indeed, during the seventh battle, God Himself "will shine forth" and show His "great hand" in the utter defeat of the wicked (i, 8–14; xviii, 1, 9f.).[53] This coming of God had been predicted by some Old Testament prophets; but its relation to the Messiah's coming was not made clear, so that most scholars regarded these variant hopes as rival expectations.[54] In the prophecy of Zech. 14, the Lord Himself will descend with all His holy angels and His feet will strike the Mount of Olives. The mountain will be rent asunder and a spring will flow from the temple mountain not

52. 1Q M xvii, 6ff.; cf. my remarks in *NTS*, III, p. 204, n. 1.

53. The language of theophany was not at first eschatological, as, for example, Ex. 34:5–7; Ps. 18:7–19; Micah 1:2–4; Isa. 30:27–33; 40:10; but in the post-Exilic prophets, theophany sometimes became an eschatological event: Isa. 35:4; 62:10—63:6; 64:1–3; Joel 3:11–12; Zech. 14:3–5. God and His angelic armies both play a part in the last two passages; and one expects a similar manifestation of God in 1Q M, but attention is focused rather upon the angels. Note that in the earliest section of I Enoch, there is no mention of a Messiah, but only the coming of God (1:3–9, of which verse 9 is quoted in Jude 14f.).

Sigmund Mowinckel has explained the expectation of a final epiphany of the Lord as arising from an eschatologizing of the Hebrew New Year's festival, at which the Lord was expected to manifest himself. See *The Psalms in Israel's Worship* (translated from the Norwegian by D. R. Ap-Thomas), 2 vols., New York and Nashville, Abingdon, 1962; *He That Cometh;* pp. 138–54, 157. Perhaps the coming of Michael replaces the coming of God Himself in Dan. 12:1; but both appear in 1Q M.

54. The coming of the Messiah and the coming of God belong to two different complexes of thought, the former belonging to a this-worldly goal of human history and the latter to the transcendental world to come. Mowinckel (*op. cit.,* p. 267) states, "Here we have two profoundly different conceptions of the future, one of which is older .and more truly Jewish than the other . . . These ideas were never systematically arranged; and any attempt so to present them would only result in an artificial picture." For an attempt to show that God's self-manifestation was to be through the Messianic king, see H. W. Wolff, *Herrschaft Jahwes und Messiasgestalt im Alten Testament, ZAW,* LIV, 1936, pp. 168–202. Note Mowinckel's rejection of Wolff (*He That Cometh,* p. 172, n. 1).

only eastward to the Dead Sea (as in Ezekiel 47), but also westward to the Mediterranean Sea, so that the whole of Palestine will spring anew with the verdure of Eden. This hope of God's own coming is fulfilled by the coming of the Messiah, Who is also God's suffering and victorious servant, of whom Paul speaks in lyric strains: [55]

> Existing in the form of God,
>   he did not count equality with God a thing to be grasped,
> but emptied himself, taking the form of a servant,
>   being found in the likeness of men.
> And being found in human form,
>   he humbled himself and became obedient unto death,
>   even death upon a cross.
> Therefore God has highly exalted him
>   and bestowed upon him the name which is above every name,
> that at the name of Jesus every knee should bow,
>   in heaven and on earth and under the earth,
> and every tongue confess that Jesus Christ is Lord,
>   to the glory of God the Father.

When this Jesus knelt in agony at Gethsemane, no mountain was rent asunder, but His own heart was well nigh broken, as He prayed to Him Who was able to save Him from death. In Him we see the agonizing love of God for sinners.

For this doctrine of Incarnation, there are no clear antecedents in the Qumrân literature; but those who have come to recognize their own foolish pride and sinfulness in the light of Christian fact and faith know that here is a divine power which can create our lives anew, so that we lose ourselves in humble, loving service. Here is disclosed the power of the new creation, that can make lilies bloom in the desolation of devastated souls. This is the earnest of the new heavens and the new earth, the guarantee of Paradise regained.[56]

55. Phil. 2:6–11, RSV, but my arrangement.
56. As a postscript, mention may be made of important studies of the Qumrân literature in relation to the New Testament which appeared too late for use in this chapter: Herbert Braun, "Qumran und das Neue Testament, ein Bericht über 10 Jahre Forschung (1950–1959)," *Theologische Rundschau,* 28. Jahrgang, 1962, pp. 97–234; Lucetta Mowry, *The Dead Sea Scrolls and the Early Church,* University of Chicago Press, 1962.

CHAPTER SIX

The Teacher of Righteousness

and

the Uniqueness of Christ

JUSTIFICATION IN HABAKKUK 2:4

"The just shall live by his faith" declared Habakkuk in the late seventh
century B.C. Probably no single verse in the Old Testament has played
a more important role in religion than this one. The Apostle Paul
found in this verse a manifesto of salvation by faith in Christ. It was
centuries later rediscovered by Luther and became the most important
text in the Reformation. In the scrolls found a few years ago near the
Dead Sea, there appears an important new chapter in the history of
this text, one that neatly fits into the picture before the Apostle Paul
played his colorful role in the early Church. In an ancient Jewish commentary (or midrash) on the Book of Habakkuk, one finds the verse
explained:

> Its meaning concerns all the doers of the Law in the house of Judah
> whom God will deliver from the house of judgment for the sake of
> their labor and their faith in the Teacher of Righteousness.

Careful analysis makes clear the details of the interpretation. The "just"
are identified with "the doers of the Law in the house of Judah." To
"live" means to escape "the house of judgment," the society of doomed
men. The Hebrew word *'emûnâh* means both *faith and faithfulness,* as
normally in Hebrew, for the law-doers are to be saved both by their
labor and by their faith in the Teacher of Righteousness.[1] One readily
sees that Paul has substituted Jesus for the Teacher of Righteousness,

1. 1Q pHab viii, 1ff.

and has narrowed the concept of *ᵉmûnâh* so as to include faith alone as the ground for justification; and yet even for him faith must inevitably show itself in fidelity to Christ.[2]

There are also fundamental differences as to the nature of the faith involved. Faith in the Teacher of Righteousness was merely belief in an authoritative spokesman for God; but faith in Jesus the Christ is trust in a Redeemer; and in view of this basic difference, belief in the Teacher was simply a meritorious work, rewarded by salvation; whereas faith in the Christ is an acceptance of redemption as a free gift. The salvation involved in each case may likewise be different, that of the Qumrân sect perhaps referring to the survival of the sect in this world; whereas that spoken of by Paul is a spiritual redemption for all eternity.[3] Despite these differences, we have an important background in the enrichment of a text preparatory for its use at a higher level of meaning in the New Testament.

CONTROVERSY OVER THE SIGNIFICANCE OF THE SCROLLS

The first encounter with this interpretation in the ancient commentary leads one to ponder the question as to who this great teacher might be, and to raise the question, could it be Jesus Himself? All the evidence opposes this view; the historical allusions in no way fit the ministry of Jesus. They are all related to an earlier age. After presenting a paper on the implied history of the sect in a national meeting of Biblical scholars in 1948,[4] I was approached by an elderly gentleman who, with sweet and gentle voice, said, "Do you suppose the Teacher can be Jesus?" My reply was, "We would be pleased, of course, to find

2. Rom. 6:1ff.; Gal. 5:6.
3. See *JJS*, VII, 1956, p. 173; *NTS, III*, 1956–57, p. 209; J. A. Sanders, "Habakkuk in Qumran, Paul, and the Old Testament," *Journal of Religion*, XXXIX, 1959, pp. 232–44.
4. In exploring possible identifications of the Wicked Priest, I examined the pre-Hasmonean priests Jason and Alcimus and certain of the Hasmonean priests. I did not publish then, believing that any publication at that time would be premature. However, when I eventually published an article, "The Historical Allusions of the Dead Sea Habakkuk Midrash," *BASOR*, No. 126 (April 1952, pp. 10–20), it was attacked by Karl Elliger (*op. cit.*, p. 288) as a mere synthesis of the theories of others. However, the theories of others dealt with phases of the problem, which, through the intervening years, I continued to study until I found what seemed to me the best solution to the varied data. Actually, Elliger's theory was only a modification of the theory of A. Dupont-Sommer. All theories, as long as they are controlled by archaeological and palaeographical data, represent valuable experiments at achieving meaning and coherence for the historical allusions. Some theories may be entirely wrong; but others may contain elements of truth.

a reference to our Lord in this ancient scroll, but I do not think he can be Jesus. There are no references to his crucifixion, to his resurrection, or to any atoning efficacy in his death. Moreover, the historical allusions do not fit the first century A.D." [5]

Professor J. L. Teicher of Britain later published a series of articles setting forth the theory that the Teacher of Righteousness was Jesus. He argues that our scrolls are really documents of the early Church, stemming from a sect of Jewish Christians, the Ebionites, who regarded the Apostle Paul as a heretic. [6] To maintain his view he has had to allegorize the allegorical interpretations of the commentary. [7] It is well enough to recognize that the commentary interprets the Scripture allegorically, but the commentary really explains nothing, if it in turn must be interpreted allegorically. His view, only tenuous at the best, has been overthrown by the excavation of the sectarian community center near the scroll caves, where the archaeological evidence indicates that this community established itself here about 100 B.C., if not earlier.

On May 26, 1950, André Dupont-Sommer, a professor of the Sorbonne, gave a lecture in Paris concerning the Habakkuk Commentary which caused a sensation in Paris and in the daily newspapers of Europe. [8] The Teacher of Righteousness was not Jesus, but a priest of the first century B.C., and one whose life closely paralleled that of Jesus. According to him, the teacher probably was crucified, was raised from the dead, and appeared in judgment over the city of Jerusalem when, on the day of atonement in 63 B.C., the legions of Rome under Pompey captured the city and put many of its inhabitants to the sword. All this

5. Whoever he was, he seemed convinced by this reasoning. H. E. del Medico, *The Riddle of the Scrolls* (translated by H. Garner), London, Burke, 1958, and Cecil Roth, *The Historical Background of the Dead Sea Scrolls*, New York, Philosophical Library, 1959, have both done an ingenious, though far-fetched, job of arguing that the sectaries of the scrolls are first-century Jewish Zealots, whose religious and patriotic opposition to Roman rule led to the First Revolt against Rome in A.D. 66–70. For criticisms of their views, see R. de Vaux, "Les manuscrits de Qumrân et l'archéologie," *RB*, LXVI, 1959, pp. 87–110.
6. These were published in the *JJS*, 1951–54.
7. Most particularly, instead of looking for a chief priest to fulfill the function of the Wicked Priest, he assigns this role to the Apostle Paul, whose bloody persecution of Jesus (the True Teacher) was only his special interpretation of the Gospel, and whose plundering of the wealth of neighboring nations was the collection of voluntary offerings in the churches of the Diaspora on behalf of the poor saints at Jerusalem!
8. Dupont-Sommer's lecture was entitled "Observations sur le commentaire d'Habacuc découvert près de la Mer Morte," which was published separately by the Librairie Adrien-Maisonneuve, Paris, 1950.

led to the conclusion: "The Galilean Master, as He is presented to us in the writings of the New Testament, appears in many respects as an astonishing reincarnation of the Teacher of Righteousness."[9] Dupont-Sommer has made many important technical and non-spectacular contributions toward the understanding of the scroll literature, but his historical reconstruction of the career of the Teacher of Righteousness is doubtless in error.

To many European Roman Catholics this was not purely an academic matter; the uniqueness of Christ seemed to be at stake also, for the humanists of France went so far as to speak of a "Christianity before Christianity" and to say that Jesus was only a pale reflection of His forebear, the Teacher of Righteousness.[10] This was going quite beyond the intention of Dupont-Sommer; but priests, scholars, and secularists tangled in the fray, which was featured prominently in the daily newspapers and magazines of Europe. The supposedly literate American public knew nothing of all this. The secular press was silent, for the differences of language between Europe and America were a barrier that held back the tidal wave. Only American scholars knew what was happening and they did not allow themselves to be drawn into *this* battle of the scrolls.

Scroll studies in this country were almost entirely confined to scholarly journals and the secular press had long regarded these as dull reading, so that questions of scroll interpretation and their importance for the New Testament were matters of which the general public had no inkling. On May 14, 1955, however, a brilliant journalist, Edmund Wilson, published in the *New Yorker* a lengthy article divulging in full and for the most part accurate detail the thrilling story of the scroll discoveries and the important researches that were being carried out in all areas of the world concerning these documents. He later published a book giving a fuller account.[11] The present popular interest in the scrolls in America is largely due to him. He did for America what Dupont-Sommer did for Europe; for not only did he tell an exciting story, but he also conveyed an impression as to the

9. *The Dead Sea Scrolls, a Preliminary Survey*, p. 99.

10. For a discussion of this journalistic debate, see J. Bonsirven, "Révolution dans l'histoire des origines chrétiennes?" *Études*, CCLXVIII, Feb. 1951, pp. 213–18; A. Gelin, "Le christianisme avant le christianisme?" *L'Ami du Clergé*, LIX, Feb. 15, 1951, pp. 101–3; H. H. Rowley, "The Qumrân Sect and Christian Origins," *BJRL*, XLIV, 1961, pp. 119–56, especially, p. 120, n. 1.

11. *Op. cit.*

signal importance of the documents for the origins of Christianity and the history of culture.

Wilson's approach was humanistic, rather than theistic, and he openly boasted of the fact that he was neither Christian nor Jew, and thus supposedly free from bias. His own humanistic presuppositions, however, together with his inadequate understanding of Christian theology, led him to pose alternatives which for the Christian do not exist: Is Christianity a dogma, or the culmination of an historical process? Supposing that the Christian view were the former, he argued that the rise of Christianity is "simply an episode of human history." [12] He did not perceive that Christianity's principal claim to validity has never been in any gnostic disavowal of the importance of historical continuities. As a matter of fact, the idea of history as a meaningful process which moves toward a goal is one of the contributions of the Hebrew-Christian Bible to human culture. This idea has often been secularized, as in atheistic evolution, humanistic democracy, and atheistic communism; but all these are debtors to the Hebrew-Christian faith, however much they have perverted it. The scrolls are an important new link between the Old and New Testaments, in addition to the Apocrypha and Pseudepigrapha of the Old Testament which were previously known and studied. They bind Christianity to pre-Christian Judaism all the more firmly and strengthen the claim that Jesus the Christ is the true fulfillment of Judaism and the key to history. Faith in divine revelation is the conviction that events of human experience (some more than others) have a divine meaning. Dogma arises in the effort to expound this meaning.[13]

THE TEACHER'S PLACE IN HISTORY

The historical allusions of the midrash (or commentary) upon Habakkuk (together with a previously known document named variously as the Zadokite Work or the Damascus Covenant) make it possible to integrate the Teacher of Righteousness and his movement into the religious history of the last two centuries B.C. In order to do this in the

---

12. *Op. cit.,* p. 107. Cf. above, p. 117. If I seem to put Wilson twice in jeopardy for the same offence, it is with no malice intended, but it is to be explained as due to the relevance of the same discussion to both chapters (which originated as separate lectures, given at different places).

13. See in this regard the statements of various American scholars in "The Dead Sea Scrolls, Their Significance to Religious Thought, a Symposium," *The New Republic,* Vol. 123, No. 15 (April 1956), pp. 12–25.

most direct fashion possible, I shall now sketch an over-all interpretation, without going into the varying lines of literary and archaeological evidence.[14]

Early in the second century B.C. there was a movement known as the Hasidim (pronounced *H^asîdîm*), a term which may be variously translated as "holy ones," "pious ones," "faithful ones," "devoted ones." [15] These Hasidim sparked a revolt against their Syrian overlords which gave rise to the Maccabean wars. First they won religious independence under Judas Maccabeus, and then some measure of secular independence under Jonathan, his brother and successor; but it was not until the rule of Simon, another brother, that the independence of the Jews was officially recognized by the Syrians themselves.[16] This was in 143 B.C. It marked an important new era for the Jews who had not been an independent state since the fall of Jerusalem to the Chaldeans in 587 B.C. The Jews heralded the event as the fulfillment of promised restoration of nationhood after the Exile, as a time when God "caused a root to shoot from Israel and Aaron to possess the land." [17]

Once secular power was fully achieved, these Maccabean (or Hasmonean) rulers became so engrossed in worldly matters that the religious ideals of their forefathers seemed to be relegated to second place, which made for growing dissatisfaction with the Maccabean leadership, or, as one of the ancient documents describes the matter, "it was a time of groping after the way for about twenty years, when God

14. For my detailed argumentation, see *BASOR*, No. 126 (April 1952), pp. 10–20; *JQR*, XLV, 1954–55, pp. 211–17; *NTS*, III, pp. 13–15, also in the present volume, pp. 101–4. See also Cyrille Detaye, "Le Cadre historique du Midrash d'Habacuc," *Ephemerides Theologicae Lovanienses*, XXX, 1954, pp. 323–43. Some critics of my view regard it as unreasonable that the historical allusions relating to the Wicked Priest in the Habakkuk Commentary as interpreted by me are largely in historical order, and find fault with my theory in a single exception (which concerns the "last priests of Jerusalem" in relation to the Kittim). However, the chronological ordering is the result and not the premise of my research. After seeking the best interpretation for each allusion, it then suddenly appeared to me that the events referred to (except those relating to the Kittim who are mentioned first) were in chronological order and that the events after 89 B.C. were all without exception in the Hebrew imperfect. The acceptance of this distinction of tenses in the Habakkuk Midrash in no way necessitates that the same distinction be observed in other literary works. There is no single key which will unlock the meaning of all the historical allusions.
15. Another transliteration of the word is Chasidim. In a Hellenized form, the word is Hasidean. The Hasidim are not to be confused with the later medieval Hasidim.
16. I Macc. 13:31–42.
17. CDC i, 5ff. (1:5).

raised up for them a Teacher of Righteousness to lead them in the way of his heart." [18] This Teacher was a priest who rallied behind him a small segment of the Hasidim consisting of both priests and laity. He had hoped to bring them all under his leadership, but his ascetic way of life was much too extreme for many of the Hasidim, so that a rift occurred between them. Those that followed the Teacher of Righteousness became the Essenes; the majority who preferred a more moderate course became the Pharisees. There was also at the same time a third religious party, the Sadducees. These consisted largely of priests, and they were the most conservative group in that they held rigidly to the letter of the Law and were less inclined to reinterpret and reapply the Scripture to the needs of later generations. Thus they rejected the developing oral tradition associated with the Law. At the same time, they were more materialistic in their outlook and more tolerant to the adoption of Hellenistic practices. The rift among the various factions of the Hasidim probably came to a head during the last years of the rule of John Hyrcanus, whose period is 135–105 B.C. Hyrcanus turned from the devout Hasidim to the non-Hasidic Sadducees. When he was rebuked by the Teacher of Righteousness (according to one explanation of the historical allusions of the Habakkuk Commentary), he found occasion therein to persecute the Teacher; and he even succeeded in inveigling the Pharisees into the clutches of his spiritual repression.

Hyrcanus died in peace, leaving the rulership to his son, Aristobulus I, who died only one year later of some intestinal disease. Then there came to the throne a priest-king, Alexander Jannaeus, another son of Hyrcanus, who ruled from 103–76 B.C. He was a man given to self-indulgence and his rule was marked both by wars of conquest and by internal dissension and civil war, as he backed the views of the worldly Sadducean priests and sought to crush all Hasidic elements, both the Pharisees and the Essenes. Many of the devout fled the country, taking refuge in neighboring countries.[19]

18. CDC i, 8ff. (1:6–7).
19. For fugitives during the reign of Jannaeus, see Josephus, J.A., XIII, xiv, 2 (¶ 383) and J.W., I, iv, 6 (¶ 98). The fugitives of Psalms of Solomon 17:16–22 are interpreted by Roger Goosens (in Les éléments messiniques des traditions sur Onias le Juste, chez Josèphe et dans le Talmud," *Bulletin de la Classe des Lettres et des Sciences Morales et Politiques,* 5th series, XXXVI, 1950, pp. 463ff.) as referring to fugitives during the reign of Aristobulus II (65–63 B.C.). Cf. the sayings of Shemiah and Abtalion in Pirke Aboth 1:10f. Frank Cross, *The Ancient Library of Qumran,* p. 141, n. 65a, cites I Macc. 15:21 as evidence for fugitives during the reign of Simon (143–135 B.C.). Yet there is nothing to indicate that these were not "political" refugees, or at most, Hellenists, against whom the Maccabees had persistently fought. However, the request for the right of

It was probably during this period that the Teacher of Righteousness fled to the region of Damascus, an event which may be referred to in one of the hymns: "They drive me from my land like a bird from its nest; and all my neighbors and friends are driven far from me." [20] He remained there for a time in this "his house of exile," and others who fled the country eventually joined him there. He had already organized a colony in the Judean Wilderness; a modestly fortified community center had been erected on an acropolis overlooking the Dead Sea at Khirbet Qumrân. He probably also had other followers residing elsewhere. In any case, rather than jeopardize the Qumrân Community, it seems he took refuge with the Syrians of Damascus who were themselves engaged in battle with Jannaeus. Not to be outwitted, Jannaeus led his army to the place of the Teacher's retreat, attacking him and his followers on the day of their annual observance of the Day of Atonement. Since the Teacher followed a different calendric system from that of the Sadducees, the Sadducean High Priest Jannaeus found it possible to be away from Jerusalem at the time of the Essene observance. His intention was to "swallow up the Teacher" and to make his followers "stumble." He was probably at least partly successful in his design. It may be that the Teacher was killed, but of this we may not be certain.

ANCIENT CENTERS OF ESSENISM

Having already sketched the early history of the Essenes under their leader the Teacher of Righteousness, it may perhaps not be considered

extradition for fugitives in Egypt reminds one of I Enoch 103:13: "We found no place whereunto we should flee and be safe from them."
20. 1Q H iv, 8f. According to Robert North ("The Damascus of Qumran Geography," *PEQ*, LXXXVII, 1955, pp. 1–14), Damascus is but a surrogate for Qumrân. This is unconvincing; for how could the Wilderness of Judea with all its Biblical associations be regarded as outside "the land of Judah" (CDC, vi, 5 [8:6])? The Military Manual (1Q M i, 3) speaks of a time "when the exiled band of the Children of Light return from the wilderness of the peoples to encamp in the wilderness of Jerusalem." To judge from the Biblical data, "the wilderness of the peoples" (Ezek. 20:35–38) should lie outside "the land of Israel"; and "the wilderness of Jerusalem" (cf. Zion's wilderness in Isa. 51:3, cited below on p. 194) should be the Judean Wilderness with all its paradisiac promises (Isa. 35). We cannot be certain, but 1Q M may have been written in Syria ("the wilderness of the peoples") during the period that Khirbet Qumrân remained in ruins. In that case, its author looked forward to a return to Khirbet Qumrân (in "the wilderness of Jerusalem") from which the eschatological war would be launched. The "Children of Light" did return and rebuild the site; but, no Messianic leadership having yet arisen, they could not begin the conquest of the Holy Land itself, let alone the subjection of the world.

too great a digression to continue this history until the destruction of Khirbet Qumrân by the Romans, although none of this directly concerns the Teacher himself.

By the time of the Teacher's death, the movement which he had led was firmly established both in Syria and in the Judean Wilderness. He had religious adherents in both regions who regarded him as the founder of their society. He had bequeathed to both certain basic beliefs and practices which they developed in their own way. From the land of Damascus came the Damascus Covenant and from the community center of Khirbet Qumrân came the Society Manual (or Manual of Discipline). The former was designed for marrying Essenes and the latter for non-marrying.[21]

There are important reasons for believing that the sectaries of Qumrân and of Damascus were Essenes.[22] Most importantly, their beliefs and practices depicted in their literature agree remarkably with the ancient descriptions of Philo and Josephus. Such discrepancies as may seem to exist are mostly explainable either as errors in the accounts of the ancient historians or as false inferences drawn from their accounts by modern scholars. Some of the minor differences may also be due to the fact that the Society Manual and the Damascus Covenant were both written and compiled before 50 B.C.; whereas, Philo and Josephus lived a century later. Another important reason for identifying these people with the Essenes is that their community center at Qumrân was such a major establishment and their literature was so extensive that it is difficult to believe that they were an unimportant sect completely passed over by all ancient hisorians.[23] In fact, the very location of Khirbet Qumrân, according to most scholars, agrees well with that of the Essene community which the Roman historian Pliny

21. CDC vii, 6f. (9:1) refers to those who "settle in camps according to the order of the earth and take wives and beget children." My restoration of 1Q S i, 1 (in *The Dead Sea Manual of Discipline, BASOR*, SS, 10–12) refers to "women and children," but this restoration was based upon 1Q Sa, which was presumed to be a part of the same composition, since it was a part of the same manuscript. The real basis of my early suggestion that 1Q S was the rule of discipline of marrying Essenes was 1Q S iv, 7, "to bear seed with all everlasting blessings." This is by no means figurative language, as a comparison with I Enoch 10:16–18 and 1Q Sb iii, 4 will show. However, the doctrinal section of 1Q S iii, 13—iv, 26 was of separate origin and doubtless served for catechetical purposes among both the marrying and non-marrying Essenes. We are probably not to think of any cleavage between those who married and those who did not, except that the latter were organized under a stricter system of discipline.
22. Cf. above, p. 111, n. 4.
23. Cf. F. M. Cross, Jr., in *IB*, XII, p. 658, n. 69.

the Elder located "On the west side of the Dead Sea, but out of range of the noxious exhalations of the coast"; for Khirbet Qumrân is on a natural terrace nearly a mile west of the Dead Sea. Pliny's further statement that "lying below the Essenes was formerly the town of Engedi" suggests a location in the hills west of Engedi. A. Dupont-Sommer, however, has noted that this reference to the Essenes occurs in the context of sites west of the Dead Sea, and that if we locate the Essenes at Khirbet Qumrân these places would be arranged from north to south: the abode of the Essenes, Engedi, Masada. This view has been widely, but not universally accepted.[24] The crux of the issue is what Pliny meant by "below." Could he have meant "down the coast from"? Khirbet Qumrân lay in ruins when Pliny wrote, except for a small Roman military fort which was built there. Did not Pliny know this? Probably not, but we should not exclude the possibility of there having been another Essene establishment near Engedi, of which Pliny heard.

Though there were many Essene communities, most of them were small. The Damascus Covenant mentions "camps"; and the Society Manual authorizes settlements with a minimum membership of ten men, of whom one must be a priest. Josephus, writing as if to correct a misconception, denies that Essenes all resided in one place, but avers that "many of them dwell in every city."[25] Palestinian locations outside the Wilderness of Judea may be explained as arising from the necessity of looking after the community property which was scattered here and there all over the country. When one joined the society, he brought all his wealth with him. Unless he had sold his property (and there is nothing in the literature to indicate that this needed to be done), he would be bringing with him real estate as well as portable goods. Such widespread community wealth would need to be administered, and it was natural that colonies should have been organized to administer it for the benefit of all. When the Qumrân Community refers to "cities of Judah where [the Wicked Priest] stole the wealth of the

---

24. Cf. A. Dupont-Sommer, *op. cit.,* p. 86, n. 1. J. T. Milik, *op. cit.,* pp. 44f. This view has been contested by Jean-Paul Audet, "Qumrân et la notice de Pline sur les Esséniens," *RB*, Vol. LXVIII, pp. 346–87. In his opinion, the Essenes resided at Hazazon-tamar (Gen. 14:7), which according to II Chron. 20:2 was located at Engedi. In fact the name Essene is to be derived from Hazazon. For a reply to his view, see E. M. Laperrousaz, " 'Infra Hos Engaddi' Notes a propos d'un Article récent," *RB*, LXIX, 1962, pp. 369–80.

25. CDC vii, 6 (9:1); xiv, 3 (17:1); 1Q S vi, 2f.; *J.W.*, II, viii, 4 (¶ 124).

Poor," it probably refers to scattered Essene properties which were confiscated by a hostile Chief Priest who sought in this way to suppress the sect.[26]

The Qumrân Scrolls do not indicate that all Essenes had to locate in the Wilderness. There was an annual ceremony of renewing the covenant in which the people congregated in large numbers. Probably this occurred at Qumrân, so that there would be at least an annual trek into the desert.[27] There may have been other festival occasions in which members from elsewhere flocked to the community center at Qumrân, just as other Jews went on pilgrimage to Jerusalem. Apart from this, the Wilderness abode of the *whole* sect remained only an eschatological ideal. In times of unusually intense Messianic expectation, the proportion of those living in the Wilderness would be larger: for their Messianic hopes were centered on this region. One will recall here the words of Matth. 24:26:

> So if they say to you, "Lo, he is in the Wilderness," do not go out; if they say, "Lo, he is in the inner rooms," do not believe it.   (RSV)

Both marrying and non-marrying Essenes seem to have settled in the vicinity of Qumrân itself; for though no skeletons of females have yet been discovered among the identifiable skeletons of the large central cemetery there, skeletons of women and children have been discovered among the remains in the peripheral cemeteries. The identification of fragments of the Damascus Covenant among the scrolls found in nearby caves points to the same conclusion.

During the early part of the reign of Herod the Great, the community center at Khirbet Qumrân and the agricultural buildings at 'Ain Feshkha were destroyed by an earthquake. From a reference in Josephus, this event is dated to 31 B.C. For some unknown reason, the Essenes did not rebuild till about the end of the century, after the death of Herod the Great. Although Josephus has described Herod as friendly toward the Essenes, it has been suggested that Herod was alarmed by this center of intense Messianic expectation which was not many miles distant from his winter palace which he had located near Jericho. Herod was so suspicious of possible contenders for his throne that members of his own family were not safe. According to Matthew,

26. 1Q pHab xii, 9f. CDC xii, 19 (15:1) mentions "dwellers in the cities of Israel."
27. See my "Appendix G" in *The Dead Sea Manual of Discipline*, p. 53, also "Light on the Manual of Discipline (DSD) from the Book of Jubilees," *BASOR*, No. 123 (Oct. 1951), pp. 30–32.

rumors of Messianic expectation focusing upon the birth of Jesus in Bethlehem led him to slaughter the infants of that town. Accordingly, Charles T. Fritsch has suggested that Herod took advantage of the earthquake by refusing to allow the Essenes to rebuild at Khirbet Qumrân, and that, like Joseph, Mary, and the infant Jesus, they needed to take refuge outside the country.[28] He suggests that the migration to Damascus occurred at this time. Though this is too late for the migration referred to in the Damascus Covenant, it is entirely possible that some of the folk of Qumrân found a haven among their brethren in Syria. Others may have dispersed to various Essene settlements in Judah itself, where they would be living under Herod's government, but would not be so likely to evoke his suspicions.

After the death of Herod, the sectaries returned and built again at Khirbet Qumrân. There they flourished until the Roman General Titus ordered the destruction of their community center and replaced it with a small garrison of Roman soldiers about A.D. 68. Before fleeing the place, the Essenes hid their scrolls in nearby caves. Some they carefully wrapped in linen and placed in covered jars; but most were simply abandoned upon the floors of the caves. In one cave they deposited the Copper Scroll containing a guide to hidden deposits of unbelievable wealth. These treasures may be only legendary, as J. T. Milik believes,[29] but somebody believed in them so firmly that he inscribed the record on copper. In any case, the Essenes clearly intended to return to the caves at a later date in order to recover their documents. As to whether the Essenes escaped to Damascus once more, or as to what became of them, there is not the slightest clue. One thing alone is clear; they never returned to claim their scrolls, and knowledge of their beloved founder, the Righteous Teacher, was doomed to oblivion.

28. *Op. cit.*, pp. 20–25. It is possible that the occupants of Qumrân were forced to flee this region during the Parthian occupation of Palestine in 40–37 B.C., as is argued by E. M. Laperrousaz, "Remarques sur les circonstances qui ont entouré la destruction des bâtiments de Qumrân," *VT*, VII, pp. 337–49; J. T. Milik, *op. cit.*, p. 94. Still one needs to explain why the Essenes did not rebuild during the reign of Herod, and it is doubtful that Laperrousaz and Milik have fully succeeded here. Even though Herod respected the Essenes, according to Josephus (J.A., XV, x, 5), he may nevertheless have not wished such a heavy concentration of Messianic-minded people so close to his winter palace. Cf. Josephus' explanation of the hostility of Herod Antipas to John the Baptist in J.A., XVIII, v, 2.
29. See "The Copper Document from Cave III, Qumrân," *BA*, XIX, 1956, pp. 60–64.

THE ROLE OF THE TEACHER

Of great importance for the background of our Lord's ministry is the concept of the true teacher's role as exemplified in the Teacher of Righteousness. For the sake of clarity I shall enumerate various aspects of his mission:

1. To be all that is suggested in the Hebrew title môrèh haṣ-ṣedeq, conventionally translated Teacher of Righteousness. This title is so full of meaning that it is really untranslatable. The term *môrèh* may mean teacher, guide, or shower of rain; and every one of these ideas is associated with the title. The primary meaning, of course, is "teacher," but the other meanings were used to enrich the concept. As a "guide," his function was "to lead" God's people "in the way of His heart." [30] As "rain," he appears as a fruitful source of the word of God (Isa. 55:10–11). One of the hymns declares: "And thou, O my God, hast placed in my mouth (teaching) like an autumn shower of rain." [31] The title itself was drawn from Joel 2:23 and Hosea 10:12. There are two possible translations of each of these verses. The former verse may be rendered either "He gave you the rain according to righteousness" or "He gave you the teacher of righteousness." The latter verse may be read either "For it is time to seek the Lord until he come and rain righteousness upon you" or "until he come and teach you righteousness." [32]

30. CDC i, 11 (1:7).
31. 1Q H viii, 16.
32. The former of these alternatives is taken in the RSV rendering of Hosea, which translates *ṣedeq* "salvation" in agreement with the context. P. R. Weis (in the *JQR,* XLI, 1950–51, p. 135) has noted that a medieval Karaite scholar, Daniel al Kumisi, commenting upon Joel 2:23, explained: "According to my view, it is the *Môrèh Ṣedeq* [Teacher of Righteousness], Elijah, who will be sent to Israel to teach them the laws, as it says [Hos. 10:12]: 'Till he come and teach you righteousness'; and it also says [Mal. 3:24] 'And he shall turn the heart of the fathers to the children,' and this will be before the coming of God, as it says [Mal. 3:23], 'Before the coming of the great and dreadful Day of the Lord.' "
There is interesting testimony concerning a medieval Dead Sea Scroll discovery which perhaps influenced the beliefs of the Jewish Karaites. The testimony comes from various quarters: (1) *Christian* — Otto Eissfeldt, "Der Anlass zur Entdeckung der Höhle und ihr ähnliche Vorgänge aus älterer Zeit," *ThLZ,* LXXIV, 1949, cols. 597–600; G. R. Driver, *The Hebrew Scrolls from the Neighborhood of Jericho and the Dead Sea,* London, Oxford University Press, 1951, pp. 25ff.; (2) *Karaite claims* as cited by medieval orthodox Rabbis — Saul Lieberman, in *The Proceedings of the American Academy for Jewish Research,* XX, 1951, p. 402; (3) *Spanish Jewish tradition* — Stanislav Segert, "Ein alter Bericht über den Fund hebräischer Handschriften in einer Höhle," *Archiv Orientální,* XXI, 1953, pp. 263–9.

Ṣedeq (translated righteousness) may refer in Hebrew quite as much to that which is religiously true as to that which is ethically right. Thus the Teacher is a teacher of truth, or a true teacher. In this role he is contrasted with his powerful enemy *maṭṭîf haḵ-ḵāzāv*, whose name may be translated as "false prophet" or "dripper of lies," and who is further described as him "who dripped to Israel waters of falsehood." [33] On the other hand, the *môrèh haṣ-ṣedeq* stands also in antithetical relationship to his opponent, "the Wicked Priest." This antithesis may be sharpened by translating "Righteous Teacher," which the Hebrew allows, just as "men of holiness" in Hebrew are "holy men." It was originally the priest's function to teach, and the scrolls carry on this tradition, so that "teacher" and "priest" are really synonymous. Thus the great Essene leader appears as the "Righteous Priest" in opposition to his enemy "the Wicked Priest." Malachi 2:7 declares: "The lips of a priest should guard knowledge, and men should seek teaching (or *tôrâh*) from his mouth." *Tôrâh* has conventionally been rendered as Law, beginning with the Jewish translators of the Septuagint. It has especially been employed to designate the Pentateuch (or Law of Moses) which is sometimes referred to in English as the Torah. The word comes from the same Hebrew root as the word *môrèh*, teacher. Consequently, Theodor H. Gaster translates "the teacher who expounds the Law aright." [34] This translation stresses his priestly function, but as an interpreter he was even more concerned with prophecy, as will appear from the next aspect of his mission.

2. *To interpret the Prophets.* The Habakkuk Commentary describes him as "the priest in [whose heart] God put [understand]ing to explain all the words of his servants the prophets." These explanations of the teacher were all concerned with the fulfillment of prophecy in the interpreter's own day or in the not distant future. In this role the Teacher was like Daniel, who was able to interpret not only dreams and the mysterious handwriting on the wall, but also Jeremiah's prophecy of seventy years (Dan. 9). [35]

3. *To enact a New Covenant.* The so-called Zadokite Work refers to "those that entered the New Covenant in the land of Damascus." The Habakkuk Commentary refers to the New Covenant as coming

---

33. CDC i, 14f. (1:10).
34. *Op. cit., passim.* Cf. my discussion of the meaning of the name in *NTS*, III, 1956–57, p. 13, and in the *JBL*, LXXVII, 1958, pp. 384.
35. Cf. F. F. Bruce, *Biblical Exegesis in the Qumran Texts*, pp. 7ff.

from the mouth of the Teacher of Righteousness,[36] and in one of the Hymns we hear the Teacher say:

> I do thank Thee, O Lord;
>   for my face Thou enlightenedst for Thy covenant's sake.
> Yea, from [evening until morning] do I seek Thee;
>   and as the sure dawn for [per]fect illu[mination]
>   hast Thou appeared to me.[37]

Here we have the Teacher's role as lawgiver, for one is reminded of Moses whose face was radiant when he descended from Sinai with the "words of the Covenant" in his hand. One is equally reminded of Jesus as depicted by Paul in II Cor. 4:

> For it is God who said, "Let light shine out of darkness," who shone in our hearts to give the light of the knowledge of the glory of God in the face of Jesus Christ.

4. *To build the congregation of God's people.* In the commentary upon Psalm 37 from Cave Four we read:

> Its interpretation concerns the priest, the Teacher of Righteousness whom . . . God has established to *build* for him the congregation of (His elect).[38]

This reminds us of Jesus' promise to Peter, "On this rock I will *build* my Church." The scroll reference to *building* the congregation is not surprising in view of the frequent references to the community as a holy house or sanctuary.[39]

5. *To be the Servant of the Lord.* In Second Isaiah (Isa. 40—55), we find the portrait of one who is called the Servant of the Lord and who probably is to be interpreted as both Israel and Israel's representative head, the Messiah.[40] The Essenes variously interpreted the Servant

---

36. CDC vi, 19 (8:15); xix, 33f. (9:28); xx, 12 (9:37); 1Q pHab ii, 7f.
37. 1Q H iv, 5f.
38. This is an interpretation of Ps. 37:23f. in 4Q Ps. 37, at ii, 14–16.
39. See, for example, 1Q S v, 6; viii, 5–6, 11; ix, 6. Cf. Ps. 114:2; I Cor. 3:16–17. See also Otto Betz, "Felsenmann und Felsengemeinde," *ZNW*, XLVIII, 1957, pp. 49–77.
40. Christopher R. North, *The Suffering Servant in Deutero-Isaiah*, London, Oxford University Press, 1948. The same distinction between personal and corporate applications of the Servant theme is also recognized by H. H. Rowley; but he prefers to distinguish the personal servant of the Great Servant Song (Isa. 52:15—53:12) from the Messiah, whom he regards as a king and warrior. See his book, *The Servant of the Lord and Other Essays on the Old Testament*, London, Lutterworth Press, 1952, Chap. 1. Between Rowley and North there is only a terminological difference, for in any case there were varieties of Messianic expectation. That of the Servant of the Lord, insofar as personal, represents one special line of expectation.

as the true Israel and as the representative heads of the community, among whom are a special group of twelve or fifteen men, the Teacher of Righteousness, and possibly the two Messiahs of Aaron and Israel.[41] In any case, the Servant was always either Israel or Israel's representative. In fact, every leader of God's people must embody certain Servant traits as described by Second Isaiah. The following traits applied to the Teacher are here worthy of note:

a.   To be set apart in infancy and youth as a spokesman for God. In Isa. 49 the Servant declares:

> The Lord called me from the womb,
>   from the body of my mother he named my name.

Also in Isa. 53 it is declared of him: "He grew up before him as a young sprout." The word which I translate "young sprout" has a literal meaning of "sucker" and can refer either to a suckling child or to the tender shoot of a plant. Only the latter meaning is contextually appropriate, but the ancient Septuagint version chose to render here "like a little boy." With these Servant passages we may compare the reference to the Teacher of Righteousness in one of the Hymns:

> For Thou hast known [or loved] [42] me from my father . . .
>   and from the womb Thou hast sanctified me,
>   and from the body of my mother Thou hast
>   bestowed kindness upon me,
> And from the breasts of her who conceived me have Thy
>   compassions come to me,
>   and in the bosom of my nurse . . .
> And from my youth hast Thou appeared to me in the
>   wisdom of Thy Law,
>   and by Thy fixed truth hast Thou supported me,
>   and by Thy holy spirit hast Thou delighted me.
>
> (1Q H ix, 29–32)

There is probably some echo in this language of the call of Jeremiah in his youth, who also grew up before the Lord like a little boy.[43] We are likewise reminded of Jesus, of whom Luke 2:40 declares: "The little

---

41. See my articles in the *BASOR*, No. 132 (Dec. 1953), pp. 8–15; No. 135 (Oct. 1954), pp. 33–8; *NTS*, III, pp. 18–20, 26, 195–8; and see below, Chaps. 9 and 10.

42. The verb "to know" in Hebrew frequently means to look upon with favor, rather than to be simply aware of. The words "from my father" probably mean "since the time my father begat me."

43. Jer. 1:4–8, with which cf. Isa. 49:1–2. Cf. I Sam. 2:21c in the text of 4Q Sam^a, *Wai-yigdal shəm[úel] lifnê Y[HWH]* ("And Samuel grew up *before* the LORD").

boy grew and became strong, filled with wisdom, and the favor of God was upon him."

b.   He possessed the Servant's gift of teaching.
       In Isa. 50:4 the Servant declares:

> The Lord God has given me the tongue of disciples,
>   that I may known how to encourage with a word
>   him that is weary.

With clear allusion to this passage the Teacher in one of the Hymns declares: "My tongue is like that of Thy disciples." [44] With reference to a time of enforced silence he declares:

> And there was none to lift the voice with the
>   tongue of disciples,
> to revive the spirit of the stumbling,
>   to encourage him who was weary, with a word.
> All my lip was dumb . . .   (1Q H viii, 35f.)

c.   He fulfilled the Servant's ministry of consolation.
       This is already apparent in the preceding reference; and it is probably to be seen in the following fragmentary passage:

> According to Thy truth a herald of glad tidings . . .
> Thy goodness, to herald glad tidings to the poor
> according to Thy abundant compassions.   (1Q H xviii, 14)

This is clearly an echo of Isa. 61:1:

> The Spirit of the Lord is upon me,
>   because He has anointed me
>   to herald glad tidings to the poor.

d.   Like the Servant of the Lord he was endowed with the Spirit.
       The gift of God's Spirit is characteristic of the Servant as announced by God in Isa. 42:1:

> Behold My servant, whom I uphold,
>   My chosen in whom My soul delights.
> I have put My Spirit upon him,
>   he shall bring forth justice to the nations.

Here we need to take note of the following passages:

> I, Thy servant, know the Spirit
>   which Thou hast put within me.   (1Q H xiii, 18f.)

44. 1Q H vii, 10.

As for me, Thy servant, Thou hast favored me
with the Spirit of knowledge.   (1Q H xiv, 25)

Thou hast shed Thy holy Spirit upon Thy servant.
(1Q H xvii, 26)

I thank Thee, O Lord, for Thou hast sustained me
with Thy strength,
And hast shed Thy holy Spirit within me.   (1Q H vii, 6f.)

e.   Like the Servant he suffers.

In Isa. 53:3f. there is figurative language which literally rendered would be:

He was despised and forsaken of men,
a man of pains and acquainted with disease . . .
Yet surely He has borne our diseases and carried
our pains,[45]
but we esteemed him plagued, smitten of God
and afflicted.

A fragmentary passage of the Hymns speaks of him

. . . dwelling with diseases;
and I underwent trial with plagues,
And I was as a man forsaken, despised . . .
(1Q H viii, 26f.)

The Contrast Between the Teacher and Jesus

In describing the role of the true teacher as understood by the Qumrân Community, we have incidentally called attention to the use of some of the same Old Testament passages in describing his significance as are employed for interpreting the meaning of Jesus in the New Testament. Lest these surface similarities (which are by no means biographical) lead one to exaggerate the similarities between the two men, it is important that we note the following fundamental points of distinction between them:

1. *Unlike Jesus, the Teacher of Righteousness was a confessed sinner who gratefully acknowledged his dependence upon the forgiving grace of God.* Listen to the following passage:

Man is involved in iniquity from the womb;
and to grey old age is in a state of guilty infidelity.

45. So literally; cf. Matth. 8:17.

I know that man possesses no righteousness;
the son of man, no perfection of way.

All righteousness belongs to God Most High . . .

As for me, shaking and trembling seized me,
all my bones were crushed,
My heart melted like wax before fire,
and my knees gave way like water plunging down a precipice,
When I became conscious of my own faithlessness
as well as the infidelity of my ancestors.
When the wicked arose against Thy covenant,
the irreligious, against Thy word,
Then I said, "It is because of my transgression that
I am left outside Thy covenant;"
But when I remembered the power of Thy hand
together with the abundance of Thy compassion,
I regained my footing and stood erect,
and my Spirit became strong in confronting affliction;
For I leaned upon Thy loyal love,
Thy abundant compassion;
for Thou dost pardon iniquity.   (1Q H iv, 29–37)

This contrast with the sinless Jesus Who need not confess sin is no disparagement of the Essene Teacher, for confession of sin in all ordinary people is a virtue; and unrepentance is the worst of sins. Like all true saints the Righteous Teacher acknowledged:

In pardon I delight;
and I repent of former transgression.

(1Q H ix, 13)

2. *Unlike Jesus, he must suffer in order to be purified from sin.* Thus the Teacher in one of the Hymns seems to be speaking of himself when he says:

In order to act mightily through me
before the sons of men,
Thou has wrought marvels with this poor man,
And Thou has put him into a crucible,
that as gold is refined by the action of fire
And as silver is refined in the furnace of the smelters,
so he may be purified sevenfold.   (1Q H v, 15f.)

The theme of the refining of the man of God is frequently employed in the Qumrân literature. There is one passage in the Society Manual which depicts a suffering man through whom will come a revelation of divine truth in the Messianic Age. The passage relating to him belongs to an important doctrinal section in which dualism of light versus error is depicted. These are in conflict, one with the other. But this shall not always be so, for God has decreed a season of judgment of which it is said:[46]

> At that time, God will purify by His truth all the deeds of a man and refine him more than the sons of men, in order to destroy every perverse spirit from the inner parts of his flesh, and to cleanse him through the Spirit of Holiness from all wicked practices; and He will sprinkle upon him the Spirit of Truth like the water of purification, so as to cleanse him from all untrue abominations and from being polluted by the Spirit of Impurity, so that he may give the upright insight into the knowledge of the Most High and into the wisdom of the heavenly beings, in order to make wise the perfect of way; for God has chosen them to be an eternal covenant, and all the glory of Adam will be theirs. There will be no more perversity, all works of fraud being put to shame.

When I first came to interpret this reference to the man of God's refining as an individual, I concluded that the reference was to the coming Messiah — a point of view already adopted by Jean Paul Audet and Bo Reicke.[47] It had already been suggested that the Qumrân sect believed in the coming of three eschatological figures of Messianic significance: a prophet, a priest, and king. Soon thereafter the relevant passages were published.[48] Consequently Géza Vermès modified my interpretation by relating it to the expected Prophet. This Prophet, according to him, was none other than the Righteous Teacher, the author of the Hymns.[49] Against this identification it might be argued that the coming of the Prophet (or the man of God's refining) is future in this Manual of Discipline, whereas the Teacher is presumably a figure already come. However, the passage in the Manual may be older and reflect an earlier point of view in which the Teacher had not yet become identified with the coming Prophet. On the other hand,

46. 1Q S iv, 20–23.
47. See below, at Appendix A.
48. 1Q Sa and 1Q Sb in DJD, I, texts 28a and 28b (pp. 107–30).
49. "Quelques traditions de la communauté de Qumrân," Cahiers Sioniens, IX, 1955, pp. 25–58, with attention here to pp. 54ff.

the finding of a personal reference at all in the above portion of the Manual has been subject to serious challenge.[50] That the theme was applied to the Teacher of Righteousness, however, is clear from the Hymn passage already quoted; so that we are in no way dependent upon the Manual for this idea.

The motif of purification through suffering is indeed applied to Jesus the Christ in the New Testament, but always in such a way as to indicate the borrowed character of the motif, for it is always distorted so that it does not mean — as applied to Jesus — self-purgation from sin. Thus in Jesus' High Priestly prayer as recorded in John, He prays:

> Sanctify them by the truth;
> Thy word is truth . . .
> And for their sake I sanctify myself
> that they may be also sanctified by the truth. (17:17, 19)

The language here is so close to that of the Society Manual that one cannot help but recognize their affinity; and yet examination of the theology of the Fourth Gospel makes it clear that when Jesus sanctifies Himself through dedication to His Passion, it is not any subjecting of Himself to needed purification, but is rather a devoting of Himself to the redemption of others whereby *they* may be truly purified from sin.[51] Similarly the Epistle to the Hebrews speaks of Jesus, the "pioneer" of our "salvation," as being made "perfect through suffering" (2:10). It even goes so far as to declare, "Although He was a Son, He learned obedience through what He suffered" (5:2). This cannot mean, however, that Jesus required sanctification from sin, for the epistle repeatedly emphasizes that Jesus was sinless. Rather, the passage means that only through much travail of soul could Jesus be matured sufficiently to know the cost of holy living in the midst of this vale of sin and tears, and only thereby could He become a High Priest fully capable of sympathizing with us in our temptations, trials, and heartaches.[52]

Similarly, in the First Epistle of Peter we recognize the same warping of the motif of the refined man:

> Since therefore Christ suffered in the flesh, arm yourselves with the same thought, that [53] whoever has suffered in the flesh has ceased

50. See below, Appendix A.
51. See further references and discussion in *BASOR*, No. 135, p. 37, n. 33.
52. See further in *NTS*, III, p. 30.
53. The Greek particle *hoti* is ambiguous and may mean "for" (as generally understood in this passage), or "that" (by way of introducing either a direct or indirect

from sin, so as to live for the rest of the time in the flesh no longer
by human passions but by the will of God.   (4:1–2)

It is clear from this passage that in some sense Christ has ceased from
sin through His Passion and that we also as His followers are challenged, through the willing acceptance of suffering for His sake, to
achieve a sinless life. And yet, this very Epistle of Peter maintains the
sinlessness of Jesus (2:22f.) It would seem, therefore, that Christ has
ceased from sin only in the sense that His own temptations to sin and
atonement for sin have ceased once and for all through His Passion;
but Christians who would follow in His steps by appropriating the
mind of Christ will be rid of sin not only as it confronts them exter-
nally, but as it has become an element of their own living. Thus, by
their constant warping of the motif of purification through suffering,
the New Testament writers indicate how impossible it was for them
to entertain the possibility that Jesus ever sinned. On the other hand,
purification from real sin through the travail of persecution was essential for the consecration of the Teacher of Righteousness to his
prophetic role.[54]

   *3. Unlike Jesus, the Essene Master founded a community vowing
hatred toward its enemies.* The Manual of Discipline indicates that
those who joined the sect assumed the obligation:[55]

> To love all the sons of light, each according to his lot in God's counsel,
> but to hate all the sons of darkness, each according to his guilt in
> provoking God's vengeance!

In one of their songs they sang:

> I will repay no man with evil's due;
>   (only) with good will I pursue a man;
> For with God is the judgment of every living thing;
>   and He will reward a man with his due![56]

This sounds very Christian, almost like Jesus' Sermon on the Mount;
but the reason for forgoing vengeance is that vengeance is a prerogative
of God. One must await, therefore, the just vengeance of God. That

---

quotation). Context seems to favor the latter alternative in I Peter — "the same
thought" being victory over sin through suffering.
54. 1Q H v, 15f.
55. 1Q S i, 9f. Cf. Ps. 139:19–22 for religiously motivated hatred, which appears as
the obverse side of the love of God.
56. 1Q S x, 18.

there is no love for one's enemies in the forgoing of vengeance is clear from the words which follow at once in this same passage:

> But my anger I will not turn back from wicked men;
> nor will I be content until He establishes judgment!

Nevertheless, this passage provides us with an interesting link between the Old and New Testaments, and, even more specifically, between the Law of Moses and the Sermon on the Mount. The Essenes went part way in forbidding vengeance, but they allowed the vengeful spirit to remain. Only Jesus forbids and removes the vindictive spirit itself.

4. *Both teachers founded a church — but only Jesus built a church which the powers of death could not overcome.* Concerning the Essene Teacher, it is declared in the commentary upon Psalm 37: "God established him to build for Him the congregation of (His elect)." This language (as we have already noted) is similar to Jesus' promise to Peter:

> I tell you, you are Peter, and on this rock *I will* build my church, and the powers of death shall not prevail against it.
>
> (Matthew 16:18, RSV)

The powers of death did prevail against the Essene community, for we know nothing of their history after A.D. 68. They passed from history and are extinct today; but the Christian Church founded by Jesus is still a religion that is dynamic and alive, sweeping to the ends of the earth, redeeming and transforming men by the grace of God.[57]

5. *Unlike Jesus, the Teacher called his followers out of the world, but Christ on the contrary sent His followers into the world.* The Essenes claimed the authority of Isaiah 40:3 for retiring into the desert, their aim being to prepare there the way for the Messianic Age. But Jesus prayed:

> I do not pray that Thou shouldst take them out of the world, but that Thou shouldst keep them from the evil one. They are not of the world, even as I am not of the world.   (John 17:15–16, RSV)

It is the outgoingness of the Christian faith which most sharply distinguishes it from Essenism.

6. *Unlike Jesus, the Teacher of Righteousness does not appear to*

---

57. In certain ages, the Church largely forgot its universal mission; but the nineteenth and twentieth centuries have seen a great expansion of the Christian missionary enterprise — with the whole Bible translated into hundreds of new languages and portions of it into more than a thousand tongues. There is nothing to compare with this in any other religion.

have been "a friend of publicans and sinners." [58] The very suggestion that the Teacher of Righteousness may have been "a friend of publicans and sinners" would in any case be out of character with the community which he founded; for it was governed by stringent rules forbidding nearly all contacts with outsiders. Provision was allowed for commerce so that the community could subsist through trade. Allowance was also made for the instruction in the faith of interested outsiders who, through careful indoctrination, rigid examination, and a period of two years' probation, might eventually gain admission into membership. Nevertheless, in view of the seclusive character of the community which the Teacher founded, it seems very doubtful that he would have associated in any intimate way with the spiritually negligent in order to reclaim them for God. The society regarded itself as a community of penitents; but we hear of no evangelistic program whereby people were won to repentance.

7. *Unlike Jesus, the Essene Master performed no works of healing, nor in other ways did he engage in acts of compassion among the needy.* There were no gospels written to tell us the story of his life; nor are there any allusions to any works of benevolence on his part. In fact, the details of his life are largely unimportant to the Essene community, since the real significance of their master was in the prophetic role which he played.

8. *Unlike Jesus, he was at most a prophet, not a redeemer.* He may have been regarded as the expected Prophet and Forerunner of the Messiah, who figured in Jewish expectation. It is possible (though not certain) that he was expected to return at the end of time in order to become the great high priestly associate of the Davidic Messiah, but there is nothing to indicate that a redemptive role was expected of him. Though it has been disputed, it is possible the Teacher was martyred, but, in any case, there was no theology built upon his death as an atonement for sin. We do find evidence of the belief that the good works and the suffering of all righteous people is in some sense atoning. The idea would seem to be that the piety of a few enables God to look with favor upon the Holy Land; but the great Essene Teacher seems to have had no uniquely redemptive work, only his rather vague share in the atoning work of all God's elect. [59]

9. *Unlike Jesus, the Teacher of Righteousness was simply preparing*

58. Matth. 11:19; Luke 7:34.
59. Cf. the doctrine of the atoning value of the suffering of martyrs in II Macc. 7:37; 8:3; IV Macc. 1:11; 6:28–29; 17:21; 18:4. See my article "Maccabees, Books of," in *IDB*, pp. 210, 212f., under sections C, 10; E, 3.

the way for one far greater than himself. Like John the Baptist, he believed that he stood upon the threshold of the Messianic Age, and, like John, he did not fully understand what its true nature would be. By saying this we intend to honor the Teacher rather than disparage him, for no prophet ever visualized fully or with complete clarity the Messianic Age. Nevertheless, the contrast remains, for Jesus appears to the Christian not as an imperfect Forerunner of the Messiah but as the Messiah Himself who brings in the Kingdom of God.

10. Unlike Jesus, the Teacher of Righteousness founded a community enmeshed in legalism. The strict rules of the Essenes' Manual of Discipline indicate their stern legalism. The Essenes appear to have been much stricter than the Pharisees. Though they acknowledged that the attainment of virtue was wholly dependent upon the grace of God, the pathway of its realization was in their view largely legalistic. Christianity appeared to the Pharisees as antinomian, but how much more so must it have seemed to the Essenes.

As a matter of fact, the New Testament provides us with no Manual of Discipline, but rather with a new way of life imparted by the Spirit of Christ. Some passages indeed stress the importance of order as well as ardor and concern themselves with the discipline of the Church.[60] There are also passages of moral counsel; but the teaching of Jesus and of the Apostles is pre-eminently the controlling power of love, "the law of liberty."[61]

60. Matth. 18:15–20 (with a partial parallel in 1Q S v, 25—vi, i); Acts 6:1–6; 14:23; I Cor. 5:1–13; 14:26–40; but especially I and II Tim. and Titus. The last three books, the Pastoral Epistles, seem to show the least kinship to the Qumrân Scrolls of the entire New Testament. To be sure, the term "bishop" (Greek *episkopos*) has an antecedent in the "overseer" (Hebrew *pâqîd*) of 1Q S, just as "bishopric[k]" (Greek *episkopê*) of Acts 1:20 (KJV) translates the cognate term *pəquddâh* of Ps. 109:8 (LXX Ps. 108:8). All this is superficial, however, for the office and functions of primitive bishops were probably patterned after the elders of the synagogues. In fact, in the earliest development of ecclesiastical government, bishops and elders were identical (Acts 20:17, 28 [ASV]; Titus 1:5–7). There were several in every church (Acts 14:23), or city (Phil. 1:1; Titus 1:5)—although sometimes churches sprang up without any regular officers, as is shown by the Teaching of the Twelve from the late first century A.D.

The theme of salvation by God's righteousness in Titus 3:5 may be compared with the theme of the justifying and cleansing righteousness of God which is found in both the Epistles of Paul and in the Qumrân Scrolls. Cf. *BASOR*, No. 121 (Feb., 1951), p. 12. Note also the similar designations "elect angels" (I Tim. 5:21) and "elect of heaven" (1Q M xii, 5).

61. James 1:25. For a study of the Epistle of James in relation to the Qumrân Scrolls, see Wallace I. Wolverton, "The Double-Minded Man in the Light of Essene Psychology," *Anglican Theological Review*, April, 1956, pp. 3–12.

11. Unlike Jesus, the Teacher of Righteousness has not risen from the dead. Professor John Allegro thinks he has found a reference to this expectation in an obscure, poorly preserved scroll fragment;[62] several other scholars have questioned his interpretation of the passage.[63] In any case, the Essenes passed from the historical scene without ever having been convinced of their Teacher's resurrection. In contrast, the disciples of Jesus were so convinced of Jesus' resurrection within two days of His death that nothing could halt the triumphant march of their faith.

62. Apparently this was presented by Allegro in television and radio broadcasts. See "Crucifixion before Christ," *Time*, Feb. 6, 1956, p. 88.
63. See the letter written from Jerusalem, Jordan, and signed by Roland de Vaux, J. T. Milik, P. W. Skehan, Jean Starcky, and John Strugnell in *The* [London] *Times*, March 16, 1956, p. 11, col. 5.

PART II

THE SIGNIFICANCE OF THE COMPLETE
ISAIAH SCROLL

CHAPTER SEVEN

The Significance of Scribal Errors

GREAT EXPECTATIONS AND DISAPPOINTMENT

When the news of the discovery of the Dead Sea Scrolls was first disclosed by the American Schools of Oriental Research on April 10, 1948, it was pre-eminently the existence of a complete copy of Isaiah from the late second century B.C. which excited the scholarly world. Scholars, to be sure, were interested also in the other documents, but here was an astonishing discovery of which one had scarcely dared to dream: that the history of the Hebrew text of the Old Testament should in a single leap be carried back a thousand years. Previously we had no manuscripts of an Old Testament prophet in Hebrew earlier than the ninth century A.D. There was, indeed, the more ancient testimony of the most ancient Greek version, the Septuagint, taking us back to the third and fourth centuries A.D.; but there we are concerned with a version, not with manuscripts in the original tongue. Consequently, there was great impatience for information concerning the readings of the Complete Isaiah Scroll.

En route from the Holy Land to America, Professor Millar Burrows, with photographs of the Isaiah Scroll in his suitcase, attempted a complete collation of this scroll. Aside from his interest in textual criticism, there was the very practical need of a careful examination of this scroll before the Revised Standard Version of the Old Testament was issued. Professor Burrows was a member of the Standard Bible Committee which prepared this translation. What he discovered in his study was utilized by him in a preliminary survey of the textual variants of the Isaiah Scroll.[1] He presented his collation more fully to the Standard Bible Committee. This preliminary disclosure of the Isaiah text, while

---

1. "Variant Readings in the Isaiah Manuscript," *BASOR*, Oct. 1948, pp. 16–24, Feb. 1949, pp. 24–32; "Orthography, Morphology, and Syntax of the St. Mark's Isaiah Manuscript," *JBL*, 1949, pp. 195–211.

presenting some interesting and valuable variants, indicated that our scroll was very close to the Massoretic tradition. This was a disappointment to many scholars who had hoped that the text would be found superior to the Massoretic (or traditional) text so that it might be corrected constantly in the light of the scroll. On the other hand, there was also a sense of elation that here we had a manuscript from before the time of Christ which was substantially the Book of Isaiah that we had always known.

Scribal Errors in the Isaiah Scroll

In the early study of the scroll, the immediate impression on the part of everyone who examined it was that our scroll was often very inferior to the traditional text. The scroll contained many scribal errors. In fact one of the important values of the scroll is to illustrate how scribal errors occurred in ancient manuscripts. There are numerous examples of the interchange of letters which are similar in appearance or in sound: the former are errors of the eye; the latter, errors of the ear. These errors in a manuscript might be cumulative from a series of copyists. On the other hand, both kinds of error might occur all in the same process. Thus a scribe in copying a manuscript directly by himself might misread certain words because of their similar appearance. If he read as much as a whole sentence to himself before transcribing it, it would be possible for him to make a few mistakes of "hearing," due to his habit of thinking orally rather than visually. Similarly, if a manuscript were being read aloud by a reader in a scriptorium, with scribes gathered about a table, each of them copying by the ear, errors of seeing and of hearing could both be made. The reader might sometimes misread; and the scribes might not always understand the words, especially if the reader did not enunciate clearly. This last danger was very real in the Qumrân scriptorium where certain of the gutturals were often confused, evidently because in their spoken dialect there was little distinction as to pronunciation.

There were also mechanical errors of inverting the order of letters (metathesis); of copying letters or words twice (errors of dittography); of transcribing letters or words only once which should occur twice (haplography); of omitting one of two phrases which began similarly (homoioarchton) or ended similarly (homoioteleuton), the eye accidentally skipping from the first occurrence of the initial or final word

to its second occurrence.[2] An example of omission through homoioarchton in the scroll is found in 2:3:

> Come, let us ascend to [the mountain of the LORD
> to] the house of the God of Jacob,
> That *they* may teach us of His ways,[3]
> and that we may walk in His paths.

The bracketed material was omitted, for after writing (or reading)
"to," the eye of the scribe accidentally completed the phrase by copying
the words of the second phrase rather than the first. An example of
omission due to homoioteleuton is to be found in 4:5–6:

> And the LORD will create over the whole site of Mount Zion and over
> her assembly a cloud by day [and smoke and the radiance of a flam-
> ing fire by night; for over all the LORD's glory there will be a canopy
> and a pavilion. It will serve as a shade by day] from the heat, and as
> a refuge and a shelter from rain and showers.

The bracketed material is omitted in the scroll through the accidental
jumping from the first "by day" to the second "by day."

Sometimes a scribe might also carelessly repeat a letter (or word)
expecting to find it in a phrase, because of its repeated occurrence in
the context. An example of this mistake occurs in the copying of one
of Isaiah's powerful puns (5:7b):

> He looked for right,
> but behold, *for* riot;

2. On various types of scribal errors, see J. Kennedy, *An Aid to the Textual Amend-
ment of the Old Testament* (edited by N. Levison), Edinburgh, T. and T. Clark, 1928.
3. The plural reading of the scroll in the place of the singular ("That *He* may teach
us") might be interpreted as an example of the third plural indefinite, so that the
meaning would be: "That we may be taught His ways." However, the interpretation
probably given by the Qumrân Community was "so that they [the priests] may teach
us of His ways." Thus 4Q pIsa[a] interprets Isa. 11:3f.: "And when it says, 'He will not
judge according to the seeing of his eyes, nor decide according to the hearing of his ears,'
its meaning is that he will not . . . ; but as they teach him, so will he judge; and
according to their judgment [the divinely guided decision will be reached] . . . One of
the priests of repute shall go forth . . ." For the restoration within the brackets, cf.
1Q S ix, 7: "Only the sons of Aaron shall have authority in matters of law and property; and according to their judgment the divinely guided decision shall be reached in
regard to every rule of the men of the Community." Cf. also v, 3 and vi, 16. For the
text of 4Q pIsa[a] see J. M. Allegro in the *JBL*, 1956, pp. 177–82. See also his article
"More Isaiah Commentaries from Qumrân's Fourth Cave," *JBL*, 1958, pp. 215–21.

> For well-doing,
> but behold, wailing! [4]

The second occurrence of "for," which makes no sense, is unattested elsewhere and is clearly an accidental intrusion.

There are likewise *memoriter* errors.[5] A mistake of this kind would best account for the interchange of parallel terms in successive phrases in 49:6a:

> He says:
> "It's too easy for you to be My legate [6]
> to raise up the tribes of *Israel,*
> and to restore the preserved of *Jacob.*"

In the traditional text one finds "tribes of Jacob" and "preserved of Israel"; but the scribe of this scroll (or a predecessor) carelessly lapsed into the familiar "tribes of Israel" and concluded by locating "Jacob" in the wrong clause. Preference in textual criticism must always be given the more unusual phrasing, in this case "tribes of Jacob." [7]

It is disappointing to find that the scroll not only contains many of the supposed corruptions of the Massoretic text where one would welcome the disclosure of a new and original reading, but is even more corrupt in places. As an illustration of this, let us examine the traditional text of 35:7–8:

> 7 Burning sand shall become a pool;
> and parched land, springs of water.
> In the jackals' haunt shall be its resting place;
> the grass, reeds and rushes.
> 8 There shall be there a highway and a way,
> and the Holy Way it shall be called.

---

4. The puns in Hebrew are respectively *mišpâṭ* and *miśpâḥ*, *ṣədâqâh* and *ṣə'âqâh*. The "wailing" referred to is that of the oppressed.

5. *Memoriter* errors may occur either through copying a book by memory, or by transcribing only a single verse after reading it as a whole — slips of memory occurring even in that brief interval. The latter, I think, to be the more likely explanation in the Isaiah Scroll.

6. "Legate," "minister," or "ambassador," is a better translation of *'eved* in the "Servant Songs" of Isaiah than "slave." Cf. II Sam. 10:2–4 for this meaning.

7. Critics basing their conclusions upon internal evidence often prefer the language characteristic of that particular book. Insofar as this procedure is valid, it must be based upon the argument that the usual phrasing *elsewhere* has modified the text of the book under consideration. Yet, even here, one must not readily assume complete uniformity on the part of any one author.

> The unclean shall not pass over it,
> but He is for them a wayfarer,
> and fools shall not stray (there).

The second half of verse 7, as emended by C. C. Torrey (and followed by the Revised Standard Version), should read:

> The jackals' haunt shall become a swamp;
> the grass, reeds and rushes.

The distich line then parallels in form the preceding one, and its final clause becomes meaningful.[8] The correction involves only a single letter of the text.[9] "And a way" at the end of the first stich of verse 8 is generally regarded as a dittograph. Considerable difficulty has been encountered with the second half of verse 8. The King James Version, in close agreement with Massoretic punctuation, rendered:

> but it shall be for those: the wayfaring men, though fools, shall not err *therein*.

Aside from the vagueness of "for those," this makes good sense; but this is prose rather than poetry. The translators of the King James Version, as also the Massoretes, were unaware of the poetic character of the material they were punctuating, and so sometimes divided the material inaccurately. In this particular case, the difficulty of the text itself was the chief contributing factor. They did a good job of making sense out of the passage as they received it. A number of emendations, not very satisfactory, have been resorted to in an effort to restore the passage to its original clarity and poetic parallelism; but to this we shall return later.

We turn hopefully to the newly found text for a solution, and this is what we read:

> 7 Burning sand shall become a pool;
> and parched land, springs of water.
> In the jackals' haunt shall be *a* resting place *of*
> 8 grass with reeds; and rushes | *shall be there*.

8. Each Hebrew poetic line consists of two or three parts (or stichs). A line consisting of two parts is a distich; whereas a line consisting of three parts is a tristich. Unfortunately, some scholars employ the obscurantist terminology of bicola and tricola to designate these lines. In the translations given here (both my own and others') I place the first stich of each new line at the left and begin it with a capital letter, but I indent the other stichs to the right.
9. Correcting *RBṢH* to *LBṢH*. The final letter is omitted in the scroll.

> There shall (a road) *be built up;*
> and *they'll call it* the Holy Way;
> *He* shall not pass over it
> but it will be *for whoever* travels the way;
> and fools shall not stray (there).

The second half of verse 7 is more intelligible than in the Massoretic text. The omission of the vague pronominal suffix "its" from "resting-place" yields the combination "a resting place *of* grass." The joining of "and rushes" with the first words of the following verse also lightens the syntactical difficulty of the verse. The adverb "there" (*ŠMH*) must then be repeated at the beginning of the next sentence (v. 8a). It is possible that the second occurrence of the word should be rendered "its name" in order to obtain a closer parallel with the next clause:

> Its name shall be Built-up; [10]
> and *they'll call it* the Holy Way.

The phrasing "they'll call it" instead of "it shall be called" reveals the influence of the Aramaic idiom where there was a fondness of the third plural indefinite form in preference to passive verbal forms. The meaning is the same in either case and a preferred English translation would obliterate the distinction, translating even the variant text "it shall be called." In verse 8b, the word "unclean" is omitted, and one is at a loss to know certainly to whom "he" refers; [11] but probably the antecedent is indefinite:

> *None* shall pass over it,
> *except he* who rightfully travels the way.

Point by point the scroll readings seem to represent a deliberate attempt to resolve the difficulties found in the Massoretic text. Yet only in the omission of "and a way" from the end of the first stich of verse 8 does the text seem to be more accurate. Still this omission might be due to haplography, rather than to a superior Hebrew prototype from which the scroll was copied.

The scroll text of 35:7–8 is nevertheless valuable as a demonstration that the difficulties encountered by modern scholars in the Massoretic text are real. The scroll's smoothing out of verse 7b cannot be original, for like the Massoretic text it gives us prose rather than poetry. The

10. For this sort of naming, cf. Isa. 62:4.
11. In the following citation, I have translated *"He shall not"* as *"None* shall."

simple emendation adopted by the Standard Bible Committee (discussed above) undoubtedly restores the original text. In the case of verse 8b, one is compelled to emend if he is to preserve any part of the second stich as an original part of the text. The reading "He is for them a wayfarer" leaves both "he" and "them" without any antecedent. Consequently a common emendation is to alter "for them" (*LMW*) into "for his people" (*L'MW*). The clause thereby obtained might be translated: "It is for His people who travel the way." The initial pronoun in the Hebrew is masculine, however, whereas in the context the antecedent "way" is referred to repeatedly in the feminine gender.[12] Therefore, some scholars would interpret "He" as a surrogate for Yahweh, and translate: *"He* Himself is for His people a traveler of the way." This would bring the passage into accord with the thought of Second Isaiah who regards this road as "the way of the Lord" Himself (40:3) Who is about to lead His people home from the Exile by means of this road (52:12). The Hebrew form of the sentence is still not very convincing, however, so that it is common practice, even after emendation, to omit the clause as a gloss, i.e. as a marginal comment which was eventually copied into the body of the text. Concerning this practice, C. C. Torrey has written, "The solution, finally, which could accept this emendation, and then pronounce the whole clause a *gloss* (!) is certainly much worse than no solution at all." [13]

In defense of the omission, we may point out that both the preceding and following lines of the passage are distichs rather than tristichs. Although Hebrew poetry is seldom consistent in its strophic pattern, the critic may feel that he has lost nothing by omitting the difficult clause; for a complete distich would be left. This is the procedure of the RSV. C. C. Torrey, on the other hand, emended radically in order to obtain acceptable sense and to even the distich form:

> The unclean and the perverse will not pass over it:
> the depraved will not lead astray him who treads it.[14]

Since emendation seems to be necessary here, I have sought a less drastic yet convincing correction of the text. It seems to me that in the first two words of the offending clause we have the scrambled

12. Both genders are attested in the Old Testament, but one would expect consistency in a given passage.
13. *Op. cit.*, p. 300.
14. *Ibid.*

letters for the name for God, Elohim (pronounced *'elôhîm*).[15] After correction, the translation becomes:

> The unclean shall not pass over it,
> but God is traveling the way,
> and the godless shall not stray (there).

Not only does this text accord with the theology of Second Isaiah in making God a wayfarer on this road, but it also introduces an element of assonance. Since *'elôhîm* (God) is traveling the road, *'ewîlîm* (fools, depraved, or godless) shall not stray thereon.

In the most extreme textual corruption, the scroll is untranslatable, except through emendation. The following is the best sense I am able to make out of Isaiah 40:20:

> [A poorer oblation] is wood that will not *ceday;*
> *and* (for it) one chooses a skillful craftsman,
> that he for his shekel may erect an idol that
> will not totter!

The bracketed portion of the text is of uncertain meaning.[16] It was omitted by the original scribe who left room for the later insertion of the words. The use of the unintelligible "ceday" in the English translation (written here as an error for the English "decay") illustrates the same kind of error as was made by the Hebrew copyist.[17] Another metathesis led to an inaccurate word combination; but this time an intelligible sense emerges.[18] The final result of this corrupted text is crass prose, rather than the beautiful poetic form of the original as preserved in the Massoretic text:

> One too impoverished chooses for an oblation
> wood that will not decay;
> He seeks out a skillful craftsman
> to erect an idol that will not totter.

After this survey of scribal errors in the scroll, it should not seem surprising that one scholar should have concluded after superficial examination of the scroll text (when it was first published by the Ameri-

---

15. Read *W'LWHYM* for the Massoretic *WHW'-LMW* and the scroll reading *HW'H WLMY*.

16. The Targum translates this as "a fir tree"; but cf. Torrey, *op. cit.*, p. 308.

17. The scribe first wrote *YDBQ* ("will [not] stick") and then corrected it to *YRBQ*, by filling in the top of the erroneous *D*. However, the correct reading is *YRQB*.

18. *YBQŠ-LW* ("he seeks for himself") thus became *WBŠQLW* ("that for his shekel").

can Schools of Oriental Research in 1950) that the scroll is not worth the paper it was printed on.[19] This is an extreme view, as is also the view of another scholar who insists that the only textual merit of our Isaiah Scroll is to confirm the traditional text.[20]

LIGHT ON PRONUNCIATION FROM SCRIBAL ERRORS

One redeeming feature of the scribal errors is that we can learn from them, not only how ancient mistakes were made, but also how Hebrew was pronounced in the Qumrân Community. We know for example from this source that the gutturals were easily confused with one another and that the community had a tendency to omit *H*'s, confusing them at times with a quiescent *'Âlef!*

There is also the interesting light shed by scribal errors upon the prounuciation of divine names. The most important word for God in the Old Testament is the Tetragrammaton, the four-lettered word *YHWH,* which according to most recent scholars was originally pronounced *yahwèh.*[21] This is the name which the Fourth Commandment sought to protect from abuse. In order to prevent the irreverent use of it, the Jews resorted to surrogates. When the word stood alone, they would substitute Adonai (pronounced *'ªdônâi,* and usually translated "Lord"); but when Adonai Yahweh stood in the text, they would substitute Elohim (i.e. "God") for Yahweh, thereby obtaining the phrase "the Lord God." We had known this practice from the traditional text, but we did not know how ancient this practice was. There are confusions as to whether to read Adonai or Yahweh in the scroll which reveal the habit of this interchange.[22] When the scribe heard "Adonai," he did not always know whether to write the consonants for Yahweh or those of Adonai which he actually heard. The order of the divine names occurring in the Massoretic text of Isa. 3:17–18 is: Adonai, Yahweh, Adonai. The order in the scroll is: Adonai, Adonai, Yahweh; but a corrector has placed dots under the first Adonai to indicate his belief that it is in error, and has placed above it the word Yahweh (contrary to the Massoretic text). He has similarly

19. Solomon Zeitlin, "The Hebrew Scrolls: Once More and Finally," *JQR,* XLI, 1950, pp. 1–58.
20. Harry M. Orlinsky, "Studies in the St. Mark's Isaiah Scroll," *JBL,* LXIX, 1950, pp. 149–66; "Notes on the Present State of the Textual Criticism of the Judean Biblical Cave Scrolls," in *A Stubborn Faith* (Edited by Edward C. Hobbs), Dallas, Texas, Southern Methodist University Press, 1956, pp. 117–31.
21. Cf. Appendix E.
22. Cf. Isa. 28:16; 30:15; 49:14 in the text of the Isaiah Scroll, where in each case a corrector has suggested an alternative to the reading of the original scribe.

corrected the third name Yahweh into Adonai, this time in agreement with the Massoretic text.

In Isa. 50:5, where the Massoretic consonantal text reads Adonai Yahweh, the scribe of the ancient scroll wrote according to the pronunciation of tradition Adonai Elohim. For the same phrase, however, at 61:11, he wrote the consonants for Yahweh Elohim, attesting thereby the same pronunciation, for he could not by ear distinguish when to write Yahweh and when Adonai, since both were pronounced *ᵃdônâi*. This may be illustrated by the current practice of many translations (including the Revised Standard Version) of capitalizing the divine name whenever the consonants are those of the ineffable Yahweh. According to this custom, the Massoretic reading of 61:11 is "Lord God," but the reading of the scroll is "Lord God." Just as in English the two different readings involve no difference in pronunciation, so also in the Hebrew. The dissimilarity between the two readings is entirely visual whether read in English or in Hebrew; but in Hebrew the visual difference is much more radical, with completely different consonants rather than merely a different type face. These confusions in the text of the scroll thoroughly substantiate the traditional use of divine nominal surrogates as early as the second century B.C.[23]

The scroll has many other important values. Many of these derive from the popular character of the text, which was designed to aid the understanding of the reader by incorporating elements of interpretation. To these values we now turn.

---

23. Actually this practice was much earlier, for one of the frequent discrepancies between the Massoretic text and the presumed Hebrew *Vorlage* of the Septuagint is whether to read in a given passage Yahweh alone, or Yahweh Adonai. This inconsistency was occasioned by the fact that originally Yahweh did stand alone, but that Adonai tended to be introduced alongside the Tetragrammaton by way of making explicit the surrogate. This was not understood by the Massoretes, however, who felt compelled to vocalize both words. Neither was it understood by the scribes of the Qumrân Scrolls, nor even by still earlier translators of the LXX. That Yahweh originally stood alone in most such passages is supported by the fact that, in Hebrew poetry, the double designation of the Deity usually adds excessive length to the poetic stich. The same sort of variations from the Massoretic text in the use of the single or the double name are frequently attested in the ancient scrolls. Curiously, both Isaiah Scrolls of Cave One agree upon inserting Adonai before Yahweh in 49:7, as against the Septuagint and the Massoretic text. Metrically, the stich is ambiguous, for *kôh 'âmar* is capable of receiving either one beat ("Thus saith") or two beats ("Thus hath said"), depending upon whether the words are combined, or given independent stress. Consequently, either reading can be accommodated here. Ambiguous passages of this kind, which are rather numerous, offer no real support for the use of both names, since in all such cases Adonai is metrically dispensable.

CHAPTER EIGHT

The Interpretative Character of the Isaiah Text

In Part I we have seen numerous illustrations of the interpretative aspects of the Qumrân Scrolls. This feature extends even to the variant readings of the Isaiah Scroll, which are a part of the vulgar (popular) character of the manuscript. I shall discuss and illustrate these features one by one.

1. The Use of Vowel Letters

It is in the lavish use of vowel letters (called *matres lectionis*) [1] that the popular aspect of the Isaiah Scroll is most readily observable. Hebrew writing as found in the most ancient inscriptions consisted wholly of consonants. Vowels were to be supplied by the reader according to context. Generally there would be little difficulty for one familiar with the tongue and the idioms of the language, but sometimes there were ambiguities to which such orthography would give rise.

In the case of a sacred text, oral tradition tended to fix the pronunciation. In the second century B.C. it became popular to adapt certain of the consonants to vowel uses. W (*Wâw*) was used for any one of a whole family of related vowel sounds, ōō [û], ŏo, ō [ô], ŏ, or °. Y (*Yôd*) was employed for ē [î], ĕ, ā [ê], or ĭ. *'Âlef* (') was employed for ä [â], in either medial or final position, but H was most commonly employed in the final position for ä. This system was imperfect, for not only were scribes inconsistent in their use of these vowel letters, but there were ambiguities as to which of various vowel sounds were intended, or even whether a vowel or a consonant was intended in a particular word.[2] Therefore Jewish scholars known as the Massoretes

---

1. The Latin means "mothers of readings."
2. Thus in II Sam. 11:1 the *'Âlef* (') of *HML'KYM*, if interpreted as a consonant would yield the meaning "messengers," but if taken as a vowel letter, as in the Massoretic vocalization, it gives the meaning "kings."

evolved a system of pointing in the fifth to the ninth centuries A.D., which employed a technique of placing dots and dashes in, above, or under the original Hebrew consonants in order to indicate the vowels.[3] This system was probably inspired by a similar practice of indicating vowels introduced by Christians into the Syriac, but it was developed to a much greater precision, so that the Massoretes achieved the most precise phonetic system of any language in human history.[4] A very interesting study would be to compare the pronunciation of Hebrew implied by the spellings of the Dead Sea Scrolls with those of the medieval Jews. Many of the pronunciations of the Massoretic Hebrew appear to have been the same as at the earlier period, but there are important exceptions. Thus for the history of Hebrew pronunciation the scrolls are invaluable. This is especially true of the Complete Isaiah Scroll, which employs vowel letters (particularly in the second half) more freely than any of the other texts so far published. In fact, there is another fragmentary Isaiah Scroll from the Qumrân Cave One whose spellings more closely approximate those of the Massoretic text, although even it contains a few of the same full spellings which characterize the complete scroll. Although we cannot go into the technical aspects of the subject here, a number of important discoveries have been made from these vowel letters. The following represents a listing of these contributions.

A. *The Recovery of the More Primitive Pronunciation of Proper Nouns*

O vowels abound in greater profusion in the Isaiah Scroll than Massoretic vocalization would indicate. A class segolate nouns are often vocalized as are those of the O class. Uncontracted O vowels also occur in the verbs where they are lacking in the traditional text. In the case of the proper nouns, the vowels of the O class, as uninteresting as they might seem, afford an important proof as to the antiquity of our scroll. The first scholar to point this out was Prof. Dewey M. Beegle.[5]

---

3. Sometimes the vowels thus supplied were intended to suggest other consonants, so that the consonants actually written represent one reading (the *kᵊtîv*) and the vowels another (the *qᵊrê'*).

4. It is even more precise than Arabic. On the influence of Syriac upon Hebrew pointing, cf. Ernst Wurthwein, *The Text of the Old Testament* (translated from the German by P. R. Ackroyd), New York, Macmillan, 1957, p. 17; Paul E. Kahle, *The Cairo Geniza*, 2nd ed., Oxford, Blackwell, 1959, pp. 65f., 72f.

5. "Proper Names in the New Isaiah Scroll," *BASOR*, No. 123 (Oct. 1951), pp. 26–30.

The presence of an O-type vowel in the first syllables of Sodom and Gomorrah (Isa. 1:9, 10; 3:9; 13:19) as found in our scroll is attested by the Greek Septuagint version, probably prepared in the third century B.C. It is from this version that our English spelling has descended. The Massoretic vocalization in each case is simply ǝ, or ᵃ, insignificant vowels like the E of our article the before a consonant.

In chapter 7 of Isaiah there are repeated references to "Rezin the king of Syria and Pekah the son of Remaliah the king of Israel" who have joined in a coalition against Judah. The traditional pronunciation of Rezin and Remaliah respectively is Rǝzîn and Rǝmalyâhû. For these the Septuagint offers Raasson and Romelios. The presence of a W in the second syllable of Rezin and the first syllable of Remaliah in the scroll supports a vowel of the O class in harmony with the Greek transcriptions of the Septuagint. In the case of the latter word, Professor Beegle suggests the original pronunciation Rûmlâyâhû with the meaning, "Be exalted, O Yahweh!"

A variant spelling of Shebna is also found in the scroll. Shebna was at first King Hezekiah's prime minister (Isa. 22:15ff.), but was later demoted to the position of secretary of state (36:3; 37:2),[6] being replaced in the former position by Eliakim in fulfillment of Isaiah's prophecy (22:20–23). In the Isaiah Scroll, Shebna is spelled with an O-type vowel in the first syllable, in agreement with the Septuagint. Beegle argues that Shebna is an abbreviated form of Shebaniah found in Neh. 9:4, 5, whose original vocalization was Shûvnâyâhû, meaning "Return, I pray Thee, O Yahweh." There is a similar Neo-Babylonian name which supports the same pronunciation of the first syllable. Shebna therefore becomes Shubna.

Isaiah 37:38 records that the great Assyrian ruler Sennacherib was assassinated by his sons Adrammelech and Sharezer, who fled to the land of Ararat, and that Sennacherib was succeeded by his son Esarhaddon. An appropriately placed W in the Isaiah Scroll supports the presence of O-class vowels in Sharezer, Ararat, and Esarhaddon where they are missing in the traditional text. In this it reflects the ancient Babylonian and Assyrian pronunciation: Sharuzer, Urartu, and Ash-shur-ahu-id-i-na.[7] The italicized u's are supported by the scroll's W's.

---

6. On this inscription, see G. E. Wright, *Biblical Archaeology,* Philadelphia, Westminster; London, Gerald Duckworth, 1957, pp. 171f.

7. Beegle, *op. cit.*

Similarly the commander in chief sent by Sargon against the Philistine city of Ashdod (Isa. 20:1) would in ancient Assyrian have been called by the title *turtannû*. In the traditional Hebrew he is called *tartân* (mistaken by the King James Version as a proper name), but the Isaiah Scroll supports *turtân*, in closer agreement with the ancient Assyrian.

The name Hezekiah is vocalized according to longer or shorter spellings in the Massoretic text as *Yəḥizqîyâhû* and *Ḥizqîyâhû*. In the Isaiah Scroll a *W* frequently follows the first *H*, supporting an *O*-type vowel here.[8]

These more ancient pronunciations implied by the orthography of our most ancient Isaiah manuscript are but a small part of the total impact of the orthographic variants of the document.

B. *The Recovery of Longer Pronominal Forms*

The Isaiah Scroll discloses the use of longer forms of the pronouns and pronominal suffixes than those of the Massoretic text. This is particularly true in the second half of the scroll, though some of the same spellings occur in the first half. There may well have been some conscious archaizing on the part of the scribe in producing these forms. Nevertheless, these longer forms are important for any study of the history of the language. It may be that longer and shorter spellings existed side by side for a considerable time, with the shorter forms of more popular speech gradually gaining the ascendancy.[9] In the traditional text, only a few scattered passages can be cited containing these longer forms, and even they do not represent all the varieties of pronominal forms abounding in the Isaiah Scroll.[10] They are merely

8. I protested rather strenuously the failure of Burrows to take note of this in the transcription which he (with the assistance of Trever and me) prepared of the Isaiah Scroll. Eventually, he came to recognize a distinction between the letters and published an article of retraction: "*Waw* and *Yodh* in the Isaiah Dead Sea Scroll (DSIa)," *BASOR*, No. 124 (Dec. 1951), pp. 18–20. He introduced many corrections in the second printing of *The Dead Sea Scrolls of St. Mark's Monastery*. Unfortunately, the photographic plates are much less clear in this printing.

9. See F. M. Cross and D. N. Freedman, *Early Hebrew Orthography. A Study of the Epigraphic Evidence*, New Haven, 1952.

10. Examples of the longer suffix forms in the Massoretic text are as follows: *bâ-hêmmâh* (Ex. 30:4; 36:1; Hab. 1:16); *lâ-hêmmâh* (Jer. 14:16); *lâ-khenâh* (Ezek. 13:18); *L-KY* (*kətív*), vocalized as *lâkh* (the *qərê'* for *L-K*) (II Kings 4:2; Song of Songs 2:13); *bətôkhêkhi* (*BTWK-KY*) (Pss. 116:19; 135:9); also *-êkhi* and *-âyəkhi* in Ps. 103:3–5 (five examples).

the fossilized remains of a past age when such spellings had full life in Hebrew literature.[11]

These pronominal forms are of more than orthographical interest; for here is a phenomenon which must be taken into account in the study of Hebrew metrics. In Hebrew poetry, as now understood, accents are distributed not according to any rigid system of syllable counting, but according to natural stresses of the sentence. *Normally a single word receives a single beat*, unless it is very brief and can be combined with another into a brief phrase (almost like a compound word) which then receives a single beat.[12] This system of accentuation is very elastic, so that sometimes for emphasis a very brief word (like the negative particle *lô'*) might receive a single beat. Syllable counting applies only insofar as the mechanics of human speech tends to limit the number of syllables that might be subsumed under a single accent. There might be only one syllable; but one would expect an upper limit of not more than five syllables to a beat. Now the addition of syllables to the pronouns and pronominal suffixes may have some effect upon future analysis of Hebrew poetic rhythm. As far as I know, no one has investigated this implication.

Monosyllabic pronouns become *dissyllabic* in the Qumrân literature, really easing the problem of giving a single beat to such a short word. At the same time, this makes less probable those scansions which combine the pronoun with another word under a single beat. Likewise long pronominal suffix forms lessen the possibility that such a word be combined with others under a single stress. In some cases, where a noun or verb is itself fairly long, it introduces the probability that two beats may be allowed, one for the principal word, the other for the pronominal suffix. This is a somewhat technical matter which we cannot illustrate here, and yet a scholar's theory of Hebrew metrics does influence his translation of the Bible into a modern language.[13] There-

11. The full spellings seem to have been most abundant in the second century B.C. See Cross and Freedman, *op. cit.*, also Eduard Yechezqel Kutscher, *The Language and Linguistic Background of the Isaiah Scroll* (in Hebrew, but with twelve pages of English summary), Jerusalem, Israel, Magnes Press, the Hebrew University, 1959.

12. In many such cases, the Massoretic text employs a hyphen (*maqqef*). In many other cases, the second word is the genitive of the former (the two words being linked together by the construct relationship in Hebrew grammar).

13. This is most noticeable where it is a matter of whether a given passage is prose or poetry. Contrast Joel 2:30–32a RSV with the same passage in Acts 2:19–20 RSV — where much of the difference in word order and phrasing is due to the treatment

fore, there may be some fruit from this source in which future Bible readers will share, without knowing the linguistic roots.

c. *The Revelation of More Extensive Use of the Plural of Majesty*

It is well known that the usual name for God in Hebrew is plural in form (Elohim), and that this does not, however, make it mean plural (gods), for this form is employed in the very Old Testament passages which assert God's unity. In fact the noun normally receives singular verbs and is referred to by singular pronouns. The Qumrân Scrolls attest a much wider use of the plural form in antiquity by adding vowel letters which suggest plural readings where the Massoretic text reads the singular.

In a critical note to Ecclesiastes 12:1 ("Remember your Creator in the days of your youth."), F. Horst notes that the text given in Kittel's *Biblia Hebraica* gives the word "Creator" in the plural and that some medieval manuscripts read the singular instead. In the Complete Isaiah Scroll from Qumrân, the opposite correction is made. The missing letter which would make the word "Creator" plural is added above the line at 43:1. Similarly the title "Maker" is possibly given a plural spelling in 17:7, while a supralinear addition to 54:5 perhaps corrects the singular to the plural. Other explanations are possible in each of the foregoing examples,[14] but such is not the case in 45:9:

---

of the passage as poetry in the New Testament and as prose in the Old Testament. This inconsistency between the two Testaments is regrettable.

C. C. Torrey (as most other translators) believed it to be impossible to represent the rhythm characteristic of Hebrew poetry in English translation. However, his distinguished student W. F. Stinespring insists that this is not only possible, but desirable. The demonstration of the feasibility of this is to be seen in the theses written under his direction at Duke University: Samuel Wilds Du Bose, *Linguistic and Literary Problems in the Book of Joel*, A.M. thesis, 1943; *The Book of Jeremiah in Recent Criticism*, Ph.D. Dissertation, 1947; William Hugh Brownlee, *The Book of Ezekiel — the Original Prophet and the Editors*, Ph.D. Dissertation, 1947; Brooks Milton Waggoner, *Studies in Hebrew Poetry with Special Reference to the Contributions of Robert Lowth*, Ph.D. Dissertation, 1952; Donald Leigh Williams, *Zephaniah: A Re-interpretation*, Ph.D. Dissertation, 1961. None of these is published.

As long as one makes the number of major words or brief phrases in English correspond with the rhythmic measure of the Hebrew, his translation has largely succeeded in representing the Hebrew meter. Reading aloud, however, may often suggest the need for smoother or rhythmically sharper English wording, so that the stresses of normal pronunciation clearly correspond with the number of beats assigned each Hebrew stich.

14. Y might be regarded as merely a vowel letter.

> Woe to him who strives with his *Moulder*,
> a pot with the *Potter* of the earth.

Both "Moulder" and "Potter" as designations of God are spelled as though plural. The former term appears as singular in the Massoretic text, and the latter, which did appear in the plural, was misunderstood by the Massoretes and vocalized as "potsherds," [15] which makes no sense.[16] C. C. Torrey suggested emending "potsherds" into the singular form "potter"; in this he assessed rightly the sense, but there was no need to omit the plural termination, except that he was unprepared to recognize the use of the plural form with reference to the Deity.[17] Even the Revised Standard Version, which was completed after the discovery of the scrolls, is puzzled — resorting to correction of the text and explaining in a footnote that the Hebrew reads "potsherds or potters." Such emendations should be abandoned in the future.

Isaiah 40:21 is tacitly emended in the King James Version so as to read:

> Have ye not known? have yet not heard?
> hath it not been told you from the beginning?
> have ye not understood *from* the foundations of the
> earth?

There is no "from" in the last stich, although the parallelism suggests it. The ancient versions and the scroll lack "from." Therefore the literal translation is to be preferred, provided it can be given an appropriate sense. Can the term "foundations" refer really to God as the Creator or *Founder* of the earth? The addition of an article in the participle which immediately follows in the scroll suggests that the participial phrases of verses 22–23 are appositional to "foundations," which term must then be regarded as an example of the plural of majesty, not a real plural:

> 21 Have you not known? Have you not heard?
> Has it not been told you from the beginning?
> Have you not understood earth's *Foundation:*

15. Vocalized *ḥarśê*.
16. Two ingenious methods of handling the clause is represented by the KJV (*"Let the potsherd strive* with the potsherds of the earth.") and ASV ("a potsherd among the potsherds of the earth!"). In both of these renderings, the contentious person is a potsherd among other potsherds (other men) — but the parallelism of the Hebrew poetry does not support either of these renderings. They are both more satisfactory, however, than the Septuagint and the Targum.
17. *Op. cit.,* p. 359.

> 22   *Him Who* thrones above the earth's dome
>   with its inhabitants as grasshoppers;
>   Him Who stretches out the sky like a canvas,
>   and spreads it out like a tent to dwell in;
> 23   Him Who reduces princes to naught,
>   making earth's rulers as nothing?

The use of the term "Foundation(s)" rather than "Founder" is in keeping with a concreteness of Hebrew usage whereby God may be called "Salvation," "Help," or "Vindication" instead of "Savior," "Helper," "Vindicator." Perhaps also the verse means that to understand truly the *foundations* of the earth one must know their *Founder*. Thus the ancient Targum in its paraphrastic rendering of verse 21 interprets correctly:

> Have you not known? Have you not heard?
> Has not the work of the orders of creation been
> announced to you from the beginning?
> Will ye not understand so as to fear before *Him*
> *Who created the foundations* of the earth?

The reading of the article with the first word of verse 22, *"Him Who* thrones" (literally, "the throning one"), rather than *"He* thrones" (or, "throning") is not essential to this interpretation. It does serve, however, to imply the interpretation of "Foundation(s)" as a designation of God, which eliminates the necessity of emendation.

D. *Recovery of New Readings of Old Words*

The supplying of vowel letters to the text generally does not alter the sense, but occasionally it may do just this. An interesting example of this sort of variant is to be found in 40:6. Where the traditional text reads "one said," the Isaiah Scroll reads "I said." This reading is supported by the Septuagint and Latin Vulgate versions. Internal evidence also supports the reading, for in this portion of chapter 40 is to be heard a faint literary echo of the call of the Prophet Isaiah in chapter 6. In the earlier passage we have all the paraphernalia of vision carefully and vividly described. There are several voices to be heard, each of which is clearly identifiable as that of the Seraphim or even of God Himself. In chapter 40 the voices heard by the later, Exilic prophet are introduced so vaguely that we can only guess whether they are those of angelic beings or perhaps of God. Yet there is the inescapable impression of some literary affinity between these chapters which is best explained as the influence of the eighth-century Palestinian prophet upon the sixth-century Exilic prophet. Now in the earlier chapter, the prophet himself responds to the voices and introduces his words with the expression "and I said." This also occurs in the new reading of 40:6. Since this agrees with the ancient versions, it is undoubtedly correct. This reading is followed in the Revised Standard Version.[18]

Another example of this helpful feature of vowel letters is to be found in Isaiah 53:9, where the Massoretic text reads:

> With wicked men *one* placed his grave,
> and with a rich *man in his deaths.*

A number of scholars had conjectured that the word rendered "in his deaths" should through a different vocalization be rendered "his tomb."[19] This spelling actually appears in the scroll:

> With wicked men *they* placed his grave;
> and with rich *men, his tomb.*

The parallelism is much superior to that of the Massoretic text, so that it is disappointing to find that the Revised Standard Version did not follow this reading.[20]

Even the absence of vowel letters may favor one reading over another. The Massoretic text of Isa. 40:26c reads:

> By the plenitude of (His) powers,
> and (because) he is strong of might,
> not one is missing.

This reading is awkward, since there is no word here in the Hebrew for "because" to smooth out the sense as in English. The Greek,

18. No footnote accompanies this rendition because of the principle employed by the Standard Bible Committee of introducing no notes where a mere change in vocalization is involved. Thus, there are more scroll readings followed in the RSV than the citation "one ancient ms." would suggest.

19. Cf. the third alternative reading suggested by Rudolph Kittel in *Biblia Hebraica,* where the first *Qâmes* is the *Qâmes Hâtûph* (a short *o*). For the use of two *O*-class vowels in the verb, cf. Isa. 14:14; 58:14; Micah 1:3. Note the same error of vocalization on the part of the MT in its handling of the last word of Ezek. 43:7 (contrasted with the Vulgate) as in Isa. 53:9.

20. The significance of the vowel letters in the scroll was not fully understood at that time. It is therefore a mistake to say that every reading of the scroll was considered by the Standard Bible Committee.

Targum, and Syriac versions vocalized one of the words differently, reading the noun "strength" (*'ômeṣ*) for the adjective "strong" (*'ammîṣ*):

> By the plenitude of (His) powers
> and *the strength* of His might
> not one is missing.

The absence of vowel letters in the scroll (*'MṢ* for *'MYṢ*) favors this reading. The parallelism is much better, so once more it is disappointing to find the Revised Standard Version holding to the traditional text.

A dramatic new possibility is opened up by the scroll vocalization of Isa. 41:1, where the traditional text may be rendered:

> Come silently to Me, far shores;
> let the peoples gain fresh strength.
> Let them approach, then speak;
> together let us draw near for judgment.

The words "gain fresh strength" (or "renew their strength") have seemed inappropriate to the context. It has been plausibly suggested that this phrase is a corruption of a similarly appearing phrase meaning "await reproof." The erroneous reading arose through a scribal confusion of this with "gain fresh strength" in the preceding verse. On the other hand, C. C. Torrey has argued that the renewing of strength is an ironical anticipation of verses 5-7, where the nations of the world are taunted into making more gods with the hope of escaping the approaching judgment depicted in the intervening verses.[21] This view now seems correct. The difficulty with the sense and parallelism of the verse lies really in another word. Instead of *yiggəshû* (*YGŠW*), "approach," the scroll apparently reads *yâgûshû* (*YGWŠW*), "harden, grow firm or bold." This verb (*gûsh*) is attested in Rabbinic Aramaic and has a cognate form in Arabic. That it was probably also an ancient Hebrew verb is seen from the existence of the related noun *gûsh* in the phrase "clod of earth" (Job. 7:5). Isaiah 41:1 may then be read:

> Come silently to Me, far shores:
> let the peoples gain fresh strength.
> Let them *grow firm,* then speak;
> together let us draw near for judgment.

21. *Op. cit.*, p. 313.

"Grow firm" provides the requisite parallel to "gain fresh strength." The over-all parallelism is of the chiastic type: A/B, B/A. The new reading might be interpreted as indicating simply a new pronunciation (*yiggôshû?*) of the same old word "approach," but the possibility of a different root is an attractive solution to the difficulty of the traditional text. This new interpretation arises solely from the addition of a vowel letter to the original consonants.

2. THE SUBSTITUTION OF EASIER READINGS FOR HARDER ONES

In Isaiah, as elsewhere in the Old Testament, there occur rare terms which might not be generally understood at a later date. In such cases our scroll sometimes substitutes a more common or better understood term. In Isa. 42:11 the verbal root for "shout" is *ṣâwah* in the Massoretic text, but the scroll employs the root *ṣârah*. The former verb occurs only here. Professor Harry M. Orlinsky argues persuasively that, in accordance with a basic rule of textual criticism, preference should be given to the more difficult reading. The rare word of the Massoretic text, as he points out, is attested in the ancient Canaanite literature preserved at Ugarit. He cites a passage which shows that the verb "lift up" (the voice) is associated with the verb *ṣâwah* precisely as in Isa. 42:11. The goddess Anat's worship of the god Il is described as follows:

> She prostrates herself and honors him,
> she *lifts up* her voice and *shouts*.

Now the word *ṣârah* does occur two verses later in the Massoretic text, and it is this verse (as Orlinsky notes) which has influenced the reading of the earlier verse.[22] The meaning is the same in either case, but we should give preference to diversity of reading in the similar verses, rather than to sameness of wording, even when it involves a word occurring but once in the Bible.

In Hebrew poetry, phrases are sometimes abbreviated by reason of metrical considerations. This occurs in Isa. 42:11 and in the Ugaritic passage quoted above, where one finds simply "lift up" used in the sense of "lift up the voice." Similarly in Isa. 41:20, the traditional text reads simply "put" for the expression "put upon [or in] the heart." The King James Version and the Revised Standard Version both render the verb as "consider":

22. "Studies in the St. Mark's Isaiah Scroll, II," *JNES*, XI, 1952, pp. 153–6.

> that men may see and know,
>   may *consider* and understand together,
> that the hand of the Lord has done this,
>   the Holy One of Israel has created it.   (RSV)

The scroll substitutes, however, the word "perceive" from the verbal root *bîn,* which means "to *penetrate* to the meaning." The second stich of the verse then becomes: "may *perceive* and understand as well."[23] The word "perceive" affords excellent parallelism with the verb "see" of the preceding stich; but it is nevertheless an error, for an ancient scribe has placed directly above the word a correction bringing the verse into harmony with the received text.[24] Nevertheless, the variant affords an interesting interpretation[25] of the idiom "put into the heart." The rendering "consider" assumes that it means "to ponder the matter in one's heart"; but the scroll variant suggests that it means "to apprehend the meaning and to store this up in one's heart." In some passages of the Old Testament the parallelism is with verbs meaning "to know, or understand," which would favor the scroll's interpretation.[26] In others, however, the parallelism is with the verb "remember."[27] In still other passages the phrase seems to mean "to take to heart," but probably without displacing the idea of perceiving the significance of that which is taken to heart.[28] Thus the scroll variant sheds an important light upon the Biblical idiom, giving the expression an area of connotation not previously understood, that of *perceptivity* in laying hold of data.

Isaiah 9:16 (9:17 in English) is rendered as follows by the Standard Bible Committee:

> Therefore the Lord does not *rejoice* over their young men,
>   and has no compassion on their fatherless and
>   widows . . .

23. Biblical translators have generally failed to notice that "as well" is frequently a better translation of *yaḥad* than "together."
24. The placing of a dot on each side of the verb was intended to show that it is to be substituted for the word below, rather than to be inserted beside it. Nevertheless, this placing of the variant reading between the lines well illustrates how conflate readings might arise — a later scribe copying both readings, rather than choosing between them.
25. One often forgets that a non-original reading may often convey the correct sense.
26. Cf. Isa. 41:22; 42:25; 57:1.
27. Cf. II Kings 19:20 (English, 19:19); Isa. 47:7; 57:11; Luke 2:50–51.
28. Cf. Deut. 32:46; Job 22:22; Ezek. 40:4 — with variations in the Hebrew idiom.

The word "rejoice" (*śâmaḥ*) is not a close parallel to "have compassion," so it has sometimes been emended into "pass" (*pâśaḥ* or *pâsaḥ*), i.e. "The Lord does not pass over their young men," sparing them as when the angel of death passed over the homes of the Hebrews in Egypt after the sprinkling of blood upon the doorposts. Another suggestion was to retain the present consonantal text but to relate the word to the Arabic root *śâmaḥ*, which means "to spare." The Isaiah Scroll confirms this meaning by its reading *ḥâmal*, which certainly means "to spare." The words are so dissimilar that we cannot explain the variant as arising from any confusion in appearance or sound. This is simply a case of substituting a common word for a rare word, which seemingly occurs only this one time in the Old Testament. The traditional text doubtless preserves the correct consonants, but the scroll reading makes explicit the correct meaning.[29] The verse should now be translated:

> Therefore the Lord does not *spare* their youths,
> nor pity their orphans and widows . . .

Still another example shows how important variants may be for interpretation, even when the variant does not preserve the original reading. Isaiah 65:11 condemns those who "fill cups of mixed wine for Destiny." The reference is to the pouring out of a libation to the god *Mənî* (Destiny). For the word "mixed wine" (*mimsâkh*) the scroll reads "libation" (*massêkhâh*). Though not giving us the original word, the new reading at least points rightly to the cultic use of the mixed wine. In so doing, it incidentally sheds light upon Isa. 30:1, where the meaning of *massêkhâh* has been in doubt. One interpretation of the phrase *linsôkh massêkhâh* has been "to pour out a libation," but another has been "to weave a web." The former was adopted by the American Standard Version and has been followed in the Revised Standard Version, with the free rendering "make a league," i.e. enter into a treaty by the pouring out of a drink-offering. The latter alternative is represented by the obscure rendition of the King James Version "cover with a covering" and by the interpretative rendering of the American Jewish Bible "form projects." [30] In the light of the use made of *massêkhâh* at 65:11,

29. See B. J. Roberts (who cites J. Hempel) in *The Friends' Quarterly*, v. 1951, p. 13.
30. *The Holy Scriptures according to the Masoretic Text, a New Translation with the aid of Previous Versions and with Constant Consultation of Jewish Authorities*, Philadelphia, Jewish Publication Society of America, 1917.

it appears that the interpretation of the American Standard Version (followed by the RSV) is correct. Thus the easier readings of the scroll, though probably not original, often make clear the meaning of the original text.

3. PARAGRAPH DIVISIONS

The text of the Complete Isaiah Scroll (as of the other Dead Sea documents) is arranged in paragraphs. As in the Massoretic text, the divisions are usually indicated in two ways, sometimes by leaving a line incomplete and beginning anew at the margin of the next line. New paragraphs are rarely indented from the margin. The paragraph divisions agree so often with those found in medieval manuscripts of the Massoretic text that one can assert with confidence that the paragraph-ings of the ordinary Hebrew Bible rest upon ancient tradition, rather than upon the whim of the Massoretes. Differences of paragraphing must therefore be regarded as textual variants.[31] We treat them in the present connection, for they have implications for literary analysis.

As an example of divergent division in the scroll, we cite the in-dentation of 10:27 which severs the verse from what precedes and links it with verses 28ff. The Massoretic text preserves no division here; but the Revised Standard Version introduces a break in the middle of the verse, thus approximating the paragraphing of the scroll.

The absence of a paragraph division may also be significant for lit-erary analysis. Modern versions of the Bible usually leave a space be-tween chapters 61 and 62, but not so the ancient scroll. Not only are the chapters continuous, but the first words of 62:1 must be treated as be-longing to the preceding verse:[32]

> 61:11 For as the earth brings forth its vegetation,
>   and as a garden germinates the seed sown,
>   So the LORD *God* will bring up vindication
>   and praise before all nations
> 62:1   on Zion's behalf.
>   *And* I will not keep silent;
>   nor on behalf of Jerusalem
>   will I keep quiet,
>   Until her vindication dawns like day-break
>   and her salvation *flames* like a torch.

31. For differences in paragraphing among medieval manuscripts of the Isaiah text, compare the text of S. Baer, *Liber Jesaie*, 1872, with the discussion of C. D. Ginsburg,

Although the Massoretic text likewise proceeds uninterruptedly, its sentence structure is different; for "On Zion's behalf" begins the new sentence of 62:1:

> On Zion's behalf I will not keep silent,
> nor on behalf of Jerusalem will I keep quiet.

The parallelism is better here and thus the text may be judged superior to that of the scroll; and yet the variant construction of the scroll adds emphasis to the ancient understanding that chapters 61 and 62 are inseparable. This is in precise harmony with the view of Alexander Gordon (in *An American Translation*), who puts both chapters together under the heading "The Year of the Lord's Favor."

4. MARGINAL SYMBOLS

In addition to the indention at the beginning of a new paragraph, there may occur a short horizontal line in the right-hand margin. This occurs at 10:27 (the indentation of which is discussed above), at Isa. 40:1, at 53:1, and at numerous other passages.

There are also a number of marginal symbols, some of which are very complicated and all of which are of uncertain significance.[33] Considerable discussion has centered upon the X-mark occurring in the scroll (and also in the Habakkuk Commentary). The Syrian Archbishop, Athanasius Samuel, noticed these before bringing the scrolls to the American School of Oriental Research for study in February 1948. He suggested that these X-marks might be crosses and that the scrolls might thus be shown as having belonged to primitive Christians. I suggested that they were more likely an ancient *T*, being similar to examples of the letter *Tâw* in paleo-Hebrew. Professor J. L. Teicher of Cambridge University identifies the symbol as the Greek letter *Chi*.[34] In his view it marks Messianic prophecies (as for example, certain of the Servant Songs) and is an abbreviation of the word *Christos* — Christ! Professor Isaiah Sonne of Hebrew Union College, however,

---

op. cit. The latter lists twenty-four sectional divisions omitted by Baer, nearly all of which are found in the Isaiah Scroll. There are about twenty-five per cent more gaps in the text of the Isaiah Scroll than in the text of Ginsburg, but many of these are small and may not mark major divisions.

32. The variants of the scroll are italicized.

33. For a list of these symbols, see J. C. Trever in Burrows, *The Dead Sea Scrolls of St. Mark's Monastery*, Vol. I, xvi.

34. "The Christian Interpretation of the Sign X in the Isaiah Scroll," *VT*, Vol. V, 1955, pp. 189–98.

has countered with greater plausibility that the supposed *Chi* is an abbreviation for *chrestos* (excellent), and that it serves simply to mark passages of special interest.[35] Thus unlike Teicher, he would find no reference to Christ in these marks.

One must consider also the possibility that some of the marginal markings (of which there were several kinds) may have indicated lectionary divisions, but it seems even more probable that these symbols were simply a device for marking key passages. In a book as large as Isaiah, with no chapter and verse numbers, they would prove particularly helpful in locating important passages and prooftexts.[36]

5. PUNCTUATION BY ADDITIONAL "AND's" (or WÂW's)

The addition of a *Wâw*, generally translated by "and," sometimes by "but," yet often adequately represented by a comma or a period, is a frequent feature of the Isaiah Scroll. It is the view of the present writer that many of these extra *Wâw*'s were added to the text to aid punctuation, just as vowel letters were often added to assist pronunciation. Thus they are another illustration of the popular character of the Complete Isaiah Scroll. In any case, they are often quite determinative of syntax. Thus in a passage quoted in the Section 3 above, we have already noted that what marks the sentence division between 61:11 and 62:1 is an *and* which compels us to relate the words "on Zion's behalf" with 61:11 rather than 62:1.[37] In this particular case we concluded that the punctuation of the scroll was wrong, but let us turn now to an illustration of correct punctuation (41:2):

> 2 Who aroused Vindication from the east
>   *and* called him to His feet,
>   *And* gave up nations before him —
>   so he subdues kings
>   *And* makes (them) as dust (with) his sword,
>   *dispersing* (them) as chaff (with) his bow?[38]

35. "The X-Sign in the Isaiah Scroll," *VT,* Vol. iv, 1954, pp. 90–94.
36. Although the division of the Hebrew and Aramaic text of the Old Testament into verses "can be traced back to the early centuries of the Christian era" (F. F. Bruce, *The Books and the Parchments,* London, Pikering & Inglis Ltd., p. 118), these were not fixed until medieval times, and they bore no numbers until the fifteenth century. See Frederic Kenyon, *Our Bible and the Ancient Manuscripts,* London, Eyre & Spottiswoode, 4th Ed., 1939, reprinted 1948, p. 226.
37. On pp. 178f.
38. The scroll reads the active participle *nôdêf* ("dispersing") instead of the passive participle *niddâf* ("dispersed," "driven"). The parallelism is a bit fuller here than in the Massoretic reading "as driven chaff with his bow."

Of the three additional "and's," only the first is important for establishing the punctuation of the sentence, for it compels us to follow the Massoretic accentuation which likewise construes the word *ṣedeq* (righteousness, or vindication) with the first stich. The American Standard Version, however, links the word with the second stich, giving it an adverbial sense; and Alexander Gordon followed suit, translating:

> Who has aroused (one) from the east,
> calling him *in righteousness* to His service? [39]

The Standard Bible Committee has likewise put *ṣedeq* in the second clause; but by making *ṣedeq* the subject, they gave the verse a radically different sense:

> Who stirred up (one) from the east
> (whom) *victory* meets at every step? [40]

The meaning "victory" for *ṣedeq* is very doubtful. Moreover, the translators made the risky assumption that the verb *qârâ'* (call) is a misspelling for *qârâh* (meet). The RSV is therefore doubly audacious at this point.[41]

The King James Version, in following the traditional text, translates in harmony with the syntax of the scroll:

> Who raised up the *righteous* (*man*) from the east,
> called him to His foot?

C. C. Torrey rendered it similarly. The King James translators probably thought the passage referred to the Messiah, and so translated "righteousness" as "righteous *man.*" C. C. Torrey's "righteous one" was interpreted by him as referring to Abraham. Most scholars, however, apply the passage to Cyrus, King of Persia, who launched a program of world-wide conquest in the middle of the sixth century B.C. The designation of Cyrus as "righteous" has seemed doubtful. Hence Gordon by his punctuation applies the term "righteousness" to the activity of God in the calling of Cyrus. Ironically, the RSV by its rendering "victory" relates *ṣedeq* to Cyrus, but follows the punctuation of Gordon who achieved the opposite result.

39. In *An American Translation.*
40. RSV, following the view of B. Duhm and T. K. Cheyne, concerning which, see the comments of C. C. Torrey (*op. cit.,* pp. 313f.).
41. The confusion of the two Hebrew roots is not unattested, however. It is the combination of factors involved which militates forcefully against the translation.

The crux of the difficulty is the meaning of *ṣedeq*. How is it to be rendered? To whom does it refer? The punctuation of the scroll compels us to take the noun as a designation of the human conqueror Cyrus, but this does not eliminate the divine reference in the word; for Cyrus is not the embodiment of *ṣedeq* by virtue of his own righteousness, but by virtue of God's righteousness. He is the agent of God's *ṣedeq*.[42]

Since the time of the King James translators, the word *ṣedeq* has become much better understood. Considerable light has been shed upon it through the study of poetic parallelism. The fact that it frequently occurs as a synonym for "salvation" (*yêsha‘* and *yəshû‘âh*) has led to the conclusion that it is often aptly rendered as "deliverance" or "salvation." This is not fully adequate, however, for associated with *salvation* in Old Testament theology is nearly always the related thought of *vindication*. God's saving acts serve to vindicate the righteous from their cruel oppressors and even to vindicate the cause of God Himself.[43] Thus *yêsha‘* and *ṣedeq* (and their cognates) occur frequently as synonyms because vindication and salvation are related concepts.[44]

In the light of the above word study, I believe that the first clause of verse 2 may be correctly paraphrased, "Who has aroused from the east the man Cyrus as an agent of divine deliverance and vindication? Is it the Lord, or some other god?" It is the simple addition of an "and" in the scroll which guides us into the riches of this interpretation.

6. ASSIMILATION TO PARALLEL PASSAGES

Nothing emphasizes more strongly the popular character of the Complete Isaiah Scroll from Qumrân than the way passages are en-

42. Cf. the name of the Messiah in Jeremiah 23:6: "The Lord our Righteousness," and note that Cyrus is called the Lord's anointed in Isa. 45:1. With God's use of Cyrus as an instrument of salvation for His people, compare His use of Assyria as an instrument of punishment (Isa. 10:5, 15).

43. Cf. Pss. 24:5; 54:1; 76:9; 79:9–12; 135:14; 138:7; 141:8–10. The so-called imprecatory Psalms are really prayers for salvation. Cf. the use of the verb *shâfaṭ* in the sense of "deliver by an act of judgment" in I Sam. 24:16; II Sam. 18:19, 31.

44. Some have tried to stress this relationship to the extent of eliminating the element of justice in *ṣedeq* and its cognates. This overlooks the fact that the very verb "to save," can mean "to avenge," particularly in the expression "his own hand has saved (avenged) him." Cf. I Sam. 25:26, 33; CDC ix, 9–10 (10:6); 1Q S vi, 27. Salvation as a work of avenging is supposed to deliver; but in the case of Samson there was only avenging (Judges 13:5; 14:19; 15:3–5, 15; 16:30). This was at first largely a matter of avenging himself; but in the end he sacrificed himself and avenged Israel as well. Since his deeds did not bring deliverance, but only the vengeful side of saving activity, his work was incomplete. He had but *begun* to save Israel (Judges 13:50), his deeds being only precursors of the ultimate deliverance through Samuel, Saul, and David.

riched and harmonized with similar passages elsewhere. We now turn to a discussion of the different forms of this enrichment and harmonization.

A. *Enrichment from Parallel Passages in Isaiah*

At the conclusion of 1:15 one finds an additional clause in the scroll:

> Though you multiply your prayers,
> I will not listen;
> Your hands are full of blood,
>   *your fingers with iniquity.*

The added clause fills out the parallelism and has therefore been viewed with favor by several scholars,[45] but the clause is really to be accounted for as a borrowing from Isa. 59:3:

> For your hands are defiled with blood
> and your fingers with iniquity.

That the last clause is an intrusion into 1:15 is apparent when one observes that the preposition "with" (*bǝ*) is normally employed with the verb "defiled" but not with "full."

Another example of this same sort of enrichment may be found in 51:6:

> Lift up your eyes to the heavens,
> and look at the earth beneath. ·

At this point the scroll adds from 40:26, "and see who created these." Again at 52:12b note the addition of the final clause:

> For the LORD will go before you,
> and the God of Israel will be your rear guard;
>   *the God of all the earth will He be called.*

The supplement which derives from 54:5 is quite appropriate immediately before the "Great Servant Song" of 52:13—53:12, in which the redemption of the whole world through the Lord's Servant is portrayed. Still, this identification of Israel's God with the God of the whole earth probably stood originally only at 54:5.

B. *Enrichment from Parallels in Other Books*

A common feature of vulgar texts is the enrichment of passages from similar materials in other Biblical books. This is a constant feature of

45. Cf. Sutcliffe's support of this reading, *op. cit.*, p. 11.

the Samaritan Pentateuch, in which the legislation of Moses in Exodus (for example) is enlarged from related material in Deuteronomy.[46] This is to be seen also in the *Textus Receptus* of the New Testament (on which the King James Version is based) wherein the text of one of the Gospels may be supplemented from material belonging originally only to the other Gospels,[47] or where Colossians may be enriched from its sister epistle, Ephesians.[48] A most striking example of this phenomenon is to be found in the scroll text of Isa. 34:3:

> Their slain shall be flung out,
>   and from their corpses their stench shall rise.
> *The* mountains shall melt down with blood,
>   *and the valleys shall be cleft.*

The last clause is a borrowing from Micah 1:4 and even the article with "mountains," which is lacking in the traditional text, may come from that source:

> And *the* mountains shall melt under him,
>   *and the valleys shall be cleft.*

The phrasing *"melt* down with blood" is so peculiar it is clear that the author of Isa. 34 was consciously conforming his language to that of Micah, despite the unsuitableness of the verb in the new context. The Isaiah Scroll through its closer agreement with Micah indicates that the two passages were correlated in interpretation.

Lest certain scholars be enamored by a presumed better parallelism of such readings of the scroll, one should point out that the tristich pattern of the original text in certain places was a contributing factor to the enrichments. The third member of a tristich line is often not

46. In this manner, Deut. 27:4–8 was inserted after Ex. 20:17 and Deut. 5:21 in order to become the Tenth Commandment according to the Samaritan reckoning. Thus the last Word of the Decalogue was the command to write the Ten Commandments upon the altar to be erected at Mount Gerizim (the Samaritan text reading Gerizim, rather than Ebal). The traditional Ten Commandments were kept to nine by combining the first two (Ex. 20:2–6; Deut. 5:6–10) after the manner of the Roman Catholic Church, which attains the number ten by dividing the last Commandment into two separate commands, through setting apart the first clause of Deut. 5:21 as the Ninth Commandment. Rabbinic Jewish reckoning makes the prefatory remark of Ex. 20:2 and Deut. 5:6 the First Word and then combines unto a single Commandment what Evangelical Christians take to be the First and Second.
47. Cf. Matth. 18:11, which was probably borrowed from Luke 19:10 and is missing from the most ancient Greek manuscripts of Matthew.
48. Cf. the marginal addition to Col. 3:6 in the RSV, which was probably derived from Eph. 5:6.

in strict parallelism with the preceding stichs, but is rather its climax or conclusion. Tristichs may appear suddenly in a distich context. In such cases there would be the temptation on the part of an ancient scribe to carry through the distich parallelism by adding a new stich derived from a parallel passage, thus producing two distichs where before there had been only a single tristich. Similarly, certain modern scholars have been loath to recognize the validity of the tristich and have in various passages suggested the loss of a stich from the original text; or, conversely, they have quite unnecessarily suspected the third stich of being an interpolation. Today the existence of this stich is generally recognized and there is no problem as to the literary propriety of such a line as the following:

> Their slain shall be flung out,
> and from their corpses their stench shall rise —
> the mountains melting down with blood!

c. *Harmonization by Alteration*

Sometimes one suspects harmonization of one passage with another through alteration. Under this category are to be included slight departures from the original forms of the words of the Hebrew text in order to make them conform more closely to another passage. Often, of course, the alteration may be accidental and unconscious rather than deliberate, but in either case such changes would contribute to the harmonious interpretation of the passages.

As an example of such assimilation of one passage to another, one may note the scroll's text of Isa. 7:14. It reads "His name *shall be called* Immanuel" rather than "*She shall call* His name Immanuel." The former reproduces precisely the verbal form of 9:6, "*His name shall be called* Wonderful Counselor, etc.*"

Similarly in 40:18 we discover a first person text where the Massoretic text reads the third person. The wording of the latter is:

> So to whom would you liken *God*,
> or what likeness compare with *Him?*

The scroll, however, reads:

> So to whom would you liken *Me*, God,
> or what likeness compare with *Me?*

The latter is certainly influenced (probably unconsciously) by 40:25:

"So to whom would you liken Me
that I be comparable?" says the Holy One.

In all cases of increased similarity in parallel texts, preference should be given to divergence of reading rather than to sameness of reading. Repeatedly this rule favors the Massoretic text over the Isaiah Scroll, even though the latter is centuries older.

Some alterations in the scroll are of such an involved character that they are explicable only as deliberate emendations. Isa. 6:9-10 in the scroll may be rendered as follows:

> 9 Keep on listening, *because* you may understand;
>   keep on looking, *because* you may perceive!
>   *Make* the heart of this people *appalled:*
> 10   stop its ears
>   and turn away its eyes —
> lest it see with its eyes
>   and hear with its ears.
> *Let* it understand in its heart
>   and return and be healed.

In the traditional (and doubtless original) text, the purpose of the prophet's ministry is described as one of hardening the hearts of the people lest they understand in their hearts and repent and be healed. The sense of the passage is reversed in the scroll text through four slight alterations. Instead of the particle *'al* meaning "not," we find *'al* which may mean "because." This could have arisen through accidental misspelling (especially likely if the manuscript were copied from dictation), but it is remarkable that the same error occurs twice in immediate sequence. The next variant involves simply the omission of a single letter from the word *HŠMN* (make fat) so as to produce *HŠM* (make appalled). The final alteration is the omission of an *and* before the last line of Hebrew poetry [49] so that the force of the negative particle "lest" is broken, so that *"and (lest)* it understand" becomes "Let it understand." [50] Singly each one of these errors can be explained as accidental, but when viewed collectively they impress one as a deliberate reshaping of the text.

We are not left to guesswork regarding the optimistic interpretation

49. On the nature of a poetic line in Hebrew, see above, p. 159, n. 8.
50. There were doubtless exceptions to this rule in Hebrew poetry, as for example, I Sam. 2:3, where a series of asyndeton clauses follow a single negative; but cf. 4Q Samᵃ on this passage.

which was given the scroll text, for a passage in one of the Qumrân Hymns is clearly dependent upon this interpretation:

> Turn my eyes away from seeing evil,
>   my ears from hearing of murder.
> Make my heart appalled at evil thoughts.[51]

Every one of the verbs of this verse comes from Isa. 6:9–10, as also the organs of perception: "eyes," "ears," and "heart." The hymnic passage is also enriched by allusion to Isa. 33:15, where the righteous person is described as one

> Who stops his ears from hearing of *murder*,
>   and shuts his eyes from looking upon *evil*.

From this passage the words "evil" and "murder" were drawn by the hymn writer as the unexpressed (but understood) objects of the verbs in Isa. 6:10:

> Make the heart of this people appalled (*at evil*)
>   stop its ears
>   and turn away its eyes —
> lest it see (*evil*) with its eyes
>   and hear (of *murder*) with its ears.

Thus Isaiah's mission is interpreted as that of producing men of the quality described in Isa. 33. He was to be a preacher of repentance.

Still another passage may have influenced the text of the Isaiah Scroll. Hos. 5:15—6:1, when corrected in the light of the Septuagint, reads as follows:

> I will return again to my place
>   until they *are appalled* and seek my face,
>   and in their distress they seek me, saying,
> "Come, let us *return* to the LORD:
>   for He has torn, that He may *heal* us;
>   He has stricken, and He will bind us up."

In this text we find the verbal sequence of *appall*,[52] *return* (or repent), and *heal*, exactly as occurs in the scroll text of Isa. 6:9–10. Thus this

---

51. 1Q H vii, 3. Cf. Meir Wallenstein, "A Striking Hymn from the Dead Sea Scrolls," *BJRL*, Vol. 38, No. 1 (Sept. 1955), pp. 241–65, with attention here to his numbered stichs 182–4 (p. 264). I had independently noted the parallel.

52. On confusion of the roots *'ŠM* and *ŠMM*, cf. the JBL Monograph Series, Vol. XI, p. 24, on Hab. 1:11, also G. R. Driver in *Occident and Orient*, 1936, pp. 75–7.

passage appears to have been of considerable influence in the shaping of the Isaiah text. The subtle accommodations of Isa. 6:9–10 to such widely separated passages as Hosea 5:15–6:1 and Isa. 33:15 are explicable only as the product of clever and *purposeful* alterations on the part of a scribe of profound Biblical scholarship.

7. UNDERLYING ALLUSIONS MADE EXPLICIT

The text of Isa. 56:10 in the Complete Isaiah Scroll differs subtly from that of the Massoretic text. It reads:

> His watchmen are blind,
> > all of them ignorant.
> They're all dumb dogs,
> > unable to bark!
> Sleeping *seers are they*,
> > loving *oracles!*

The last line in the Massoretic text reads:

> Sleeping *dreamers*,
> > loving *to slumber*.

Apart from the addition "are they," which is metrically helpful, the scroll differences are slight. Instead of *hôzîm* ("delirious dreamers"), the scroll reads *ḥôzîm* ("seers"); and instead of *nûm* ("to slumber"), it reads strangely *nû'm* ("oracle," or perhaps "to enunciate oracles").[53] In each case it is simply a difference of a single letter, and in the pronunciation of the Qumrân Community there would have been practically no difference between the words.[54] Yet the writing of the word "oracle" instead of "slumber" involved the addition of an extra letter whose intent was clearly to suggest the former. Most scholars will agree that the Massoretic text is more accurate, especially since the other, fragmentary Isaiah from the first scroll cave preserves the traditional wording.

These variants may or may not have arisen as scribal blunders; but they are not to be lightly dismissed as only that, for in truth they bring to the surface the underlying allusions of the original text. Third Isaiah (who composed this passage) is indicting the false prophets of

---

53. The verbal use of the root is attested by Jer. 23:31.
54. '*Âlef* (') in Qumrân usage tended to be quiescent, so that it was a matter of indifference as to which side of an '*Âlef* the vowel letter was inserted. Thus *Wâw* may occur on either side of the '*Âlef* in the word *M'D(H)* in the scroll.

Judah who claimed to be "seers," but he substitutes his sarcastic pun "delirious dreamers." They claimed to receive "oracles," but the prophet will recognize only that they "slumber." They doubtless did sleep in some shrine where their dreams were interpreted as "oracles." This kind of sleep is referred to by students of religion as incubation. The erroneous readings of the scroll correctly interpret the spurious claims of the false prophets. This may be regarded as purely accidental, or as another example of the interpretative character of the scroll text.

With our eyes open to the prophet's use of punning surrogates for the spurious claims of self-styled "seers," we may look for other examples of his sarcasm. The following verse offers possibilities:

> The dogs are gluttonous,
>   knowing no satiety.
> They are shepherds
>   who know not how to discern.
> They've all turned to their own way,
>   each from all quarters to his profiteering.

In the scroll there is a scribal ambiguity in the writing of the word "satiety" ($\acute{S}B'H$), whose second letter, though squat like the scroll's B, is in the formation of its left side similar to the scroll's M.[55] This last would allow for the alternative reading $\check{S}M'H$ (sound, report, message) and one could translate:

> The dogs are gluttonous,
>   recognizing no sound
>   (or, discerning no message).

"Discerning no message" affords actually a better parallel to the following "who know not how to discern," and yet "satiety" fits better the description of these watchdogs as "gluttonous." The other Isaiah Scroll, moreover, attests the traditional reading.

In this same verse we find the use of the word "shepherds" ($r\acute{o}'\hat{\imath}m$), where actually a word for "seers" ($r\acute{o}'\hat{\imath}m$) would fit better the statement that they "know not how to discern" God's purpose. At this point the ancient Greek and Syriac translators read $ra'\hat{\imath}m$, "evil ones," which is a possible reading of a purely consonantal spelling as found in the Fragmentary Isaiah Scroll. The Targum rendered the word as "evil doers," as though reading $r\acute{o}'\partial'\hat{\imath}m$, but it is not impossible that $r\acute{o}'\hat{\imath}m$ was.

55. Another example of the ambiguous writing of a letter is probably to be seen in the *Dâlet-Rêsh* of the last word of 1Q pHab xi, 3.

regarded as a contracted form of this. In his choice of this ambiguous word, the original prophet may have resorted once more to a punning surrogate, rejecting the spurious claim of those who called themselves *rô'îm*, "seers."

Isaiah 56:9–12 is but one part of the prophet's condemnation of cultic abuses. The theme is carried forward into the next chapter. Verses 7–8 require consideration here:

> 7 On a hill, aloft and lifted up,
>   you set your *bed!*
>   There also you *retired*
>   to perform sacrifice.
> 8 Behind the door and the doorpost,
>   you erected your symbol;
>   For not with me
>   you disrobed and *retired*.
>   You enlarged your *bed*
>   and *contracted marriages* with them.
>   You loved their bed;
>   you *visioned naked strength!*

Here the prophetic irony is brought to a climax. The reference is to an ancient high place, which its priesthood claimed to be a "tabernacle" (*miškân*), but which the prophet by perversity calls a "bed" (*miškâv*). In the Hebrew text, only the last letter was different. As a matter of fact, Professor H. L. Ginsberg of the Jewish Theological Seminary (New York), has proposed emending the text so as to read either "tabernacle" or "sanctuary." [56] This, however, would in effect be an alteration similar to those of 56:10 in the Isaiah Scroll; for, far from restoring the original text, it would put into writing the spurious claim which the original prophet disdained to concede. Related to the parody of the supposed "tabernacle" as a "bed" is the prophet's use of the verb "go up" which was commonly used in both connections; for the "tabernacle" was upon a high hill and the bed was frequently in an upper chamber (or when weather permitted, on the roof). "To go up," therefore, in association with bed may mean "to retire." [57]

The "symbol" (*ZKRWN*) which is set up in the place of cult involves a play upon the word "male" (*ZKR*).[58] The contracting of mar-

---

56. "Some Emendations in Isaiah," *JBL*, lxix, (1950), pp. 51–60, with attention here to pp. 59f.
57. Cf. the use of this verb with a sexual connotation in Gen. 49:4.
58. Cf. James Muilenburg in *IB*, V, p. 667.

riages alludes to the rites of religious covenant-making with alien gods. The enlargement of the bed in order to make room for these lovers alludes to the enlargement of the tabernacle in order to provide space for more idols. The words "you visioned naked strength" may also be translated "you saw a hand." The verb for "see" (*hâzâh*) is that from which a word for "seers" is derived (*hôzîm*) and refers to the seeing of a vision. The "hand" is the symbol of divine power; but it is also a euphemism for the male phallus, in keeping with the bed motif.[59] That *idolatry is adultery* is a common prophetic theme. Third Isaiah carries the thought further, *the idolatrous sanctuary is not a Bethel, but a brothel!*

There are other examples of the sarcastic surrogate in the Old Testament. The best known is a parody of the name *Ba'al Shâmêm* ("Lord of Heaven") in the Book of Daniel. An image of this Syrian god, identified with the Greek Zeus, was erected by King Antiochus Epiphanes in 168 B.C., on or beside the altar of burnt sacrifice in front of the Jewish sanctuary at Jerusalem. This event is referred to as the "setting up of the desolating and/or shocking abomination" (9:27, 11:31, 12:11) and as "the desolating and/or shocking transgression" (8:13). Here the name Baal is replaced by the dissimilar words "abomination" and "transgression"; but *Shâmêm* is parodied as *shômêm* and *məshômêm,* words which probably conveyed both of two possible meanings — "desolating" and "shocking." Since the prophet cannot concede that Zeus is really "Lord of Heaven," he perverts his name into "desolating and shocking abomination." [60]

There are other illustrations of parody which have escaped general notice. When Zephaniah 3:4 declares: "Her prophets are wanton, faithless men," the word "wanton" (*pôhªzîm*) is a surrogate for their false claim of being "seers" (*hôzîm*). Likewise Jeremiah 23:32 attributes to the false prophets "wantonness" (*pahªzût*) rather than "vision" (*hâzût* or *hâzôt*).[61] Similarly in the Qumrân literature true prophets are called "seers of testimonies" (*hôzê təʻûdôt*), but false prophets are called "seers of error" (*hôzê taʻût*).[62] Again Malachi 2:11 condemns the men of Judah for "profaning the sanctuary of the LORD" and for "marrying the daughter of a foreign god." There is no easily apparent

59. Cf. below, p. 235, n. 41.
60. See H. H. Rowley, *op. cit.,* p. 249.
61. Cf. Isa. 21:2; 28:18; 29:11; Dan. 8:5, 8 for the former, but II Chron. 9:29 for the latter.
62. 1Q M xi, 7; 1Q H iv, 20.

connection between these two charges in English, but the phrase "daughter of a foreign god" (*bat 'êl nêkhâr*) is in Hebrew a parody of "house of God" (*bêt 'êl*) and is therefore a fitting antithesis to "sanctuary of the LORD." Perhaps this indicates that the marrying referred to involves attachment to an idolatrous temple, or even to a god named Bethel.[63] On the other hand, the surrogate *bat 'êl* may stand only formally related to *bêt 'êl* and refer rather to idolatrous women. More probably, there is veiled allusion to both. In this case the old equation *idolatry equals adultery* is literal fact, and no mere figure of speech. The men of Judah are guilty of both crimes.

The punning surrogate is not at all uncommon in the Old Testament, but it can be detected only in the original language, and even then it is usually overlooked.[64] We are therefore profoundly grateful to the Complete Isaiah Scroll, the variants of which have made clear for the first time the nouns which Third Isaiah parodied in 56:10. The recognition of these has given us the eyes to see more deeply into the prophet's message at 56:11 and 57:7f.

63. See W. F. Albright, *From the Stone Age to Christianity, Monotheism and the Historical Process*, Baltimore, Johns Hopkins Press, 1940, p. 188. See also J. P. Hyatt, "Bethel (Deity)," *IDB*, Vol. A–D, p. 390b.
64. Cf., however, the excellent article "Humor" by W. F. Stinespring in *IDB*, Vol. E–J, pp. 660–62.

CHAPTER NINE

1 he Creation of New "Servant Songs"

One of the problems connected with the literary analysis of Second Isaiah (usually defined as Chapters 40–55) has been the number of "Servant Songs" and their literary extent.[1] The four generally recognized are 42:1–4, 49:1–6, 50:4–9, and 52:13–53:12. Some scholars would add to these units a few more verses; some would recognize other passages as "Songs," for example 61:1ff.

In the present chapter, we shall examine two passages which in the peculiar text of the Isaiah Scroll require consideration as "Servant Songs." In the preceding chapter, under point 6, we have already seen how the Isaiah text of the scroll has been assimilated to parallel passages. Similarities of language already existing were increased in order to make the passages more alike. It is this procedure which has resulted in the creation of new "Servant Songs."

ISAIAH 51:4–6

In 1903 Henri Roy argued that 51:1–8 is to be interpreted as a "Servant Song."[2] He assumed the Servant to be the persons described in 51:1 and 51:7, a people devoted to the pursuit of righteousness and vindication. These people are then presented as the personified figure of the Servant who speaks in the first person singular in verses 4–6. The passage as a whole, according to the Massoretic text, reads as follows:

1 Listen to me
you pursuers of righteousness [or vindication],
you seekers of the LORD.
Look to the rock you were hewed from,
to the quarry from which you were dug.

1. For the history of this problem, see Christopher R. North, *op. cit.*
2. *Israel und die Welt in Jesaja 40–55*, Leipzig, 1903. Gerhard Füllkrug, *Der Gottesknecht des Deuterojesaja*, Göttingen, 1899, had argued that verses 4–6 were composed by the author of the "Servant Songs," whom he distinguished from Second Isaiah.

193

2   Look to Abraham your father,
        and to Sarah who bore you;
    For when he was one I called him,
        and I blessed him and multiplied him.
3   For the LORD has consoled Zion,
        has consoled all her ruins.
    He will make her wilderness like Eden,
        her desert like the LORD's garden.
    Joy and rejoicing will be found in her,
        thanksgiving and the sound of song.

4   Listen to me, my people,
        and give ear to me, my nation;
    For law proceeds from me,
        and my just rule for a light to the peoples.
5   I speed my vindication ever nearer,
        my salvation has gone forth,
        and my arms will rule the peoples;
    Far shores wait for me,
        and for my arm they hope.
6   Lift up your eyes to the sky,
        and look at the earth beneath;
    For the sky will vanish like smoke,
        the earth will wear out like a garment,
        and its inhabitants will die like gnats;
    But my salvation will be for ever,
        and my vindication will never be abolished.

7   Listen to me, you knowers of righteousness,
        the people in whose heart is my law.
    Fear not the reproach of men;
        and at their revilings be not alarmed.
8   For the moth will eat them like a garment,
        and the larva will eat them like wool;
    But my vindication will be for ever,
        and my salvation for succeeding generations.

If we assume that the Servant is speaking in verses 4–6, he is clearly differentiated from the Hebrew nation whom he addresses. Though this distinction between the people and the Servant is possible, even with a corporate interpretation of the Servant,[3] those finding a "Servant Song" here cite the authority of the Syriac version for reading:

3. Cf. Isa. 49:6; 50:10; 52:14 (in unemended text); 53:8.

Listen to me, O peoples,
and give ear to me, O nations.

The passage thus begins with an address to the world similar to that
of 49:1. The unemended text, however, with its distinction between the
speaker and his people, would most naturally be understood as referring
to the Messiah who addresses Israel.

Immediately after Roy's identification of this passage as a "Servant
Song," William B. Stevenson in his interpretation restricted the "Song"
to verses 4–6, pointing out that the Lord's Servant is completely personified in the other "Songs" and not addressed in the plural as he
would be in 51:1–3, 7–8.[4]

Stevenson's view was further developed by A. Van Hoonacker, who
suggested linking 51:4–6 directly with 50:10a, the latter serving as an
introduction to the "Song," as follows:[5]

50:10a   Who is among you that feareth *Jahweh?*
         Let him obey the voice of His servant:

51:4–6   "Hearken to me, my people,
         and give ear to me, my nation:
         For a law shall proceed from me
         and I will make my judgment shine . . ."

This critical reconstruction of the passage treats 50:10b–11 as a later
addition and 51:1–3 as misplaced.

Later writers on the subject recognized the real affinities between
verses 4–6 and the "Servant Songs," but they argued that they were an
editorial addition to the text on the part of someone who borrowed the
vocabulary of the "Servant Songs."[6] They set the tone for present-day
criticism which agrees with them in this and interprets the words as an
address by God Himself, rather than as a speech of the Servant. In
the context God addresses His people with a message of comfort at
51:1ff. and also at 51:7f. and it is most probable that He does also at
51:4ff. (Consult the translation of 51:1–8 given above.) Moreover the
possessive pronoun "my," if applied to the Servant, is not suitable to
the nouns "vindication" and "salvation"; for *"my* vindication" and
"my salvation" in the mouth of man (even though he be the Servant)

4. In the *Expositor*, Vol. 6 of the 8th series, 1913, pp. 216ff.
5. "The Servant of the Lord in Isaiah 40ff.," *Expositor*, Vol. 11, 8th series, pp. 182–210,
with attention here to pp. 192f.
6. W. Rudolph in *ZAW*, 1931, p. 108.

would be most naturally interpreted as that which he is to receive rather than that which he is to convey. This difficulty might be overcome by supposing that God is the speaker and that He refers to His servant by the titles "Law," "Just Rule," [7] "Vindication," and "Salvation"; but this identification would seem to be forced as long as verse 5 concludes with the divine declaration:

> *My* arms will rule the peoples;
> far shores wait for *Me,*
> and for *My* arm they hope.

At this point, however, the Qumrân Isaiah substitutes third person pronouns for the first person. The whole passage in the scroll should be examined:

> 4 Listen to Me, My people,
> and give ear to Me, My nation;
> For Law proceeds from Me,
> and My Just Rule for a light to the peoples.
> 5 I speed My Vindication ever nearer,
> My Salvation has gone forth,
> and *his* arms will rule the peoples;
> Far shores wait for *him,*
> and for *his* arm they hope.
> 6 Lift up your eyes to the sky,
> and look at the earth beneath,
> *and see Who created these!*
> [Yet the sky will vanish like smoke,
> the earth will wear out like a garment] [8]
> and its inhabitants will die like gnats;
> But My Salvation will be for ever
> and My Vindication will never be abolished.

7. "Justice" (*mishpâṭ*) should be interpreted as "just rule," both here and in 42:1–4, not as "religion" (or "religious truth").

8. The bracketed words are missing in the text of the scroll, but they were omitted because of damage suffered by the lower margin of the manuscript from which it was copied. The scribe left an incomplete line here for a later insertion of the missing text from another manuscript, but this was never done. For numerous examples of such losses from the text of Isa. 34—66, with the lacunae sometimes filled in later, see my article, "The Manuscripts of Isaiah from which DSIa was Copied," *BASOR*, No. 127 (Oct., 1952), pp. 16–21.

The italicized words represent the scroll's variants. The clause immediately preceding the bracketed omission of the scroll is an addition from Isa. 40:26.

The third person "his" and "him" in verse 5 are differentiated from God who refers to Himself in the first person and also from God's people Israel who are addressed in the second person. The passage is strikingly similar to another "Servant Song," Isa. 42:1–4, which in the scroll reads as follows:

1 Look!
   My Servant whom I uphold,
     My Chosen in whom My soul delights.
   I have put My spirit upon him
     that *his* just rule he may extend to the
     nations.

2   He does not rant or rave,
     or make his voice heard in the streets

3   The down-trodden reed he crushes not,
     and the flickering wick he quenches not —
     in very truth extending justice;

4   *but* he flickers not, nor is downcast,
     ere he establish justice in the earth,
     and far shores *inherit* his law*s*.[9]

The affinities between the two passages is emphasized by their common use of the Servant designations "Law" and "Just Rule." His role as "a light to the peoples" may be compared with the similar language of 42:6 and especially that of 49:6:

   I make you a light to the nations,
     to be My salvation to earth's end*s*.

Here the Servant is described as an agent of God's saving work, in exact accord with the title "My Salvation" of 51:5. Similarly, the name "My Vindication" may be paralleled by the title of Cyrus at 41:2, although the possessive pronoun is lacking there. The declaration that "far shores" await the Servant's coming agrees more closely with the Massoretic text of 42:4, "far shores *wait for* (not inherit) his law." The traditional reading is undoubtedly correct.

Superficially, therefore, we have an acceptable "Servant Song" in the scroll text of 51:4–6. God is the speaker as the context requires, and the attributes and functions of the Servant are proclaimed by God Himself precisely as they are in 42:1–4 and 49:6. It is not surprising there-

9. The variants are italicized.

fore that D. Barthélemy, who was the first to point out the significance of the variants in 51:5, should believe that the scroll's third person pronouns are original and that the Jews later altered them to the first person in order to avoid a Messianic interpretation.[10] For my part, I believe quite the opposite to be the case: some scribe of the Qumrân Community (or a predecessor among the Hasidim) altered the text in the interest of assimilating the passage to the "Servant Songs." In fixing the Massoretic text at a later date, the Jewish authorities followed manuscripts which did not contain these Messianized readings.

Some reasons for rejecting the scroll variants at 51:5 as original readings are: (1) The defective spelling of "his arms" in the Hebrew (*ZRW'W* rather than *ZRW'YW*) would suggest that the original reading was "My arms" (*ZRW'Y*) which has been simply converted by changing the last letter. On the other hand, these readings are no mere slip of the pen; for no such explanation can account for the full spelling of "for him" (*'LYW*) which replaces "for Me" (*'LY*).[11] (2) The Messianizing of the passage is in accord with the eschatological interests of the sect which prepared the scroll, as also with their practice of making parallel passages even more similar to one another. (3) The

10. "Le grand rouleau d'Isaïe trouvé près de la Mer Morte," *RB*, LVII, 1950, pp. 530–49, with attention to p. 548.
11. Note that the variant calls for the addition of an extra letter, and that further the *Wâw* and *Yôd* are clearly distinguished. R. E. Brown rejects these variants (in Stendahl, *op. cit.*, p. 204), but he fails to note the additional letter. The scholars whom he cites on the confusion of the letters both agree on their clear distinction in this scroll! That *Wâw* might appear in place of *Yôd* by reason of a confusion in pronunciation (as he also suggests) is impossible, since *i* and *ai* are not similar in sound to *ô* and *âw*. If one asks, "How can we know which readings represent Qumrân interpretation, since the other Isaiah Scroll (1Q Isa^b) follows closely the Massoretic text?" the answer is that only where there are interpretative variants, as in 1Q Isa^a, may we discern the interpretation from a Biblical manuscript! That such variants really exist in 1Q Isa^a, see Arie Rubinstein, "The Theological Aspect of Some Variant Readings in the Isaiah Scroll," *JJS*, VI, 1955, pp. 187–200, especially pp. 198–200; John V. Chamberlain, "The Functions of God as Messianic Titles in the Complete Qumrân Isaiah Scroll," *VT*, V, 1955, pp. 366–72.
  A. S. van der Woude, *Die messianischen Vorstellungen der Gemeinde von Qumrân*, pp. 168f., has argued that the variant readings are merely personifications, not without parallel in Wisdom Literature. A close parallel (not cited by van der Woude) is given by Helmer Ringgren, *Word and Wisdom, Studies in the Hypostatization of Divine Qualities and Functions in the Ancient Near East*, Lund, Hakan Ohlson, 1947, p. 54. That such hypostatized attributes of God may find expression through a human agency is well illustrated by the title *ṣedeq* ("Vindication") used of Cyrus in Isa. 41:2 (cf. above, pp. 181f.) and by "the Word of the LORD in the land of Damascus" employed for Alexander the Great in Zech. 9:1. See M. Delcor, "Les allusions à Alexandre le Grand dans Zach IX, 1–8," *VT*, I, pp. 110–24.

extreme apocalypticism of 51:6 sounds more like Third Isaiah (author of chapters 34–35, and much of 56–66) than Second Isaiah (author of chapters 40–55), so that 51:4–6 appears to be an interpolation made by Third Isaiah. There are those, to be sure, who assign all the "Songs" to Third Isaiah, and yet one never encounters the title Servant as a collective figure in chapters 56–66, the word always occurring in the plural, and not by way of designating men with a divine commission but only as His subjects and worshippers. It is therefore more likely that 51:4–6 is a little section composed by Third Isaiah, who repeatedly speaks of God's direct intervention to bring salvation, without any reference to a Messianic mediator.[12] The author as a disciple of the Second Isaiah was influenced by his master's language, but never himself wrote "Servant Songs." [13]

In our approach to 51:4–5, we have assumed a unity of reference in the titles "Law," "Just Rule," "Vindication," and "Salvation"; for if the scroll be cited on behalf of an *original* "Servant Song" here, this alone could be the meaning. These terms standing in parallelism must in that case be synonymous. However, the Qumrân Community sometimes disregarded the laws of parallelism, interpreting each phrase as a detached entity. There is, therefore, no special difficulty in accommodating 51:4–5 to the Messianic expectation of the Essenes. These terms could easily have been distributed among its several eschatological figures. Thus "Law" (Torah) could have been applied to the historical Teacher of Righteousness, to the coming Prophet, or to either of the two expected Messiahs. The term "Just Rule" would most aptly fit the royal Messiah. The same reference is possible for the term "Vindication" (or "Righteousness"), but it might just as easily have been applied to the Righteous Teacher. The term "Salvation" was doubtless interpreted as the militant royal Messiah, for the Book of Jubilees and the Testaments of the Twelve Patriarchs with their many affinities with Essene literature attest the use of his title for the Davidic Messiah.[14]

12. Isa. 35:4; 59:16–20; 62:11—63:3; 64:1–3.
13. Second Isaiah is basically Chaps. 40—55, and Third Isaiah may be loosely defined as Chaps. 34—35 and 56—66; but Third Isaiah is not necessarily a unity. The nearest thing to a Servant Song written by Third Isaiah is 61:1ff.; but the Targum probably understands this passage correctly as the prophet speaking in the first person of himself. It was his personal mission "to proclaim the year of the Lord's favor, and the day of vengeance of our God." With 61:2, cf. 34:8 and 63:4.
14. Cf. *NTS*, iii, pp. 195–7, especially, p. 197, notes 2–4. On the salvific role of Davidic Messiah, cf. 4Q Midrashim i, 13, as published by Allegro in the *JBL*, lxxvii, 1958, p. 353, and cf. the *JBL*, lxxv, 1956, p. 177.

ISAIAH 62:10–12

As a corollary to the designation of the Servant as Salvation in 51:5, the term "Salvation" could have been interpreted as his title also in other passages, such as Isa. 62:11; but it must be studied in context.

10   Pass out through the gates,
        clear the way for the people.
      Build up, build up the highway;
        free it from stones *of stubbing*.
      Say among the peoples:

11   "Behold, the LORD!"

      Proclaim to the end of the earth;
        say to Maiden Zion:

      "Look! your Salvation has come.
        See, his reward is with him,
        and his recompense before him.
12   They shall be called the Holy People,
        the Redeemed of the LORD;
      and you shall be called Sought Out,
        a city not deserted."

The differences in verse 10 are to be accounted for by the influence of literary parallels. "Stones *of stubbing*" for simply "stones" reflects Isa. 8:14, where we have the parallel phrases "stone of stubbing" and "rock of stumbling." "Say among the peoples" is a radical departure from "Lift up an ensign over the peoples." Perhaps the manuscript from which our scroll was copied was illegible at this point and the scribe merely guessed what belonged here.[15] In any case what he wrote seems to have its closest parallel in Psalm 96:10: "Say among the nations, 'The LORD reigns!'" The result is most impressive, a perfect balancing of "Say among the peoples" with "Say to Maiden Zion." This ingenious product could not have arisen without design. "Behold, the LORD! Proclaim . . ." differs only by a single letter from the Massoretic text, "Behold, the LORD has proclaimed . . ." The variant could also be translated, "Behold, the LORD has *summoned* him" by

15. Cf. n. 8 above.

vocalizing the word as *hishmî'ô* instead of *hishmî'â*.[16] Thereby the "him" (of "summoned him") becomes the Messianic Servant of the Lord referred to explicitly in the address to Maiden Zion as "Salvation." In both addresses there is the same proclamation of the Messianic deliverer. The parallelism is complete. The reference to the Servant may be reinforced by citing again Isa. 49:6*b*:

> I appoint you to be a light to the nations,
> to be *My salvation to the end of the earth*.[17]

Isaiah 62:11a announces the fulfillment of this promise:

> Look! the LORD has summoned *him*
> *to the end of the earth.*

The reading *hishmî'ô* ("has summoned him") is refuted by other Isaianic passages which influenced the wording of 62:11. Note the following:

> Say to the cities of Judah,
> *"Behold, your God!"*　　　　　　　　　　　　　　(40:9c)

> With resounding voice *proclaim* this;
> send it forth *to the end of the earth.*　　　　(48:20b)

In 40:9 we see an analogy to "Behold, the LORD" of 62:11. Likewise, 48:20 was the inspiration for "Proclaim [*hishmî'â*] to the end of the earth." The parallel addresses "among the peoples" and "to Maiden Zion" may well equate "the LORD" and "your Salvation." Yet in the light of 51:4–5, the latter could be interpreted as the Messianic agent of the former.[18]

SALVATION AS A MESSIANIC TITLE IN THE NEW TESTAMENT

The transformed, Messianic sense of 62:11 is attested by Matthew's combining of Scriptures. Compare the following:

> Say to Maiden Zion:
> Look! Your salvation has come.　　　　　　　　(Isa. 62:11)

16. For the meaning "summon," cf. Jer. 50:29: "Summon archers to Babylon."
17. Cf. the LXX, KJV, and ASV. The construction is ambiguous, but the parallelism here is better than in the RSV.
18. Note that in Isa. 41:2 the Lord's agent of vindication (Cyrus) follows at the Lord's "feet." Both are on the move. Cf. above, pp. 180ff.

> Rejoice greatly, O Maiden Zion;
> shout, O Maiden Jerusalem:
> Look! your king is coming to you.   (Zech. 9:9)

> Say to Maiden Zion:
> Look! Your king is coming to you.   (Matth. 21:5)

This putting together of Zech. 9:9 and Isa. 62:11 tacitly identifies the promised "salvation" with the Messianic "king." The interpretation must have been especially attractive to Matthew, who elsewhere puns the name Jesus (*Yêshû'a* from *Yəhôshû'a,* meaning *"Yahweh* saves") by declaring: "You will call his name Jesus, for He will *save* his people from their sins." [19]

Likewise Luke records that when the priest Simeon took the infant *Yêshû'a* into his arms, he chanted his *Nunc Dimittis,* saying:

> Lord, now lettest Thou Thy servant depart in peace,
>   according to Thy word;
> For mine eyes have seen Thy Salvation
>   which Thou hast prepared before the face of all people;
> A light to lighten the nations,
>   and the glory of thy people Israel.[20]

The song is replete with allusions to the language of the Second Isaiah, especially the "Servant Songs" (Isa. 42:6; 49:6; also 52:10); and, as in the sectarian readings of the large Isaiah Scroll from Qumrân, "Salvation" is clearly a Messianic title, for Simeon's expectation of living to *"see* the Lord's Christ" (Luke 2:26) was fulfilled in the *seeing* of God's "Salvation." [21]

Similarly, in Luke's story of Zachaeus, the Master invited Himself to Zachaeus' house, saying, "Today, I shall stay in your house." [22] When Zachaeus later promised to make fourfold restitution for any fraudulent exactions of taxes of which he had been guilty, Jesus said: "Today, Salvation has come to this house, inasmuch as he also is a son of Abraham; for the Son of Man has come to seek and to save the lost." [23]

---

19. Cf. *NTS,* III, pp. 197f.
20. Luke 2:25–32.
21. Cf. *NTS,* III, p. 196.
22. Luke 19:5.
23. Luke 19:9–10. The clause, "inasmuch as he also is a son of Abraham," means "because he is still a Jew, despite his present lost condition." Cf. Matth. 10:5–6.

The "I" of Jesus' self-invitation is replaced by the titles "Salvation" and "Son of Man" in the later words of Jesus.

In the Fourth Gospel also, there is probably an example of "Salvation" being employed as a Messianic title. When in John 4:22 Jesus says to the woman of Samaria that "Salvation is from the Jews," he means that the Messiah is to spring from the tribe of Judah rather than from the Israelite (and allegedly half-breed) tribes of Samaria; for the term "Jew" in this Gospel is employed in its original meaning "Judean." The impression which Jesus' personality makes upon this woman leads her to say to the Shechemites, "Is not this the Messiah?" When they hear Him for themselves, they confess, "This is indeed the Messiah, the Savior of the world!" Now between "Salvation" and "Savior" as titles there is very little difference. In fact, where Old Testament writers speak of God as their "Salvation," the ancient Jewish translators sometimes render the word as "Savior." [24] In this they interpreted correctly, because of the personal character of the "Salvation." It is not surprising, therefore, that the New Testament should generally prefer the personal title "Savior" to the more abstract designation "Salvation."

The occasional use of "Salvation" as a Messianic title in the Gospels does not in any way indicate that the Gospel writers were familiar with the Qumrân Scrolls, but rather that the Messianic use of the title (and probably, also, the Messianic interpretation of certain passages in Isaiah) was of wider currency than the society at Qumrân. [25]

24. For the translation of *yêsha'* and *yoshû'âh* as *sôtêr* in the LXX, cf. Deut. 32:15; Ps. 24:5 (Heb. and Eng. 25:5); Isa. 12:2; Micah 7:7. In the reading of S at Isa. 25:9, *epi tô sôtêri* appears for the usual *epi tê sôtêria*. Similarly, the two recensions of the Testament of Joseph 19:11 differ as to whether to render the Semitic original as *sôtêr* or *sôtêria*. In the Targum, the rendering *pârîq* ("savior") is also common. Cf. Exodus 15:2; Isa. 12:2b; 62:11.

25. Cf. my comments in the *New Republic*, Vol. 134, No. 15 (April 9, 1956), p. 22b. See also L. Cerfaux, "Influence de Qumrân sur le Nouveau Testament," Rech. Bib., iv, pp. 233-44.

CHAPTER TEN

A Messianic Variant of the "Great Servant Song"

The "Great Servant Song" (52:13—53:12) in which Christians from the most primitive times have seen a prophecy of the death and resurrection of Jesus is a chapter which naturally elicits particular interest. Its text is difficult at a number of points and seems to differ considerably from the Hebrew prototype of the Greek Septuagint. This fact alone naturally draws particular attention to the text of the scroll. As we shall see later, although there are a few significant readings in harmony with the Septuagint version, by far the greatest interest has been focused upon the text of Isa. 52:14. For here we seem to have the reading "anointed" rather than "marred." When first sampling the text of the scroll in February 1948, I was unimpressed by it, recognizing that such a reading would be for classical Hebrew both unintelligible and unsuited to the context. I thereby surmised that the reading could be a double reading in which were combined the words "I marred" and "was marred." Remove the first letter of the word MŠḤTY and the former reading would be obtained; remove the last letter of the word, and the latter meaning would be obtained. This was my explanation of the reading for a number of years, even after D. Barthélemy in 1950 (following the publication of the text of the scroll) argued that Isa. 52:14 is a Messianic variant. I was unimpressed by Barthélemy's argument in view of the forced translation of the passage to which he had to resort in order to obtain an acceptable sense:

> Whereas many remained astonished before your calamity,
> I, by my anointing have given him a countenance more than
> human, its splendor eclipsing the sons of Adam.

The difficulty which I encountered was occasioned by Barthélemy's zeal in the recovery of original Messianic readings which had been altered by later Jews in an effort to expunge from the Scriptures material affording Messianic prooftexts for the Christians.[1] Having for many years given up the direct Messianic significance of the "Servant Songs," I was not prepared to recognize at once Messianic variants in the Isaiah Scroll, especially where they were less agreeable to the context than the Massoretic readings. It was not until August 1953, when to my amazement there came the recognition of the use of Isa. 52:14–15 in depicting the role of an expected Messianic Prophet in the fourth column of the Manual of Discipline, that my eyes were suddenly opened to the vital significance of these Messianic variants; but my fresh understanding was one wholly different from that of Barthélemy, for far from recognizing these variants as representing the original text of Isaiah, I argued rather that these variants represented deliberate alteration of the Hebrew text in order to produce the desired Messianic interpretations. This about-face led to a publication of a series of articles dealing with the Servant of the Lord.[2] My understanding of Isa. 52:14–15 at that time admitted a certain amount of unintelligibility in 52:14, which was rendered as follows:

14 As many were astonished at you —
    I so *anointed* his appearance beyond any one (else),
    and his form beyond that of (other) sons of men —
15 So shall he *sprinkle* many nations *because of himself,*
    and kings shall shut their mouths;
    For that which had not been told them they have seen,
    and that which they had not heard they have understood.[3]

No sooner was this interpretation published than it was subject to attack on the ground of its unintelligibility, and a rival explanation of the supposed "anointed" was given.[4] It seemed quite inappropriate for one to speak of anointing a man's *appearance.* At the same time it was argued that here was an archaic form of the participle so that the reading "I anointed" might (despite the new spelling) be interpreted as "was marred." This explication would have been convincing, even though the alleged participial form is not characteristic of Qumrân

1. In the *RB*, lvii, 1950, pp. 546f.
2. In the weekly issues of the *UP*, the last five issues of 1953 and also of 1954; in the *BASOR*, Nos. 132 (1953) and 135 (1954), and in *NTS*, iii, October and April, 1956–7.
3. Variants of the scroll are italicized.
4. Joseph Reider, "On MŠḤTY¹ in the Qumrân Scrolls," *BASOR*, No. 134 (April, 1954), pp. 27f. This interpretation had been suggested earlier by H. Yalon, in *Kirjath Sepher*, Vol. xxvii, (1951), p. 171, n. 84.

orthography,[5] if it were not that it failed to deal with the evidence which led to the recognition of the truly Messianic character of the reading. This evidence may be analyzed under several heads:

1. *The correlation of the Messianic reading of Isa. 52:14 with other Qumrân texts.* Most important of all is the correlation of this variant with the general interpretive character of the Isaiah Scroll itself (as shown in Chap. 8 above) and with the Messianic variants of Isa. 51:4–5 in particular (as discussed in Chap. 9 above).

In the Qumrân Society Manual (or Manual of Discipline) there is a passage which had first of all been translated in a non-Messianic manner: "Then God will purge by His truth all the deeds of *man, refining for Himself some of mankind."* [6] This translation was open to question inasmuch as the word rendered "man" is employed elsewhere with an individual rather than a collective reference, so that "a man" would have been the natural translation if it had not been for the parallel clause with its presumed reference to "some of mankind" (literally, "some of the sons of men"). Jean-Paul Audet (a French Canadian) and Bo Reicke (a Swedish scholar) each independently advanced a Messianic interpretation of the text. Audet translated, "Then God will purify by His truth all the deeds of *man* and will put in the refining furnace *a certain one* from among the sons of men." [7] This "certain one" is the Messiah, but discordantly "man" of the preceding phrase according to Audet means men in general. Reicke translated: "Then God will purify by His truth all the deeds of *a man* and will separate (*him*) out for himself from the children of men." [8] Audet's interpretation with its disparity of rendering between the two clauses seemed quite tenuous, and Reicke's supplying of an object to the verb in his parenthetical "him" seemed to be a fatal weakness. Consequently the translation of neither made a strong impression, being set aside by me, until quite unexpectedly I got the insight that the passage was to be properly rendered: "At that time God will purify by His truth all the deeds of *a man; and He will refine *him more than* the sons of men." [9] The individual reference in "a man" is to be con-

5. Cf. John V. Chamberlain, "Toward a Qumrân Soteriology," *Nov. Test.*, iii, 1959, pp. 305–313, especially p. 307, n. 1. See Appendix D.
6. 1Q S iv, 20, in *Supplemental Studies*, Nos. 10–22, *BASOR*, 1951, p. 16.
7. In the *RB*, lix, 1952, p. 232.
8. *Handskrifterna från Qumrân*, Symbolae Biblicae Upsalienses, No. 14, 1952, p. 70, and n. 54; "Nytt ljus över Johannes döparens förkunnelse," *Religion och Bibel*, 1952, p. 14.
9. *UP*, Vol. 111, No. 50 (Dec. 14, 1953), pp. 7f.

tinued in the second clause by the recognition of an Aramaism in the Hebrew usage, the word *lô* to be translated "him" rather than "for Himself." The preposition "from" was to be given another common Hebrew meaning of "more than." The whole passage was seen to be an interpretation of the "Great Servant Song." The suffering of the Lord's Servant was interpreted as a refining, as precisely in the free rendering of Isa. 53:10 in the Targum:

> And it was the Lord's good pleasure *to refine* and *to purify* the remnant of his people, in order to cleanse their soul from sin; they shall look upon the kingdom of their Anointed One (or, Messiah), they shall multiply sons and daughters, they shall prolong days, and they that perform the law of the Lord shall prosper in his good pleasure.[10]

Similarly the Manual of Discipline referred to the suffering of the leaders of God's community as designed "to *expiate* iniquity through doing the right and through the anguish of the refining furnace." [11] The "refining furnace" recalls Isa. 48:10 and the work of expiation is reminiscent of the Servant's atoning work in Isa. 53. In the fourth column of the Manual, allusion is made to one whose refining will exceed that of all others, one whom God will "refine *more than* the sons of men." This last seemed to echo Isa. 52:14:

> As many were astonished at you,
>   so his appearance was marred *more than any man,*
>   and his form *than the sons of men.*[12]

Furthermore, it was in accord with the Messianic reading of the scroll at this point, since in the continuation of the same passage there is a promise: "And He *will sprinkle* upon him the Spirit of truth." The verb "will sprinkle" interprets "anoint," indicating the gift of the Spirit to the "man" for a prophetic role (as in Isa. 61:1); and it is precisely the same word found in Isa. 52:15:

> So shall he *sprinkle* many nations because of himself,
>   *and* kings shall shut their mouths.[13]

10. The translation is that of J. F. Stenning, *The Targum of Isaiah*, Oxford, Clarendon Press, 1949, p. 180.
11. 1Q S viii, 3f.
12. The verse is translated here so as to make easy comparison in English with the Manual of Discipline. However, it is capable of a much different translation. Cf. the RSV.
13. In *BASOR*, No. 132, p. 10, I wrote, "For the anointing of the Servant would indicate his consecration for the priestly office so that he could 'sprinkle' others." On the basis of that statement, F. F. Bruce (*Biblical Exegesis in the Qumrân Texts*, p. 51)

This passage seems to say, if one takes seriously the distinction between "you" and "his":

> Just as many were astonished *at you*, the community of God, by reason of your suffering in the destruction of your nation and in the humiliation of the Exile, so also is God's Servant the Messiah an object of amazement by reason of *his* marring which exceeds that of any other.

The differentiation in person is attested in both the Isaiah Scrolls found in the first Qumrân cave and also in the most ancient version, the Septuagint, and thus it seems to be fully verified, beyond question. The Targum and the Syriac appear to be quite secondary in their easier reading of "him" for "you," and are therefore not to be relied upon for the emendation which has been followed by modern versions.[14]

Further description of the man of God's refining in the Manual promises that God "will *sprinkle upon him* the Spirit of truth." The words "sprinkle upon him" are identical with a phrase occurring in Isa. 52:15 in the text of the Complete Isaiah Scroll:

> So shall he sprinkle many nations *upon him* (?),
> *and* kings shall shut their mouths.

The words "upon him" are of doubtful interpretation here, perhaps meaning "because of himself" (that is, because of his own anointing referred to in the preceding verse of the scroll), or perhaps again meaning "unto himself." [15] In any case, the use of the same words in the Manual makes clear an allusion to the Lord's Servant. Sprinkling with *the Spirit of truth* interprets the anointing as a qualification for a prophetic role as in Isa. 61:1; and precisely this role is assigned to the man whom God will refine and endow with the Spirit of truth:

> to give the upright insight into the knowledge of the Most High and into the wisdom of the heavenly beings, in order to make wise the perfect of way.

In one of the Essene Hymns (or Thanksgiving Psalms) is a reference to "a man" who is about to be born through the travail of his

---

has suggested that the reference in the sectarian reading of Isa. 52:14 is to the priestly Messiah. Actually the language of the "Servant Songs" was applied in various ways (including the corporate), so that it would probably be a mistake to restrict the Qumrân understanding to this eschatological figure alone.

14. For a discussion of the various versions in relation to the text and syntax of Isa. 52:14f., see Appendix F.

15. Cf. I Cor. 10:2, "were all baptized *unto* Moses."

mother. Her womb is referred to as her "refining furnace." He is none other than the "Wonderful Counselor" of Isa. 9:6. It seemed only natural at first to think of the mother as the Virgin Israel and of her offspring as the Messiah, and to identify the "man" in each passage as one and the same, combining in himself the roles of Davidic ruler and prophet. Later study, however, has shown that the Messianic hope of Qumrân was tripartite, with the expectation of a prophet like Moses, a priest like Aaron, and a king like David. It has also shown that the motif of the travailing mother was applied to the author of the Hymns and that the Messianic child was interpreted as the religious community to which the author's suffering had given birth.[16] Efforts have been made to show that the passage of the Manual of Discipline should also be interpreted corporately. If so, both passages would refer to the people of God, but to the people with a Messianic mission. However, the challenges to the individual interpretation of 1Q S iv, 20 are not well founded. It now seems probable that this passage refers to an anointed prophet, rather than to a royal Messiah.[17] In either case, the Manual definitely establishes a Messianic interpretation of Isa. 52:13–15.

2. *The correlation of "anointed" and "sprinkle."* The recognition of the reading "anointed" as an original reading in 52:14, according to Barthélemy, may be reinforced by its excellent correlation with the word "sprinkle" in the following verse. Even if we regard the variant as non-original, this correlation certainly serves to reinforce the validity of the sense "anointed" as a real textual reading.

3. *The literary parallel of Psalm 45:8.* By way of reinforcing the possibility of a Hebrew text reading "I *anointed* his appearance *beyond* that of any man," Barthélemy quoted Psalm 45:8 (45:7 in English):

> Therefore God, your God has *anointed* you
> with the oil of gladness *beyond* your fellows.

This parallel passage, however, can equally be claimed as support for the theory that the scroll passage has been harmonized by accommodation to that of the Psalms. Psalm 45, like all royal psalms, came to be interpreted as a Messianic prophecy.[18] Therefore, the parallel is im-

16. See Appendix C.
17. G. Vermès, *op. cit.,* pp. 54ff. See also *NTS,* III, pp. 25f.
18. See Harold Eugene Hill, *Messianic Expectations in the Targum to the Psalms,* Ph.D. thesis, Graduate School of Yale University, 1955 (unpublished).

portant not for the original sense of Isa. 52:14, but for Jewish interpretation of the passage.

4. *The Messianic interpretation of Isa. 52:13 in the Targum.* One need not be unprepared for a Messianic reading in 52:14 in view of the Jewish Aramaic version of the preceding verse:

> Behold, my servant, the Anointed One (or, *the Messiah*), shall prosper; he shall be exalted, and increase, and be very strong.[19]

The origin of the Targum in its traditional roots is pre-Christian. Its insertion of the word "Messiah" (which is lacking in the Hebrew text) is not easily accounted for as the result of Christian influence. More naturally, the differentiation of Judaism from Christianity would have tended to produce the opposite effect. The very retention of the Messianic interpretation of the "Great Servant Song" shows how deeply rooted in tradition this understanding must have been.

5. *The Ambiguity of the Massoretic reading.* The vocalization of *MŠḤT* in the Massoretic text as *mishḥat* is an oddity which has been explained in various ways. The usual explanation of lexicographers is that we have here a nominal form meaning "marring." A very literal rendering of 52:14 would therefore be:

> As many were astonished at you,
> so his appearance was *a marring* beyond man,
> and his form beyond sons of men.

The usual translation "was marred" is simply a paraphrastic translation of this reading, except in the case of a few modern scholars who have followed an ingenious explanation of C. C. Torrey that the word *mishḥat* is a sort of composite reading combining two separate verbal readings: *moshḥât* and *nishḥat,* both of which have the literal meaning "marred."[20] This view was followed by the present writer prior to the autumn of 1953. Since then he has reverted to the older interpretation, having noticed that if the word *mishḥat* is indeed nominal, it is an ambiguous form which in the present construction can mean either "marring" or "anointing."[21] If this ambiguity is as ancient as the second century B.C., and we are now inclined to grant antiquity to many features of the Massoretic text, one may allow that in an interpretative text like the Complete Isaiah Scroll this ambiguity may

19. Stenning, *op. cit.,* p. 178.
20. *Op. cit.,* pp. 415ff.
21. *BASOR,* No. 132, p. 11.

have been resolved on the side of Messianic allusion by the addition of a single letter in order to produce the reading "I anointed." In fact, in the light of the Messianic rendering of the Targum in the preceding verse and the apparent Messianic reading of the scroll, one might suspect an intentional ambiguity in the Massoretic text for the very purpose of suggesting a possible Messianic interpretation alongside the contextual meaning of "marring." This view of the matter was adopted earlier by S. D. Luzzatto in his commentary, who followed a suggestion of one of his students that "the punctuators designedly vocalized the word *mishḥat* in order to alter a meaning alleging blemish and fault to one suggesting the anointing oil of his God."[22]

6. *The Pun "Marring-Anointing" in Daniel.* The above-mentioned facts opened my eyes to an interesting phenomenon in the Book of Daniel, where the presence of the Lord's Servant has not been sufficiently recognized.[23] The most direct Servant allusion is in 12:3:

Teachers of wisdom will shine like the brightness of the sky; and those who make many righteous, like the stars for ever and ever.

Here the term "teachers of wisdom" (*maśkîlîm*) is a participle of the verb *yaśkîl* employed in Isa. 52:13, as though the passage means, "Behold, My Servant shall teach wisdom." "Those that make many righteous" is a parallel expression drawn from 53:11, "My Servant shall make many righteous." These devout teachers are referred to in Dan. 11:33–35 as a persecuted group among whom there are many martyrs who "fall, to refine and cleanse them and to make them white, until the time of the end." Here is the theme of refining associated with the Lord's Servant precisely as in the Manual of Discipline and in the Targum. One may further notice that what is declared of the "teachers of wisdom" is also said of the "many" in 12:10, and that the term "many" (or "great ones") drawn from Isa. 53:11–12 is frequently employed in the Book of Daniel for the persecuted righteous. In Dan. 8:24–25 we find the parallel expressions concerning the action of the fearsome "little horn" that "he shall destroy the *strong* and the people of the saints" and "he shall destroy the *great* (or many)." The Hebrew words "strong" and "great" (or "many") are drawn from

---

22. I have not seen Luzzatto's commentary, but this fact is reported by Arie Rubinstein, Isaiah lii, 14 — *Mishḥat* — and the DSIa Variant," *Biblica*, xxxv, 1954, pp. 475–9, with attention here to p. 475.

23. Cf. *BASOR*, No. 132, pp. 12–15; H. L. Ginsberg, "The Oldest Interpretation of the Suffering Servant," *VT*, iii, No. 4 (Oct. 1953), pp. 400–404.

Isa. 53:12, and the verb "destroy" is of the same root as the noun "marring" of Isa. 52:13. Thus it would appear that the Suffering Servant motif was applied both to the "wise teachers" and to their "many" (or "great") adherents.

The most important fact of all for the present connection concerns the seventy weeks of Dan. 9. The seventy weeks were decreed "to atone for iniquity, to bring in everlasting righteousness, to authenticate both vision and prophet, and to anoint the most holy." *After* the sixty-ninth week, "an anointed one shall be cut off" and "the city and the sanctuary shall be *marred* (or destroyed) along with the coming prince." [24] The seventieth week which was supposed to conclude in anointing, ends rather in marring, the only anointing referred to being that of the "anointed one" (or Messiah) who is to be cut off, and who likewise appears to be the same as the "coming prince" who is to be *marred* at the same time as the city and the sanctuary. This juxtaposition of mar-anoint points doubtless to a punning interpretation of Isa. 52:14 wherein the roots "mar" (*ŠḤT*) and "anoint" (*MŠḤ*) were both seen in the word *MŠḤT*.

This servant theme in Daniel is profoundly important for the scroll texts, for Daniel was written in the same pietist (or Hasidic) circles from which the Essenes emerged. The affinities in this particular case are not hard to find. The members of the sect are frequently called "Many" or "Great Ones." Their priestly instructors are called "the Teachers of Wisdom." [25] Their suffering is often explained in terms of refining. The community itself is sometimes identified with the "sanctuary" and the "most holy." [26] It is in complete consistency with these facts that we acknowledge that both the Hasidim and the Essenes recognized in *mishḥat* (however vocalized) a double reference to marring and anointing. Both groups, moreover, apply the Servant motif to the community at large, to its leaders, and to the Messiah(s).[27]

<hr/>

24. Both Theodotian and the Septuagint versions so interpret the verse, reading '*im*, rather than '*am*. The Septuagint clearly understands the passage as referring to the Messiah.
25. Cf., above, pp. 104ff.
26. Cf. above, Chapter 6, n. 33.
27. In the Targum, also, there are varied interpretations of the Lord's Servant. He appears to be the Messiah in 42:1ff. (see v. 7) and 49:1ff. (see 8b) and is certainly so at 52:13. In the following chapter, the role of the servant according to the Targum is primarily that of the Messiah, but the righteous remnant also make their appearance along with him. In 43:10, the language of the Targum is ambiguous; for one finds there either Israel *and* the Messiah (the former addressed as God's witnesses, the latter

7. *The Concrete Meaning of "Appearance" (mar'èh).* The above arguments seemed quite sufficient in 1953 to warrant reading "I anointed" in the scroll text of Isa. 52:14, but it was open to the charge of being disconsonant with the noun "appearance"; for in the abstract sense an appearance may be marred, but not anointed! This argument seemed fatal to Barthélemy's desire to find here an original reading, but not so to the view that at best this reading represented a subtle textual alteration by way of making explicit a secondary allusion to "anoint" in the word ostensibly meaning "mar."

Later investigation, however, seems to confirm an unexpressed suspicion that the Hebrew word "appearance," like the English word "visage," may have passed from an original meaning of "appearance" to the concrete meaning "face." In this case, there can be no objection to the word on the grounds of incongruity, for a face can be anointed.

The concreteness of the Hebrew word *mar'èh*, seems quite clear in the Songs of Songs 2:14, where the Septuagint translated it by *opsin,* which originally meant "appearance" but came to have the concrete meaning "face." The King James Version employed the word "countenance" which may refer vaguely to one's bearing but may also mean "face." The Revised Standard Version actually translates *mar'èh* as face:

> O my dove, in the clefts of the rock,
>   in the covert of the cliff,
> let me see your *face,*
>   let me hear your voice,
> for your voice is sweet,
>   and your *face* is comely.
>
> (Song of Solomon, 2:14)

Context strongly favors a concrete meaning for *mar'èh* here, for the youth who comes seeking a glimpse of this maiden probably already knew what she looked like, what he wishes to do here is to feast his eyes upon her person. Thus her "appearance" must be as concrete as her "voice"; and "face" is a good guess, better than Moffatt's render-

as God's Servant the Messiah), or Israel *as* the Messiah (interpreting the varied expressions along the line of synonymous parallelism). At 50:10, the Targum applies 50:4ff. to God's "servants the prophets." For the evidence of Jewish Messianic interpretation of Isa. 52:13—53:12 in the Septuagint and in post-Septuagintal Judaism, see W. Zimmerli and J. Jeremias, *The Servant of God,* Studies in Biblical Theology, No. 20, 1957, Chaps. II and III.

ing "form," for the Oriental attire of women is not very form-revealing! Daniel 1:13–15 most strikingly illustrates the inadequacy of "appearance" as a translation of *mar'èh*. The King James translators chose the word "countenance":

> Then let our *countenances* be looked upon before thee, and the *countenance* of the children that eat of the portion of the king's meat. . . . And at the end of ten days their *countenances* appeared fairer and fatter in flesh than all the children which did eat the portion of the king's meat.

At this point the Revised Standard Version represents a retrogression. The translators recognized that a supposed literal rendering: "Let our appearances appear before you" would be tautological, so they paraphrased, "Let our appearance *be observed* by you." The intolerable "their appearances appeared fairer and fatter of flesh" in verse 15 should have driven them to a concrete meaning for "appearance" like "countenances" of the King James Version; but instead they resorted to paraphrase in order to preserve the abstract sense: "They were better in appearance and fatter in flesh." The Septuagint employed the word *opsis* which may mean face. These illustrations are all from late Hebrew; they simply serve to illustrate the propriety of anointing a *mar'èh* in the second century B.C.

Actually the same difficulty of propriety might have been supposed for the word "form" (*tô'ar*), for the root meaning would suggest shape, and anointing in contrast with marring can in no way affect shape; but just as "form" in English can mean either shape or body, so also in Hebrew the word *tô'ar* came to be used concretely for the body itself. An example of this is Lamentations 4:8, where the Revised Standard Version and the King James Version translate with the word "visage":

> Now their *visage* is blacker than soot,
>   they are not recognized in the street.
> Their skin has shriveled upon their bones,
>   it has become as dry as wood.   (RSV)

Here "form" in the abstract sense of "shape" is entirely unsuitable, for shape does not possess color. The word "body," however, would be entirely satisfactory: "Their *body* is blacker than soot." This need not be limited to the face, but naturally the face as the exposed part of the body is involved in the problem of recognition, so that the use of "visage" as a translation is not to be disparaged.

In the light of the above evidence, one may feel justified in translating Isa. 52:14 in the scroll text as follows:

> As many were astonished at you,
> so I anointed his *face* more than any man,
> and his *body* more than the sons of men.

In the original context the astonishment of the many would concern the shocking appearance of the Servant's marred body and equally the Servant's unexpected triumph depicted in the following verse. In the scroll text the astonishment would concern only the Servant's anointing and triumph, despite his terrible affliction depicted in the next chapter.

Professor Alfred Guillaume of Princeton University, who regarded the anointing of an appearance as "intrinsically unlikely," suggested that another meaning for the verb *mâshah* must be found. To find it he resorted to an Arabic root which in the primitive sense meant "to gall the back of a camel and to exhaust it." It is this word which he would read in Isa. 52:14:

> So did *I mar* his appearance from that of man,
> and his form from that of the sons of men.

In fact, he regards the new reading as on the whole more satisfactory than that of the Massoretic text.[28] This suggestion must appear very tenuous, for nowhere else is this root attested in the Old Testament, whereas *mâshah* regularly means "anoint." In the last analysis the difficulty lies not in the *verb* but in the *nouns* which are its object, and these as we have seen came to have concrete meanings, "face" and "body." Guillaume's view is that of pedantic literalism which fails to see that in the readings of the scroll our concern is not simply with the text of the original book, but also with the interpretative alterations of that text. We are dealing with a sectarian Isaiah, almost as truly as the Samaritan Pentateuch is a sectarian Torah.[29]

28. "Some Readings in the Dead Sea Scroll of Isaiah," *JBL,* lxxvi, 1957, pp. 40–43, with attention here to pp. 41f. Cf. the reaction of Bruce, *Biblical Exegesis,* p. 50.
29. Cf. also the alterations of the Soferim, concerning which Jacob Lauterbach, *Rabbinic Essays,* Cincinnati, 1951, pp. 191ff., wrote: "The Soferim were able to do this because they were also the actual scribes whose business it was to prepare copies of the Book of the Law. If they desired to teach a certain law, custom, or practice, because they considered it as part of the religious teachings, although it could not be found in, or interpreted into, the Book of the Law, they would cause it to be indicated by some slight change in the text. For instance, by adding or omitting a letter, or by peculiar spelling of a word they could bring about the desired result. They did not hesitate to do so, because they did not in any way change the law as they understood it."

CHAPTER ELEVEN

Superior Readings in the Isaiah Scroll

THE PROBLEM OF EVALUATING THE TEXT

The Complete Isaiah Scroll from Qumrân is by no means a flawless manuscript. Besides large numbers of accidental scribal mistakes, it contains many interpretative variations. One may even say that almost any medieval manuscript of Isaiah, or even a twentieth-century Isaiah, will on the whole be more accurate than this document coming from the second century B.C. On the other hand, paradoxically, there is more to be learned from this scroll than from a less popular but more accurate text. The reason for this is that we may safely assume that the traditional Hebrew text is very close to the best manuscripts of the second century B.C. A fragmentary document of Isaiah (also from Cave One) reads almost word for word and letter for letter the same as the Massoretic text, although it does contain a few important variants. Several other Isaiah Scrolls from the other Qumrân caves tell the same story. Lest one exaggerate the differences between the great Isaiah Scroll and the traditional text, it must be pointed out that more often than not, except for the free use of vowel letters, even this document supports Massoretic readings. Its disagreements, moreover, are so often inferior that indirectly they attest the superior character of the familiar text. Therefore as proof of the general accuracy of the transmission of the *Massôret* it does almost as well as if it were more accurate, while at the same time it affords us the immense riches of its explanatory variations. Sometimes the interpretations indicated by vowel letters and by more popular phrasing are accurate, sometimes they are not; but in either case they are valuable for the history of Isaiah exposition.

It would be a mistake, however, to conclude with Prof. Harry Orlinsky:

Its text is worthless to the student who wishes to get behind the Massoretic text or to recover the Hebrew *Vorlage* of the ancient primary versions; it is a vulgar text, largely, if not wholly, orally contrived.[1]

Professor Moshe Greenberg evaluates the scroll more fairly in his criticism of Orlinsky's view:

> That Orlinsky may have overstated the case against the textual value of the Isaiah *a* scroll appears to be indicated by the occasional, rare reading which is original and seems superior both to the received Hebrew and the Greek.[2]

It would indeed be most amazing if a scroll so ancient should preserve no superior readings. Conversely, readings which appear superior according to well-established principles of textual criticism, instead of being judged worthless because of the inferior quality of the scroll in which they are found, should rather be treasured because of the antiquity of the document. A variant is not necessarily a doubtful reading just because it occurs in the scroll, for then its prevailing attestation of Massoretic readings must also be judged worthless. It would also be arbitrary to insist that its readings are of value only when they agree with the Massoretic text, for certainly agreement with the Septuagint, with the Targum, and with other ancient versions may be just as valuable. Each reading must stand or fall on its own merit; on the other hand, the worth of each reading must be weighed with care, with due consideration for the popular character of the text.

In earlier portions of this book, certain readings have been judged as superior, or more likely original. Others remain to be considered. The following are especially worthy of note, for some of them may eventually win acceptance in the scholarly world.

The Calf and the Young Lion

An important new reading recognized by Greenberg is in Isa. 11:6:

> Wolf and lamb shall dwell,
> and leopard and kid shall couch.
> Calf and young lion *shall fatten* together,
> while a little child leads them.

---

1. "Studies in the St. Mark's Isaiah Scroll, IV," *JQR*, xliii, 1952–53, pp. 329–40, with the citation here from p. 338.
2. "The Stabilization of the Text of the Hebrew Bible, Reviewed in the Light of the Biblical Materials from the Judean Desert," *Journal of the American Oriental Society*, lxxvi, 1956, pp. 157–66, with the citation here from p. 164, n. 51.

Instead of the verb "shall fatten" (*yimrû,* contracted from *yimrə'û*), the Massoretic text reads "and fatling" (*ûmərî'*).[3] The verbal reading would seem to be attested by the Septuagint, but until the scroll was found, it was uncertain what Hebrew verb should be read. Because of the similarity of the verb (*YMR'W*) and the noun (*WMRY'*) in the original consonantal text (where in one stage of transmission *W* and *Y* were somewhat similar), it was easy for the words to become confused — especially in view of the rarity of the intransitive form of the verb "fatten" which occurs only here in the Old Testament. Poetic parallelism and intelligibility favor the new reading.

"SEER," RATHER THAN "LION"

Isaiah 21:8 in the Massoretic text begins enigmatically, reading either "and a lion cried," or "he cried, 'A lion!'" The ancient versions were of no help here for they were obviously dependent upon the same reading. Therefore, a number of conjectural emendations were proposed, one of which was to substitute "the seer" (*HR'H*) for "lion" (*'RYH*). This reading has at last been discovered in the Isaiah Scroll and is one of thirteen scroll readings whose adoption is recognized with a footnote in the RSV. The text reads:

> The *seer* cried:
> "On a watchtower, O my Lord,
> I do stand
> continually by day;
> And at my post
> I am stationed
> whole nights."

The word "seer" is employed as a synonym for the word "watchman" of verse 6, and it also serves to designate the prophet; for, as most interpreters believe, the watchman is the prophet himself.

GRASS ON THE HOUSETOP

Another superior reading of the scroll overlaps 37:27f. The Massoretic text reads here:

. . . .

> 27b   like grass on the housetops,
> *a field* before it rose up (or, grew up).

3. *Ibid.*

> 28   And your sitting down
>   and your going out and coming in I know,
>   and your raging against me.

The source passage as preserved in I Kings 19:26 was more intelligible, "a blighting before it rose up." The Standard Bible Committee corrected Isaiah according to Kings, translating "blighted before it is grown." The Isaiah Scroll's reading is more probable, however:

> 27b   like grass on the housetops
>   *which is blighted before the east wind.*
>   *Your rising up* and your sitting down
>   and your going out and your coming in I know,
>   and your raging against me.

Here we have a verbal form which really means "blighted" instead of the dubious noun "blighting." Haplography occurred here in the transmission of the traditional text, the two words *QDM QMKH* ("east wind. Your rising up") were carelessly reduced to a single word QMH ("it rose up"). The new reading correctly restores the reference to the "east wind," or sirocco, which is so dangerous to vegetation in the Holy Land, and it also restores the lost antithesis to "sitting down." There can be little doubt as to the accuracy of this reading.

MEASURING THE WATER OF THE SEA

There are interesting, and possibly significant readings in 40:12:

> 12   Who ever measured in his palm the *ocean,*
>   or ruled off the sky with *his* span,
>   or enclosed the earth's dust in a measure,
>   or weighed mountains in scales,
>   or hills in a balance?

The traditional text reads, "Who ever measured water in his palm?" This seemed to many scholars a pointless question, for a mere dipping up of water in the palm is common experience.[4] Therefore it was suggested that the text be corrected from *mayim* (water) to *yâmîm* (seas). The scroll reads *mê yâm,* "(the) water of (the) sea," which is a slighter emendation (with *MY YM* replacing *MYM*) and one which

---

4. This difficulty is obscured by the translation "waters," but the only word for water (whether much or little) in the Hebrew is a dual (English plural).

affords an excellent parallel to "dust of the earth." Although many scholars favor this reading, my first reaction was to distrust it, for would not the word "sea" have been written with the article *"the"* to parallel *"the* earth"? However, the omission of the article is common in Hebrew poetry, particularly in Second Isaiah's writing,[5] and it is too much to insist upon perfect consistency in its use. Whether or not the reading is original, it conveys the proper sense, for even if we do not adopt this reading, we must nevertheless interpret "water" as meaning the "ocean." Another minor variant in this verse is the addition of the pronoun "his" with "span." This affords better parallelism, and yet we should not insist upon its originality unless some further attestation can be found for it.

The Lord's Unfathomable Mind

The text of 40:13 in both the Massoretic and the Qumrân texts make an interesting comparison:

MASSORETIC TEXT

Who ever directed the mind of the Lord,
    or what man of His counsel made Him know?

SCROLL

Who ever *fathomed* the mind of the Lord,
    or (what man of) His counsel *has made
    it known?*

This text is best approached from the end. The simple difference of gender in the suffix to the last verb is the only fundamental difference. If the suffix is masculine, "made *Him* know," the challenge means, "Who has instructed God?" Since in Hebrew parallelism both clauses should mean the same thing, the verb *tikkên* of the first stich must in this case be translated "directed." However, if the suffix is "it" (a Hebrew feminine), the line refers to the revelation of the "mind of the Lord." Then, the verb *tikkên* is best taken in its other meaning, "measure, rule off." For the figurative expression of this sense, the English word "fathom" is most appropriate. One must be able to fathom the Lord's mind, if he is to make it known. This brings the text into closer accord with the preceding verse, where *tikkên* certainly means "to measure, rule off." The sense of verse 13 is thereby reversed

5. Helen Genevieve Jefferson, "Notes on the Authorship of Isaiah 65 and 66," *JBL*, LXVIII, 1949, pp. 225–30, especially p. 226.

with resultant greater consistency with verse 12. When we examine verse 14 we find the twice repeated challenge of "Who has instructed God?" That is quite sufficient expression of the theme, so we not only lose nothing, but actually gain in richness of thought if we reserve verse 13 for the other challenge of "Who has so fathomed the Lord's mind as to be able to reveal it?" The true prophet, according to Jeremiah, is one who has stood in the council of God and declares what he has heard from God Himself. Second Isaiah was familiar with this thought and had no intention of contradicting it. For him also a true prophet is one "taught of God," but a prophet learns ever so little compared with the boundless reaches of the Spirit of God, "whose ways are past tracking out." [6] No mere man, therefore, can fully reveal God's mind.

Corpses of Israel

Inadequacy of parallelism in the usual text of 41:14a has led many to emend the text. It reads:

> Fear not, you worm Jacob
> you men of Israel!

Since "worm" and "men" are very far from being synonyms, it has been suggested that for "men" (*mǝtê*) we substitute "maggot" (*rimmat*) — "you maggot Israel!" [7] This same parallelism is attested in Job:

> Behold, even the moon is not bright
> and the stars are not clean in His sight;
> How much less man, who is a *maggot*,
> and the son of man, who is a *worm!*   (25:5–6, RSV)

The scroll, however, offers a different parallel term, "corpses":

> Fear not, you worm Jacob,
> *and you corpses* of Israel!

Curiously, in the Hebrew text, "men" and "corpses" would be spelled exactly alike (*MTY*). Their pronunciation would be very similar,

---

6. Cf. Romans 11:33–34, which is based on this passage of Isaiah. For the "taught of God," see Isa. 50:4; 54:13; and cf. 8:16 and Jer. 31:34.
7. This emendation, first suggested by G. H. A. Ewald, was followed by C. C. Torrey, *op. cit.*, p. 317, and by Alexander Gordon in *An American Translation*. Cf. James Muilenburg, in *IB*, Vol. v, p. 457, for various explanations of the word.

mətê (men), *mêtê* (corpses). It is only the use of a vowel letter in the scroll (MYTY) which determines the meaning. Although "worm" and "corpses" are not synonymous, they are certainly related terms and might well have been used together in a sort of complementary parallelism. It calls for no emendation, only a different vocalization, and it is supported by the second century A.D. Greek version of Aquila.[8]

CLARIFICATION OF THE CYRUS ORACLES

The oracle concerning the Persian ruler Cyrus in Isa. 41 has already been partially examined in another connection.[9] It is worth quoting again, at greater length:

> 2 Who aroused Vindication from the east,
>   and called him to His feet,
>   And gave up nations before him —
>   so he subdues kings
>   And makes them as dust with his sword,
>   dispersing them as chaff with his bow,[10]
> 3 And pursues them and passes on in peace
>   down the pathway at His feet?
>   (*They discern not!*)
> 4 Who has wrought or done this,
>   announcing history in advance?
>   It is I, the LORD, the first;
>   and with the last, I am He.

At the end of verse 3, there is the interesting variant, "They discern not," where the *Massôret* reads, "He does not come." The difficulty in understanding the Massoretic text may be seen by comparing the different English versions. The verb "come" as an imperfect would be naturally translated as either present or future, but the King James Version reads, "by the way he had not gone with his feet." The Revised Standard Version similarly renders with a perfect, "by paths his feet *have not* trod." C. C. Torrey rendered more agreeably with

---

8. So states Robert H. Pfeiffer, *History of New Testament Times with an Introduction to the Apocrypha,* New York, Harper & Bros., 1949, p. 417, in connection with Baruch 3:4.
9. Above, pp. 180ff.
10. The traditional text reads, "as dispersed (or driven) chaff with his bow." The reading of the scroll is *NWDP,* not *NYDP.* This was not corrected in the second printing of the *DSS,* Vol. I.

the tense, "No path shall he tread with his feet." [11] Yet the translation "tread" is too strong for an ordinary word like *bô'*, which means simply to "come"; and, conversely, the verb is too weak to bear the weight of what appears to be the interpretation of Torrey that Cyrus is proceeding so rapidly that his feet scarcely touch the ground. The traditional reading is therefore improbable, for either the tense is unsuitable to the context (as in the KJV and the RSV) or the verb is inappropriate to the desired meaning (as in Torrey's rendering).

Instead of the obscure "he does not come," the scroll reads, "they discern not" (*yâvînû* replacing *yâvô'û*). The new reading, according to Arie Rubinstein, serves to introduce verse 4 rather than to conclude verse 3. One should read consecutively: "They discern not who wrought or did this." [12] At first I too was inclined to connect the clause with verse 4; but this requires that the pronoun *mî* be understood as a relative rather than an interrogative, which would represent late usage. Although Rubinstein's construction is possible at the date of the scroll, it seems better to interpret the words as originating as a scribal comment which by accident came to be incorporated into the text; for the Septuagint omits the clause altogether. The new reading is superior to the Massoretic text, in that it gives us the original wording of the comment, but the Septuagint's omission is better yet, with verse 3 concluding originally with the word *bəraglâw*, "at His feet." This expression is to be interpreted as strictly parallel to *ləraglâw*, "to His feet," in verse 2. Both are familiar idioms which mean respectively, "in His service," and, "to His service." God is on the march in the international scene, and Cyrus as God's agent of deliverance for the Jewish exiles is following in God's steps, doing His bidding.

In the description of Cyrus at 41:25, God says that "he calls on My name." Historically this occasions difficulty, for there is no evidence that Cyrus ever embraced the Jewish religion, and it seems to be contradicted by 45:4b where the opposite is expressed:

> I call you by your name,
> I surname you, though you do not know Me.

Consequently some would emend 41:25 to read, "I call you by your name." In the place of this radical emendation, the scroll offers another possibility, "he is called (i.e. summoned) by *his* name." The only con-

---

11. *Op. cit.*, p. 228.
12. *JJS*, Vol. vi, 1955, p. 193. I had independently reached the same conclusion.

sonantal difference in the Hebrew is in the pronoun *his* instead of *my*.
Only a single letter is involved, a confusion of the two similar letters
W and *Y,* which are clearly distinguished in the scroll on the side of
the *W* (*his* name).

Few texts have been more obscure than Isa. 41:27a, which in crude
literalism seems to say, "First to Zion, behold, behold them." The following clause with its reference to a "herald of glad tidings" made it
apparent that here also is the proclamation of news, but the obscure
phrasing suggested that the text was corrupt. To what does "first"
refer? C. C. Torrey thought of the beginnings of Zion's history as a
temporal antithesis to new things about to be proclaimed.[13] Most interpreters, however, have thought "first" referred to the Lord. A common emendation for clarifying the text is that of the Revised Standard
Version: "I first have declared it to Zion." The Isaiah Scroll offers us
a strange variation (*HNWMH*) from the standard "behold them"
(HNM). The significance of this new reading has been discerned by
Alfred Guillaume, who recognizes in the word a participle of a
Semitic verb not previously attested in Hebrew. It means "informer,
announcer." [14] This is an impressive suggestion, for it yields a good
parallel term to "herald" of the following line. The word "first" remains undefined, but since the new reading provides us with the
herald, perhaps it refers to the news. With this assumption, we may
translate:

> Zion gets the first report:
>   behold, the news bringer;
> to Jerusalem I give a herald of glad tidings.

Perhaps this "news bringer" is Second Isaiah, who as God's prophet
divines the future where the Babylonian gods and priests have failed.
Cyrus is coming to destroy Babylon and to release the Jewish exiles.
In still another Cyrus oracle, God identifies Himself as He

> Who says of Cyrus, "My shepherd,
>   and all My purpose he shall fulfill":
> And says of Jerusalem, "She shall be built";
>   and (of) the temple, "You shall be founded."   (44:28)

In this, the traditional text of 44:28, there are three declarations made
by God: of Cyrus, of Jerusalem, and of the temple. The third is quite

13. *Op. cit.,* p. 320.
14. *Op. cit.,* pp. 40f.

suspicious, for not only is there no "of" before "temple," as before Cyrus and Jerusalem, but also it is in the second person instead of the third person as in the preceding promises.[15] Here the scroll offers a convincing improvement:

> Who says of Cyrus, "My friend,
> and all My purpose he shall fulfill";
> And says of Jerusalem, "She shall be built,
> and (My) temple *she shall found*."

Not only are the difficulties of the Massoretic text resolved, but there is perfect symmetry between the two lines, both Cyrus and Jerusalem being given a promise and a mission in the scroll text. The pledge given Cyrus is that he is God's "friend," or perhaps "shepherd," but the absence of a vowel letter in the scroll allows (and perhaps favors) "friend." He who is so honored is commissioned to fulfill God's purpose. Similarly, Jerusalem is promised rebuilding and is then assigned the task of laying the foundations of the temple. The over-all parallelism is better than that of the Septuagint where in the second line, it is all promise and no mission:

> Who says to Jerusalem, "She shall be built,
> and My holy house I shall found."

The Septuagint agrees with the scroll in that there are only two declarations made by God, the supposed third being a part of the second. It also read the possessive "My" with the word "temple," precisely as in a supralinear correction in the scroll. The basic difference between the scroll and the Massoretic reading is that of the verb, and it is the very slight difference of *TYSD* ("she shall found") and *TWSD* ("you shall be founded"). The *W* and *Y* are readily confused in some ancient manuscripts, but happily in the Isaiah Scroll they are easily distinguished.

No Reference to China

A slight scribal error in the transmission of 49:12 has occasioned voluminous writing, beginning as early as the Middle Ages. What is the "land of Sinim"? Does Sinim mean "Chinese"? Whole books have

---

15. If the temple could be regarded as of feminine gender, this difficulty could be overcome. However, this would be the sole exception to the rule that *hêkhâl* is of masculine gender. See *BASOR*, No. 127 (Oct. 1952), p. 21.

been written on the pro and con of this. It is exceedingly doubtful whether China was known in Babylonia or Palestine as early as the sixth century B.C. Therefore, most scholars have preferred the emendation of *Sînîm* to *Sǝwênîm,* the only consonantal difference being that of the often confused *W* and *Y.*[16] The scroll's clear distinction between the letters settles the issue on the side of *Sǝwênîm,* Aswanites:

> Lo, these shall come from afar,
> and lo, these from the north and from the west,
> and these from the land of the Aswanites.

The passage appears to have been written from the standpoint of the Holy Land, having been written by Second Isaiah after the return from the Exile, which is referred to at the end of the preceding chapter. In any case, "afar" means Babylonia, which from Palestine is the most remote part of the region known as the "fertile crescent," which arches around the Arabian desert. Thus, in encompassing all the directions, the prophet refers first to the east. Next comes mention of the north and the west, and this leaves the south. The Targum actually reads, "the land of the South," but this is doubtless a free rendering, properly locating for us the city of Aswan which lies far south on the Nile.[17]

The Resurrection of the Lord's Servant

A reading of considerable importance in the Great Servant Song is the first clause of Isa. 53:11: "From his soul's travail he shall see." This is construed in the King James Version to mean: "He will see *of* the travail of his soul." The same sense is more fully expressed in the Revised Standard Version: "He will see *the fruit of* the travail of his soul." This represents the best that can be done with the traditional Hebrew, but its textual basis is open to challenge. It is possible to demand of the Hebrew a more explicit object for the verb "see." At this point both scrolls from the first Qumrân cave supply a suitable object: "From his soul's travail he shall see *light.*" The ancient Septuagint also adds "light," but in a text which is otherwise very different.[18]

16. The RSV presents this as a correction of the Hebrew ("Cn: Heb Sinim"); whereas it should have cited "One ancient Ms." The reason for this omission of documentation was the initial failure to distinguish *Wâw* from *Yôd.* Cf. at this point the first and second printings of *DSS* I.
17. Cf. G. Lambert, "Le livre d'Isaïe parle-t-il des Chinois?" *NRTh,* Tome 85, 1953, pp. 965-72.
18. In the LXX the last words of verse 10 are attached to verse 11, and the passage is rendered: "And the Lord wills to deliver him / from the travail of his soul, *to show*

Since the two Isaiah Scrolls and the Septuagint are our three most ancient sources and represent three different text types, their agreement on the word "light" is the strongest sort of textual support. The Revised Standard Version was prepared too early for the worth of this variant to be realized, so it is not recognized there even as a marginal alternative. Today, however, many scholars accept the reading as original.

Quite as important as the reading "see light" is its interpretation. This must be found through an investigation of the manifold figurative uses of "light," which we analyze as follows: (1) truth and instruction, (2) moral and spiritual guidance, (3) guidance through trials and difficulties, (4) prosperity and happiness, (5) divine favor as the source of all blessing, (6) deliverance from misfortune (or salvation), and (7) life itself. Very often there are shades of more than one meaning in the same passage. Each of these significations will be examined below, especially as regards the usage of Second Isaiah.

1. *Can "light" in Isa. 53:11 mean "truth"?* Preliminary examination would favor this, for its apparent parallel in the extant text is "knowledge." Consequently Prof. Sheldon H. Blank of Hebrew Union College (Cincinnati) translates:

> As a consequence of his life's distress he shall see light,
> he shall be sated with knowledge.[19]

Similarly, H. H. Rowley of the University of Manchester renders:

> And after his travail of soul he shall see light,
>   and be satisfied with the knowledge of the Lord.[20]

The identification of "light" with "knowledge" would certainly have been congenial with Essene theology, where "light" and "darkness"

---

him light, to mould his understanding, to justify the just one who serves the many well; and he himself bears their sins." The same word *yir'èh* ("he shall see") may be vocalized *yar'èh* ("he shall show") — but not in the context of either 1Q Isaᵃ or 1Q Isaᵇ.

Other Septuagintal agreements in the Great Servant Song are as follows: "upon him, *and* kings shall shut their mouths, for . . . ." (52:15), "smitten to death" (53:8), the plurals "rich men" (53:9) and "sins of many" (53:12), also "for their transgressions" (rather than "for the transgressors") in 53:12.

For the relationship of Complete Isaiah Scroll to the Septuagint, cf. Joesph Ziegler, "Die Vorlage der Isaias-Septuaginta (LXX) und die erste Isaias-Rolle von Qumrân," *JBL*, lxxviii, 1959, pp. 34–59.

19. *Prophetic Faith in Isaiah*, New York, Harper and Bros., 1958, p. 88.
20. *The Unity of the Bible*, Philadelphia, Westminster Press, 1953, p. 56, n. 3.

are the figurative representations of "truth" and "perversity." The Essene understanding, however, is not necessarily authoritative for the original meaning. In fact, if it were not for the support of the Septuagint, which is earlier than the scrolls, one might well suspect this reading as being sectarian in origin.[21] Other possible interpretations must be examined before we may simply accept the equation of "light" and "truth."

2. *Closely associated with "light" as "truth" is the thought of light as a source of moral and spiritual guidance.*[22] This relationship is perhaps to be seen in Psalm 43:3:

> Oh send out Thy light and Thy truth;
> let them lead me,
> Let them bring me to Thy holy hill
> and to Thy dwelling!   (RSV)

3. *The meaning may be, however, "Send out Thy light and prove Thy faithfulness in bringing me safely to Thy holy hill."* In this case, the psalm illustrates better the theme of *guidance through trials* and difficulties, which seems to be the thought of Isa. 42:16:

> And I will lead the blind
> in a way that they know not;
> In paths that they have not known
> I will guide them.
> I will turn darkness before them into light,
> the rough places into level ground.   (RSV)

The turning of darkness into light is a figurative way of saying that all obstacles will be overcome.

4. *Light as a figure for prosperity and happiness is well exemplified by Isa. 45:7.* Here God describes Himself as:

> The Fashioner of light and Creator of darkness,
> the Maker of welfare and Creator of disaster.

21. I. L. Seeligmann, "The Epoch-making Discovery of Hebrew Scrolls in the Judean Desert," *Bibliotheca Orientalis,* vi, 1949, pp. 1–8, suggested (p. 7) the pre-gnostic, or sectarian, origin of the word "light" both in the LXX and in 1Q Isa[a]. Although he was doubtless wrong regarding this, his prediction on the following page has proved true: "It may be that, to arrive at a true assessment of the text-critical value of our manuscript, its origin from a sectarian milieu will have to be taken into account; i.e., the possibility that sectarian variants have been allowed to creep in." The only passage of the Bible in which "light" explicitly refers to "knowledge" is II Cor. 4:6.
22. Cf. Ps. 119:105.

Here the antitheses of "light" and "darkness" are clarified as "welfare" and "disaster," respectively. These are rather prevalent meanings of the terms throughout the Old Testament.[23]

5. *Since God is the author of all well-being, His favor is essential to its realization, and consequently divine favor is sometimes represented under the symbolism of light.* This is well illustrated in the Aaronic benediction:

> The LORD bless you and keep you;
> The LORD make His face to *shine* upon you,
>   and show you *favor;*
> The LORD lift up His countenance upon you,
>   and grant you *well-being.*   (Num. 6:24–26)

God's gracious, smiling face is said to shine when it looks upon one with favor. Thus God as light is the source of *shâlôm,* not simply "peace" (as in most translations), but "well-being." The same association of "light" with "favor" is to be found in the case of the earthly ruler:

> In the *light* of the king's face there is life,
>   and his *favor* is like the clouds that bring spring rain.
>   (Prov. 16:15)

This usage is not particularly helpful in expounding Isaiah; but, naturally, wherever God is identified as Israel's light,[24] his favor is presupposed, except where the prophet may desire to give the term an ironical twist, as in Isa. 10:17:

> The light of Israel will become a fire,
>   and his Holy One a flame;
> And it will burn and devour
>   his thorns and briers in one day.

Here the "light of Israel," instead of being a boon, becomes the fire of divine judgment.

6. *Light may denote deliverance from misfortune, or restoration to welfare.* It is therefore a synonym for "salvation." An example of the literary form known as hendiadys makes clear the identification:

23. Cf. Job 12:25; Isa. 30:26; 58:8, 10; and 60:1 as an introduction to the entire sixtieth chapter. In Gen. 1:3–4, light is the first gift of the Creator in bringing order out of chaos — perhaps by way of symbolizing the emergence of well-being.
24. Cf. Isa. 2:5; 60:1, 19–20.

The LORD is my Light and my Salvation;
whom shall I fear?   (Ps. 27:1)

The equation of "light" with "salvation" suggests that, in Isa. 53:11, "to see light" might mean "to see deliverance," a thought which is most agreeable to the context. This is especially suggestive, since Second Isaiah does use elsewhere the expression "see the salvation of God." [25] One may compare here Micah 7:9b:

He will bring me forth to the *light;*
I shall *see* His *vindication* (of me).

Since "vindication" and "light" are parallelistic synonyms, there is an indirect indication that "to see light" may mean "to experience deliverance." Certainly the Servant of the Lord, when represented as a light, appears with a salvific mission:

I have appointed you to be a covenant to the people,
to be a light to the nations,
to open the eyes that are blind,
To bring out the prisoners from the dungeon,
from the prison those who sit in darkness.   (42:6)

I appoint you to be a light to the nations,
to be My salvation to the earth's ends.   (49:6b)

The Servant as a light is not acting primarily as a prophet, but as a redeemer.

7. *Finally, "light" may stand for "life" itself.* This equation is common in the Book of Job:

Or why was I not as a hidden untimely birth,
as infants that never *see the light?*   (3:16)

Why is light given to him that is in misery,
and *life* to the bitter in soul?   (3:20)

"To see light" in this context means "to live." "Light" and "life" are synonymous. This language brings us back to the literal meaning of light, for *to live is to see the light of the sun.* The abode of the dead, referred to variously as Sheol and the Pit, is in the thought of Job a land of darkness.[26] When the life of the wicked is extinguished, it is his

25. Isa. 52:10 and (in the Septuagint) 40:5. Cf. Luke 3:6, also II Esd. 6:25.
26. Cf. Job 10:21f.; 17:13; Sirach 22:11; I Enoch 9:4–6; 10:5; 46:6; 63:6; 102:8.

"light" which is "put out," and he himself is "thrust from light into darkness and driven out of the world."[27] Similarly Ecclesiastes 11:7 can declare, "Light is sweet, and it is pleasant for the eyes to behold the sun." This proverb was not written by a sun worshipper, but by a man who loved life.[28]

"Light" as "life" may be related also to the theme of deliverance:

> He has *redeemed* my soul from going down into the Pit,
> and my life shall *see the light.*

> Behold, God does all these things,
> twice, three times, with a man,
> *to bring back* his soul from the Pit,
> that he may *see the light of life.*   (Job 33:28–30, RSV)

God's redeeming work results in life, the seeing of light.

After consideration of all the above meanings of "light," we return to Isa. 53:11 to determine which meaning best suits the context of the words, "he shall see light." "Truth" and "guidance" (either spiritual or physical) are not suited to the needs of one who is dead and buried, since even Sheol was to the Hebrew a land of darkness which knew not the praise of God.[29] Well-being, or happiness, would be most desirable; but such is not to be found except under the light of the sun. What the context requires, therefore, is redemption from the blackness of the netherworld into the light of this earth.[30] From the very first, J. M. P. Bauchet proposed that what the passage in Isaiah refers to is resurrection: "After his soul's travail he shall see (again) the light (of this world)."[31] This interpretation alone fits well the context; and it becomes even clearer, if we accept an emendation of C. C. Torrey whereby we reverse the order of two similar Hebrew words, reading ṢDYQ YṢDYQ for YṢDYQ ṢDYQ.[32] In fact, if the verse is to be scanned as poetry at all, some such alteration is necessary. The resultant text may be translated:

---

27. Job 18:18. Baruch 3:20, speaks of youths who "have seen the light of day, . . . but have not learned the way to knowledge."
28. The author of the proverb is thereby not necessarily the author of the Book of Ecclesiastes, with his oft repeated "vanity of vanities."
29. Ps. 6:5; 30:9; 88:10–12; 115:17; Eccles. 9:10.
30. He was "cut off from the land of the living" (v. 8) and buried (v. 9).
31. "Notes on the Newly Discovered Hebrew Manuscripts," *Scripture,* Vol. iv (Oct. 1949), pp. 115–17. For the association of "light" with resurrection, cf. Isa. 26:19; Ephes. 5:14.
32. *Op. cit.,* pp. 421ff.

> After his mortal suffering he shall see light,
> and shall be satisfied in knowing himself vindicated.
> My servant shall vindicate many,
> since it is their iniquities that he bears.

Here is perfectly regular Hebrew rhythm. Here is the association of "light" with "vindication" in a characteristic Hebrew fashion; and here "deliverance" results in life itself. Here therefore is an explicit prophecy of the Servant's resurrection and ultimate well-being. The author of Job contemplated the possibility of resurrection, but Second Isaiah makes of it a reality.[33]

Studies of the identity of the Lord's Servant have picked first one and then another of the Lord's great Old Testament figures as Second Isaiah's portrait model. In my view, not one, but several such great models were employed. Moses, David, Jeremiah, Jehoiachin, and Job were all probably in the prophet's mind as he thought of now one feature and now another of the Lord's Servant. The one who figures more than any other in Isa. 53 is God's "servant Job." A Swiss professor, B. Duhm, in 1892 advanced the theory that Second Isaiah was describing a leprous teacher of the Law, a figure contemporary with himself.[34] Careful examination of the text, however, points rather to Job [35] — not that Job is the servant, but that he is the model for important features. He is the sick man from whom men hide their faces (v. 3), whom men supposed was smitten by God (v. 4). He is the exemplar of perfect patience, the man who never opened his mouth to complain against God (v. 7a).[36] Though men supposed his family line to be cut off, he lived to see his seed (v. 10). He is the one who, after deliverance from suffering and death, made intercession for the transgressors (v. 12). So like-

33. However, if one is convinced of a corporate understanding of the Servant in Isa. 53, having in mind the historical Israel, he will necessarily interpret the resurrection as figurative, precisely as in Ezek. 37. For the view that the doctrine of the resurrection in Dan. 12:2 was inspired partly by Isa. 53, see H. L. Ginsberg, in *VT*, iii, 1953, pp. 402, 404.

34. *Das Buch Jesaja*, Göttinger Handkommentar zum Alten Testament, Göttingen, Vandenhoeck & Ruprecht, 1892, on Isa. 42:1.

35. I follow Robert H. Pfeiffer (*Introduction to the Old Testament*, pp. 467ff.) and Samuel Terrien (in *IB*, Vol. 3, pp. 889f.) in the opinion that the Book of Job antedates the composition of Second Isaiah, since the latter was often dependent upon the language of Job (and not vice versa).

36. There are two portraits of Job in the Book of Job, one in the opening chapters in which he exemplifies perfect patience, the other in his debates and soliloquies in which he is very impatient.

wise verse 11 gathers up the distinctive Joban terminology.[37] "After his suffering of soul, he shall see the light," crystallizes the language of Job 3:16 and 20, from which every Hebrew word (with slight modification) can be drawn:

> Or why was I not as a hidden untimely birth,
> as infants that never *see the light?*

> Why is *light* given to *the sufferer,*
> and life to the bitter of *soul?*

"Suffering of soul" is a phrase coined by Second Isaiah from the separate words "sufferer" and "soul." The resultant expression probably means "mortal suffering." The phrase, "see the light," is also in near context. Still another link is Job's assurance at 13:18: "I know that I shall be vindicated."[38] The precipitate of Job's speeches therefore produces:

> After his suffering of soul, he shall see light,
> and shall be satisfied in knowing himself vindicated.

This is almost entirely the vocabulary of Job, but applied to a Servant far greater than Job, or, indeed, than all the portrait models put together. Moses, David, Jeremiah, and the rest serve only to suggest the grandeur of the ideal Servant and Ambassador of God, whoever he may be.[39]

37. Aside from the general similarities, which call for no documentation, one may note that Job 16:10 and 17:6 are combined in the picture of the Lord's Servant in Isa. 50:6, and that Job 6:30 and 16:17 combine in their influence upon the language of Isa. 53:9b. "He shall see his offspring" (v. 10) finds its closest Old Testament parallel in Job 42:16, according to Christopher R. North, *op. cit.,* p. 153.

38. So is the passage well translated in the RSV. Cf. KJV, "I know that I shall be justified." The ASV rendered less suitably, "I know that I am righteous."

39. Like Moses, the Servant is to be a deliverer in a New Exodus, like him, he has a Torah (42:4), and like him he is willing to lay down his life for others (cf. Ex. 33:30–32) — only the Servant's deliverance and Torah (law) are for the whole world and not just Israel; and he really dies, not merely offering his life. Like Jeremiah, the Servant was consecrated before his birth to a prophetic mission (Jer. 1:5; Isa. 49:5); and like him he was led as a lamb to the slaughter (Jer. 11:19a; Isa. 53:7) by those who wished to "cut him off from the land of the living" (Jer. 11:19b; Isa. 53:8). There is a Jewish tradition that Jeremiah was really martyred in Egypt, so that this may be more than a linguistic similarity. Like David, the Servant is anointed with the Spirit (I Sam. 16:13; Isa. 42:1, with which cf. 61:1), and is to be an international leader (Ps. 18:43f.; Isa. 55:4–5). Like the dynasty of David, he suffers but is exalted (Ps. 89:38–51); and like the Messianic Branch of David, he deals wisely (Jer. 23:5; Isa. 52:13). Like Isaiah

A Shocking Text (65:3)

Chapter 65 alludes to strange rites of some pagan nature cult, which are regarded as shocking and abhorrent. The third verse is of interest by reason of the radical differences in our three main textual sources. The Septuagint reads as follows:

> *This* people which is so provocative
> toward me always,
> *They* sacrifice in gardens
> and burn incense upon bricks
> *to non-existent demons.*

The first word "This" may represent only the definite article of the Hebrew which our English versions generally omit. The insertion of the word "they," however, is supported by the Complete Isaiah Scroll. The final phrase, "to non-existent demons," reflects a feeling of revulsion for the heathen practice; but it is so far not represented in any Hebrew text.

The scroll reading of the passage differs considerably in the contents of its last stich:

> The people who provoke me
> to my face continually,
> *They* sacrifice in gardens
> and *suck̟* the hands upon the stones.

It has been suggested by Arie Rubinstein that "hands" in the last half-line is a euphemism for the male phallus, similar to the way in which "hand" seems to be employed in 57:8.[40] He does not venture a suggestion for "stones," probably feeling that this is an obvious reference to the testicles. This interpretation may be correct, but one wishes for corroboration from a parallel passage. I have found no evidence as yet for the use of the Hebrew word '*BNYM* ("stones") in this conjectured sense; but the same word is vocalized as a dual in the expression, "upon the birthstool" (Exodus 1:16), and this too hints at some rela-

and his children, he is a disciple of God (Isa. 8:16–18; 50:4) — the Lord being the speaker in 8:16, both in the text of the scroll and in the Massoretic text. The Servant of the Lord is not to be identified with these, or with any other historical figures of the Old Testament; but several of the more prominent servants of the Lord contributed to the portrait of the Servant (or Ambassador) *par excellence* in Second Isaiah.

40. "Notes on the use of the Tenses in the Variant Readings of the Isaiah Scroll," *VT*, III, 1 (Jan. 1953), pp. 92–95, with attention here to pp. 94f.

tionship with the genitals.[41] We do not at present know exactly what the new reading of the last half-line says, but it seems to refer to an obscene practice which was so revolting as to be practically unmentionable. Because the variant is shocking, we may regard it as preserving an original reading. Other lines of textual transmission effaced it because of its obscenity. This revolting, though obscure, reading should make us aware that there is still much in the Book of Isaiah which we do not yet understand, despite the brilliant new light of ancient scrolls.

41. I wonder whether this can mean "upon their knees," a posture for childbirth in antiquity. Cf. Gen. 30:3, in the case of proxy maternity. The phrase *'al hâ-'ovnâyim* (a dual) appears also in Jer. 18:3 where the KJV renders "on the wheels." One thing in common between a potter's wheel and a kneecap is their disk-like shape. On the use of *yâd* ("hand"), see above, p. 191, also 1Q S vii, 13.

CHAPTER TWELVE

Stepping-Stone Readings

The Isaiah Scroll contains a few readings which in themselves do not completely rectify corrupted texts, but which in certain cases may serve as the first clue toward amended readings.

AN UNSUSPECTED CULTIC REFERENCE (ISA. 6:13)

The last verse of chapter 6 is full of obscurities, some of which are reflected in the American Standard Version margin. By interpolating the marginal renderings within brackets we obtain the following result:

> And if there be yet a tenth in it, it also shall in turn be eaten up [or, burnt] [or, But yet in it shall be a tenth, and it shall return, and shall be eaten up]: as a terebinth, and as an oak, whose stock remaineth [or, when they cast (their leaves)]; so the holy seed is the stock [or, substance] thereof.

Despite the uncertainties of the ASV, this verse reads as a promise of survival for the remnant of the nation. The Revised Standard Version, with less bewilderment as to the meaning of the verse, turns the whole into an oracle of doom:

> "And though a tenth remain in it,
>   it will be burned again,
> Like a terebinth or an oak,
>   whose stump remains standing
>   when it is felled."
> The holy seed is its stump.

Even the last clause in this version, through its present dangling construction, seems to serve the purpose of merely identifying the stump which is to be burned, rather than that of suggesting that a stump will survive the burning. In order to bring out the import of the last clause, it would be necessary to start a new sentence with "Like" and place a comma after "felled," and then move the close of the quotation to the very end of the verse. The reason the Standard Bible Committee refrained from doing this is that according to literary criticism the original oracle of the prophet ended on a note of doom and did not include the last clause (which is absent from the Septuagint).[1] In loyalty to the prophet Isaiah, the revisers obscured the sense of the editorial addition.

Even if one agrees with the critical point of view of the Standard Bible Committee, an examination of their translation in close comparison with the Hebrew will show that the poetic arrangement of the second half of the verse is untrue to the text. The RSV is right in arranging what precedes this as poetry and is therefore right in expecting the oracle to be completed in poetic form. The extant text, nevertheless, will not permit a natural division of words into poetic stichs. It is obvious, therefore, that the original poetic structure has been disturbed.

When I first gave serious study to 6:13 in the scroll, the verse seemed to read:[2]

> And if there be yet a tenth in it, it in turn shall be for burning, as a terebinth and an oak, when *the sacred column of a high place is overthrown.* [And like a terebinth and an oak, when (their) *stock at a high place sheds* (leaves)], (so) the holy seed is its stump.

The portions of the verse italicized exhibit the new readings of the scroll: *MŠLKT MṢBT BMH* replacing the traditional *BŠLKT MṢBT BM.* A different initial letter of the first word transformed it from a unique noun of uncertain meaning (such as "in felling" or "in shedding") into a verb, a reading which still opens up two possibilities: a passive ("is overthrown") or an intensive active ("throws off, sheds"). The second word remained unaltered from the ambiguous *maṣṣêvet* ("stump, stalk, substance, or sacred column"); but the third word opened up the possibility of establishing a new context which would

---

1. Some scholars, however, argue that the clause was in the Hebrew prototype of the Septuagint (or at least in one of its Hebrew ancestors); for the omission can be explained as an error of *homoioteleuton,* the scribe omitting the bracketed material, as follows: *M[MṢBT BM ZRʻ QDŠ] MṢBTH.* However, the Septuagint translation may have been made from a text which read: *MMṢBT BH* — the latter word being a variant found in one hundred medieval Hebrew manuscripts. The first *M* (Greek *apo*) is absent in all our Hebrew sources.

2. "The Text of Isaiah vi, 13 in the Light of DSIa," *VT,* I, No. 4 (Oct. 1951), pp. 296–8.

resolve the ambiguities of the two preceding words (insofar as the sense of the original prophet is concerned), for *bâmâh* is the word for "high place," and sacred columns were often located at cultic high places. That Isaiah should speak of such columns being hurled down fitted the iconoclastic viewpoint of much of the Old Testament.[3] Naturally the final clause, when added, was intended to transform the sense. This is indicated in the above display by repeating the preceding portion of the text in varied translation, within brackets.

The new readings seemed to solve everything except the poetic scansion. By separating the phrases "as a terebinth and as an oak" into two separate stichs, where they would appear in poetic parallelism, I was able to solve the metrical problem. This involved the transposition of only one word in Hebrew.[4] The result was as follows:

> And if there be yet a tenth in it,
>   it in turn shall be for burning,
> As a terebinth when it is thrown down,
>   and as an oak by the sacred column of a high place.

This seemed to solve all the problems, except for the last clause of the verse ("The holy seed is its stump."). When this clause was added to the verse (at a more ancient date than the Isaiah Scroll which also contains it), the entire sense was changed along the lines of the American Standard Version. In fact, the transposition of the phrase "and as an

---

3. Lev. 26:1; Deut. 7:5; 12:3; 16:21–22; II Kings 3:2; 10:26–27; 14:22–23; 17:9–10; 18:4; 23:14; II Chron. 12:2f.; 31:1; Isa. 1:29; Hosea, 4:13; Micah 5:13–14 (12–13); Ezek. 6:13; 20:28f.

4. Samuel Iwry, "*Maṣṣēbāh* and *Bāmāh* in 1Q Isaiah[a] 6:13," *JBL*, lxxvi, 1957, pp. 225–32, avoided this transposition by making four emendations. His argument that the particle *'ŠR* ("when") never occurs in poetry, and should therefore be emended to *W'ŠRH* ("and an Asherah") increases by one the cultic terms of the passage. However, it is a mistake to make an invariable rule out of the tendency of poetry to omit particles. They may sometimes be included for the very purpose of filling out the rhythmic value of a stich. For the use of *'ŠR* in Isaianic poetry, cf. the following examples from the first eleven chapters: 1:29 (twice); 1:30; 2:20, 22; 5:5; 7:25; 11:16 (the last two passages being later additions). The double emendation which Iwry has to perform upon the word at 6:13 makes his results even less convincing.

More convincing is the restoration of W. F. Albright, "The High Place in Ancient Palestine," *SVT*, IV, 1957, pp. 242–258, with attention here to pp. 254f. He was able to solve the metrical problem by making only two emendations. His translation, also, identifies the cultic trees with fertility goddesses (which in any case must hover in the background of the passage): "Like the terebinth goddess and the oak of the Asher[ah], / Cast out [with] the stelae of the high place." See also Millar Burrows, *More Light on the Dead Sea Scrolls*, pp. 144–150.

oak" (one word in Hebrew) to its position in the extant text may have been done deliberately by the editor who added the last clause. This editor apparently had no concern for the integrity and beauty of the text of Isaiah as originally composed.

No sooner had I published the above suggestion for restoring the true text of 6:13 than I became aware of the significance of a space in the scroll between *maṣṣêvet* and *bâmâh*. This was seen to be a punctuation device designed to prevent us from taking the verse in the manner just discussed. In fact, this punctuation corresponds with the Vulgate (and Douay) Version.[5] Thus *bâmâh* in the understanding of the scribe of our document did not mean "high place" at all, but it was a longer spelling of *bâm* ("in [or among] them"), and not at all to be connected with the preceding *maṣṣêvet*. It seems probable, therefore, that the scribe of the Isaiah Scroll (or the tradition back of it) would have us construe the verse somewhat as follows:

And though a tenth remain in it, it in turn shall be for burning. Like a terebinth and like an oak, when (their) stalk sheds (leaves) — (so shall there be) among them the holy seed, its stalk.

The dash in this translation corresponds with the space in the Isaiah Scroll; and the meaning with which one ends by following this lead is similar to that of the ancient Targum and of the King James Version. Nevertheless, this interpretation cannot be that of the original prophet Isaiah, whose language here was doubtlessly poetic and lacked the obscurities which are resolved by the parenthetical additions in the translation above. To arrive at the original text, therefore, we must dare to depart from ancient tradition and combine *bâmâh* with what precedes (as I had done previously) and use this as a stepping-stone for the recovery of the true text of Isaiah.

The restored text of Isa. 6:13 probably indicates that the chapter's concluding verses were written late in his career, after the iconoclastic reform of King Hezekiah.[6] Conversely, it reinforces the historicity of Hezekiah's reformation, which has often been brought into question. Isaiah used the destruction of the high places as a simile for the future ruin of Judah. This indicates that he did not consider the reforms of Hezekiah sufficient to avert the wrath of the Lord. Perhaps this was because they were mainly cultic, rather than ethical. When Sennacherib

5. Cf. Barthélemy, in the *RB*, 1950, p. 537.
6. II Kings 18:4, 22; II Chron. 30:14; 31:1; 32:12; Isa. 36:7.

sent his ambassador (the Rabshakeh) to Jerusalem to taunt the God of Israel, and Hezekiah turned to earnest prayer, the spectacle of the humbled king may have moved the prophet to promise deliverance.[6a] On the other hand, the new reading of Isa. 6:13 may seem to some scholars to make this reversal on the part of the prophet even more incredible.

The new reading also reinforces the suggestion that the description of the people's deafness to the prophet's message, which would continue until the nation was destroyed (vv. 9ff.), was composed in retrospect, after years of disheartening experience.[7] Throughout his ministry the prophet never forgot the Holy One of Israel who commissioned him. In the face of new hostilities and callous indifference, he heard God's commission afresh, sending him ever again to preach, even though his preaching seemed to make his hearers all the more determined to pursue their willful disobedience of the Lord.

HEZEKIAH'S SIGN (38:8)

When Hezekiah asked the Lord what sign He would give that he should be recovered from his illness (II Kings 20:8; Isa. 38:22), the Lord answered (according to the American Standard Version):

> Behold, I shall cause the shadow of the steps, which is gone down on the steps [or, dial] of Ahaz with [or, by] the sun, to return backward ten steps. So the sun returned ten steps on the dial whereon [or, by which steps] it was gone down. (38:8)

The marginal renderings have been placed within brackets in this display; for they reveal many of the uncertainties. The Revised Standard Version made its choice between alternative interpretations, but it commented: "The Hebrew of this verse is obscure." One of the uncertainties is whether "steps" means sundial,[8] or refers to the stairs of the royal palace where one might observe the shifting of the sun's shadow. The passage also has its grammatical problems. In the above translation, the verb "is gone down" has as its indirect subject the noun "shadow," although they do not agree in gender.

6a. For a survey of the problem relating to this history, and for an excellent critique, see H. H. Rowley, "Hezekiah's Reform and Rebellion," *BJRL,* Vol. 44, 1962, pp. 395–431.

7. Cf. the Lord's command to Hosea to marry a harlot and have harlotous children (Hos. 1:2), which is probably also the language of retrospect — an interpretation of past events as the will of God.

8. As interpreted by the Targum.

In the Isaiah Scroll the text reads, if we adhere closely to the language of the ASV:

Behold, I shall cause the shadow of the steps, which is gone down on the steps of *the upper chamber of* Ahaz, *even* the sun, to return backward ten steps. So the sun returned ten steps, by which steps it was gone down.

There are two new elements in this form of the text: (1) the reference to Ahaz's "upper chamber," and (2) the sign of the accusative ("even") before "the sun," replacing the ambiguous preposition ("with," or "by") of the Massoretic text. The latter is a bit awkward, since it ascribes two objects to the same verb; and yet by the repetition of the verb, which appears in this location in the Septuagint, this difficulty can be overcome. The reference to Ahaz's upper chamber is an addition which is convincing for three reasons: (1) This chamber is known from II Kings 23:12. (2) The Septuagint reads "the house of your father" here, which may be fully synonymous with "the upper chamber of Ahaz" — since this chamber of Hezekiah's father Ahaz may have been a separate building situated at a height requiring stairs.[9] (3) The scribal omission of "upper chamber" is readily explained since it resembles the last part of the immediately preceding word, thus BM'LWT 'LYT.

Samuel Iwry has suggested a restoration of the original wording by interpolating additional elements of the Septuagint version into the Hebrew text of the scroll, with the following result:[10]

Behold, I shall cause the shadow of the steps to return where [the sun] is gone down on the steps of the upper chamber of Ahaz, [your father]. [I shall cause] the sun [to return] backward ten steps. So the sun returned ten steps, by which steps [the shadow] was gone down.

In this restoration I have bracketed the interpolations based upon the Septuagint. By its addition of "the sun" in the first part of the verse it provides the feminine verb with its required feminine subject. If we use the Septuagint's evidence for repeating the verb "I shall cause to return," the accusative case of "the sun" is given clarity also. The addition of "your father" after "Ahaz" is unimportant, and simply may be a variant for Ahaz. The double interpolation of "the sun" and "the

9. Cf. W. F. Albright as cited by Samuel Iwry, "The Qumrân Isaiah and the End of the Dial of Ahaz," *BASOR*, No. 147 (Oct. 1957), pp. 27–33, with attention here to p. 33, n. 15.
10. *Op. cit.*, p. 33.

shadow" at opposite ends of the verse results in a neat balancing of subjects and verbs in the two halves of the verse: (1) The shadow is to return, where the sun is gone down. (2) The sun returned where the shadow was gone down. The nouns used with the verbs are different in each half. The purpose of so much repetition, relieved somewhat by the alternation of subjects, was to emphasize the spectacular character of the miracle. Still it is not surprising that editors (and/or scribes) should have tried to cut through the redundancy to something simpler. In so doing they obscured the sense. It is wonderful, if this restoration of Iwry is really correct, that all the elements of the original text have survived in order to be fitted together again in this restoration. It is the Isaiah Scroll with its stepping-stone reading in the verse which has led to the insights of Iwry in reconstructing its text. Its sense can be brought out with greater clarity if we abandon the ASV wording (which was chosen for comparison) and rephrase it in modern English:

> See, I am about to cause the shadow on the stairs where the sun has gone down to come back up the steps of the upper chamber of Ahaz, your father. I am about to bring the sun backward ten steps. So the sun came back up the ten steps by which the shadow had already gone down.

THE THIRSTY POOR (41:17)

A beautiful verse of the Exilic prophet Second Isaiah promises that God will answer the unspoken prayers of those whose mouths are too parched to speak. In the Revised Standard Version it is rendered as follows:

> When the poor and needy seek water,
>   and there is none,
>   and their tongue is parched with thirst,
> I the LORD will answer them,
>   I the God of Israel will not forsake them.

The last three stichs in the Hebrew are all three beats in length, one beat for each major word. The same rhythmic scheme appears in the preceding verse, so presumably a three-beat clause should appear at the beginning of the verse; but the words "When the poor and needy seek water and there is none" by normal scansion measure five beats. This is too long for any type of Hebrew poetry; and they cannot be broken up into two stichs (despite the appearance of the RSV), for the only natural syntactical division "and there is none" is only a single Hebrew word — too short for a poetic half-line (or stich).

The excessive length of the first potential stich doubtless indicates that it has suffered from scribal additions. In arriving at the original text, therefore, we must trim it to size. The question is, which words should be omitted. Rudolph Kittel in his *Biblia Hebraica* suggested omitting the Hebrew word translated "and needy" and changing the grammatical form of the word rendered "seek" so that it might be combined with the next word into a single beat. His emendation may be represented in rhythmic English as follows:

> The poor who seek water in vain,
> whose tongue is parched with thirst,
> I the LORD will answer them,
> as Israel's God I will not forsake them.

Partial confirmation of this perfect versification is to be found in the Isaiah Scroll, where the first stich reads: "The poor, *the needy, those* who seek water in vain." In this text the "and" that is prefixed to "the needy" in the traditional text is missing. This indicates that "the needy" is a parenthetical explanation of the word "poor." Now the word translated "poor" in the above renditions can also mean "afflicted," so the additional word "needy" was brought into the text as a marginal comment explaining the sense in which the word should be taken. The meaning of the interpolated gloss may be brought out more forcefully in English by a fresh translation: "The afflicted (that is, the poor) who seek water in vain." One is tempted to regard the gloss as erroneous, to think that the word really means "afflicted"; but one may imagine a drought year in which some villages needed to buy water, with the destitute unable to pay. In this case, the gloss represents correct interpretation of the preceding Hebrew word. That the word is a gloss seems to be confirmed by the syntax of the scroll. Unfortunately, the scroll does not abbreviate the form of the verb "seek," but curiously this participle is even lengthened by the prefixing of the article.[11] Nevertheless, I am convinced that Kittel's emended text is correct and that the reading of the scroll provides a stepping-stone toward the confirming of his perfecting of this prophetic poem.

11. The MT reads *MBQŠYM* and the Scroll reads *HMBQŠYM*, whereas Kittel would read *MBQŠY*.

THE REBELLIOUS AND CONTRARY (65:2)

The Massoretic Hebrew text of 65:2 is well translated in the Revised Standard Version:

> I spread out my hands all the day
> to a rebellious people,
> who walk in a way that is not good,
> following their own devices.

The second stich is longer in the Septuagint text quoted by Paul in Romans 10:21. The underlying Hebrew of that version may be translated as follows, italicizing the addition attested by the Septuagint:

> I spread out my arms all day
> to rebelling *and revolting* people.

The Hebrew text of the two participles of the second stich of this line, according to Kittel (in his *Biblia Hebraica*), should read *sôrêr û-môreh* for a mere *sôrêr* of the Massoretic text. At this point the scroll reads *sôreh*, which is a combination of the two words — the eye of the scribe having jumped from the beginning of the one word to the end of the other. This error was facilitated by the similarity of *m* and *s* in the ancient handwriting. Therefore, it seems clear that behind this scroll was an earlier Hebrew manuscript which read precisely as the Hebrew prototype of the Septuagint. In other words, we have found a variant which in itself is inaccurate, but which may be used as a stepping-stone toward an emended text.

The corrected text calls for examination in the light of its metrical context. The first stich contains three principal words, each receiving a separate poetic stress; and the same is true of the second stich, with the result that we obtain a line of 3/3 rhythm. The shorter reading of the Massoretic text yields only a 3/2 line, and the remainder of the verse is presumably to be read as a 3/2 line. The preceding verse (65:1), however, consists of two 3/3 lines, so the result of the emended text is the carrying forward of the 3/3 rhythm at least as far as 2a. A re-examination of the final stich of 2b indicates that its last word is very long and that it is a compound one at that, since it contains a pronominal suffix. Consequently one may entertain the possibility (even in the Massoretic text) that two rhythmic beats should fall upon this single word. The reading in the scroll adds an extra letter to the suffix, raising the number of syllables to six, so that certainly in this text the final word should receive two stresses. Therefore, the second stich of 2b must receive a total of three beats, although it contains only two principal words.[12] The result of this scansion is to extend the 3/3 rhythm of verse 1 to the very end of verse 2. There is nothing extraordinary in the change of rhythm between verses 1 and 2 in the Massoretic text; and certainly the first line of verse 3 is of the 3/2 rhythm and its second line is either a return to 3/3 rhythm (the scroll's reading), or a shift to 2/2 meter (the Massoretic text), or perhaps a shift to 2/3 rhythm (if we follow partly the Massoretic text and partly the scroll).[13] The point we make is not that the extension of the regular 3/3 meter into the second verse proves the accuracy of the longer reading, but rather that it indicates its rhythmic congruity, so that there can be no objection to it on metrical grounds. The first three verses of chapter 65, when translated into English which imitates the rhythm of the Hebrew, may be rendered as follows:

> 1 So eager for those who requested Me not,
> so available for those who sought Me not,
> I said, "Look here! Look here!"
> to a nation not calling on My name.
> 2 I spread out my arms all day
> to rebelling and revolting people —
> Who walk in a way not good,
> following devices of their own!
> 3 The people who thus vex Me,
> constantly to My face,
> Sacrifice in gardens
> and suck the "hands" above the knees![14]

This passage is the first one read by John C. Trever and me in Jerusalem in February, 1948; and with it I conclude the present study of the textual variants of the Isaiah Scroll. My treatment has been only analytic of the sort of text this scroll contains and of the sort of uses it may serve in future study of the Book of Isaiah. There are many im-

12. Cf. above, p. 169.

13. The scroll (as also the Septuagint) reads a resumptive *"They* sacrifice in gardens," with the added pronoun serving to bridge the distance between the subject and the predicate: "The people . . . / Sacrifice." The pronoun is probably to be rejected as an easier reading. Moreover, two-three rhythm after three-two is not an uncommon pattern in Hebrew metrics.

14. The first "Me" of verse 1 is absent from the Massoretic text, but it is attested by the ancient versions as well as by this scroll. For the uncertain meaning of the last stich of verse 3, cf. above, p. 235, n. 41.

portant readings and many important labors by others upon the scroll which it has been impossible to include within the present study; but these samples of the scroll are presented with the hope and the prayer that they may help others (especially non-linguists) to understand the Book of Isaiah better and to appreciate the varied meanings of this priceless manuscript for an understanding of the Bible.

CHAPTER THIRTEEN

The Literary Significance of the Bisection of Isaiah

AN IMPORTANT MIDWAY GAP

The gap between chapters 33 and 34 in the Complete Isaiah Scroll, together with orthographic peculiarities of each half, point to the practice of bisecting the Book of Isaiah into two scrolls: (1) chapters 1–33 and (2) chapters 34–66. The usual division of Isaiah into the so-called First and Second Isaiah makes chapters 1–39 First Isaiah and chapters 40–66 Second Isaiah. The latter is sometimes divided into Second Isaiah (chaps. 40–55) and Third Isaiah (chaps. 56–66). Paul Kahle, who first called attention to the deliberately large space between chapters 33 and 34 of the Isaiah Scroll, claimed that this division supported the old theory of C. C. Torrey that chapters 34–35 are to be ascribed to Second Isaiah along with chapters 40–66.[1] However, he did not explain why chapters 36–39 came to be included in this so-called Deutero-Isaiah scroll. The position set forth here is that the Book of Isaiah in its present form is the product of an Isaianic school, whose final product was the achievement of a two-volume edition of Isaianic material. These two books of Isaiah are amazingly parallel in their overall structure and outline, which I analyze tentatively as follows:

THE TWO VOLUMES OF THE BOOK OF ISAIAH

Volume I of Isaiah (chaps. 1–33)

I. The Ruin and Restoration of Judah (chaps. 1–5)
  1. First cycle (1:1 26)
    a. Ruin (1:1–24)
    b. Restoration (1:25–26)
  2. Second cycle
    a. Restoration (1:27)
    b. Ruin (1:28–31)

---

1. *Die Hebräischen Handschriften aus der Höhle*, Stuttgart, Kohlhammer, 1951, pp. 72f.

3. Third cycle
   a. Exaltation (2:1-4)
   b. Debasement (2:5—4:1)
4. Fourth cycle
   a. The glorious branch (4:2-6)
   b. The disappointing vineyard (chap. 5)

(After the first cycle, the sequence ruin-restoration is reversed. This may have no special meaning, but it does provide a somber background for chap. 6.)

II. Biography (chaps. 6-8)
   1. Isaiah's Call, or Inaugural Vision (chap. 6)
   2. Isaiah's encounter with Ahaz (the sign of Immanuel) (chap. 7)
   3. Isaiah's sons and disciples (chap. 8)

III. Agents of Divine Blessing and Judgment (chaps. 9-12)
   1. The ideal king (9:1-6 in Heb.; otherwise 9:2-7)
   2. Israel's neighbors (9:7-20 Heb.; 9:8-21)
   3. Assyria (chap. 10)
   4. The ideal king (11:1-10)
   5. The Second Exodus (11:11-16)
      (In this passage Judah and Ephraim avenge themselves upon their neighbors.)
   6. Songs of Salvation (chap. 12)
      (This may be a doxological conclusion to part III.)

IV. Anti-foreign Oracles (chaps. 13-23)
   (Including anti-Babylonian oracles: 13:1—14:23; 21:1-10)

V. Universal Judgment and the Deliverance of God's People (chaps. 24-27)

VI. Ethical Sermons, Indicting Israel and Judah (chaps. 28-31)

VII. The Restoration of Judah and the Davidic Kingdom (chaps. 32-33)

Volume II of Isaiah (chaps. 34-66)

I. Paradise Lost and Regained (chaps. 34-35)
   1. Paradise lost for the world at large, especially Edom (chap. 34)
   2. Paradise restored in the Judean Wilderness (chap. 35)

II. Biography (chaps. 36-40)
   1. Isaiah's ministry during the reign of Hezekiah, ending in the prediction of the Babylonian Exile (chaps. 36-39)
   2. Deutero-Isaiah's inaugural sermon in the Exile (chap. 40)
      (Chap. 40 opens in the divine assembly, just as chap. 6. The voices may be compared, as also the prophetic response, "I said." In chap. 6 the whole earth is full of God's Glory, but Isaiah alone sees it. In chap. 40, all flesh sees it.)

III. Agents of Deliverance and Judgment (chaps. 41-45)
   1. Cyrus (chap. 41)
   2. The Lord's Servant (42:1—43:13)
   3. The Second Exodus (43:14—44:5)
   4. The Lord the only God (44:6-20)
   5. Cyrus 44:21—45:13)
   6. The Lord the only Savior for the world (45:14-25)

IV. Anti-Babylonian Oracles (chaps. 46-48)

V. Universal Redemption through the Lord's Servant, also the Glorification of Israel (chaps. 49-54)
(This section is only doubtfully parallel to part V of Volume I, since in that section there is nothing to correspond to the Lord's Servant.)

VI. Ethical Sermons, the Ethical Conditions for Israel's Redemption (chaps. 56-59)

VII. Paradise Regained: The Glories of the New Jerusalem and the New Heavens and the New Earth (chaps. 60-66)

It must be emphasized that these outlines of the two volumes of Isaiah are not intended as a scientific analysis of all the literary units which went into the structure of the book. They are rather a way of viewing the completed book in order to exhibit possible parallelism, or balanced structure, as seen from the standpoint of the ancient editors who had no scientific interest in literary origins.

By presenting these exploratory outlines of Isaiah at this point, I wish to call attention to chapters 36-39. They are a biographical section which was perhaps introduced from Kings (with supplementation and rearrangement); or, even more probably, it was independently borrowed from the same stream of Isaianic tradition from which the author of Kings derived his material.[2] The section was inserted in order to parallel chapters 7-8, and even Isaiah's inaugural vision (Chap. 6) finds some literary echoes in Deutero-Isaiah's inaugural sermon (Chap. 40). The chapters are therefore roughly parallel within the two volumes of Isaiah. This theory of the literary significance of the bisection of Isaiah explains how chapters 36-39 came to be included in a so-called Second Isaiah Scroll. The two halves of the book possess a unity which

---

2. The author of Kings made use of the annals of the kings of Judah and Israel and other royal records; but he doubtless supplemented them with prophetic tradition, as in the stories of Elijah, Elisha, and Isaiah. In the present case, II Kings 18:13—20:19 are nearly identical with Isaiah 36—39.

is derived from the Isaianic school, which continued to reinterpret the significance of the great eighth-century prophet to succeeding generations. The ancient practice of bisecting books is well discussed by H. St. John Thackeray in his Schweich Lectures of 1920.[3] The division of books, according to him, was made for the convenience of handling, by a purely mechanical division of large works into two scrolls. Some of the better constructed books of antiquity, however, were so composed as to yield a natural literary division at about the mid-point of the work.

THE TWO VOLUMES OF EZEKIEL

An analogous case is the Book of Ezekiel, of whom Josephus says, "He left behind him in writing two books."[4] This is generally interpreted to mean that the present work was understood as consisting of two halves, to be separated on the basis that the first twenty-four chapters of Ezekiel are primarily oracles of doom for Judah, while the remaining twenty-four chapters are primarily prophecies of the restoration of Judah — though they do include anti-foreign oracles as well.[5]

Not only are the two halves of Ezekiel antithetical in their relationship, they also exemplify some parallelistic features which further support the view that the work of Ezekiel is to be viewed as two books. Thus Ezekiel's call to be a watchman is found in 3:16-21 and also in 33:1-9. In the former case the prophet's commission is followed by dumbness (3:25-27). In the latter case his call is followed by release from dumbness (33:21-22) — a release which was anticipated by 3:27 and 24:25-27 of the first volume.[6] Volume I of Ezekiel concludes with a prophecy of the destruction of the temple (24:15-27); whereas Volume II concludes with a prophecy of the restoration of the temple

---

3. *The Septuagint and Jewish Worship,* London, H. Milford, 1923, Appendix IV, pp. 130–36.
4. *J.A.,* X, v, 1 (¶ 79).
5. From the standpoint of post-Exilic Judaism, these could be regarded as hope passages of a strongly anti-Gentile type.

Thackeray, *op. cit.,* pp. 28, 37, notes that in the Septuagint a different translator took over in Ezekiel "at or about the beginning of Chapter xxviii." In the Massoretic text, the halfway mark is at 26:1. This purely mechanical division of approximately half of the book ignores the more logical division between chapters 24 and 25. For the suggestion of an earlier division, cf. note 7, below.
6. On the use of chapter 33 to bind the two parts of the book together, see Carl Gordon Howie, *The Date and Composition of Ezekiel,* Journal of Biblical Literature Monograph Series, Vol. IV, 1950, p. 98.

and the cult, the life-giving power of which will bring fertility to the land itself (Chaps. 40–47).[7] The "glory of the Lord" which leaves the temple in the vision of chapters 8–11 returns to the restored temple in the final vision (43:1–5) and will give sanctity to the whole land, especially Jerusalem, which will be called "*Yahwèh Shâmmâh*"—"the LORD is there" (48:35).

Not everything in each book of Ezekiel finds a parallel or contrasting counterpart in the other book; but the structure of the books is at least partially explained through parallelism. It is certainly helpful to interpretation to know the reason for the repetition of the prophet's commission to be a watchman and to understand the cause of the dispersion of the materials concerning the prophet's dumbness (however defined). No longer need we suppose that the experience of dumbness extended to the major part of the prophet's ministry. It is apparent that this mutism belonged wholly to the period shortly before the destruction of the temple (Chap. 24), and that only editorially has this theme been read back into the very beginning of Ezekiel's ministry.[8]

EVIDENCE FOR THE BISECTION OF ISAIAH

Of the prophet Isaiah, Josephus also says that "he wrote down all his prophecies and left them behind in books." [9] The plural "books" is reasonably explained as meaning "two books," the two volumes corresponding to the two halves of the Complete Isaiah Scroll. Each is divided into thirty-three chapters in our modern Bibles. In the scroll, each consists of twenty-seven columns, and the point of division lies between two sheets of skin, so that, if it were not that they happen

---

7. Another possible arrangement would begin Vol. II at chapter 24:1 or 24:15. This would have the advantage of beginning the second volume with a portion of text dealing with Jerusalem, rather than with foreign nations. According to this arrangement, the antithesis between the destroyed and the restored temple would lie between the beginning and the end of Vol. II. It would also place the second and last mention of the prophet's name (24:24) near the beginning of the latter volume. Cf. the renewed claim to authorship by Thucydides in his History at V, 26, at the probable beginning of the second roll of his work. Thackeray, *op. cit.*, p. 132.

8. This understanding of the editorial process renders invalid the ingenious hypothesis of Moshe Greenberg, "On Ezekiel's Dumbness," *JBL*, lxxxvii, 1958, pp. 101–105.

9. *J.A.*, X, ii, 2 (¶ 35). Similarly Josephus states that Daniel left "books" (*biblia*), in *J.A.*, X, xi, 7 (¶ 267). In the case of Daniel one could think of the diverse character of the last six as opposed to the first six chapters; but since the Biblical work is relatively small, one should rather think of apocryphal works assigned to Daniel as justifying the plural "books."

Section of the Complete Isaiah Scroll, showing the lower half of Column 27 (Chapter 33) and portions of other columns to the right and left.

to be sewed together, they could easily circulate as two separate scrolls. An unprecedented gap of three lines occurs at the bottom of Col. 27, separating the two volumes. This gap, it is maintained, preserves the tradition of the separate "books" of Isaiah.[10]

In an article already published, I have presented evidence to show that the scribe of IQ Isa[a] began his copying with a manuscript containing only the first thirty-three chapters and concluded with another containing sixty-six chapters. When he had exhausted the contents of the first scroll he turned to another manuscript for the completion of the book. The latter was badly worn and had crumbled at the margin; this accounts for the gaps within the scroll where portions of text are missing. I was uncertain whether the former manuscript preserved the tradition of a First Isaiah Scroll or should be regarded as Volume I of Isaiah, which had become separated from Volume II.[11] I now feel certain that it is to be regarded as Volume I, that indeed this body of material never existed in its present form except as the first tome of the larger work.

THE LITERARY ORIGIN OF THE TWO VOLUMES

The Book of Isaiah is the product of a school organized by the prophet Isaiah (8:16-17; 28:9-10), who doubtless included among his disciples his own children. The Exilic prophet, commonly called Deutero-Isaiah, arose within this school (cf. 50:4).[12] His disciples in turn continued to add to and edit the Isaianic material — the final product of which is the two-volume work, with some intentional parallelisms between the two volumes. This parallelism need not be pervasive. As in the case of Ezekiel, it is not necessary that everything have its parallel. However, the above outline is an experiment which seeks to see possible parallel relationships between all the major sections, the same numbered division of one book corresponding to that of the other.

---

10. The midpoint of Isaiah according to the Massoretes is at 33:20, only shortly before the end of the chapter.
11. "The Manuscripts of Isaiah from which DSI[a] was copied," *BASOR*, No. 127, Oct. 1952, pp. 16-21.
12. Cf. Aage Bentzen, *Introduction to the Old Testament*, Copenhagen, G. E. C. Gad, 2nd Edition, 1952, Vol. II, pp 103-115; Martin Buber, *Prophetic Faith*, New York, Macmillan, 1949, pp. 147, 202ff.; Sigmund Mowinckel, "Prophecy and Tradition," *Avhandlinger utgitten det Norske Videnskaps-Akademi*, 1946. The curious statement of the Babylonian Talmud (Baba Bathra 15a) that "Hezekiah and his colleagues wrote Isaiah,

Sufficient to establish this thesis, it seems, is the presence of biography after other introductory material in each volume, the appearance of the Second-Exodus motif in both parts (III, 5, and III, 3,
respectively), and the balancing of anti-foreign oracles with anti-
Babylonian oracles. It should also be observed that prophecies against
Babylon are included among the anti-foreign oracles of the first part.
The two books were probably developed simultaneously, Exilic and
post-Exilic material being added to Volume I and pre-Exilic tradition
(chaps. 36–39) being inserted into Volume II — thereby creating literary
balance. It is not impossible that there are some pre-Exilic prophecies
among the oracles of Volume II. Note especially 56:9—57:13 and
58:1–9 as being of possible pre-Exilic origin.[13] The final form of the
book was achieved after, or in conjunction with, the composition of
Isa. 24—27, a section of disputed date, but which certainly must antedate
the second century B.C.

The bisection of Isaiah between chapters 33 and 34 puts chapters
34–35 in their proper place as an introduction to Volume II. Chapter
34 is, in its linguistic and apocalyptic character, most intimately related
to chapters 56–66; and chapter 35 finds its closest verbal parallels in
chapters 40–55.[14] Together they make a superb introduction to chapters

---

Proverbs, the Song of Songs, and Ecclesiastes" preserves the tradition of collective authorship of Isaiah. For Hezekiah's role as a patron of literature, cf. Prov. 25:1.
13. Cf. Bentzen, *op. cit.,* pp. 109f. He notes that "in like manner 63, 7—65, 25 may
be connected with the events of [587 B.C.], just as the Book of Lamentations."
14. Marvin Pope, in his fine study ("Isaiah 34 in Relation to Isaiah 35, 40–66," *JBL,*
LXXI, 1952, pp. 235–43), argues that "As to style, . . . 34 certainly corresponds as
closely with 40–55 as does 35." Still, the apocalyptic themes of chapter 34 connect it
more closely with chapters 56–66, than to 40–55. The "day of vengeance" and "year
of recompense" anticipate 61:2 and 63:4. Chapters 34 and 63 also hold in common the
fearsome doom of Edom. The collapse of the heavens at 34:4 finds a more dramatic
connection as an antithesis to the New Heavens and New Earth of chapters 65–66. The
desolation of Edom's streams in 34:9 may be compared with 42:15 and 50:2; but the
last two references are but figurative allusions to the Exodus, whereas the first reference
is literal apocalyptic expectation.
    Chapter 35 finds many verbal parallels with 40–55. Compare the last line of 35:2
with 40:5; compare 35:4 with 40:9d–10; compare 35:6f. with 41:18 and 55:12f.;
compare 35:8 with 40:3 and 43:19 (but also with 57:14 and 62:10). Isaiah 35:10 and
51:11 are identical verses. These linguistic connections relate chapter 35 most vitally
with 40–55. Still, this chapter may be of the same authorship as chapter 34; for the
"Wilderness" of chapter 35 is a definite geographical area of Judea (as in Joshua 15:61)
and stands in antithesis to Edom of chapter 34. Their connection finds a neat summary
in Joel 3:19–21 (Heb.; otherwise, 4:19–21). Though references to the wilderness road
and to streams in the desert in the writing of the Exilic prophet mostly refer to release

40–66, as rightly emphasized by C. C. Torrey.[15] One may note further the appropriate balancing of the first and seventh major divisions. The collapse of the old heavens and old earth in chapter 34 prepares the way for the New Heavens and New Earth near the end of Volume II (65:17–25; 66:22). The message of the Babylonian prophet Deutero-Isaiah (presumably chaps. 40–55) is framed by materials which give it more of an eschatological and apocalyptic sense than was intended by the Exilic prophet. His message may be occasionally interpolated by later members of the Isaianic school. Thus 51:4–6, which concludes with an apocalyptic note (v. 6) similar to that of chapter 34, may be such an interpolation.[16]

The late Robert H. Pfeiffer noted correctly that chapter 1, which is one of (First) Isaiah's last oracles, was prefixed in its present place prior to the heading of chapter 2 as a sort of introduction to the book.[17] When this was done, the more elaborate heading of 1:1 was also prefixed. Its extension of the ministry of Isaiah down to the time of Hezekiah quite naturally suggested that there may have been a Book of Isaiah concluding with the historical appendix of chapters 36–39, so that the arrangement was similar to that of the Prophet Jeremiah. This carried with it, however, the assumption that chapters 40–66 originally stood in no connection with chapters 1–39. If, however, the whole is the product of an Isaianic school, 1:1 might be understood as the heading of the entire two-volume work — being intended to indicate the period of the great master's prophetic career, rather than to define the total scope of the book. It is possible that chapter 1 is to be regarded as the preface to the complete work, and that chapters 2–5, with their heading at 2:1, are the introduction to Volume I proper. In that case, the portrayal of the New Jerusalem in the final chapters (60, 65–66) is anticipated already in 1:26–27, with the nexus between ruin and future blessedness being the refining process of divine judgment (1:24–25).

---

from the Exile, with figurative allusions to the Exodus as a type of redemption, 51:3 has in mind Judean wasteland which will be transformed; but here the author specifies *"her* wilderness" and *"her* desert."

15. *Op. cit.,* pp. 279–82, 295f.

16. Verses 4–5 are made up of phrases borrowed from the so-called "Servant Songs" and were converted into a Servant Song by the alteration of the pronominal suffixes in the Isaiah Scroll. Cf. above, pp. 195ff.

17. *Op. cit.,* p. 448.

DUAL STRUCTURE AND FORM CRITICISM

This discussion should be regarded as a contribution to the form criticism of books. Form criticism has too often been applied to the individual units of books, rather than to their organization into a larger whole.

For other examples of dual structure, one should note that certain New Testament books can be analyzed as containing parallelistic halves. H. St. John Thackeray believed that the Acts of the Apostles consists of two parts. Certainly the Gospel and the Acts represent complementary volumes.[18] The Book of Revelation, it seems to me, is best understood as consisting of two volumes. Both begin with a vision of Christ (chaps. 1 and 12) and both conclude with the ultimate triumph of Christ's kingdom.[19] This dichotomy explains why already at Rev. 11:15 "The kingdom of the world has become the kingdom of our Lord and of his Christ, and he shall reign for ever and ever"; and yet the following chapter starts afresh with the birth of Christ and his conflict with Satanic power. The message of the whole work can be grasped in its general principles by any reader stopping at the end of the first volume. The second volume however, is no mere repetition of the first; but it carries the apocalyptic drama through with heightened intensity which calls for many original elements. In this regard one may compare the two volumes of Isaiah, noting the more miraculous and apocalyptic character of Volume II — even in the biographical section.[20]

It is not suggested that dual structure is the only book form. Pentateuchal structure is witnessed to by the Psalms, by II Maccabees, and by the Gospel according to Matthew. II Maccabees may also, however, be divided into approximately two equal parts: the first part

18. *Op. cit.,* p. 132. Here he mentions likewise the natural division of Joshua into twelve chapters of conquest and twelve of the allocation of the land. One may recall also the Wisdom of Jesus Son of Sirach, which divides naturally between chapters 23 and 24. Both volumes of Sirach begin with a chapter praising wisdom. Indication of a fresh beginning in chapter 24 is pointed to specifically by verses 32f.

19. Since writing the above, I have discovered that Hugh J. Schonfield (*The Authentic New Testament,* a Mentor Book, New York, The New American Library, 1958, p. 439) also divides the Revelation of John into two books.

20. The destruction of Sennacherib became a type of the ultimate defeat of the last great foe of God's people. With the miraculous intervention of the angel deliverer, cf. Daniel 12:1 and 1Q M xvii, 5–9. There is thus an affinity between this event and later apocalyptic expectation.

concluding with the institution of the Feast of Dedication; the second, with the institution of the Feast of Nicanor.[21] In addition, many of the doublets of the Old Testament literature are to be explained as stylistic, even when the parallel passages may come ultimately from different sources. I believe the love of parallelism to be characteristic of Hebrew literature, not merely in poetic verse structure, but also in larger units. It is therefore not accidental that Moses received his divine commission, first at the burning bush and again in Egypt (chaps. 3 and 6); nor is it merely by reason of doublets in the sources that the Ten Commandments were given to Moses twice (Ex. 21:18; 32:15f. and 34:1, 27-29) at Sinai-Horeb; for editors have often shown themselves capable of combining two accounts of the same event into a simple narrative. In these particular illustrations from Exodus, it is a case of literary parallelism within the same half of the book, rather than between halves. Similarly the two interrogations of Job by the Lord who appeared to him in the whirlwind may be there for stylistic reasons. The first examination is in the area of the natural world; the second is in the area of mythology (chaps. 38-39 and 40:1—43:6, respectively). In both cases Job must confess his ignorance. Such parallelism may have been intended by an editor, or even by the original author. Why should the Lord's double questioning of Job be any more suspect than the two appearances of Satan before the divine assembly and Satan's twice testing of Job in the first two chapters? There may well be an intended parallelism between the beginning and the end, in the fact that the book opens with Job's twofold trial by Satan and concludes with his double examination by Yahweh.

In the Gospels, also, Jesus' sayings are sometimes arranged in couplets. In the Sermon on the Mount, "the salt of the earth" and "the light of the world" stand side by side as parallel representations of the redemptive role of Christ's disciples (Matth. 5:13, 14-16). Two figures are employed to reinforce the necessity of singleness of devotion: the clearly focused eye (6:22-23) and the serving of one master (6:24). In Luke's presentation of the Sermon on the Plain, the Beatitudes (6:20-23) are paralleled by a series of woes (6:24-26).

Jesus' parables are also sometimes grouped in pairs. The parables of the soils and of the tares (Matth. 13:1-23, 24-30) both concern the varied experiences of a sower. The parables of the mustard seed and

21. Cf. my entry "Maccabees, Books of," in *IDB*, Vol. K–Q, sections C, 2 and 7, on pp. 206, 208.

of the yeast (13:31-32, 33) jointly reinforce the thought of the rapid growth of the Kingdom of Heaven. The joyful abandonment of discipleship is doubly illustrated by the parables of the discovered treasure and of the prize pearl (13:44, 45-46). The necessity of calculating the cost of discipleship is set forth by the stories of the man building a tower and of the king going to war (Luke 14:23-30, 31-33). Sometimes there are more than two illustrations of a given point. Thus the two brief parables of the shepherd who found a lost sheep and of the woman who found a lost coin (15:4-7, 8-10) are followed by the longer story of the spendthrift son who had been lost and was found (15:11-32). Some of these groupings may be due to the Evangelists; others may be due to their sources. Thus one suspects that the first two parables of Luke 15 may have stood together in a Lukan source and that the next one which is concerned with the wayward son was placed here by Luke himself.

The principle of parallelism between halves may apply to the book structure of the Gospel according to Mark.[22] Peter's confession of Jesus as the Messiah near Caesarea Philippi (8:27-29) is the climax of the first half of the book, just as the Roman centurion's confession of Jesus as God's son (15:39) climaxes the second half. The latter is given extra emphasis by the cruel mockery of Jesus as king of the Jews in what precedes (15:16-26). Jesus' transfiguration, with the divine voice owning Jesus as Son (9:2-7), is a parallel to the account of Jesus' baptism recounted at the beginning of the book (1:9-11); but at the same time it may be an anticipation of the resurrection of Jesus at the end of the book (chap. 16).[23]

The Meaning of Duplication

Duplication may have had a special meaning, as in the dreams of Genesis; e.g. Joseph's own dreams were two in number (37:5-11), and while in prison he interpreted the dreams of the butler and the baker (40:9-19). Each had only one dream; but the two are linked together in the story. Pharaoh also had two dreams (chap. 41). In this last case the Biblical text says explicitly: "The dream of Pharaoh

---

22. This was brought to my attention by the Rev. Mr. Theodore J. Weeden, a Ph.D. candidate at the Claremont Graduate School.
23. See Mark 9:8. Cf. II Peter 1:16-19. On the problem of interpreting the transfiguration story, see B. Harvie Branscomb, *The Gospel of Mark*, The Moffatt New Testament Commentary, New York and London, Harper and Bros., no date, pp. 159-163; and Frederick C. Grant, *IB*, VII, pp. 774ff.

is one . . . And the doubling of Pharaoh's dream means that the thing is fixed by God, and God will shortly bring it to pass." Thus the meanings of divine certainty and imminent fulfillment are attached to the duplication of Pharaoh's dream.

Returning then to the duplicates already mentioned, one may suggest that the doubling of Joseph's dreams emphasizes their divine origin and certainty of fulfillment. The dreams of the two Egyptian officials, both of which were correctly interpreted by Joseph, authenticate Joseph as a true interpreter of dreams. The two commissions of Moses to deliver the Hebrews from bondage strengthen the divine authorization of Moses. The two givings of the Ten Commandments reinforce their divine origin and authority. The double testing of Job by Satan confirms the piety of Job; and his twofold interrogation by the Lord shows how doubly ignorant he was and utterly audacious in his charges against the Lord. Similarly, within the two parallel halves of Isaiah, one may suggest that to a certain extent the visions are one, so that, in the clarification of the message of the total work, corresponding parts of each book (insofar as truly parallel) need to be expounded together. The dualistic structure may also confirm the divine authority of the Isaianic message and stress the certainty and the imminence of its fulfillment. Yet, in so stating, one must not forget that the massiveness of the literature of the Isaianic school made it advantageous to divide it into two volumes. Rules of literary parallelism, therefore, came in secondarily to determine the fashioning of these two balanced volumes.

POSTSCRIPT: For the original, lecture form of this chapter (cf. above, p. xii), see now *Trudy Dvardtsat Pyatogo Mezhdunarodnogo Kongressa Vostokokovedov,* Moscow: Tzolatel'stvo Vostochnoi Literatury, 1962, Tome I, pp. 431–7.

The Man of God's Refining

An important passage in the Manual of Discipline is a doctrinal section concerning the dualism of human existence (1Q S iii, 13—iv, 26). Two spirits (the Spirit of Truth and the Spirit of Perversity), or angels (the Prince of Light and the Angel of Darkness), are struggling for the loyalty of man. The good spirit and his hosts seek to lead man to moral perfection and to eternal glory, but the evil spirit and his demonic legions seek to lead man into greater and greater sin and thereby to eternal ruin. The society of men is divided into two groups, according to which spirit they follow: the Children of Light and the Children of Darkness. The latter are wholly dominated by the Angel of Darkness; and, though the former have the Prince of Light and the God of Israel as their helper, they have to give battle constantly with the opposing Angel of Darkness who is perpetually trying to trip them. As a matter of fact, no good man is entirely free from the taint of sin or the defiling presence of a demonic spirit. The God of Israel who created both angels will ultimately triumph over the evil angel and his hosts who are arrayed against His will. This victory over Satanic power is what is featured in the climax of this doctrinal section, which reads as follows:

iv, 18　　Now God, in the mysteries of His understanding and in His glorious wisdom, has assigned a limited time for the existence
19　of perversity; and at the season appointed | for divine intervention, He will destroy it for ever. At that time, the truth on earth will emerge victorious; [1] for it has become polluted by the ways of wickedness, under the dominion of perversity, un-
20　til | the season of the decreed judgment. At that time, *God will purify by His truth all the deeds of a man and refine him more than the sons of men,* in order to destroy every perverse

1. Or, "The truth will emerge victorious on earth." On earth, truth is mixed with error, because man's insight is obscured through sin; but in the eschaton there shall be revealed the untarnished wisdom of heaven.

21 spirit from the inner parts of | his flesh, and to cleanse him
through the Spirit of Holiness from all wicked practices; and
He will sprinkle upon him the Spirit of Truth like the water
of purification,[2] (so as to cleanse him) from all untrue abom-
22 inations and from being polluted | by the Spirit of Impurity,
so that he may give the upright insight into the knowledge of
the Most High and into the wisdom of the heavenly beings, in
order to make wise the perfect of way; for God has chosen them
23 to be an eternal covenant, | and all the glory of Adam will be
theirs. There will be no more perversity, all works of fraud being put to shame.

The italicized portion of the above text is of disputed interpretation.
One needs to compare it with six other translations. It appears as **D**
in the following list:

A, 1 God will purify by His truth all the deeds of man
   2   and refine for Himself some of the sons of men.

B, 1 God will purify by His truth all the deeds of man
   2   and refine for Himself [a certain one] from among the
          sons of men.

C, 1 God will purify by His truth all the deeds of a man
   2   and separate [him] out for Himself from among the sons
          of men.

D, 1 God will purify by His truth all the deeds of a man
   2   and refine him more than the sons of men.

E, 1 God will purify by His truth all the deeds of each man
   2   and refine for Himself the body of each man.

F, 1 God will purify by His truth all the deeds of a man
   2   and refine for Himself the body of a man.

G, 1 God will purify by His truth all the deeds of man
   2   and refine for Himself the body of mankind.

There are three different Hebrew expressions involved in the variant
translations. The FIRST of these is *gever* at the end of the first clause,

2. The "water of purification" (*mê niddâh*) was apparently the purifying water mixed
with the ashes of the red heifer according to Num. 19 and 31:23. Cf. Brownlee in
Stendahl, *op. cit.*, p. 38; J. Bowman, "Did the Qumrân Sect Burn the Red Heifer?" *RQ*,
I, 1959, pp. 73ff.

which has been given three different renderings: (a) "man" (as in A, 1; B, 1; and G, 1), (b) "a man" (as in C, 1; D, 1; and F, 1), (c) "each man" (as in E, 1). The SECOND Hebrew word is *LW* (*lô*), which may mean "for Himself" (as in A, 2; B, 2; C, 2; E, 2; F, 2 and G, 2) or it may be an Aramaism for the accusative "him" (D, 2). The THIRD Hebrew expression is *MBNY 'YŠ*, which if read *mib-bənê 'iš* may mean variously: (a) *"from* the sons of men" (as in B, 2 and C, 2), (b) *"some of* the sons of men" (as in A, 2), or (c) *"more than* the sons of men" (as in D, 2). Another treatment of the phrase is to regard it as an irregular spelling for *mivnêh 'iš,* "the *body* of a (?) man" (as in E, 2; F, 2; and G, 2). All three of these disputed Hebrew expressions are interrelated, according to the interpretation adopted. It is therefore best to examine each translation in sequence.

TRANSLATION A, which represents my initial understanding of the passage, has been followed by nearly all translators, including P. Wernberg-Møller, who was aware of the controversy over the passage.[3] The translation of *gever* as "man" in the general sense of "mankind" was a departure from Old Testament usage which one standard Hebrew lexicon defines as: "man as strong, disting[uished] fr[om] women, children, and non-combatants whom he is to defend . . . = each (of locusts) Jo[el] 2⁸."[4] The corporate and generic sense of *gever* seemed to be necessitated by the plurality of reference in the expression *mib-bənê 'iš,* "some of the sons of men." Whatever uneasiness I may have felt concerning the collective interpretation of *gever* was disspelled by the logic that the general, or indefinite usage of *gever* as "a man" "any man," or "each man" elsewhere in the scrolls had prepared the way for this corporate usage.[5]

TRANSLATION B represents the rendering of Jean-Paul Audet.[6] It modified my translation by finding an individual reference in the second clause, though oddly enough not in the first. The author doubtless felt compelled to interpret *mib-bənê 'iš* as singular ("a certain one from among the sons of men") rather than as a plural ("some of the sons

3. *Op. cit.,* pp. 27, 85f.
4. *A Hebrew and English Lexicon of the Old Testament,* based on the Lexicon of William Gesenius, as translated by Edward Robinson, edited by Francis Brown, and revised by S. R. Driver and Charles A. Briggs, Oxford, Clarendon Press, corrected impression, 1952, p. 150a.
5. This indefinite usage is attested in 1Q S iv, 23; x, 18; 1Q H ix, 15; xi, 20. In the last two passages it is used as a parallel term with *'ənôsh,* but in the sense of "a man," "a human being."
6. Cf. above, p. 206, and n. 7.

of men") by reason of singular pronouns in the following clauses
("his flesh," "cleanse him," "upon him"). In this, Audet was wrestling
with a real grammatical difficulty in Translation A. It seems strange,
however, that if an individual is referred to he is not specifically mentioned, as indeed he is if *gever* of the preceding clause is understood
to mean an individual.

TRANSLATION C represents the rendering of Bo Reicke.[7] It eliminates
the principal objection of Translation B in that the person referred to
receives specific mention in the first clause. However, the sense assigned the verb refine (*ZQQ*), "separate out," seems unlikely. There
appears to be no precise analogy for refining a desired product *from*
an inferior substance; for one seems to speak rather of smelting away
the *dross* from the precious metal (Isa. 1:25; Jer. 6:29, using the verb
ṢRP), or of purging away *impurities* (Ezek. 20:38, using *BRR;* 22:15,
using *TMM*).

TRANSLATION D is my revised understanding, which I adopted in
August 1953.[8] It improves upon Bo Reicke by discovering the true
object for the verb "refine" in *lô* ("him"). However, it did not arise
by way of attempting to improve upon anyone's rendering; for mo-
mentarily, I had forgotten about Audet's translation (which I had read
when it first appeared) and I recalled only Reicke's treatment of
gever, when suddenly it occurred to me in examining the passage in
another connection, that *lô* might be the object of the verb "refine."
It was a whole day before I had an opportunity to check Reicke's
translation to see how he had handled *lô*.

TRANSLATION E represents that of Yigael Yadin, which was proposed
immediately after I published translation D in the *BASOR*.[9] He disparaged Translation A as "somewhat forced," and described B and C
as "unsuccessful efforts of others." He objected to the Aramaism of *lô*
("him") and proposed a new solution based upon the discovery in
the Qumrân Hymns of the word *mivnèh* ("frame," or "structure")
in the sense of "body."[10] These Hymns did not appear in print until

---

7. Cf. above, p. 206, and n. 8.
8. Cf. above, p. 206, and n. 9.
9. No. 135 (Oct. 1954), pp. 35–38; Yadin, "A Note on DSD iv, 20," *JBL*, lxxiv, 1955,
pp. 40–43.
10. This occurs twice (1Q H i, 23; xiii, 15); but Yadin lists indiscriminately with
these also the cognate word *mavnît* (1Q H vii, 4; fragment 47, line 5), which occurs
also in 1Q S xi, 8, but not in the sense of "body." The most interesting passage is 1Q
H i, 21–23, where the concept of the "body of sin" is discussed. Cf. Rom. 6:6.

after my article was published, so that this solution to the problems was not available to me.[11] Several observations must be made regarding Yadin's proposed solution.

(1) Its ascription of the meaning "each" to both *gever* and its presumed parallel *'ish* is in full accord with Old Testament usage and is entirely possible in the Qumrân literature; but the unqualified promise that God will purify the body of *each* man is unsuited to its dualistic context where a clear distinction is constantly drawn between the fate of the righteous and the wicked. The wicked are not to be refined, but scourged and destroyed by the wrath of God. Of course, Yadin understands the present passage to refer to the righteous alone; but if this be so, then there is a surprising lack of precision in the Manual at this point.[12]

(2) The treatment of *MBNY* as an irregular spelling for *MBNH* is *a priori* possible in view of similar misspellings elsewhere in the Qumrân literature, although this one is as yet unattested, unless it be here. However, within this doctrinal passage one encounters repeatedly the phrase *banê 'ish*, so that *a priori* one would expect this to be but another example of the characteristic phrase "sons of men." It is not surprising, therefore, that A. M. Habermann in his pointed Hebrew text disregards the suggestion of Yadin.[13]

(3) Yadin's claim that his translation presents a rendering truer to the author's intended parallelism rests upon faulty literary analysis, as may be seen by comparing his translation with mine:

And then God will purify by His truth all the deeds of each man,
And He will refine for Himself the body of each man,
In order to consume every spirit of wrongdoing from the midst of his
flesh.

(Yadin)

11. I was privileged to study for a short while one of the first copies to reach America, brought directly from Israel in December 1954. The text did not become generally available until 1955.
12. J. Licht, in his mostly excellent study ("An Analysis of the Treatise on the Two Spirits in DSD," in *Aspects of the Dead Sea Scrolls*, p. 97, n. 37) notes this difficulty, but dismisses it by saying that the author "expresses his view on the subject clearly enough in his curses, IV, 13–14." Indeed he does there, but the present lapse is noteworthy.
13. *Megilloth Midbar Yehuda, The Scrolls from the Judean Desert,* Tel-Aviv, Machbaroth Lesifruth Publishing House, 1959, p. 63. For occurrences of *banê 'ish* in the context, see IQ S iii, 13; iv, 15, 26.

Then God will purify by His truth all the deeds of a man
and refine him more than the sons of men.
In order to consume every perverse spirit from the midst of his flesh
and to cleanse him through the Spirit of Holiness from all wicked
practices.

(Brownlee)

In displaying the parallelism, Yadin did not quote the last clause which
I have included, perhaps feeling that it was irrelevant to the present
discussion. However, syntactically, it is quite relevant; for we are
confronted with two distichs rather than with a single tristich.[14] This
affects the interpretation of the parallelism; for there is obviously a
chiastic (ab/ba) parallelism, in which the closest parallel to the first
half of the first line is to be found in the second half of the second line,
and the closest parallel to the second half of the first line is to be found
in the first half of the second line. Failing to note this, Yadin argued:
"the construction of the whole sentence compels us to see in *MBNY*
'IŠ an object parallel to *M'ŚY GBR*." Yadin neglected to take into
account, however, "the whole sentence." Had he done so, he would
have noticed that the true parallel to "all deeds of a man" is to be
found in the phrase "all wicked practices," and not at all in *MBNY*
'IŠ ("more than the sons of men")! Similarly, although all the verbs
are parallel to one another, the first verb ("purify") finds its closest
parallel in the fourth ("cleanse"); and the second ("refine") is paralleled most closely by the third ("consume.") Likewise "by His truth"
of the first stich is balanced by "through the Spirit of Holiness" in
the fourth, in full confirmation of the chiastic character of the verse.
One may try to turn the edge of this argument by noting that the
reading of "body" in the second stich of the first line would provide
an appropriate anticipation of "flesh" in the first stich of the second
line. However, there is nothing intrinsically wrong with the progressive,
synthetic parallelism of these stichs as I read them. The chiasmus does
not exhaust the parallelism, and thus structurally there is also parallelism (though of a supplementary type) between both halves of each
line. It is also interesting that "refine him" may be compared contextually with "cleanse him," although this lies outside the chiastic

14. The passage as a whole, though characterized by considerable parallelism, is only
doubtfully to be considered as poetry. Yet see the translation of A. Dupont-Sommer
in *Revue de l'Histoire des Religions,* cxlii, 1952, pp. 7–12. Be that as it may, the literary
structure of the present fragment of text is regular enough to admit of poetic analysis.

relationship, so that little is to be made of this. The fundamental observation is that there is plenty of parallelism in the various varieties of interrelatedness of the four stichs, without forcing MBNY 'IŠ into a structural equivalence with M'ŚY GBR.

(4) There is nothing incredible in translating WZQQ LW as "refine him." Although the use of L as the sign of the accusative is an Aramaism, it is well attested in late Hebrew (even that of the Old Testament), and its use in the Qumrân literature is beyond question.[15] The most dramatic demonstration of Qumrân usage is the substitution of L for 'T, the classical sign of the accusative, in the quotation of Isa. 50:4 in 1Q H viii, 36.[16]

TRANSLATION F represents that of Géza Vermès, who sought to combine elements of truth in both Yadin's position and mine.[17] Its advantage over the rendering of Yadin is that it gives a lucid text in which there is no apparent suggestion of the purification of the whole human race, contrary to the doctrinal setting; for Vermès interpreted this passage, despite Yadin's supposed improvements, as referring to an eschatological prophet of Qumrân expectation.

TRANSLATION G represents the interpretation of J. Licht, A. P. Hastoupis, and A. S. van der Woude.[18] It departs from the understanding of Yadin by assigning a collective sense to gever and 'ish, rather than an individual application ("each"). It therefore has this dubious feature in addition to other unsound aspects of Yadin's treatment. If one is to ascribe this sense to gever, he will be on surer ground to return to Translation A, where the second clause may be claimed as an appropriate qualification of the first — only "some of the sons of men" to be benefited by the divine purgation.

In conclusion, the best rival to Translation D is Translation A, and I prefer D to A for the following reasons: (1) The singular pronouns of iv, 20f. agree with the singular gever, thereby showing that mib-bənê 'ish was not construed as giving a plural denotation ("some of the sons of men") to the sentence. (See the passage in context on p. 261.) In

15. 1Q S viii, 36; x, 6f.; xi, 16; 1Q H i, 18; v, 33. For the last two passages see J. Baumgarten and M. Monsoor in the JBL, lxxiv, 1955, p. 118, n. 23; lxxv, 1956, p. 112, n. 48.
16. L'WT L' 'P DBR rephrasing the Massoretic L'WT 'T Y'P DBR, where ' 'P ('YP) appears for Y'P. Cf. my comments in NTS, iii, 1956–7, p. 19, n. 3.
17. Op. cit., pp. 54–58.
18. J. Licht, op. cit., pp. 96f.; A. P. Hastoupis (Professor of Old Testament at the University of Thessalonica), To en tois Cheirographois tês Nekras Thalassês Egcheiridion Peitharchias (a Greek translation of the Dead Sea Manual of Discipline), Athens, 1957, p. 20; van der Woude, op. cit., p. 89.

harmony with this, an alternative may be found to interpreting *ZQQ LW* as "refine *him*," by assigning a singular significance to *mib-bənê 'ish;* for the partitive use of *min* (here *mib*) is sometimes (though less often) employed as a singular.[19] If we allow that usage here, we may obtain the following translation:

> God will purify by His truth all the deeds of a man
> and refine for Himself *one* of the sons of men.

This reading, which may be compared with Translation B, not only offers an important modification of Translation D, it allows those who object to the Aramaism of *LW* to find another appropriate singular object for the verb *ZQQ* ("refine") in the words *mib-bənê 'ish*. This latter would provide a term parallel to *gever* — not, however, with *M'ŚY GBR* (as Yadin would wish it), for its full parallel is to be found in the second half of the next line (as we have already shown). This revision, be it noted, would sharpen rather than lessen the clarity of the personal reference.

(2) "A man" with definiteness of meaning is well attested in the Old Testament and is illustrated in the Qumrân interpretation of the *gever* of Psalm 37:23 as referring to the Teacher of Righteousness, although in this particular place the psalm probably meant originally, "The steps of *every* man are from the Lord." [20]

(3) The individual reference in iv, 20 points to a prophetic figure, who as a man made perfect through suffering, will mark the beginning of the final triumph of truth over error. This Messianic expectation looks like an Essene modification of the Zoroastrian belief in the ultimate triumph of truth over error through the coming of a prophet-savior (or *saoshyant*). This Iranian belief had a long, rich development; and it is difficult to know exactly at what stage this doctrine had arrived in the first two centuries B.C. However, its pre-Christian inception seems assured.[21] No other passage in the Qumrân Scrolls is so shot through with

19. Cf. Ex. 6:25: "Eleazar, Aaron's son, took *for himself one of* the daughters of Putiel to be his wife." Cf. also Lev. 25:33; Neh. 13:28; Ez. 17:5, 13; Ps. 132:11; Dan. 11:5.
20. Note that this usage is not the same as a collective or corporate usage, for men are viewed individually, as also in the passages referred to above in note 5.
21. See A. V. W. Jackson (in Hershey Sneath, *Religion and the Future Life,* New York, Fleming H. Revell, 1922, pp. 132f.) who states: "At all events, there is no doubt on one point, the Saoshyant doctrine in Zoroastrianism is pre-Christian as is shown by its occurrence in metrical compositions."

Zoroastrian ideas and concepts as IQ S iii, 13—iv, 26, and the discovery of another important (though partial) [22] parallel between Essenism and Zoroastrianism is in striking accord with the general character of the section.

(4) The correlation of this reading with Isa. 52:13–15, as discussed above, points to a Messianic interpretation of that passage. In this connection, one should not make too much of the word Messiah; for the Qumrân sect expected the coming of a prophet and two anointed ones, and one of their titles for the Old Testament prophets was "the anointed ones." [23] Anointing, in this connection, refers to the gift of the Spirit (cf. Isa. 42:1; 61:1) and does not necessarily point to a royal figure. On this point, one should recall that H. H. Rowley has argued strenuously that Isa. 52:13—53:12 referred originally to an individual who was to be a prophet and redeemer, but not a royal Messiah.[24] Essene interpretation is apparently in accord with that point of view; although, one must not forget that the Servant motif was applied in many different ways, including the corporate, so that the application of this theme in one manner in one scroll passage does not exclude its application in another way in other places. Such variety of application is to be found also in the Targum.

(5) The concept of the man sanctified, or made perfect, through suffering underlies some important Christological passages of the primitive Church. In each case the motif is obviously warped in order that it may be made to fit the case of a Christ Who was always without sin. The Christian use of this theme, despite the necessity for modification, points to a pre-Christian doctrine like that of 1 Q S iv, 20f.[25] The birth of the Messianic community through the suffering of the Teacher of Righteousness seems to be set forth in 1Q H iii, 5ff., where the sectarian society is personified as a *gever* ("a man") and as a *zâkhâr* ("a male"). In that case, such specific terms have a corporate meaning not by definition of the words themselves, but because they stand as metaphors for God's "mighty people." There is nothing in the present context to

22. There is no suggestion of a series of such prophetic saviors as in Zoroastrianism, nor any suggestion that the prophet is to be descended from the seed of Zoroaster (or Zarathustra). The production of the perfect man through the refining process of suffering (as in persecution) is only vaguely reminiscent of the refinement of the final judgment in Zoroastrianism. Yet the eschatological suffering of the righteous in the Qumrân Scrolls is a precursor of the Judgment Day, precisely as in I Pet. 4:17ff.
23. CDC ii, 12 (2:10); vi, 1 (8:2) (following Rabin's edition); 1Q M xi, 7f.
24. Cf. above, p. 140, n. 40.
25. See above, pp. 146f.; NTS, III, 1956–7, pp. 28–30.

indicate that *gever* is a metaphor; and hence, the passage is most reasonably interpreted as referring to an individual.[26] Although there
is an indefinite usage of *gever* to be found in the scrolls, its meaning
of "any, or every, man" (including the evil as well as the good) [27] is
too broad to suit 1Q S iv, 20. Nevertheless, that there should be a
thematic agreement between the emergence of the *gever* as a corporate
figure and also as the eschatological prophet shows that the passages
are mutually compatible; for both corporate and personal *gever* must
pass through the refining furnace of affliction in order to be equipped
for their prophetic role.

26. Whichever way we read "refine him *more than* the sons of men," or "refine for
Himself *one* of the sons of men" the language suits an individual better than a group;
but in the former translation, which I prefer, the group as well as the individual are
both refined. P. Wernberg-Møller, *op. cit.*, pp. 82f., states that "the section ll. 15–26 is
nothing but a variation of the same theme" as preceded in iii, 13—iv, 14. There, however, only the personal destinies of the sons of light and the sons of darkness were dealt
with. Nothing was said of the eschatological triumph of truth over error. It is this
denouement in iv, 15–26 which distinguishes it from what precedes. The appearance
of a Messianic prophet in this setting is wholly congruous.
27. Note especially iv, 23f.

Christian Prophets

It has been argued above that Old Testament prophecy originated in the cult in the context of music and psalmody, that in fact Old Testament prophecy has two branches: inspired praise and oracular preaching.[1]

According to Luke, the priest Zechariah "prophesied" (Luke 1:67) when he gave inspired praise to God after the birth of his own son John. This hymn is characterized also by an oracular (or revelatory) element, wherein the roles of Jesus (Luke 1:68–75) and John (1:75–79) are described.[2] The prophetess Anna (the Hellenized form of Hanna) "who gave thanks unto God" (Luke 2:36–38) is doubtless also thought of as singing her thanksgiving. With this, one may compare the opening clause of the Qumrân Hymns, "I thank thee, O Lord, because . . ."[3] The singing of a thanksgiving psalm at the presentation of Jesus was doubtless recorded here because of its reminiscence of the earlier Hannah who sang a thanksgiving psalm upon the dedication of her own son at the temple of Shiloh (I Sam. 2). The similarity between the two stories would have been closer had Mary sung a hymn of

---

1. Pp. 70f.
2. If Luke has employed here a Hebrew, or Aramaic, source (as some believe), this song would appear to be an adaptation of a Jewish hymn which spoke of the royal Messiah (1:68–75) and the Messianic Prophet (1:76ff.). It is even possible that "the dayspring" in verse 76b may have referred to the Messianic Priest. Cf. the Testament of Levi 18:2ff. and my discussion of the Messiah of Aaron in *NTS*, iii, pp. 198ff.
3. *Tôdâh* ("thanksgiving") is a well-known class of psalm in the Old Testament and also the name of a class of sacrifice. Presumably both were originally associated with the cult. Hannah's dedication of Samuel seems to be the presentation of her own son as a living *tôdâh*, or sacrifice, and her song is her hymnic *tôdâh*. Its contents seem hardly appropriate for Hannah's situation, but it was placed editorially in I Sam. 2 in order to suggest this cultic interpretation. In Luke, Jesus is the sacrificial *tôdâh* of Joseph and Mary, and the hymnic *tôdâh* was sung by Anna. For the eschatological "thanksgiving," see Isa. 12; Rev. 11:17f. This element is prominent also in 1Q H.

thanks at this point; but her name was not Hannah. Actually, Mary's earlier Magnificat (1:46–55) is strikingly similar to the song of Hannah in its phraseology and content; and the description of the development of the child Jesus (2:52; cf. 2:40) is patterned after that of Samuel (I Sam. 2:26), where Luke's translation is much better than that of the Septuagint. My suspicion is that the aged priest Simeon in Luke is a sort of counterpart to Eli, only the departure of Simeon from this world in peace (Luke 2:25–35) is an antithesis to the demise of Eli (I Sam. 4:12–18) — the contrast being occasioned by the receipt of good news on the one hand and bad news on the other.

For many years, I have suspected that the prophets of the primitive Church were in some way connected with the inspired praise of God, since the offering of an inspired song is one of the gifts of the Spirit (I Cor. 14:26), in a chapter which contextually deals with prophecy (I Cor. 14:4, 22–24, 31) and prophets (14:29, 37). In an unpublished article, James M. Robinson notes that speaking in tongues is closely associated with prophecy and the unintelligible utterance of unknown tongues is interpreted as the praise, or blessing of God (I Cor. 14:2, 13–16).[4] Actually, of course, the latter passage, against the background of 14:1, is contrasting tongues with prophecy. Both consist of praying, singing, blessing, and thanksgiving (which are largely synonymous terms); but in prophecy the worshipper gives intelligible utterance, wherein he employs his mind as well as his spirit. With "I will sing with the mind" (I Cor. 14:15) one may compare 1Q S x, 9: "I will sing with knowledge." For the hymnic character of thanksgiving, Robinson refers to Col. 3:16f. and Eph. 5:19f.[5] He calls attention to the role of the prophet in such thanksgiving (or blessing) in the Teaching of the Twelve (Didache 10:7, against the background of 9:1—10:6).

This is not to say that the role of the New Testament prophet was wholly hymnic; for as in the case of Old Testament prophets it could also be oracular (Acts 11:28; 13:1–2; 21:10–11; Eph. 3:5; Rev. 1:3;

4. His article is entitled, "Primitive Christian Hodayoth." He read it in preliminary form at a meeting of the Pacific Coast Section of the Society of Biblical Literature and Exegesis which was held at Berkeley, Calif., the spring of 1960.

5. These passages were once interpreted by Presbyterians (among others) as referring to the Biblical Psalms, since the words "psalm," "hymn," and "ode" (or "song") appear in the superscriptions of the Psalms in the Septuagint. These passages were, therefore, used to argue the case for the exclusive use of Biblical songs (primarily the Psalms) in Christian worship. Fundamentally, this was an argument for the sole use of inspired praise (cf. I Cor. 14:26). In accord with Protestant theology, it limited inspiration to the canon of Holy Scriptures.

22:6, 9; Didache 11:7–12). In this sense the Book of Revelation is the outstanding example of New Testament prophecy; but even it (like the Old Testament prophetic books) contains its hymnic sections.[6] H. Greeven has emphasized the instructional side of the prophet's work (I Cor. 14:18, 31) as well as its revelatory side (I Cor. 14:6, 30). He defines the work of the primitive Christian prophet thus:[7]

> To prophecy belongs all speech which to appearance breaks through the mute or illusory foreground and makes visible the underlying activity of God, whether it deal with personal destiny or the way of the entire community, whether it serve as reprimand or as consolation.

Greeven's treatment is sound and deals with important aspects of the prophet's task not treated here. On the other hand, he does not treat the relationship of prophecy to the hymning of God's praise.[8]

In the continuing life of the Church, one may note that sometimes persons of prophetic stature are not only great preachers but also the authors of great hymns, as for example, Francis of Assisi and Martin Luther. The Wesley brothers, also, revived England quite as much through their hymns as through their sermons; and the Methodist Churches, which have never produced an elaborate and detailed formulation of their beliefs, are content to point to the sermons and the hymns of the Wesleys as examples of Biblical faith and piety.[9]

6. Note the portions which are arranged as poetry in the RSV: esp., 4:8, 11; 5:9f.; 7:15–17; 11:17f.; 15:3f.; 16:5–7; 19:1–8. Note also the doleful dirges of Rev. 18.
7. "Propheten, Lehrer, Vorsteher bei Paulus, zur Frage der 'Ämter' im Urchristentum," ZNW, Vol. 44 (1952–3), pp. 1–43, with the quotation here coming from p. 11.
8. This neglect was occasioned by his judgment that I Cor. 14:14–19 is fundamentally directed against speaking with tongues, rather than to the extolling of the advantages of prophecy. Luke 1:67; 2:36–38 were overlooked in this discussion.
9. In CDC x, 6; xiii, 2; xiv, 7 (11:2; 15:5; 17:5) and 1Q Sa i, 7 there are references to the importance of being learned in *sêfer ha-hᵃgî* ("the book of meditation"). In CDC the text read an enigmatic HHGW for the last word (but the Y of the last letter seems clear enough in 1Q Sa.); and, from the context, it was surmised that the reference was to some sort of manual of discipline. If, however, Qumrân's Manual of Discipline was called rather *serekh hai-yahad,* one is at a loss to identify the discipline book to which reference is made. At 1Q H xi, 2, the author refers to "the meditation of my heart," and I have wondered whether the Qumrân Hymns could not be the "Book of Meditation." They combine worship with sectarian doctrine, and if authored by the Righteous Teacher, they would have considerable prestige for the Covenanters of Damascus and of Qumrân, similar to that of the hymns and sermons of the Wesleys to Methodism. Theological education in the Methodist Church once gave a large place to the study of these Wesleyan materials.

The Wonderful Counselor and the Virgin Mother

A CONTROVERSIAL HYMN

Considerable controversy has raged around one of the Qumrân Thanks-giving Psalms (IQ H iii, 7ff.). The purpose of the present treatment is not to give a complete exposition of the passage, but to eliminate an overly extended footnote from an earlier chapter. The Hymn may be translated as follows:

And I was in distress,
    as a woman in travail bringing forth her first-born;
For her birth-pangs wrench;
    and sharp pain, upon her birth canal,
    to cause writhing in the crucible of the pregnant one.
For sons have come to the deathly birth canal,
    and she who's pregnant with a man is distressed by her pains;
For, through deathly contractions, she brings forth a man child;
    and, through infernal pains, there bursts forth from the
        crucible of the Pregnant One:
A Wonderful Counselor, the people of His might;
    and a man is delivered from the birth canal by the Pregnant One.

Three schools of interpretation relate to this Hymn. According to the first, the author compares his sufferings with those of the true Israel through whom the Messiah is born, and therefore the "Wonderful Counselor" is the Messiah who is predicted by Isa. 9:6.[1] This interpreta-tion translates the first part of the last line quoted above as "a Wonder-ful Counselor *with* His might;" — the Hebrew '*M* being ambiguously either '*im* ("with") or '*am* ("people").

---

1. John V. Chamberlain, "Another Qumran Thanksgiving Psalm," *Journal of Near Eastern Studies* (hereafter abbreviated as *JNES*), xiv, 1955, pp. 32–41; "Further Elucida-tion of a Messianic Thanksgiving Psalm from Qumran," *op. cit.*, pp. 181f.; Brownlee, "Messianic Motifs of Qumran and the New Testament," *NTS*, iii, 1956–7, pp. 23–5, and already in the *BASOR*, No. 135 (Oct. 1954), p. 37, n. 30.

According to the second school of interpretation, the author is not concerned with a birth at all, but he introduces an extended metaphor to describe the suffering from which, thank God, he has been delivered. Only this interpretation, it is alleged, suits the *Gattung,* or literary type, of the thanksgiving psalm (*tôdâh*).[2] In rebuttal to this interpretation, one may reply that all the Qumrân Hymns are shot through with eschatological interests, so that Messianism cannot be excluded on dogmatic grounds from being a real element of this particular thanksgiving psalm.[3] Furthermore, the author would have all the more reason for being thankful, if his sufferings are really thought of as issuing in a birth — as the text plainly says!

According to a third line of interpretation, the author thinks of himself as travailing to give birth to his own disciples, who are referred to here under the designation "Wonderful Counselor, the people of His might."[4] This interpretation seems to be assured by the author's portrayal of himself elsewhere as a father and as a nurse of his spiritual children. It also accords with the frequent designation of the Qumrân Community as the "Council" or "Council of God."

If the Wonderful Counselor is to be interpreted as a people, it must be as a people with a Messianic mission, otherwise one is at a loss to give adequate explanation for the use of Messianic terminology to describe the child. Contrary to Mowinckel, we need not look for "some mythological being" from which the author has "taken many traits of his picture"; for we know the sources of the author, the Messianic prophecies of the Old Testament! Particularly important was the Book of Micah, where the Maiden Zion is portrayed as a woman in travail (4:10) who gives birth to the Davidic Messiah (5:1f., in English 5:2f.). The "Wonderful Counselor, the people of His might" doubtless echoes Isa. 9:5 (in English, 9:6). The "man child" (or "male") was drawn from Isa. 66:7; and probably also the title "Pregnant One" was based upon Isaiah 7:14: "Behold, the young woman is pregnant [or, will conceive] and is about to [or, will] give birth to a son, and she will call his name God-with-us." One may surmise, not unreasonably, that it was because God was believed to be with the Teacher and his followers that these folk could

2. Lou H. Silberman, "Language and Structure in the *Hodayot* (1Q H 3)," *JBL,* lxxv, 1956, pp. 96–106; S. Mowinckel in the *JBL,* lxxv, 1956, p. 276.
3. See *NTS,* iii, pp. 209f.
4. O. Betz, "Die Geburt der Gemeinde durch den Lehrer," *NTS,* iii, 1956–7, pp. 314–26; "Das Volk seiner Kraft zur Auslegung der Qumran-Hodajah iii, 1–18," *NTS,* v, 1956–59, pp. 67–75; Matthew Black, *op. cit.,* pp. 129f.

be thought of as "the people of *His* might." Thus, at this point, the Hymn reflects the influence of Isa. 7:14 and 9:5. Similarly, in 1Q Isaᵃ, the text of the former verse is assimilated to that of the latter by the utilization of the same wording, "his name will be called."[5] Thus, we seem to have here the doctrine of a Messianic community. This in no way excludes belief in personal Messianic figures; but the author is not here concerned with them. He simply wishes to equate his own sufferings and those of others associated with him with what Rabbinic Judaism called "the birth-pangs of the Messiah."[6]

The Corporate Interpretation of Isaiah 7:14

The corporate interpretation of Immanuel need not surprise us; for, in Isa. 7:21–22, the experience of this child in eating curds and honey (7:15) is applied to "every one who is left in the land." The identity of Immanuel with what scholars call the Righteous Remnant was long ago suggested by Miss Annie E. Skemp.[7] She argued that the mother also is corporate; for " 'the young woman of marriageable age,' 'just come to maturity' (mistranslated 'virgin,' we are told), must represent *Judah* (or Israel as a whole), of whom the faithful 'remnant,' 'Immanuel,' is about to be born." In her view, the corporate interpretation was intended by the original prophet, Isaiah, who in symbolic language was telling King Ahaz that through the travail of the Syro-Ephraimitish War (734–732 B.C.) a new Israel would be born. This was hinted at, according to her, by the prophet's taking with him his own son Shearjashub when he called upon Ahaz (7:3); for this child's name means either (or both) "a remnant will survive," or "a remnant will repent." This corporate interpretation also helps us to understand how the territory of Judah can be called Immanuel's land in Isa. 8:8.[8]

---

5. Cf. above, p. 185.
6. See Joseph Klausner, *op. cit.*, pp. 440ff.
7. " 'Immanuel' and 'the Suffering Servant of Jahweh': a Suggestion," *Expository Times*, xliv, 1932, pp. 94f.
8. B. Duhm and many others (including James Moffatt in his popular translation) have emended the text of 8:8 from 'RSK ("your land") to 'RS KY ("the land, for"), from "your land, O Immanuel" to "(the) land; for God is with us." The result is to produce a brief refrain with verse 10. The text of 1Q Isaᵃ in each case writes the two words '*immanû* '*ēl* ("With-us God") as a single word, thereby forcing the reader to recall the name of the child in 7:14, where the scroll (in opposition to Massoretic text) follows the same practice. This combining of words seems singularly inappropriate in 8:10, where a sentence is called for, rather than a proper noun. For an attempt to resolve the difficulty by a different word division, see Frank Zimmermann, "The Immanuel Prophecy," *JQR*, lii, 1961–2, pp. 154–9.

One may well be skeptical of whether Isaiah could expect such an unobvious meaning to be apprehended by King Ahaz. He may therefore argue that the corporate interpretation of the passage was not intended by Isaiah at all. Moreover, the language employed is that found commonly in annunciations in real life situations and involves the following elements: (1) announcement of the present, or future, pregnancy, and of the forthcoming birth; (2) the prescribing of the child's name and the explanation of his name; (3) his manner of life and the reason therefor; and (4) his mission, or destiny.[9] The fourth element is sometimes absent, or perhaps is left to be inferred from the significance of the name. The original prophecy of Isaiah, in the light of this pattern, may be restored to a more logical order, as follows:[10]

9. See the following annunciations: to Hagar concerning Ishmael (Gen. 16:11f.); to Abraham with regard to Isaac and Ishmael (17:15-21), and also with regard to Isaac alone (18:9-13 — the references to laughter alluding to the meaning of "Isaac"); to Manoah's wife regarding Samson (Jud. 13:3-5); to Manoah (13:12-14); to Joseph concerning Jesus (Matth. 1:20f.); to Zechariah as regards John (Luke 1:13-20); to Mary with respect to Jesus (1:28-38). These are referred to above as "real life situations" by way of stressing that these concern the birth of individuals from real parents (whether or not the stories are historical). Isaiah is the only instance of a prophet delivering an annunciation. In all other cases it is either an angel, or God Himself. In Isaiah's inaugural vision, he responded to the summons sounded in the divine assembly (Isa. 6:8) in precisely the same way as the spirit (or angel) in Micaiah's vision (I Kings 22:20-22). In other words, he is fulfilling a heavenly (or angelic) mission. By a clever dissection of Isa. 7, Sheldon H. Blank was able to divide the material of the chapter into legendary and historical, the annunciation belonging to the former (op. cit., pp. 16-30). There doubtless are interpretative layers in this chapter; but the basic stratum includes the annunciation. If, as I argue below, Isaiah's oracle concerning Immanuel is partially one of judgment (as in 8:8) and not merely one of consolation (as in 8:10), then the oracle is not at all one which contradicts the faith of the historical Isaiah. Blank's removal of verse 15 eliminates an element which belongs to the form-critical structure of the annunciation (as I restore it below), and this is not simply "eschatological" as he believes, but it reflects the situation of judgment. One of the principles for Blank's dissection is the alternation between the singular and the plural number of the second person pronouns; yet his removal of verse 13 from the annunciation makes for a more violent alternation between the singular (addressed to Ahaz in verse 11) and the plural second person of verse 14, than in the Massoretic text where the broadening of the address to the "house of David" well explains the change to the plural. In Blank's analysis, the annunciation belongs to a legendary, pious Ahaz, who for orthodox reasons refused to ask a sign. The idea of a pious Ahaz is so refuted elsewhere as to make it seem unlikely that such should develop. Moreover, in tradition and legend, the pious sometimes ask for signs (as in the case of Gideon and Hezekiah); for this sets the stage for miracle. It seems more likely that Ahaz's refusal to ask for a sign rested upon his unbelief. The sign he was offered was not any wonder, but an omen of the divine presence which would be manifest in, through, and beyond judgment. Isaiah's annunciation was historical.

10. With this restoration, cf. that of Julius A. Bewer, Literature of the Old Testament, New York, Columbia University Press, rev. ed., 1933, p. 105. In the above restora-

(1) [v. 14] See, the young woman is pregnant and is about to bear a son; (2) and she will call his name Immanuel, [v. 16b] (for) the land before whose two kings you stand in dread will be deserted. (3) [v. 15] Curds and honey will he eat, *when* [or, *until,* or *so that*] he know[s] to refuse the bad and to choose the good; [v. 16a] for before the lad knows to refuse the bad and to choose the good, [v. 17] the LORD will bring upon you and upon your father's dynasty such days as have not come, since the day that Ephraim departed from Judah.

In this translation, the sequence of the form-critical elements is indicated by the numerals within parentheses, and the numbers of the verses (or parts thereof) which are thus rearranged are placed within the brackets. This rearrangement of the text, if regarded as a true restoration of the passage, would indicate that the child's name is to be given him because Israel will fail in her attack upon Judah because she in turn will be attacked by Assyria. This will make the mother of the newly born child conclude that God is with Judah and name her child accordingly, Immanuel (God is with us); however, Judah will herself be engulfed by Assyria and be reduced to a primitive pastoral state in which Immanuel (and all others who are left) will eat curds and honey. The Hebrew is ambiguous, but it is possible that the prophet entertained the hope that this judgment would serve an educative purpose of teaching Immanuel (and others as well) "to refuse the evil and to choose the good." [11] Thus God would be truly with His people, but it would be a presence to be realized through the discipline of divine judgment. By analogy with other annunciations, we should be concerned here with the prediction of a real birth which was made to one of the child's parents. The child himself, furthermore, should be either of patriarchal significance (as Ishmael and Isaac) or of personal importance (as Samson, John, and Jesus). Most probably, therefore, Ahaz (to whom the annunciation was delivered) is Immanuel's father; and this well accords with the fact that the "sign" is offered to

---

tion, the reason for the prophet's name (16b) is in its proper place. It was later transposed (as in our Bibles) by an editor who believed that the doom of Israel and Judah represented a common disaster and should be presented together (16a, 16b, 17). The explanation of the child's name (16b) became therefore connected with the explanation of his diet (16a, 17); but it was not Israel's forthcoming devastation, but Judah's, which accounts for the diet.

11. If this means *"so that* he know" the idea is that ethical perceptivity will come through judgment and the simplicity of pastoral life. The Vulgate and the King James Version support this interpretation. See here the profound study of Karl Budde, "Das Immanuel-zeichen und die Ahaz-Begegnun Jesaja 7," *JBL,* lii, 1933, pp. 22–54.

the "house (or dynasty) of David." It is also possible that this forthcoming child became the object of Isaiah's hopes concerning the ideal king in chapters 9 and 11; however, we cannot be sure of this.

THE "VIRGIN" MOTHER

If Isa. 7:14 be given an historical setting in the eighth century B.C., as nearly all scholars insist must be done, then there can be no thought of a virgin birth in the passage for a Christian; for in Christian theology there is only one virgin birth, that of Jesus who became the Christ. Yet the ancient Septuagint version translated the Hebrew word 'almâh into the Greek parthenos, meaning "virgin"; and this prophecy is said to be fulfilled by Jesus (Matth. 1:23). It has been pointed out that some annunciations at ancient Ugarit use bətûlâh ("virgin") in parallelism with 'almâh.[12] The significance to be drawn from this is doubtful; but from this some have concluded that the words mean exactly the same, "virgin," or that the Septuagint was influenced by such an ancient background in its translation.[13] Yet no one would argue that these passages in Ugaritic literature really speak of a virgin birth; and one authority on this literature asserts "There is no word in the Near Eastern languages that by itself means virgo intacta." [14] Even the technical term for virgin (if bətûlâh be that) is frequently qualified in the Old Testament by the assertion that the maiden had not been known by man.[15] This is probably not merely pleonasm, but a safeguarding of the term in its strict sense. It would appear that bətûlâh, like "maid" in English meant "a maiden; esp., a virgin." [16] The word "esp[ecially]" indicates in this dictionary definition that there are possible exceptions to the strict usage of the term.

12. To be more precise, it is rather a matter of the terms cognate with them, btlt and ğlmt. I. Engnell, *Studies in Divine Kingship in the Ancient Near East*, Uppsala, 1943, p. 133; E. Hammershaimb, "The Immanuel Sign," *Studia Theologica*, Vol. iii, Fasc. 2, 1951, pp. 124ff.; Mowinckel, *He That Cometh*, pp. 113f.; E. J. Young, *Studies in Isaiah*, Grand Rapids, Eerdmans, 1954, pp. 166–70. Cyrus Gordon, " 'Almah in Isaiah 7:14," *Journal of Bible and Religion* (abbreviated as *JBR*), Vol. 21, 1953, p. 106; "The Patriarchal Age," pp. 238–43, with attention here to pp. 240f.; E. R. Lacheman, "Apropos of Isaiah 7:14," *JBR*, 22, p. 43.
13. E. J. Young, *op. cit.*, pp. 167, 184; Mowinckel, *op. cit.*, p. 114.
14. Cyrus R. Gordon, *Ugaritic Manual*, I, Grammar, Analecta Orientalia, 35, Rome, Pontificium Institutum Biblicum, 1955, 375, p. 249b. See also his discussion of ğlmt, 1483, p. 310a.
15. As in Gen. 24:16 and Jud. 21:12. Yet bətûlâh in II Sam. 13:2, 18f. clearly means "virgin" without such explicit language.
16. As the word is defined in *Webster's New Collegiate Dictionary*, a Merriam-Webster, Springfield, Mass., G. & C. Merriam Co., 1961, p. 506b.

That the idea of virginity does attach to *bətûlâh* and not to the Hebrew synonyms *na'ǎrâh* and *'almâh* seems clear from the fact that the abstract noun "virginity" (*bətûlîm*) is drawn from the first and that the idea of "youth" (*nə'ûrîm* and *'ǎlûmîm*) is drawn from the other words. Thus, if one is thinking etymologically, one should expect *bətûlâh* at Isa. 7:14, if Isaiah had in any strict sense been thinking of a virgin. The Syriac version actually employs the cognate term *bəthûltâ'*.

My suspicion is that the Septuagint's translation of *'almâh* as *parthenos* was not based upon traditions deriving from Canaanite culture, as some have argued by appealing to the Ugaritic parallels; but that it was rather based upon a popular corporate interpretation which identified Immanuel's mother with the nation which through travail would give birth to the ideal king.[17] The term *parthenos* was chosen because this term in the Septuagint (as also *bətûlâh* in the Hebrew Bible) occurs frequently in such expressions as "Virgin Zion," "Virgin Daughter Judah," and "Virgin Israel." The idea of the corporate mother who gives birth to the Messianic king is found as early as Micah 4:10 and 5:2 (in English, 5:3); and this passage may well have influenced the translators of the Septuagint.

The idea of the corporate mother is found likewise in Rev. 12, where the heavenly woman is none other than Israel travailing to give birth to the Christ.[18] It is found also in John 16:21f.,[19] where the community of Christ and His disciple band suffers in order to give birth to the resurrected Redeemer. In striking agreement with this understanding of the Messianic birth, the Christ of Rev. 12 is caught up into heaven as soon as He is born (v. 5); for in the thought of John (or that of the

---

17. See *NTS*, iii, p. 24, n. 2.

18. The woman is described as "clothed with the sun, with the moon under her feet, and on her head a crown of twelve stars," by way of alluding to Joseph's dream of Gen. 37:9 where similar language is employed of the patriarchal family of Israel. The suggestion that this passage should in any way allude to the assumption of Mary, even though she be regarded as a matriarchal head and representative of the Church, is ridiculous; for it is the child of this woman (not she herself) who is "caught up to God and to His throne" (12:5f.). Her offspring is described in language borrowed from the Old Testament as follows: *"And she gave birth to a son* (Isa. 7:14 with altered tense), *a male* (Isa. 66:7), who is destined *to shepherd* all the nations *with a rod of iron* (Ps. 2:9, LXX). The pleonasm of "a son, a male" is to be explained on the basis of the author's deliberate combination of as many prophetic allusions as possible. Only the American Standard Version avoids glossing over the apparent redundancy. "A male," or "man child," appears also in the Hymn of 1Q H iii. Likewise, the haven in the "wilderness" of Rev. 12:6 is reminiscent of Qumrân.

19. See Chamberlain's discussion in *JNES*, xiv, p. 41*b*.

Johannine school) Jesus did not become fully the Christ until He had achieved redemption through His death and resurrection.[20] The reason that the Gospel according to John has no nativity story is probably to be explained by the view that the real birth of the Christ into the world was through the redemptive event of His death and resurrection. In Matthew, there seems to be both the human mother Mary and the travailing corporate mother Israel, the latter being personified by the weeping of Rachel (Matth. 2:16–18); but in this case the suffering of the corporate mother is read back into the events attendant upon the physical birth of Jesus. The Virgin Mary was probably regarded by Matthew as not merely the physical mother of Jesus, but as a symbol of the true Israel from which He sprang.

20. See my discussion in *NTS*, iii, p. 29.

Variants in the Text of Isaiah 49:7

The text of Isa. 49:7 as it appears in the Complete Isaiah Scroll can be profitably compared with that of other ancient texts and versions, as follows:

MASSORETIC TEXT

1a   Thus says the LORD,
b   the Redeemer of Israel, his Holy One,
2a   To him whose life is despised,
b   to him who abhors nations,
c   to the slave of rulers:
3a   "Kings shall see and shall arise;
b   nobles, and they shall do obeisance —
4a   For the sake of the LORD Who is faithful,
b   of Israel's Holy One and He chose you."

SEPTUAGINT

1a   Thus says the Lord
b   Who redeemed *you, the God* of Israel:
2a   "*You have sanctified him* who despised his life,
b   him who is *abhorred by* the nations,
c   by the slaves of rulers.
3a   Kings shall see him and shall arise;
b   rulers, and they shall do obeisance to him
4a   For the Lord's sake — since Israel's Holy One is faithful,[1]
b   and He chose you."

1. This radically different translation is an entirely possible rendering of the Massoretic Hebrew text, by taking 'ŠR in the sense of "since" rather than "who," and by ignoring the Hebrew parallelism. However, the Septuagint's translation of this verse reduces it to prose — the present display being intended solely for the comparison of clauses and syntactical structure.

as an accusative.[2] Despite this agreement, the reading is surely in
; for it compels one to construe the title "holy one" as a designa-
of Israel, which is contrary to the proper usage of this term as a
e for the Lord (as is clear from 4b and from other passages in
h).

eneath the differences between the variant texts and renditions of
second line is an uncertainty as to whether the participles are transi-
or passive. The first in the Septuagint (2a, "who despised") is
sitive, and the consonants of the Massôret (BZH) also favor this
ding (bôzèh); but the Massoretes have vocalized them as bəzôh
way of suggesting the passive, which, however, should rather be
ûi — a reading which is implied by BZWY in 1Q Isaᵃ.

The second participle of 1Q Isaᵃ is MT'BY, which should be passive
d of singular number if it is to agree with the preceding participle of
s text. This is possible, if we read a Ḥireq compaginis, as Rubinstein
s suggested.[3] However, the added Yôd on the end of the word could
an indication of the plural construct. As such, it could have arisen
rough carelessness, under the false impression that the Yôd at the end
the preceding participle was also a plural construct. Or, again, it
uld have been deliberately altered to the plural in order to insinuate
e corporate interpretation of the verse. In this regard, one will note
e plural "slaves" in 2c of the Septuagint and the free rendering of the
ntire second line in the Targum which repeatedly uses the plural. An
nalogy to an inconsistent alteration with an interpretative intent is to
e found in Hab. 1:13 in the Habakkuk Commentary, which reads as
ollows:[4]

> Why do *ye* look on faithless men,
>   and (why) art *thou* silent when the wicked swallows up the man
>   more righteous than he?

2. The participle gô'êl is viewed virtually as a noun and therefore receives possessive,
rather than accusative, suffixes — where such are distinguishable. Thus W, rather than
HW, is employed as the third person masculine singular suffix in Isa. 44:6; and Y,
rather than NY, is employed in Ps. 19:15; Job 19:25. The text of stich 1b in Isa. 49:7
has been influenced by Isa. 48:17 both in the Septuagint and in 1Q Isaᵃ.
3. *Biblica*, Vol. 35, 1954, pp. 478f.
4. 1Q pHab v, 8–12. Another example of the inconsistent plural and singular is to be
seen in Isa. 50:10, 1Q Isaᵃ: "Who among you are fearers of the LORD / Who hearkens
to the voice of His legate? / Those who walk in darkness / and he who has no illumination / let him trust in the name of the LORD and lean upon his God." The first variant
YR'Y ("fearers") may have arisen simply as an orthographic peculiarity for the singular; but the second HLKW ("they walk") cannot be so explained.

TARGUM

1a Thus says the LORD,
 b   the Savior of Israel, his Holy One,
2a To *those* who are despised among the nation[s]
 b   to *those* who are cast out among the king[s]
 c   to *those* who were slaves to rulers.
3a "Them shall kings see and then rise up;
 b   nobles, and they shall do obeisance —
4a For the sake of the LORD Who is faithful,
 b   of Israel's Holy One and He chose you."

1Q IsA[a]

1a Thus says the *Lord* GOD,
 b   *your* Redeemer, O Israel, His only one,
2a To him whose life is despised.
 b   to him [or, *those*] *abhorred by* nations,
 c   to the slave of rulers:
3a "Kings *have* seen and arisen [or, and shall aris[e]
 b   *and* nobles *shall do*(ne) obeisance —
4a For the sake of the LORD Who is faithful,
 b   of Israel's Holy One [Who] *shall* choose you.[”]

1Q IsA[b]

1a Thus says the *Lord* GOD,
 b   the Redeemer of Israel, his Holy One,
2a . . . .
 b   . . . .
 c   . . . . rulers:
3a "Kings shall see, *shall* arise;
 b   . . . .
4a . . . .
 b   of Israel's Holy One, and He chose you."

It is curious that both the Complete Isaiah Scroll (1Q Isa[a])
Fragmentary Isaiah Scroll (1Q Isa[b]) should agree with reg[ard]
interpolation of Adonai ("Lord") alongside Yahweh (LORD, o[r]
1a, although the texts are otherwise quite different. In the sec[ond]
of this line (1b), 1Q Isa[a] reads "*your* Redeemer" in agreem[ent]
the Septuagint's rendering "Who redeemed you" — only [the pro]
nominal suffix of the participle is better interpreted as a p[ro]

Its meaning concerns the House of Absalom and the men of their council, who were silent during the rebuke of [or, by] the True Teacher and did not help him against the False Man, who had rejected the Law in the midst of their whole [council].

The Habakkuk quotation is correctly preserved in the Massoretic text where both verbs are of the singular number ("Why dost *thou* look . . . art *thou* silent") and are addressed to God! The author of the commentary insinuated his interpretation by altering the number of only one verb; and it is reasonable to suggest that the same thing may have happened in the treatment of the participles of Isa. 49:7 in the text of 1Q Isa^a.

Underlying line 3 in the text of 1Q Isa^a there seems to have been the reading which is to be found in the first printed transcription of this passage:

> Kings *have* seen and arisen;
> and nobles, and they *have done* obeisance.

This text with its perfect tenses throughout is the exact opposite of all the other texts and versions; and it failed to please even the scribe of 1Q Isa^a, who undertook to suggest a future reference by converting a *Wâw* into a *Yôd* before the verb in perfect tense *HŠTḤWW*.[5] This more accurate reading of what the manuscript actually reads appears in the second printing of the published text. The alteration results in a solecism in Hebrew, which is similar to "*shall do*(ne)" in English. This scribal error might conceivably be a mere slip of the pen; but the future tense is in accord with the scroll's treatment of the verb in 4*b* which is altered into a clear future by the omission of the prefixed *Wâw* ("and"): "Israel's Holy One *shall* choose you."

The idea of the future election in 4*b* is not fortuitous, for it accords with the sectarian doctrine of the future elect with whom God will renew His covenant, according to an important scroll passage:[6]

> Yet Thou wilt choose for Thyself a people
> in the time of Thy favor;
> For Thou hast remembered Thy covenant,
> and wilt make them to be set apart for Thyself
> as a holiness distinct from all peoples;

5. One may compare the retention of the *Hê* after the *Yôd* of the imperfect tense in the case of the *haf'êl* stem in Aramaic; but the present word cannot even be explained as an Aramaism since it is not of a corresponding stem.
6. Cf. above, p. 115, n. 18.

> And Thou wilt renew Thy covenant with them
> with a manifestation of glory and words of Thy Holy Spirit,
> with deeds of Thy hand and a script of Thy right hand,
> To make them know glorious ordinances and eternal heights . .
>
> . . . .
>
> And Thou wilt appoint for them a faithful shepherd,
> who will . . . . the afflicted.

Not only does this passage speak of God's future choice of a people, but it also uses the expression "in the time of Thy favor" which is reminiscent of Isa. 49:8. Even the references to the covenant are consonant with Isa. 49:8 and 42:6; but here the New Covenant of Jer. 31:31–34 is even more influential. Separation as a thing of holiness accords with the sect's interpretation of themselves as a "holy house" (or "sanctuary") in the Manual of Discipline, and also with the first line of Isa. 49:7 in 1Q Isaᵃ (at 1b) where Israel is referred to as the Lord's "holy one." It agrees also with the stich 2a in the Septuagint rendition where the Servant is one to be "sanctified" (or "made holy").

The theme of the New Covenant in the sectarian expectation of the newly elect people stands related to that of the Second Exodus (a prominent motif in Second Isaiah) and it carries with it also the expectation of a Second Moses and a new revelation of divine law, which are associated with the Lord's Servant in Second Isaiah.[7] Reference to the Second Moses (or the Prophet like Moses) is to be seen in the expectation of the coming "faithful shepherd," which is reminiscent of Isa. 63:11:

> Then He remembered the days of old,
> of Moses His servant.
> Where is He who brought up out of the sea
> the shepherds of his flock?
> Where is He who put in the midst of them
> His holy Spirit?   (RSV)

7. On the theme of the Second Exodus, note that the oppressor (Babylon) is sometimes alluded to in language which is reminiscent of Egypt, Israel's first oppressor (43:3, 14, 17); that Israel is said to be led by God unharmed through water in order to remind one of the crossing of the Reed Sea (43:2, 16; 50:2; 51:9–11); and that God prepares a way in the wilderness (40:3; 43:19) and provides streams in the desert (43:20) — all by way of recalling Israel's experiences in the Wilderness of Sinai. The Servant's role in the Second Exodus seems to be set forth in 49:8–12; 42:6f. His mission with respect to mishpāṭ (justice) and tôrâh (law) are set forth in 42:1, 4. These features suggest that the Servant is in part a Second Moses.

In this verse, Moses and Aaron both appear as shepherds, as is made clear by comparing the passage with the last verse of Ps. 77. If the New Covenant passage were fully preserved, it is possible that the Second Aaron (or Messianic Priest) would also receive mention as well as the Prophet like Moses. In any case, enough is preserved to indicate the influence of the Book of Isaiah upon the author's concept of the newly elect people and of their "faithful shepherd." [8]

8. On "Salvation through Election" in the Scrolls, see M. Mansoor, *The Thanksgiving Hymns,* Studies in the Texts of the Desert of Judah, III, 1961, pp. 62–65.

The Meaning of the Divine Name YHWH

Since there are a number of references to the sacred Tetragrammaton in this book, it is well that we include a summary of the better positions as to its pronunciation and meaning.[1] Our only tradition as to the original pronunciation is that of the Church Fathers. Clement of Alexandria, who was of the late second and early third centuries A.D., transliterated the vocalized YHWH as Iaoue, employing the letters ou to represent the consonantal sound w. Theodoret, who was of the fifth century A.D., transcribed the word as Iabe, employing the Greek b [Béta] for the v sound, as in the late pronunciation of the Hebrew w.[2] These traditions are believed to support an original pronunciation Yâhwêh (or better, Yaḥwèh).

The pronunciation Yəhôwâh (whence the English Jehovah) was a misunderstanding on the part of medieval Christian scholars who based it upon the vowel points of the Massoretic text. Since the name Yahweh was not to be misused (Ex. 20:7), Jews became afraid to use it at all, even in the reading of the Scriptures. Therefore, they substituted Adonai (ᵃdônâi), meaning "[my] Lord." When at a later date they devised a system of vowel points to indicate the pronunciation of the text, they supplied the Tetragrammaton with the vowels of Adonai. They did this somewhat anomalously, however, for instead of vocalizing Yᵃhôwâh, in full accord with ᵃdônâi, they pointed the word as Yəhô-wâh. Curiously, they followed the rule that though an 'Âlef (') cannot take a simple Shəwâ', a Yôd can — despite the fact that this particular

1. For a survey of the literature, see A. Murtonen, *A Philological and Literary Treatise on the Old Testament Divine Names,* Studia Orientalia, Helsinki, Societas Orientalis, Fennica, 1952. For a summary treatment of the subject, see B. W. Anderson's entry "God, Names of" in *IDB,* Vol. E–J, pp. 407ff., with special attention to section B, 3, p. 410.
2. For discussion of this evidence, see Gustave Lambert, "Que signifie le nom divin YHWH?" *NRTh,* Nov., 1952, pp. 894–915, especially pp. 904f.

Yôd (Y) is to be replaced in pronunciation by an *'Âlef!* In some cases the Tetragrammaton is vocalized *Yəhôwîh,* employing the vowels of Elohim (*'elôhîm*) (meaning God), except again for the same anomalous difference in the first vowel. This form occurs in the combination "Lord Yahweh," giving us "Lord GOD" instead of the repetitious "Lord LORD." The translators of the Septuagint were consistent and translated regularly *Kurios Kurios* ("Lord Lord").[2a] The Revised Standard Version (as the King James Version before it) translates the word *YHWH* as either LORD or GOD, according to the Massoretic vocalization. The American Standard Version had introduced the fallacious pronunciation Jehovah.

Probably the most widely held modern theory as to the original meaning of the divine name is that of W. F. Albright, who accepted and developed the suggestion of Ed Dhorme that Yahweh is a noun derived from the causative form of the verb *HYH-HWH,* "to be." Thus the meaning of Yahweh would be "He Who causes to be."[3] This, to be sure, contradicts the Massoretic text of Ex. 3:14, where in response to a query from Moses as to His name God replies: "I AM WHO I AM." Then the Lord gives Moses two parallel commands: "Say this to the people Israel, 'I AM has sent me to you.'" "Say this to the people Israel, 'Yahweh, the God of your fathers . . . has sent me to you.'" Here we obviously have I AM (*'ehyèh*) as an interpretation of *YHWH,* which may readily be vocalized as the third person *yihwèh* (HE IS, or HE WILL BE). The testimony of the Church Fathers, however, supports *yahwèh* (HE CAUSES TO BE); so Albright adopted this vocalization. The general feeling has been that HE IS (inferred from the first person I AM) is too abstract a meaning for the primitive Hebrew meaning of the word; but precisely this is the understanding of the Septuagint at Ex. 3:14:

> And God said to Moses, "I am HE WHO IS;" and He said, "Thus shall you say to the sons of Israel, 'HE WHO IS sent me to you.'"

This rendering of the LXX doubtless influenced Moffatt to translate YHWH as "the eternal." However, if one is to follow Albright, "the

---

2a. In the earliest Septuagint manuscripts, the Tetragrammaton was written in paleo-Hebrew script; but the pronunciation of the word as *Kurios* led to its substitution in later manuscripts. Strictly speaking, this was not a translation of the sacred name, but of its surrogate (Adonai). See W. G. Waddell, "The Tetragrammaton in the LXX," *JThS,* XLV, 1944, pp. 158ff.; also the *BA* XVII, 1 (Feb., 1954), p. 13.
3. *From the Stone Age to Christianity,* pp. 197-99.

Creator" would be a better rendering. One may lay emphasis here upon the expression *Yahwèh Ṣəvâ'ôt* (traditionally rendered "Lord of hosts") which would mean "the Creator of Armies." [4] To be sure, however, "Creator and Sustainer" would be an even better translation of "He Who causes to be"; for this includes maintenance of being as well as bringing into being.

Although Dhorme had first suggested the causative meaning of the name *YHWH*, he later abandoned this view in favor of taking seriously Ex. 3:14, "I AM WHO I AM." According to his new view Yahweh is a segolate noun derived from the verb *HWH* ("to be"); but the import of the name was not to assert beingness, or eternity, but was rather to assert indefinableness. Ex. 3:14, with its I AM WHO I AM, was an avoidance of definition out of reverential reserve. The name Yahweh, therefore, is an assertion of the ineffable nature of the God of Israel.[5]

Another etymology of the name Yahweh is that of S. D. Goitein.[6] According to his view, the name is to be derived from the Semitic root *HWY*, meaning "to be passionate." This root, insofar as used elsewhere in the Old Testament, means "desire" (especially, "lust"); but in Arabic it has a much wider range of meanings centering around the meaning "to be passionate." A key text for Goitein is Ex. 34:14: "*YHWH*, His name is Jealous; He is a jealous God." Accordingly, he suggests that "Jealous" is a translation of YHWH. Yahweh is a God who loves so passionately that he may be described as *qannâ'*, jealous! A better translation of *'êl qannâ'*, however, would be "a God exacting exclusive devotion," [7] not "a jealous God." Therefore, *'ehwèh 'asher 'ehwèh* (the original reading of Ex. 3:14) would be: "I will be passionately devoted to whom I am so devoted." A parallel to such language is to be found in Ex. 33:19 in the sentences: "I will be gracious to whom I will be gracious and I will show mercy on whom I will show mercy." Similarly, Ex. 34:5-7, in which Yahweh discloses His

4. On this designation see B. N. Wambacq, *L'épithète divine Jahvé Ṣəbâ'ôt: Étude philogique, historique et exégétique*, Brussels, Desclee De Brouwer, 1947; also the review of W. F. Albright in the *JBL*, lxvii, pp. 377–81.
5. "Le nom du Dieu d'Israel," *RHR*, cxli, 1952, pp. 5–18.
6. "YHWH the Passionate. The Monotheistic Meaning and Origin of the Name YHWH," *VT*, vi, 1956, pp. 1–9.
7. Citing here the translation of the Jehovah's Witnesses in their *New World Translation of the Hebrew Scriptures*, Watchtower Bible and Tract Society, Inc., 1953. Cf. F. F. Bruce, *The English Bible, A History of Translations*, New York, Oxford University Press, 1961, p. 184, who states, "Some of the renderings which are free from a theological tendency strike one as quite good."

name, emphasizes the passionate, loving, and zealous nature of God. As Goitein explains, the Lord devotes Himself fully to those who are fully devoted to Him, and this is the real meaning of YHWH.

Though Goitein says nothing about the phrase YHWH Ṣəvâ'ôt (traditionally, "Lord of hosts"), it is clear that according to his theory one cannot make Yahweh the "Creator of Armies." One will most probably need to take Ṣəvâ'ôt as attributive. He will then, perhaps, translate "Yahweh, the Omnipotent," or, "Yahweh, the Militant." [8] The latter gives an appellative more closely synonymous with the Passionate and also a meaning more closely related to the eventual interpretation of the title as "Yahweh, the God of the armies [ṣəvâ'ôt] of Israel." [9] Against the attributive interpretation, as also against Goitein's interpretation of YHWH, is the supposed support of the Greek transcriptions for the causative vocalization of YHWH; but Goitein answers this objection by pointing out other anomalous transcriptions and by alluding to the uncertainty as to the exact pronounciation of Hebrew in the most ancient times.

Each of the principal interpretations of the etymology of YHWH assigns a meaning to the name capable of motivating, or expressing, Israel's monotheism. In each case, moreover, one must reckon with the fact that the translators of the Septuagint, and the Massoretes, as well, misunderstood the original sense. Far more important to the Hebrews than the etymology, as important as that may have been at one time, was the nature of Yahweh as they came to understand it through a long history of revelatory deeds. This included faith in Yahweh as Sovereign and as Redeemer; so that one is inclined to agree with Hans Walter Wolff that the Greek translation of the Tetragrammaton as Kurios ("Lord") shares the inner sense of the name.[10]

8. For the first translation, see Wambacq, op. cit. and Gerhard von Rad, Old Testament Theology, Vol. I (translated by D. M. G. Stalker), New York, Harper and Bros., 1962, pp. 18f. For the second rendering, see the translation of Robert H. Pfeiffer in The Hebrew Iliad, the History of the Rise of Israel under Saul and David (with general and chapter introductions by Wm. G. Pollard), New York, Harper and Bros., 1957.
9. See here B. W. Anderson's entry, "Lord of Hosts," IDB, Vol. K–Q, p. 151b.
10. In ZAW, liv, 1936, p. 170.

The Syntax of Isaiah 52:14–15

Reference has already been made to the syntactical distinction between Israel and the Servant in Isa. 52:14–15.[1] This distinction occurs in all our Hebrew texts. The text of the Massoretes, which is supported here by 1Q Isaᵇ, is apparently to be construed as follows:

14 *As* many were astonished at *you* —
  So will *his* appearance be a marring from [that of] a man,
    and his form from [that of] the sons of man;
15 *So* will *he* sprinkle [purify, or startle?] many nations;
    because of him kings will shut their mouths;
  For what had not been told them they will have seen,
    and what they had not heard they will have contemplated.

The protasis seems to be introduced with *as* and to be followed by two apodoses, each of them introduced with *so*. C. C. Torrey recognized this implication, but he immediately sought to avoid it by emendation of the first "so" (Heb., *kên*) to "for" (*kî*).[2] This produced the well-balanced structure of "As . . . For . . . So . . . For . . ." This is rather impressive; yet this suggested reading has not been discovered as yet at Qumrân, where both Isaiah scrolls from the First Cave support the Massoretic text This means that the differentiation "you" and "his" is in any case ancient and must be interpreted; for it surely meant something to ancient Jews.

Two ancient versions take the first clause with its *kên,* or "so," as parenthetical. They are the Septuagint and the Targum:

SEPTUAGINT

14 In the same way as many will be astonished *at you* —
    so much less glorious will *your* face be than men
    and *your* glory than men — ³

1. Above, p. 208.
2. *Op. cit.,* p. 415.

15 So will many nations be astonished *at him,*
and kings will shut their mouths;
For they who received no announcement concerning him will see,
and they who have not heard will understand.

TARGUM

13 Behold, My servant, the Anointed, will succeed;
he will mount, grow great and be uniquely strong.
14 *Like what the house of Israel* had hoped *for him* many days —
since their appearance was poor among the peoples,
and their visage worse than the sons of man —
15 *So will he* disperse [startle?] many nations;
because of him kings will keep silent,
placing their hands over their mouth;
For what had not been told them they will have seen,
and what they had not heard they will have contemplated.

The Septuagint was able to take 14*b* as parenthetical by reading consistently second person pronouns in verse 14, and the Targum was able to do likewise by translating consistently in the third person. The particle *kên* caused no difficulty in the Septuagint, since the Greek word *houtôs* may be used either adverbially or as a conjunction. The Targum, however, translates the first Hebrew *kên* with *də* ("for" or "since") and reproduces the second as *kên*. This version might be claimed as full support for the consistently third-person reading of verse 14 and for the emendation of the first *kên* to *kî;* however, the Targum is so obviously free in its rendering, one cannot rely upon it with full confidence, especially since it is in full agreement with the Septuagint in applying verse 14 in its entirety to Israel and verse 15 to the Messianic servant of the Lord.[4] Thus both these versions support the distinction of the Hebrew texts, despite the fact that they delay the apodosis to verse 15! The distinction which the Targum found in verses 14–15 may well have been in a Hebrew text comparable to the Septuagint. In any case, the discovery of both the Messiah and Israel in the introduction of the Great Servant Song led the Targumists to carry through references to both in the rest of the Song (Chap. 53).

3. The Greek preposition *apo* is difficult to interpret here. Perhaps one should translate upon the assumption that the verse makes sense only when its idioms are interpreted as Hebraisms.
4. For a discussion of the LXX and the Targum in relation to the Servant Songs, see Zimmerli and Jeremias, *op. cit.,* pp. 40ff., 66ff.

The Syriac version has also been claimed as support for the emendation of the Hebrew text. It reads as follows:

> 14 In order that [5] many may be astonished *at him,*
> *so will he* disfigure his form from that of a man,
> and his visage from that of the sons of man.
> 15 *He* himself will purify many nations,
> and at him kings will shut their mouths . . .

This version gives the text a curiously different sense; and though it has only one apodosis, it finds it in 14*b* rather than in verse 15. One valuable contribution of the Syriac version is its translation of *yazzèh* (from *NZH*) as *mədhakê'* (from *DKY*),[6] "he purifies," or "he makes a purificatory sacrifice for." It has generally been assumed that the Hebrew *NZH* takes as its object mediums like blood, oil, and water, but never people. Thus any liquid might be sprinkled *upon* people, but people are never sprinkled *with* a liquid. However, J. Lindblom inferred that this was not always so by calling attention to such Hebrew proper names as Jeziel (I Chron. 12:3) and Izziah (Ezra 10:25), which must mean "besprinkled by God [or, Yahweh]."[7] This usage is now confirmed by the Dead Sea Manual of Discipline (iii, 8f.):

> It is through the submission of his soul to all God's ordinances that his flesh will be cleansed by being *sprinkled* with water-for-impurity and by being sanctified with purifying water.[8]

Allusion here is to being sprinkled with the special water, called "water-for-impurity," which was prepared from the ashes of a red heifer. Thus this purifying water was linked with a sacrificial victim, which

5. In some contexts the Syriac particle *'aikh* may mean "as," in agreement with the Hebrew. However, the tenses do not make sense when so interpreted: "As many will be astonished at him, so will he [or, does he] disfigure himself. . . ." On this word see J. Payne Smith (Mrs. Margoliouth), *A Compendious Syriac Dictionary,* Oxford, Clarendon Press, 1903 (reprinted lithographically, 1957), p. 13a: "With *D* and a verb, expresses the subjunctive with *that,* or *to, that I may, that thou mayest,* etc."
6. Syriac always aspirates the letters *BGDKPT,* when they follow a vowel, except where gemination occurs — which in current usage hardens the letter without doubling it.
7. *The Servant Songs in Deutero-Isaiah, A New Attempt to Solve an Old Problem,* Lund, C. W. K. Gleerup, 1951, pp. 40ff. Lindblom distinguishes in his discussion between "sprinkle" (employed of a liquid) and "besprinkle" (employed of persons). Unfortunately, this serves to obscure his meaning, since the latter word is practically unused in English and the former word is used in both senses.
8. In my initial translation I emended *LHZWT* (*ləhazzôt*) to *LHZKWT* (*ləhizzakhôt*), in order to obtain the meaning "to be purified." However, I later perceived that this was unnecessary. See *BASOR,* No. 132, p. 10, n. 12.

shows the possibilities of a sacrificial as well as a purificatory connotation for the Hebrew root NZH when used of sprinkling people, precisely in line with the Syriac version of Isa. 52:15!

If we try to apply this understanding of *yazzèh* to Isa. 52:14f., we discover that the element of suffering is present in both apodoses, and that hence they are somewhat parallel. The sense may be paraphrased as follows:

> *As* many were appalled at you, Israel, by reason of your downfall and exile, *so* will My servant be an object of astonishment by reason of his marring beyond recognition as a man, or a human being; *and so also* will he through his suffering make a purificatory sacrifice for many nations, and their kings will be so astonished that they will shut their mouths; for what had not been foretold to them (as is now foretold to you Israel) they will have seen, and what they had not heard from the mouths of prophets, they will have contemplated.[9]

In the first apodosis, the effect of the Servant's suffering upon himself is stressed. In the second, it is the effect of this suffering upon others. Both are compared with the effect of Israel's own suffering. The only real difficulty with this syntactical explanation is the extreme brevity of the protasis; but the devastation of Judah and her exile were commonly referred to as an occasion of astonishment to others, so even this very brief allusion was expected to be understood.[10] It is characteristic of Hebrew poetry, moreover, that it can be terse almost to

9. *Suppar* of v. 15 means "foretold," precisely as in Hab. 1:5; 1Q pHab ii, 9f.; 1Q H i, 23. Cf. Isa. 41:26f.

10. That the divine judgment upon Judah caused the nations of the world to be amazed, appalled, or horrified, is a commonplace. For the use of the verb ŠMM, see Lev. 26:32; Jer. 18:16; 19:8; 49:17; 50:13. For the use of the cognate noun *shammâh*, see Deut. 28:37; Jer. 15:4; 24:9; 25:9; 29:18; 42:18; 44:12. Cf. also Lam. 4:12. This particular type of amazement is not congenial to the idea "I anointed" in 52:14 of 1Q Isaᵃ, so that this reading can not possibly be original; but it is defensible as a Qumrân procedure of atomizing the text. Cf. Millar Burrows, "Prophecy and the Prophets at Qumrân," in Bernhard W. Anderson and Walter Harrelson, *Israel's Prophetic Heritage,* New York, Harper and Bros., 1962, pp. 223–32.

More important is the fact that the verb ŠMM is really not congenial to the conjectured meaning of *yazzèh* as "startle," if (as is generally understood) the amazement in verse 14 concerns the Servant's suffering and that of verse 15 concerns his future triumph, for there is nothing in his triumph at which one may be "appalled." Much better suited to the context is the Syriac understanding "make a purificatory sacrifice," for this involves such excruciating suffering as to cause one to turn away in revulsion (53:3). Thus, if 52:15 is an apodosis to the preceding verse, it must refer to the Servant's suffering, not his deliverance.

the point of obscurity. It is this unfortunate fact which demands that we be slow to emend. As Jacob wrestled with his heavenly visitor by the Jabbok River, saying, "I will not let thee go, except thou bless me," so we must persistently wrestle with difficult texts of the Bible until they at long last impart to us their meaning and their blessing.

Semitic Word Index

This selective index of Hebrew and Aramaic words is arranged according to the order of the Hebrew alphabet, for which see above, p. xxx. However, in view of the fact that, in transliteration into English, we have inserted vowels that were not used at the time the scrolls were written, the words are arranged here according to the English alphabetic order under each Hebrew letter. In alphabetizing, the schwa is not distinguished from the *e*.

[*'Âlef*]
'ᵃdônâi, 163
'ahᵃvat ḥesed, 107f.
'aiḵh, 294
'ᵃsher, 238, 282
'ᵉlôhîm, 162, 170
'ᵉmûnâh, 126f.
'ovnâyim, 234
'ŠM = ŠMM, 187

[*Bêt*]
bâmâh, 238
Ba'al Shâmêm, 191
bat 'êl, bêt 'êl, 192
bᵊtûlâh, 279
bîn, 176

[*Gimel*]
gever, 263
gô'êl, 284
gûsh, 174
G'R, 'TG'R, 120

[*Dâlet*]
dâvâr, 64

[*Hê*]
hayyân, hawwân, 25
hôzîm, 188

[*Wâw*]
distinction from *Yôd*, 25, 198; as punctuation, 180ff.

[*Zayin*]
zâḵhâr, ZKR, 190, 269, 275

[*Ḥêt*]
ḥâmal, 177
ḥesed, 108
ḥôzîm, 188

[*Yôd*]
Cf. *Wâw*
Yahwèh, cf. Tetragrammaton
yaḥad, 104, 176
Yam Sûf, 56
Yamma' Simmûqa', 56
yâqah, 91
yêṣer sâmûḵh, 108f.
yêsha', yᵊshû'âh, 182
yiqqᵊhat, 91

297

[*Kaf*]

ķên, 292
ķətîv, 166
ķətûvîm, 27
ķôh 'âmar, 164
ķôhên, haķ-ķôhên hâ-r'ôsh, 63

[*Lâmed*]

L (*lə*), accusative, 267

[*Mêm*]

mar'èh, 213f.
mâshaḥtî, 204f.
maśķîl[îm], 104ff., 211
massêḵhâh, 177
Massôrâh, Massôret, 3
maṭṭîf haķ-ķâzâv, 139
mavnît, 264
mənê təķêl ûfarsîn, 40
Mənî, 177
mə'ôdâh, M'D(H), 188
midbâr, 84
mimsâḵh, 177
mishḥat, 210
mishpaṭ, 158, 196
mivnèh, 264
môrèh haṣ-ṣedeq, 138

[*Nûn*]

nâśâ', 175
nâvî', 71
N'M, 188
NZH (yazzèh), 294

[*Sâmeḵh*]

samaḥ, 177
sêfer ha-hᵃgî, 273
sereḵh hai-yaḥad, 273
suppar, 295

['*Ayin*]

'*al*, 186
'*âlâh, 'LH*, 190

'*almâh*, 280
'*arâvâh*, 84
'*eved*, 116, 158

[*Pê*]

pâqîd, pəquddâh, 150
pêsher, 64

[*Ṣâdê*]

ṣârah, ṣâwaḥ, 175
ṣədâqâh, 158
ṣedeq, 181
Ṣədûqî, 86

[*Qôf*]

qârâ', qârâh, 181
qâwâh, 91
qərê', 166
qêṣ, 104

[*Rêsh*]

rûaḥ, 74

[*Śîn*]

śâmaḥ, 177
śîm, 175f.

[*Shîn*]

shâfaṭ, 182
shallîṭ, 91
shâlôm, 82, 229
shammâh, 295
shêveṭ, 91
shîlôh, 91
shômêm, məshômêm, 191
ŠMM, 295

[*Tâw*]

tartân, 168
tel, 52
tôdâh, 271
Tôr = Tauros, 56
tôrâh, 139

Author Index

299

Subject Index